# Tree Ferns

# Tree Ferns

Mark F. Large
&
John E. Braggins

Timber Press
Portland • London

Copyright © 2004 by Mark F. Large and John E. Braggins
All rights reserved.

Published in 2004 by
Timber Press, Inc.

The Haseltine Building
133 S.W. Second Avenue, Suite 450
Portland, Oregon 97204-3527
www.timberpress.com

2 The Quadrant
135 Salusbury Road
London NW6 6RJ
www.timberpress.co.uk

ISBN 978-1-60469-176-4

The Library of Congress has cataloged the hardcover edition as follows:

Large, M. F.
  Tree ferns / Mark F. Large, John E. Braggins.
    p. cm.
Includes bibliographical references (p.   ).
  ISBN 0-88192-630-2 (hardcover)
  1. Ferns. I. Braggins, J. E. II. Title.
QK522 .L37 2004
587'.3—dc22

2003016919

A catalog record for this book is also available from the British Library.

*To my parents, O. V. and F. E. Large*
—M.F.L.

# Contents

**Foreword** by David J. Mabberley   9

**Preface**   11
    Acknowledgments   12

Chapter 1. **Introduction**   15
    The Tree Fern Habit   15
    Distribution   24
    Evolution   25
    Conservation   28
    Ethnobotany   29

Chapter 2. **Cultivation and Propagation**   34
    Temperature   35
    Humidity, Soils, and Moisture   36
    Fertilizers and Nutrition   37
    Light   37
    Vegetative Propagation   38
    Propagation from Spores   39
    Diseases and Pests   42
    Landscaping   45

Chapter 3. **The Tree Ferns**   47
    Families   49
        Cyatheaceae   52
        Dicksoniaceae   55
        Athyriaceae   56
        Blechnaceae   56
        Marattiaceae   57
        Osmundaceae   58
        Thelypteridaceae   58

  Hybrids 58
  Genera and Species 59
   Key to Tree Ferns 59
    *Calochlaena* 60
    *Cibotium* 63
    *Cnemidaria* 69
    *Culcita* 79
    *Cyathea* 81
    *Cystodium* 280
    *Dicksonia* 282
    *Leptopteris* 295
    *Lophosoria* 297
    *Osmunda* 299
    *Sadleria* 301
    *Thyrsopteris* 305
    *Todea* 307

Appendix 1. **Tree Ferns That Require Further Study** 309
Appendix 2. **Tree Ferns by Geographic Region** 313
Appendix 3. **Tree Ferns for Gardens** 323

 **Conversion Tables** 325
 **Glossary** 326
 **Bibliography** 332
 **Index** 339

 Gallery of Tree Ferns 161–220

# Foreword

For those people growing up in the temperate regions of the Northern Hemisphere, tree ferns, like palms, cycads, and epiphytic orchids, are quintessentially exotic: plants of botanical gardens and specialized collections. Seeing tree ferns in situ for the first time, as I did as an impressionable student on a university expedition to Kenya, is an unforgettable experience. In a montane forest with the calls of turacos, the whelps of monkeys, the lofty canopy of flowering trees and lianas down to the ground cover of colorful Acanthaceae in the clearings—all the trappings of the modern tropical forest—the tree fern strikes an ancient note, a successful survivor from distant times.

In New Caledonia the tree ferns bear some of the most primitive of living ferns as epiphytes, a relationship perhaps of the greatest antiquity. Yet the pachycaul tree fern structure is beautifully adapted to rapid colonization of clearings in modern forests, and to the harsh environments above tree line in New Guinea and on the cinders of Hawaiian volcanoes. Tree ferns are still rapidly evolving, yet as a group they have survived the changes that paved the way from dinosaurs to the modern fauna of mammals, birds, and insects, so intricately coevolved with the angiosperms. To study and to grow tree ferns is thus to associate with some of the most remarkable of living things.

Mark Large and John Braggins have produced a book to do justice to tree ferns: there is nothing else like it. A guide to all the known tree ferns is a must for fern gardener and pteridologist alike, yet no one has ever before attempted such a thing. Living in New Zealand, where tree ferns are familiar in both forest and garden, Mark long had in mind tackling such a project, but it was only in 1994, when working as a Royal Society postdoctoral fellow in my laboratory in Oxford, did the spur come. Triggered by questions concerning *Dicksonia arborescens*, a tree fern of St. Helena, the project was begun. Once he was back in New Zealand, Mark studied the genus, using both morphological and molecular techniques.

Mark's doctoral thesis was a spore atlas of New Zealand ferns and so-called fern allies. John had written on the tree ferns of the Auckland region of New Zealand. John was Mark's dissertation supervisor, and together they have written scientific papers on ferns, so their collaboration on this book was a natural result. In writing the book, Mark and John have drawn on their extensive travels, studying and photographing tree ferns in the wild—in New Zealand, Australia, New Caledonia, Hawaii, Fiji, Tahiti, the Cook Islands, the United States, Mexico, Panama, Sri Lanka, and the Seychelles—in addition to observing tree ferns in collections in Europe and North America.

And so *Tree Ferns* is a scientifically accurate yet accessible book. It deals particularly fully with species cultivated in the United States and the Pacific, but little-known and rare tree ferns are also included. Because of the importance of tree ferns in horticulture and the increasing trade in them, particular attention is paid to those listed protected, according to international import and export conventions. The importance of tree ferns to humans in ways other than horticulture is also dealt with, as is the folklore associated with them, notably the fabulous "vegetable lamb."

DAVID J. MABBERLEY
Leidsuniversiteitsfonds Professor,
University of Leiden, The Netherlands,
and Honorary Research Associate,
Royal Botanic Gardens, Sydney, Australia

# Preface

I have spent most of my life in New Zealand, where tree ferns are a familiar part of the forest and an important part of the national identity: *Cyathea dealbata* is a Kiwi icon (Plates 41, 44). Sports teams, including the national rugby team, the All Blacks, wear this "silver fern" as a team emblem.

My interest in botany and the origins of these seemingly primitive ferns eventually guided me to postgraduate study at the University of Auckland, with John Braggins. In 1992 I returned to the United Kingdom to do postdoctoral study at Oxford with David Mabberley. It was there that I met Quentin Cronk and came across his story of *Dicksonia arborescens*. Quentin spent several years studying the flora of the Atlantic Ocean island of St. Helena, where Joseph Banks first discovered this tree fern when he accompanied James Cook aboard the *Endeavour* in 1771. Our original scientific interest in the origins of this isolated plant and in the genus *Dicksonia* itself, combined with growing up in an environment surrounded by tree ferns, later inspired the development of this book with John Braggins.

Tree ferns superficially resemble palms, yet they represent a group of true ferns of ancient ancestry, with some members dating back at least to the Jurassic period. Today these plants are usually grouped into two families, Cyatheaceae and Dicksoniaceae, and include more than 500 known species. They have become sought after for their striking appearance and are cultivated in public and private gardens. In the wild, tree ferns occur in subtropical to tropical submontane environments and Southern Hemisphere temperate forests, where they give an immediate and characteristic flavor to the vegetation. These plants are commonly grown in warmer regions of the world, but various species grow well in cooler climates, even on the western islands of Scotland.

Increased forest clearance and collection of tree fern trunks for fiber have reduced some populations and resulted in many species becoming endangered. Their plight has engendered an upsurge of interest in their conservation and biology. At the same time, plantation forestry in the Southern Hemisphere has resulted in a large number of common tree ferns being shipped as trunk cuttings to the temperate Northern Hemisphere, raising the profile of these primeval-looking ferns.

*Tree Ferns* is intended as the source of information about these plants, and it includes information on the living tree ferns, including the families, genera, and species. Also included are other ferns with an erect trunk-like rhizome that may be cultivated by enthusiasts or that are suitable for the home garden. Although some emphasis is placed on those species cultivated in Australasia and the United States, unusual or little-known species from around the world are also included. The taxonomic treatment is based on up-to-date research and includes information on tree fern use, conservation, and cultivation.

MARK LARGE

## Acknowledgments

We sincerely thank all those people and institutions that have helped with *Tree Ferns*, in particular, staff at the Royal Botanic Gardens, Kew, Edinburgh, and Sydney; the Botanic Gardens, Singapore; and the Museum of New Zealand, Te Papa Tongarewa, and the National Library of New Zealand, Te Puna Mātauranga o Aotearoa, both in Wellington.

We are indebted to David Mabberley for his constant support throughout this project and are grateful to Rosemary Wise, Patrick Brownsey, Barbara Parris, Quentin Cronk, Elizabeth Brown, Bob Johns, John Dawson, Robbin Moran, and Alison and Kevin Downing. We thank Thelma Braggins, Nigel Taylor, Sandra Van der Mast, Brian Parkinson, and Noel Crump for help with various aspects of the text and in finding references. We are also grateful to Ross Beever and Kerry Everett for their comments on plant pathogens.

Andrew Wooding has provided indomitable assistance in many areas, including pre-editing and proofreading, compiling the Glossary and Index, and helping with the word processing software. We have no doubt that this work would not have been completed without his participation. We thank Elizabeth Nickless for her help with the diagrams, Susan Wright for her comments on the text, and Liz Grant for her illustrations.

Finally, we thank Peter Jeffreys, Rob Bielby, Will Bunker, and the crew from Kyabobo (in particular, Jen and David Bowes Lyon, Ed O'Keefe, and Jack Tordoff) for early stimulus and entertainment; and Rob Lewis, Leon

Perrie, Pete Lockhart, Trish McLenachan, and David Penny for their inspirational research.

Illustrations are by the authors unless otherwise acknowledged; however, we particularly thank Peter Bellingham, Ewen Cameron, John Engel, Martin Gardiner, Carlos Lehnebach, Rob Lucas, David Mabberley, John Mickel, Robbin Moran, Blanca Pérez-García, Magaly Riveros, and Fanie Venter for additional photographs.

# CHAPTER 1

# Introduction

## The Tree Fern Habit

"Tree fern" is a somewhat arbitrary term that has been applied to any fern with a large erect rhizome, the portion of the fern that bears the leaves. Thus tree ferns are all true ferns in that they are flowerless plants that reproduce by the production of spores, developed in sporangia on the underside of the leaves or fronds. The fronds of tree ferns also exhibit circinate vernation, that is, the coiled young fronds uncurl as they grow.

Most tree ferns have a distinctly primeval appearance with a tall trunk-like rhizome holding a palm-like group of fronds (Moran 1994). This plant form has an ancient origin. Tree-like ferns were present in Carboniferous swamps, and by the Permian period, some 275 million years before the present, forms very similar to those we see alive today were abundant. The major modern groups of tree ferns such as the family Dicksoniaceae have a fossil record dating back to the Triassic and Jurassic periods, more than 144 million years ago. A few of these tree ferns may be regarded as relicts of a time when dinosaurs were common. Other ferns achieving a tree-like habit are more modern, undergoing active speciation (the development of new species) and adapting to changing environments. Many of these more recent plants, such as members of the families Blechnaceae and Thelypteridaceae, evolved in the late Cretaceous period some 80 million years ago, alongside the first flowering plants.

## Life Cycle

Ferns have a complex life cycle with two separate and independent plants, living and growing successively (Figure 1; P. Bell 1992, 167–197). The dominant leafy plant we are most familiar with produces spores on the underside of fronds in small packages called sporangia. This plant is called the sporo-

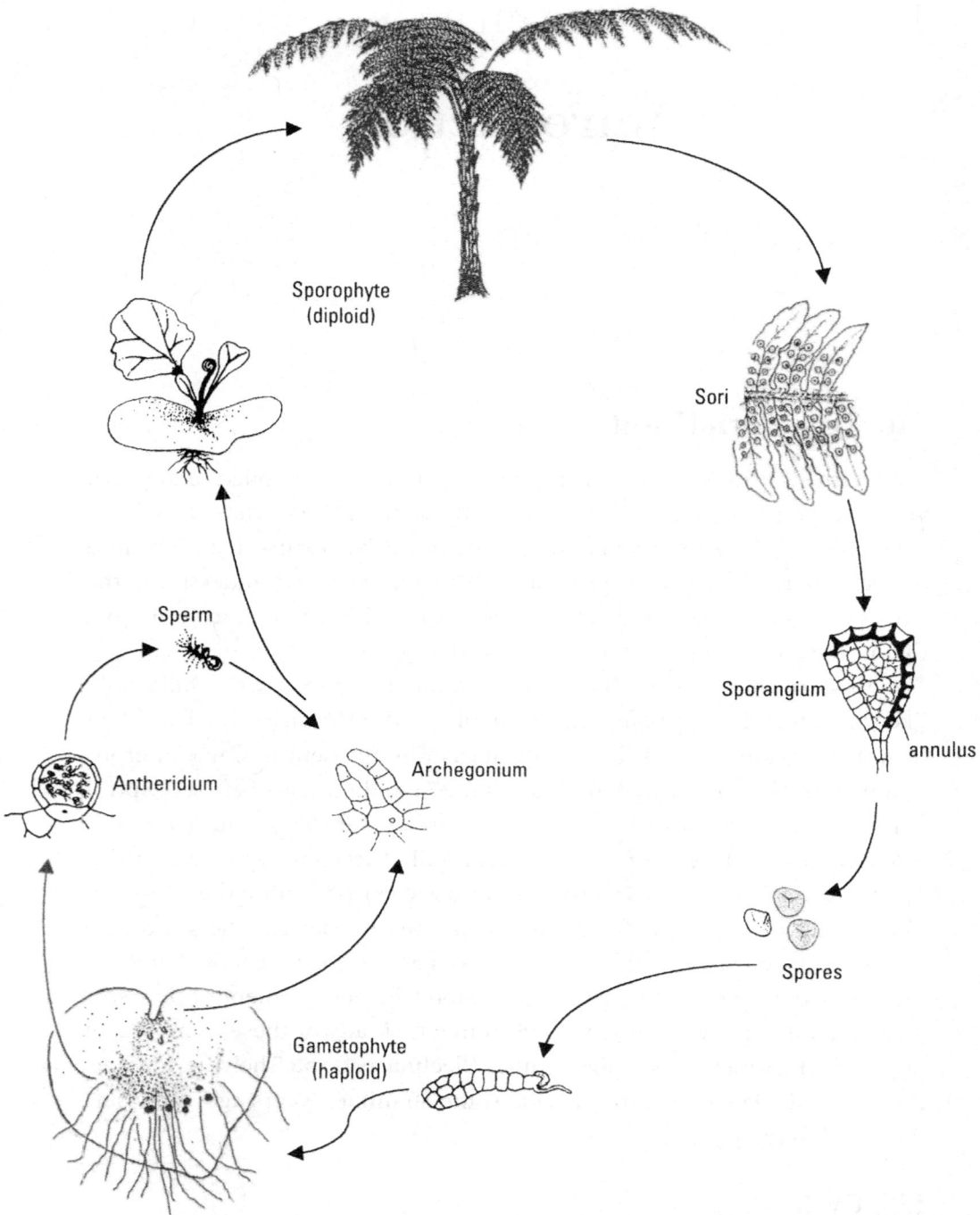

Figure 1. Alternation of generations in a tree fern between the dominant diploid sporophyte, which produces spores from sporangia on the underside of fronds, and the ephemeral haploid gametophyte, which produces male and female gametes from sex organs on its underside. Fertilization of the egg by the sperm results in a zygote that grows into a new sporophyte.

phyte. It is diploid; each of its cells contains two sets of chromosomes in the nucleus. Spores are the product of the cell division process known as meiosis. This process results in spores with half the chromosome complement (that is, one set of chromosomes in the nucleus) of the parent sporophyte. This is known as the haploid state.

A spore germinates and grows into a new green plant that is normally small (a few millimeters in diameter), thin, and heart-shaped. This is called the gametophyte (Plate 1), and it produces sex organs, each of which develops eggs or sperm amid fine hair-like rhizoids on its underside. All cells of the gametophyte are haploid, including the sperm and the eggs. Sperm cells are motile and require water to swim to the eggs. Hence, the gametophyte must live in a moist situation. At fertilization the egg and sperm join together to produce a zygote, which is now diploid. This zygote develops into a new sporophyte that, for a short time, is partially parasitic on the gametophyte.

Gametophytes are an essential part of the life cycle of all ferns. They are rarely noticed in the wild, yet these small, short-lived plants dictate where the adult sporophyte—the plant we recognize as a tree fern—will eventually grow.

## Rhizomes and Trunks

"Tree fern" implies the presence of a trunk. However, this trunk (or caudex as it is called in ferns) is unlike the woody structure found in many other land plants such as conifers and flowering trees. In those plants the trunk has a secondary cambium (Esau 1977, Fahn 1982), which is an actively dividing layer of cells that produces bands of vascular tissue (the wood). Instead, tree fern trunks (Figure 2) contain a large central area (or pith) and an outer region (called the cortex) of soft, thin-walled cells (called parenchyma), which often stores starch (Plates 66, 106). The cortex is punctuated by a ring or crescents of vascular tissue composed of cells specialized for transport of water and sugars. Cells that conduct water are collectively called the xylem and occur in the midst of each vascular bundle. These are surrounded by cells, collectively called the phloem, that conduct sugars. Each bundle is usually in turn surrounded with a dark black-brown sheath of hard cells, collectively called sclerenchyma (Plates 66, 67, 106). These cells are impregnated with a substance called lignin and act primarily as supporting structures, rather like reinforcing rods, for the stem. These tissues are frequently fused between vascular bundles, forming a complex network. Such an arrangement in a fern rhizome is called a dictyostele (P. Bell 1992). Outside all these tissues there may be a further band of sclerenchyma thicker than the others, providing a firm cylinder that produces the hard exterior of the trunk and provides the main support for the whole structure (for further information see Ogura 1927, Godwin 1932, Lucansky 1974, Lucansky and White 1974, D. Adams 1977, Moran 1994).

Old leaf bases are often retained in a cluster around the outside of the rhizome. Although the arrangement of vascular bundles and supportive tissues within a stem is often variable, the general configuration and organization of tissues may be unique to a genus or, occasionally, species. However, cutting a tree fern down to examine a slice of trunk is not a desirable method of identification!

Tree ferns, like palms and cycads, have a single dominant growing region (or meristem) at the top of their trunks. This is a region of actively dividing cells that produces new leaves and, in some species, new roots. Roots may also appear from near the leaf bases; these combine with those

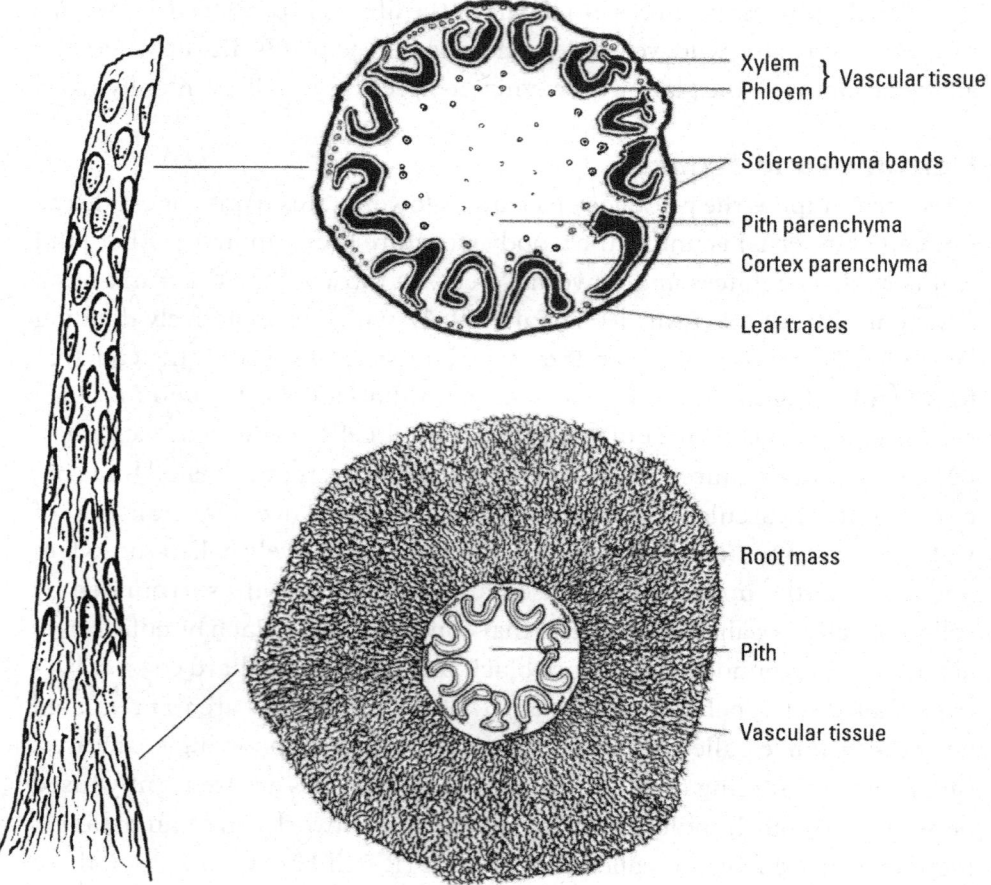

Figure 2. A tree fern trunk (left) with cross sections through the younger part of the trunk above and the older portion below, covered by a thick layer of roots.

from the apical region and grow along the outside of the rhizome toward the ground (Plate 56). These roots often build up and bury old leaf scars, giving the trunk a fibrous appearance (Plate 106). This whole root system may form a dense mass that steadily splays out toward the base of the plant and supports the plant, keeping it from falling over.

Fern rhizomes may take many forms: some creep (Plate 109), climb, or produce short tufts. There are many intermediates, and a tree fern habit is not always easily defined. Some tree ferns may branch (Plate 130) and develop offshoots or pups along their main rhizomes (Plate 18). In species in which this does not occur, damage to the main or apical meristem frequently brings about the death of the plant. Several species that otherwise produce an upright trunk as tall as several meters (Plate 39) may also produce plants with a lateral creeping rhizome (for example, *Cyathea dealbata*).

## Age and Growth Rates

Tree fern trunks do not produce annular vascular rings, so unlike most plants that produce a trunk, there is no easy method of estimating longevity. In some cases the age of mature plants has been estimated by counting leaf bases on the external surface of the trunk. Unfortunately, this method is often inaccurate, with highly variable results, depending on species and even the circumstances in which a particular plant is grown.

Many species may experience an early growth spurt, producing many fronds and gaining height quickly before slowing when a certain size is reached. For example, in the first few years of growth, *Cyathea medullaris* (Plates 68, 69) and *C. brownii* (Plate 28) may increase in height by 40–50 cm or more per year, slowing to a few centimeters per year as the plant ages (Large, unpublished data). Similarly, when young and growing under optimal conditions, *C. arborea* and *C. cooperi* are reported to grow some 30 cm per year. This early-phase development depends on available light, water, nutrients, and even temperature. Growth spurts are often related to survival strategy in the wild. Plants from a cloud forest or deep forest environment may maintain a steady growth rate. For example, *Alsophila bryophila* (Appendix 1) may grow slowly at a rate of 5 cm per year and live as long as 150 years (Tryon and Tryon 1982).

Faster-growing tree ferns such as *Cyathea medullaris* and *C. brownii*, adapted to take advantage of light and nutrients by growing rapidly, are characteristic of forest margins or clearings. Even these tree ferns may reach an age of 50–100 years or more. Large, slow-growing tree ferns (for example, *Dicksonia antarctica*, Plate 100, and *D. fibrosa*, Plate 107) adapted for forest growth may be reach a much greater age, possibly in excess of 200 years (Seiler 1981, 1995, Holttum and Edwards 1983, Tanner 1983).

Overall size may vary, from small plants less than 1 m tall to large, palm-like plants 15 m or more in height. The greatest height and leaf size is encountered in members of the family Cyatheaceae. Among the largest tree ferns are *Cyathea brownii*, *C. contaminans* (Plate 34), *C. cunninghamii* (Plate 39), and *C. medullaris*, which may produce trunks more than 20 m tall and individual fronds greater than 5 m long. The greatest trunk girth occurs in the Dicksoniaceae. Massive and dense trunks as much as 2 m or more in diameter are produced by several of the Southern Hemisphere species of *Dicksonia*, including *D. antarctica* and *D. fibrosa*. This dense structure is often enhanced by a massive buttress of fibrous roots, tapering out toward ground level.

## Fronds

Tree ferns produce some of the largest leaves (called fronds) of any plant. Fronds may function in both photosynthesis and reproduction. Although most tree ferns produce fronds that serve both purposes, in some ferns there may be a distinct morphological difference between fertile and sterile fronds. Often, the fertile fronds are more dissected (divided) than the sterile leaves.

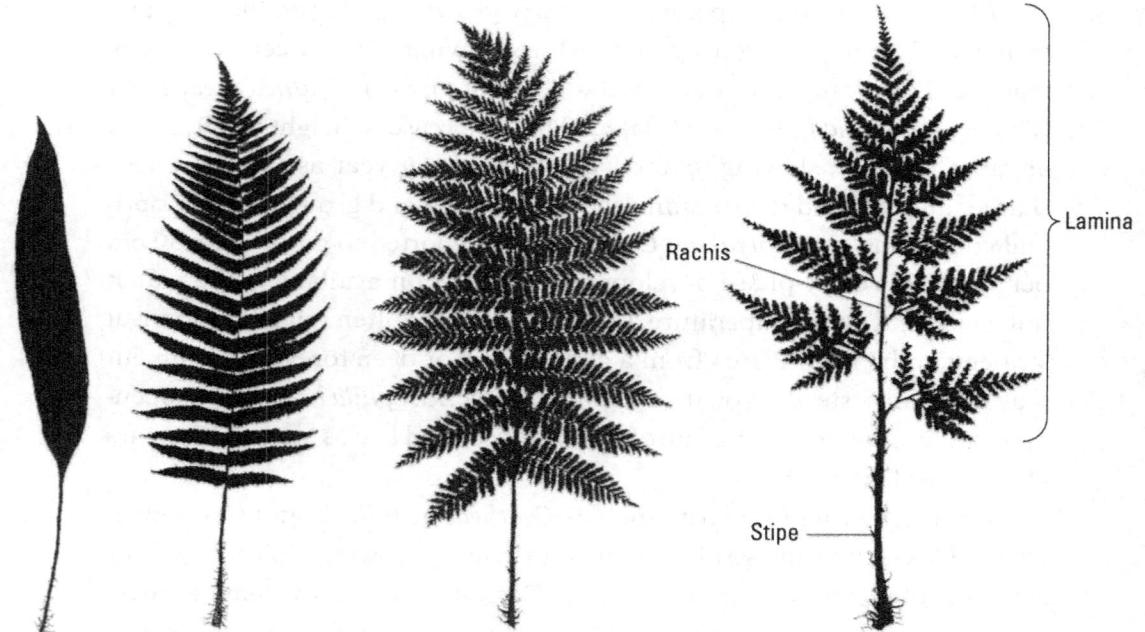

Figure 3. Frond shape and form, including the degree of lamina division. Left to right: frond simple (or entire), pinnate (once divided), bipinnate (twice divided), and tripinnate (three times divided).

Fronds consist of a flat green photosynthetic area called the lamina with a central stalk (Plate 89). This stalk is called the rachis when it occurs within the lamina, or the stipe when it extends below the lamina and eventually attaches to the rhizome (Plates 23, 55).

In tree ferns the lamina is usually dissected into small segments called pinnae; rarely is the frond entire. When the frond is dissected, the pinnae (or smaller subunits of the lamina) look like small leaflets attached to a stem. The degree of frond division has its own terminology and is often species-specific (Figure 3). Sometimes it can be difficult to distinguish between complete and partial division (incomplete division is called pinnatifid).

The trunk apex bears many uncoiling fronds (Plates 4, 5, 8, 63, 72, 82, 93, 101, 114, 118). These usually occur in compact spirals or, in a few cases, are whorled. Expansion of the new fronds can be synchronized or occur successively. Uncoiling involves a complex process of controlled growth (Voeller 1966). Cells on the inner side of the young frond elongate at a much quicker rate rather than those on the outer side. This process, circinate vernation, begins at the base of the frond stem and gradually proceeds upward, resulting in an expanded leaf.

## Aphlebiae

In some tree ferns (particularly those of the *Alsophila* clade in *Cyathea*) the lower pairs of frond pinnules (that is, those nearest the crown) may be specialized, finely divided, and/or reduced, with small pinnules intersecting each other. In the extreme form, these are highly branched outgrowths with the appearance of small bird-nest-like thickets about the growing apex of the plant. In some cases these may be transient, occurring only in juvenile plants. These structures are often called aphlebiae, a term meaning "without veins" and originally used to describe a condition in fossils (Holttum 1981). The use of this term to describe the reduced pinnae that are veined is subject to debate and is perhaps technically inappropriate. (For further discussion see Goebel 1930, Tardieu-Blot 1941, Tindale 1956, Tryon and Tryon 1982, 187–188; Conant 1983.)

## Hairs and Scales

The stipe, rachis, rhizome, and indeed, almost any part of the fern plant, may be covered with hairs and/or scales (paleae). Their presence or absence and the form that these structures take are often useful in tree fern identification.

Hairs comprise a single file of cells and may be star-shaped (stellate) or simple with a pointed apex, or may also be glandular. Scales are multicellu-

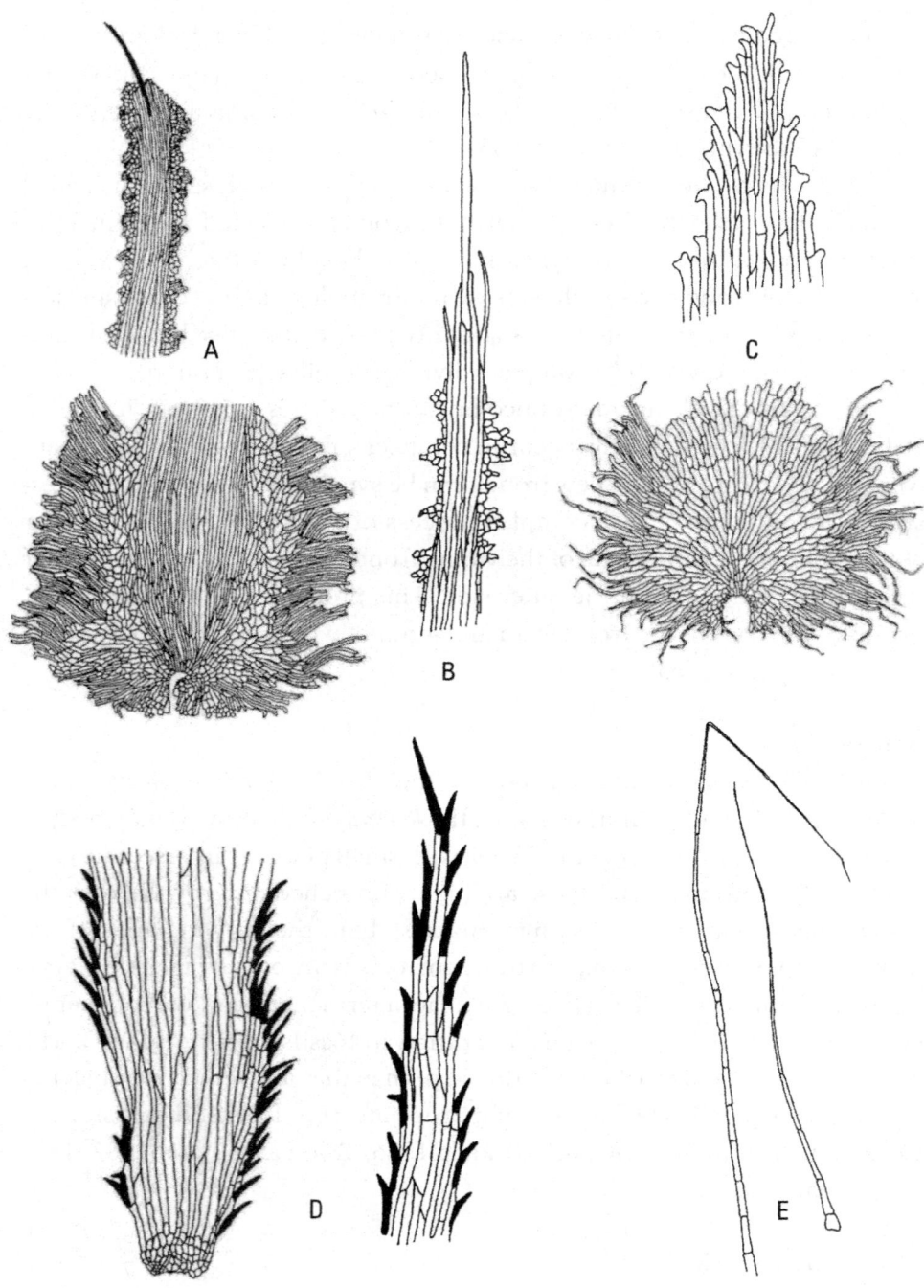

Figure 4. Hair and scale morphology in the families Cyatheaceae and Dicksoniaceae. A, *Cyathea smithii* (*Alsophila* clade), above, scale apex; below, scale base. B, *Cyathea cunninghamii* (*Alsophila* clade), scale apex. C, *Cyathea decurrens* (*Cyathea* clade), above, scale apex; below, scale base. D, *Cyathea medullaris* (*Sphaeropteris* clade), left, scale base; right, scale apex. E, *Dicksonia fibrosa*, stipe hairs.

lar, usually many cells wide and often tapering from a wide base to a narrow point. Stipe and rachis scales are of particular use in the classification and identification of the Cyatheaceae. The margin may be smooth, serrated, or even bear extensive hair-like projections (often called setae).

## Sori, Sporangia, and Spores

Spores are borne in sporangia ("small packages" of spores) on the underside of fertile fronds (Plates 115, 117, 131). Sporangia in turn are clustered into compact groups, each group called a sorus. The shape of the sorus is an important diagnostic feature in the determination of species and genera. Sori may be circular or linear, and marginal (as in the family Dicksoniaceae) or set away from the margin on the frond lamina (as in the Cyatheaceae).

The sorus may be protected by a covering called an indusium. This structure is formed by extensions of the frond lamina, resulting in an umbrella- or cup-like structure. In some species the margin of the lamina itself may also be involved (see Tryon and Feldman 1975 for a discussion of development). Indusia vary in form and may be naked or bear scales and/or hairs. Similar types of indusia occur in different genera. This is particularly true of the Cyatheaceae, in which indusia were previously considered to be important in the classification, as discussed in the introduction to *Cyathea*.

As in most ferns, tree fern sporangia are specialized to disperse their spores via a slingshot mechanism (P. Bell 1992, Fig. 7.22); such sporangia are called leptosporangiate (illustrated by the sporangium in Figure 1). This process is aided by the presence of a row of specialized cells called an annulus. The inner and side walls of these annulus cells are thickened whereas the outer walls are thin. This pattern of thickening allows shrinkage in only one direction, thus bending the annulus backward as the cells dry. The sporangium is ripped open as the annulus bends backward. Then, when the tension is released, the annulus flicks back to its original position and the spores are suddenly released in slingshot fashion.

Spores are always produced in groups of four by the cell division process known as meiosis. This process results in the reduction of the cellular chromosomal complement to half that of the parent sporophyte plant. In the majority of tree fern groups, spores are tetrahedral and round to rounded-triangular. The few exceptions are bilaterally symmetrical and ovoid or bean-shaped (for example, Blechnaceae). Spores are highly ornamented, the ornamentation often being genus- or even species-specific (Gastony and Tryon 1976, Liew and Wang 1976, Gastony 1979, Tryon and Lugardon 1990, Large and Braggins 1991).

Most tree ferns produce about 64 spores per sporangium (although some may produce 16) and many thousands of sporangia per frond. As early as 1834, Karl Martius estimated spore production in a frond of *Cyathea delgadii* (as *C. vestita*) to be 6 billion. A large tree fern like *C. medullaris* has been estimated to produce as much as 2 kg of spores in a year (Large, unpublished data), and one frond from *C. delgadii* was reported to produce 600 million spores (Tryon and Tryon 1982).

## Distribution

Tree ferns are found in tropical lowland to submontane environments, as well as subtropical and Southern Hemisphere temperate forests (Tryon and Gastony 1975, Moran 1995a). The majority form a component of humid forests in the Caribbean, Central and South America, Africa, Asia, New Guinea, the islands of Oceania, Australia, and New Zealand. Several reach cool latitudes in southern South America, Tasmania, and southern New Zealand. *Cyathea smithii* is known from some of the subantarctic islands (Auckland Islands) south of New Zealand and is the most southerly occurring tree fern in the world (Plate 90). Distribution maps are provided in the introduction to each genus. Several species (particularly those native to southern Australia and the islands of New Zealand) may form large single-species stands, excluding all other vegetation (Plate 70). In tropical areas, tree ferns may reach high montane zones, as high as 4200 m in elevation (for example, in the Andes).

Members of the family Cyatheaceae (and groups within the Blechnaceae and Thelypteridaceae) are the most widespread tree ferns. Many species show a high degree of local endemism. Centers of diversity include the Greater Antilles, Central America, the Andes, Madagascar, Malesia, including Indonesia, Philippines and New Guinea (for example, Goy 1943, Proctor 1977, 1985, Jones 1987, Goudey 1988, Mickel and Beitel 1988, Lellinger 1989, and Andrews 1990).

The family Dicksoniaceae is Pantropical with a high degree of diversity in Indonesia and New Guinea. Some (species of *Dicksonia* in particular) have a relictual distribution, with different endemic species occurring in places as isolated as St. Helena in the Atlantic Ocean and Juan Fernández Islands off the coast of Chile (Kunkel 1965).

# Evolution

Much of what we know about the origins of the ferns and the tree fern habit is based on an extensive fossil record (Table 1). The fossils include sections and compressions of fronds, pinnules, trunks, and roots. Fern spores in particular make good microfossils. Spores have a wall composed of a substance

**TABLE 1.** Selected fossil genera attributed to the families Cyatheaceae and Dicksoniaceae. Ages of geologic periods are given in millions of years ago. Key: ?, *Cibotium* affinity; 1, *Dicksonia* smooth-granulate spore form; 2, *Dicksonia* tuberculate spore form. After Lewis (2001) and compiled from Tidwell and Nishida (1993), Tidwell and Ash (1994), Collinson (1996), Hill and Jordan (1998), and Lantz et al. (1999).

| FAMILY AND GENUS | AUTHORITY | FOSSIL LOCALITY | TRIASSIC 248–208 | JURASSIC 208–144 | CRETACEOUS 144–65 | TERTIARY 65–2 |
|---|---|---|---|---|---|---|
| **Cyatheaceae** | | | | | | |
| Extinct | | | | | | |
| *Cyatheocaulis* | Ogura | Korea | | | Early | |
| *Oguracaulis* | Tidwell, Nishida & Webster | Tasmania | | Late | | |
| *Alsophilocaulis* | Menendez | Argentina | | | | Early |
| *Cibotiocaulis* | Ogura | Korea | | | Late | |
| Extant | | | | | | |
| *Cnemidaria* | C. B. Presl | Australia | | | | Early |
| *Cyathea* | J. Smith | U.S.A. | | | | Early |
| **Dicksoniaceae** | | | | | | |
| Extinct | | | | | | |
| *Coniopteris* | Brongniart | Iran | Early | | | |
| *Nishidicaulis* | Tidwell & Nishida | Australia | | | Early | |
| *Onychiopsis* | see Tidwell & Ash | Denmark | | | Early | |
| *Conantiopteris* | Lantz et al. | U.S.A. | | Late | | |
| *Erboracia* | H. H. Thomas | England | | Late | | |
| *Lophosoriorhachis* | Nishida | Japan | | | Early | |
| Extant | | | | | | |
| *Calochlaena* | Turner & White | Australia | | | | Early |
| *Cibotium* | Kaulfuss | Australia, U.S.A. | | Late ? | ? Early | |
| *Dicksonia* | L'Héritier | Europe | | Early 1 | | 2 |
| *Lophosoria* | C. B. Presl | Antarctica | | | Late | |

called sporopollenin, which is highly resistant to chemical erosion and biological decay. Spores are often highly ornamented and can be identified to the level of genus or even species with considerable accuracy (Tryon and Lugardon 1990, Large and Braggins 1991).

The earliest fossils of fern and fern-like plants date to the middle Devonian period, some 385 million years before the present. These early ferns evolved under very different ecological conditions from those seen today. Flowering plants and mammals were absent, and during the Triassic, Jurassic, and Cretaceous periods the land was dominated by reptiles. Fern colonization of open habitats was a widespread occurrence. This culminated in the formation of fern prairies in the Jurassic and Cretaceous and can be seen later in the abundance of ferns (known as the "fern spike") at the KT boundary, that is, the boundary between the Cretaceous and the Tertiary about 65 million years ago. This point in the Earth's history, which marks the final extinction of the dinosaurs, was characterized by dramatic events indicative of a major meteoritic impact and by complex changes in the Earth's ecosystems. Extensive areas were disturbed and colonized by an opportunistic fern community. This ability to rapidly colonize open areas is still seen in many ferns and tree ferns today.

The tree fern form was already well established by the late Carboniferous (340 million to 305 million years ago) and is particularly well represented in the Mesozoic–Cainozoic fossil record (about 245 million years ago until the present). This fossil evidence (reviewed by Collinson 1996) suggests that the tree fern habit has come and gone independently in various groups, many of which have no surviving descendants. Such tree ferns included *Tempskya* (Figure 5) an unusual tree fern of the Cretaceous (144 million to 65 million years ago) with a distinctive trunk composed of multiple stems surrounded by roots (Andrews and Kerns 1947, Tidwell and Herbert 1992, Moran 1994). These false trunks, which have no modern equivalent, reached 6 m in height and bore fronds along their length, unlike modern tree ferns that usually bear a crown of fronds. This plant seems to have disappeared, along with the last of the dinosaurs, at the end of the Cretaceous.

Of the ferns living today, those with Carboniferous relatives include members of the order Marattiales. The surviving genera, including *Angiopteris* (Plate 2) and *Marattia*, are now mostly large tropical plants with slow-creeping, or short-trunked rhizomes rather than the 10-m-tall or more trunks of ancestral forms. By the Permian (286 million to 248 million years ago) and Triassic (248 million to 208 million years ago) periods, other orders of ferns, including the Osmundales, included large plants with tall trunks. The

Figure 5. *Tempskya,* an unusual tree fern of the Cretaceous. Artist's reconstruction by Liz Grant, Massey University, New Zealand.

remains of these osmundaceous plants are represented by *Palaeosmunda, Thamnopteris, Zalesskya,* the fossil trunks of *Osmundacaulis* (Plate 124), and fossil fronds of *Cladophlebis* (Plate 19). The two latter genera are now reported to be parts of the same tree fern. Some of these ferns had large stems with a diameter of 45 cm. However, modern representatives of this group (including *Leptopteris, Osmunda,* and *Todea*) are clumping or only produce short trunks.

The modern tree fern families Dicksoniaceae and Cyatheaceae also have a long fossil record with the earliest members of Dicksoniaceae appearing in the Triassic. The modern genus *Dicksonia* appeared in the Jurassic (208 million to 144 million years ago), when members of the family were particularly diverse. The modern distribution of Dicksoniaceae, predominately tropical to Southern Hemispheric, is probably the result of a retreat in distribution at the close of the Cretaceous and during the Tertiary (65 million to 20 million years ago). The Cyatheaceae is apparently a younger family than the Dicksoniaceae, with fossils appearing for the first time in late Jurassic to early Cretaceous sediments. Modern genera of this family may even have an origin in the Tertiary.

## Conservation

CITES, the Convention on International Trade in Endangered Species, is based on an international treaty drawn up in 1973. This convention is designed to protect against overexploitation of natural living resources and prevent trade from threatening species with extinction.

In 1975 two families of tree ferns, Cyatheaceae and Dicksoniaceae, were listed in CITES (Oldfield 1995). A database of CITES listings is now available on the Web at *www.cites.org*. Since 1975 there has been an obligation for member states (146 countries, including members of the European Union, the United States, Japan, South Africa, Australia, and New Zealand) to report any trade in tree ferns. Countries exporting tree ferns or tree fern products include those in parts of Africa and Australia, New Zealand, Vanuatu, Indonesia, the Philippines, Paraguay, Taiwan, Brazil, Costa Rica, and the Netherlands. Primary importing countries include those in Europe (in particular, the United Kingdom, the Netherlands, Germany, and Italy), Japan, and the United States. Identification of species in the field and correct application of names for CITES are difficult. Unfortunately, the level of reporting often reflects this lack of taxonomic knowledge, with different countries reporting tree fern trade at different taxonomic levels. Species names are often mixed up or incorrect; thus the information on the conservation status of many tree ferns is unfortunately incomplete.

Many tree ferns must join the growing list of plants that are endangered through collection from the wild and from loss of rain forest habitat. This is particularly true in the Tropics of underdeveloped countries, where fiber, trunks, or living specimens provide the basis for quick cash income. However, it is not always in the underdeveloped world where tree ferns suffer from overcollection. *Dicksonia antarctica* has been used in Australia for many years as fencing, for fiber, and in landscaping. This plant is not endangered, but collection and land clearance for farming from the end of the 19th century onward have contributed to the disappearance of the species in many parts of South Australia. Australian exports of *D. antarctica* are now controlled by the Australian National Parks and Wildlife Service. Programs for the export of wild Tasmanian *D. antarctica* have been approved by law. However, this species is now protected on mainland Australia (Neyland 1986).

# Ethnobotany

## Fiber

There are regions in the world where tree ferns are not endangered. In New Zealand and southern areas of Australia, tree ferns are common, reproducing and growing quickly. These plants often colonize the extensive plantation forests (even as an understory beneath Monterey pine, *Pinus radiata*, which has been introduced from the United States for cultivation in New Zealand). When the plantation forests are harvested, the tree ferns are available as a secondary crop. Removal from these areas does not in any way endanger the wild populations or the survival of the species.

Tree fern fiber (along with *Osmunda* fiber) is used as a potting mixture particularly suitable for orchids. The fiber is produced by shredding the trunk rhizome and leaf bases of mature plants and is available through the nursery industry. In several regions of the world, these plants are harvested from the wild. Although the trade in many countries is controlled through CITES and local permits, this industry has still caused the depletion of natural tree fern populations. This is particularly true of the slower-growing species, some of which have been brought to the brink of extinction. It is always wise to ascertain the source of the fiber when purchasing supplies. In some areas, alternatives are available, including coconut fiber, granulated bark (from production forestry), cork bark, sphagnum moss (although this, too, is discouraged in some regions for conservation reasons), vermiculite, and perlite.

Tree fern fiber and hairs produced on the trunk have secondary uses other than as a substrate for growing plants. Dried rhizome hairs from *Cibotium barometz* (Plate 12) have long been used to stuff pillows in China and Malaysia, though these are known to cause respiratory problems in some people. This particular use is most apparent in the genus *Culcita,* even the name of which means pillow in Latin. In Madeira, fluffy rhizome hairs of *Culcita macrocarpa* are still used as stuffing.

## Construction

Tree fern trunks may be used in light construction of fences and shade houses. Although the trunk rhizome does not have true wood as such, in many species the internal structure (see Rhizomes and Trunks) and associated root mass provides a strong and surprisingly durable construction material. Hawaiians are known to have used trunks from tree ferns of the genus *Cibotium* to pave tracks through boggy ground. *Dicksonia squarrosa* is sometimes used in the same way in New Zealand. Traditionally, Maori in New Zealand were able to use the dense, fibrous tree fern stem bases to build food storage houses that had walls too thick for rats to invade. Trunks also formed the walls of cooking sheds and lined storage pits for sweet potato, *Ipomoea batatas* (known by Maori as kumara; discussed further by Orbell 1996). Early European settlers to New Zealand likewise recognized the durability of these stem bases for construction. Fern Tree Lodge in Dunedin is a large house built in the 1860s with external walls made partly of tree fern trunks. Today, tree fern fences are common in New Zealand (Plate 116), and these may be seen sprouting from the apex if that has not been damaged, or from buds on the stem if they are present. In New Zealand and Australia, much of this construction material is procured from plantation forest and would otherwise be destroyed during logging operations. In Australia, the same applies to many of the *D. antarctica* stems that are now marketed internationally.

The fibrous properties of the trunk may also help maintain a damp, humid environment and provide an in situ substrate for the cultivation of epiphytic plants (Plate 60). Garden troughs and fiber pots carved from whole trunks may be found for sale in garden centers. These are suitable for growing many epiphytic plants, particularly bromeliads and orchids

Other commercial products are common, and there are unusual vases, coasters, and a variety of boxes carved out of tree fern trunks that are distinctive and different (Plate 67). In New Zealand, these are usually produced from *Cyathea dealbata* and, to a lesser extent, the trunks of *C. medullaris.*

Garden ornaments and statues are also becoming more available. The best of these are handsome structures, costing large sums of money, whereas others are much simpler, cheaper, and often carved from inferior material. The best raw material seems to come from the aged remnants of tree ferns felled some time in the past and left to weather and harden. The true trunk of the tree fern is only a small portion of these structures; it is the dense mat of interwoven and fused roots from the base of the stem that provides a suitable material for carving. These carved trunks are exported from Mexico (where they are called maquique; Plate 27) and the Pacific Islands (including Vanuatu) as well as from Australia and New Zealand.

## Food and Medicine

Young uncurling fronds of tree ferns are often eaten in the wild by animals and birds. Humans have also used tree ferns as a food source. The Aboriginal peoples of Australia, the peoples of Hawaii, India, Madagascar, New Guinea, New Caledonia, and the Maori in New Zealand are known to have used the pith from the center of the trunk as a starch source. The young uncurling fronds have also been eaten. This material is often full of silicates and resinous compounds and remains an acquired taste. For a short period in the 1920s, *Cibotium* starch was extracted in Hawaii commercially for laundry and food use (Nelson and Hornibrook 1962).

Several tree ferns have toxic or therapeutic properties; some have been explored for antiviral and medicinal uses. About 300 B.C., Theophrastus recommended oil extracted from ferns to expel internal parasites. *Cyathea manniana* (Plate 64; also called *C. usambarensis*) from East Africa has been used by the Chagga and by German troops in the First World War as an anthelmintic (Mabberley 1997). However, excessive or prolonged use is reported to cause blindness. The sappy gum from the large tree fern *C. medullaris* (native to the New Zealand region) is likewise a vermifuge. This gum is happily also a treatment for diarrhea.

*Cyathea medullaris* has many further uses, with extracts used for easing boils (T. Bell 1890). The slimy material from the interior of a young uncurling frond has also been rubbed on wounds or used in various ways to relieve sores, saddle sores on horses, swollen feet, and sore eyes (three applications per day were advised). The young fronds have also been boiled and the liquid drunk to assist the expulsion of afterbirth (O. Adams 1945). The small scales on the fronds of this species are often an irritant and are reported as having been used by inventive children as itching powder. Other members of the genus *Cyathea* provide a variety of medicinal uses. In Fiji, infusions made from frond material of *C. lunulata* (Plate 63) were used to treat headaches as well as taken by expectant mothers to shorten the period of labor. On Pohnpei, also in the Pacific, fronds of *C. nigricans* were pounded, squeezed, and the liquid drunk as a contraceptive; there is no record of its success or otherwise. In Malesia, stems and frond extractions of *C. moluccana* have been used to poultice sores. (For further discussion see Burkill 1935, Cambie and Ash 1994, and Cambie and Brewis 1997.)

The use of tree fern fronds, stipes, scales, and trunks to treat wounds is widespread. Frond material of *Cyathea mexicana* (Plate 75; also known as *Alsophila firma*) has been used in Mexico to treat hemorrhaging. The four Hawaiian species of *Cibotium* are also traditionally used as a wound dressing, as is *C. arachnoideum* in Malaysia and the Indonesian portion of Borneo. Rhizome hairs from this latter species have also been used to staunch blood loss from open wounds. Similar use as a wound dressing has been made of *Cyathea dealbata* by the New Zealand Maori. The pith of this plant was used as a poultice for cutaneous eruptions. Ponga powder, probably from *C. dealbata*, was used by early New Zealand settlers for the reduction of fever, though its effectiveness is not recorded. A surviving package of "Mrs Subritzky's Ponga Powder" can still be found in the Wagner Museum, Northland, New Zealand (Brooker et al. 1981).

*Cibotium barometz*, from China and Malaysia, is still used medicinally. Hairs of the rhizome and stipe may be charred or used fresh as a wound dressing, and the fronds are used to ease fainting. This short fern, with its distinctive furry trunk (Plate 12), has long been considered to have magical properties. The rhizome (turned upside down with bud and four leaf bases) was passed off as the "vegetable lamb," a strange beast that was thought to be half animal and half plant. Stories of a vegetable lamb, or organism sharing both plant and animal characteristics, date to the time of Christ. One of the early descriptions may be found in *Talmud Ierosolimitanum* (A.D. 436). In the 14th century, John Mandeville brought to England the story of a fruit that enclosed a "a beast as it were of fleshe and bone and bloud, as it were a lyttle lambe without wolle" (Ashton 1890). There is no direct proof that these early stories specifically concern *C. barometz*, and they may refer to cotton or some similar plant. However, these descriptions have become mingled with later stories, specifically those concerning the Scythian lamb or lamb of Tartary, from India and Asia; the specific name *barometz* is a Tartar word, meaning lamb.

By the 16th century, even respectable scholars believed in the existence of this beast. Many early illustrations (Figure 6) seem to show a dead dog supported on a stalk. In the early 18th century, several vegetable lambs were exhibited at the Royal Society, London. One of these specimens remains in the 18th-century collection of Hans Sloane, now in the Natural History Museum, London. There is little doubt that this lamb is formed from a rhizome of *Cibotium barometz*. In the 17th and 18th centuries, these lambs were fashioned by the Chinese to use as toys and charms to ward off evil.

Human pharmacological use of tree fern compounds, from birth throughout life, continues to the grave with extracts employed as preservatives. This is particularly true in Hawaii, where *Cibotium* (*hapu'u*) has been used for embalming, with bodies reportedly lasting for as long as 8 months.

Figure 6. The barometz or vegetable lamb, from Lee (1887), redrawn from Johann Zahn's *Specula Physico-Mathematico-Historica Notabilium ac Mirabilium Sciendorum, in Qua Mundi Mirabilis Oeconomia, . . .* Norimbergae, 1696.

CHAPTER 2

# Cultivation and Propagation

Like palms and cycads, tree ferns provide a distinctive and dramatic element to a garden landscape. They may conjure up images of the Tropics, or of a primeval forest filled with dinosaurs. This tropical image suggests that tree ferns are climatically delicate and grow best in warmer regions. Indeed, most do well in regions with a moderate climate, from the Tropics to the Subtropics and warmer temperate areas. Even in the cooler climates of the British Isles, Europe, and the United States, however, tree ferns have long interested gardeners and horticulturists.

In Britain, this interest reached a peak during the Victorian fern craze of the early to mid-19th century. A number of species, including *Dicksonia antarctica, D. squarrosa, Cyathea dealbata,* and even *C. medullaris,* were brought from the Southern Hemisphere into the collections of the wealthy. In Europe, many of these introductions were pioneered by Jean Jules Linden (see the introduction to Chapter 3). By 1869, William Bull of Chelsea, London, had become a specialist in tree ferns. Bull, who counted no less a person than Queen Victoria as a customer, sold his plants by size (or trunk length, as is still current practice). An especially large specimen fetched as much as 40 guineas.

Today, many of the more than 500 species of tree ferns in the wild are endangered because of habitat destruction and the introduction of pests. Only 50–60 species are regularly cultivated. *Cyathea cooperi* and *Dicksonia antarctica,* both from Australia, are among the most common garden tree ferns. Cultivars of *C. cooperi* are available; 'Brentwood' and 'Robusta' are the most frequently planted in the United States. This tree fern, a rain forest species native to Queensland and New South Wales, has become naturalized in Mauritius, northern New Zealand, South Africa, and Hawaii, where it arrived sometime before 1960. In Hawaii (Plate 36), it has since been recommended for classification as a noxious weed. Its potential to become a weed must be kept in mind when its cultivation is considered.

# Temperature

In their natural habitats, tree ferns range from tropical and cold-sensitive to warm temperate and semihardy. Most species do best when night temperatures are cooler than those experienced during the day. However, there are species that will grow in regions where night and day temperatures are similar.

## Cool Climates

In general, extremely cold and dry areas are not suited to tree fern cultivation unless a glasshouse or conservatory can be provided. However, some tree ferns inhabit a wide geographic range, encompassing elevational and latitudinal differences. Species from elevated regions in countries with temperate climates such as New Zealand or Australia, and possibly those from alpine areas in more tropical areas such as New Guinea, may best survive Northern Hemisphere conditions. Plants sourced from higher elevations or from the coolest limits of their range can be expected to be hardier in cultivation. Some species are known to survive occasional snow, and frosts of −5°C (23°F) or lower. These more robust plants, including *Dicksonia antarctica* (from Australia), *D. fibrosa*, *D. squarrosa*, and to a certain extent, *Cyathea smithii* (all from New Zealand), will survive outdoors in maritime areas of Britain and Ireland (Best 1986, Rickard 1987), Europe, Japan, and the United States, especially where there are fewer than 20 frosts per year.

*Cyathea cooperi*, *C. woollsiana* (both from Australia), *C. muelleri* (New Guinea), *C. dealbata*, and the semiprostrate *C. colensoi* (Plate 33; it and *C. dealbata* from New Zealand), will also survive in cooler climates. However, these plants are susceptible to exceptionally cold or dry years. The giant *C. medullaris* of New Zealand, and *C. brownii* (Norfolk Island) and *C. robusta* (Lord Howe Island) of islands between New Zealand and Australia, have been known to survive outdoors in the Channel Islands off the southern coast of England, but these plants are best suited to temperate regions where frosts are rare as they are easily damaged. *Lophosoria quadripinnata* from South America has been known to grow outdoors as far north as Edinburgh, Scotland.

In regions where frosts are a consideration, only mature specimens (plants with a trunk 1 m high or more) should be planted outdoors. These larger plants are less susceptible to ground frost than younger ones with a small or no trunk. Most tree ferns will benefit from frost protection; this may be achieved with paper, sacking, or straw wrapped about the trunk and also protecting the apical growing region in winter. Some species naturally protect their trunk with a skirt of dead fronds (Plates 22, 92, 108, 113). Unfortunately, in the interests of overly tidy gardening, this skirt is often removed from cultivated plants. This action may be a serious mistake, resulting in the loss of even a mature specimen as a result of frost damage or drying. If frost or drought does cause damage, fronds may be cut back without significant long-term damage, provided the apical meristem of the plant is protected.

Many tree ferns grow naturally in montane forest or lowland rain forest environments where conditions are rarely dry. Even those Southern Hemisphere species that may endure occasional frosts and snow rarely experience long periods of drought or, more importantly, low atmospheric humidity. Plants brought into cultivation will do best in any situation that approximates this natural environment. In cooler situations, cold drying winds are probably the main tree fern enemy. High atmospheric humidity is advantageous, and artificial misting or fogging may help plants survive.

### Warm Climates

A warm, moist, tropical or subtropical climate will suit many tree ferns as long as moisture and some shade are available. Such tree ferns include members of the genera *Cibotium*, *Cyathea*, and *Dicksonia*. Although there are potentially many species that could be grown, only a few are in general cultivation or readily available commercially. It is also wise to consider that even those species that come from seemingly tropical countries may only inhabit the montane regions. In the Tropics, these plants would be best suited to high elevations and may not survive in cultivation at low elevations. (For further discussion see Benzona et al. 1994.)

## Humidity, Soils, and Moisture

Most tree ferns are sensitive to low humidity and drought. This is partially due to the nature of the rhizome trunk and the presence of roots along the outside of this structure. The effects of low humidity and the consequent reduction of roots may be accentuated as the plants get taller, with the longer trunk increasing the stress on the water system. Many species have mechanisms to maintain higher humidity around the trunk and growing apex. This includes the retention of old fronds and frond bases, producing a skirt (Plates 22, 92, 108, 113). The skirt is often removed in cultivation, much to the detriment of the health of the tree fern. The skirt may also aid in frost protection and discourage the growth of epiphytic plants (Page and Brownsey 1986).

Most tree ferns do best in soils with a large content of humus and a tendency toward an acidic nature. Clay soils benefit from the addition of organic matter and sand for drainage. Sandy soils also benefit from the addition of organic material to increase water-retention properties. Although some plants will continue to exist in drier conditions, most tree ferns do best in consistent soil moisture. This does not necessarily imply that tree ferns enjoy consistently wet conditions; soil drainage is essential. Container-grown plants also do best in a rich organic mixture with sharp drainage.

If tree ferns are grown indoors or where air humidity may be low, care should be taken to maintain humidity along the exterior of the trunk. This is particularly true of new plantings. Trunk humidity can be maintained automatically with a simple mist irrigation system and ground watering. The installation of an overhead watering system is not desirable, as accumulated water in the crown can promote rot of the apical growing region.

## Fertilizers and Nutrition

Ferns are often sensitive to high concentrations of mineral salts. This is particularly true of container-grown plants. Young plants may even be susceptible to the presence of chemical additives usually used in drinking water.

In general, high-nitrogen fertilizers will favor frond growth whereas high-phosphate fertilizers will favor spore production. However, excessive amounts of either may cause root damage. Slow-release inorganic fertilizers are usually the safest to use and minimize the risk of burning. Organic fertilizers such as bone meal, well-rotted manure, fish meal, treated animal manure, seaweed, or combinations of these, also release nutrients slowly into the soil and are favored by ferns, but even these compounds can cause root and leaf damage. They should be applied in diluted form in spring or at the beginning of the main growing season.

As with all rapidly growing plants, tree ferns will suffer from deficiencies of major and minor nutrients. Container-grown plants often show deficiency problems as a result of their restricted root mass. These problems may be easily remedied by repotting, or adding slow-release fertilizers.

## Light

Most tree ferns enjoy medium or filtered light. Few exist naturally where light is either very intense or dim, and few grow in fully open locations. Almost all tree ferns in cultivation are forest or forest-margin plants. However, there are exceptions. Some tree ferns are aggressive colonizers and increase their growth rates in higher-light conditions, for example, *Cyathea brownii* and *C. medullaris*. These plants can grow with full exposure to the sun, but even they will benefit in appearance by being shaded during the hottest part of the day. Too much sun will result in yellowing and eventual browning of the fronds.

## Vegetative Propagation

Trunk cuttings have often been used to propagate tree ferns and reduce the height of large specimens. In cooler climates, the cultivation of large tree ferns often depends on the provision of a glasshouse or conservatory. These constructions usually come with limited roof height; consequently, size reduction of a prized tree fern specimen may become a priority.

The ability to take a trunk cutting depends on the production of small roots (Plate 56) from the apical meristem and from among the frond bases along the trunk (anatomy is discussed in Chapter 1, under Rhizomes and Trunks). The production of roots depends on species, specimen age, and seasonal growth patterns. Stem cuttings are best planted in spring or when growing conditions are ideal, such as the wet season in the Tropics and Subtropics. Some tree ferns (such as mature specimens of *Cyathea brownii*, *C. medullaris*, or *Dicksonia lanata*) do not propagate well from trunk cuttings and do not readily produce roots beyond their juvenile phase of growth. Care should be taken to determine how plants will react before a prize specimen is topped and possibly lost! Topping is an easy way to control the height of members of the genus *Dicksonia*, in particular, *D. antarctica* and *D. fibrosa*.

In species that easily produce roots (such as *Cyathea australis*, *C. dealbata*, *C. smithii*, *Dicksonia antarctica*, *D. fibrosa*, and *D. squarrosa*), the trunk may be cut with a sharp saw and the upper trunk region, with intact crown, replanted. The fronds should be cut back or removed entirely to reduce transpiration stress while new roots form.

More delicate or difficult specimens benefit from a slower process. A plant pot may be cut into two halves and tied around the trunk. This pot may then be filled with coarse potting mix and sphagnum moss (or some other water-retentive material) and the trunk partially cut with a sharp saw. The potting mix must be kept damp until new roots fill the pot. The old trunk can finally be severed, providing a shortened and already-rooted plant. If the plant shows signs of water stress during the process, the crown fronds should be pruned back.

Tree ferns may either have one growing region at the top of their trunk, or produce side shoots (offsets or pups, Plate 18) from their main stem as well as at the apex. Most commonly cultivated tree ferns are of the first type, with one apical growing point. A trunk cutting from such plants represents a restructuring of the original, rather than a duplication of the plant.

Side shoots may be basal or occur anywhere along the trunk. For example, *Cibotium glaucum, Cyathea baileyana, C. capensis, C. rebeccae, Dicksonia youngiae, D. squarrosa,* and *D. antarctica* to a certain extent, all produce offsets. These provide an excellent alternative source for propagation material and have the added benefit that the parent plant will not be destroyed if they are removed. Side shoots may be removed from the main trunk and potted in a humus mixture with good drainage. On no account should the side shoots be allowed to dry out.

## Nursery Plants

In many countries the nursery trade is now able to provide large tree ferns. These plants are almost always grown from trunk cuttings. Only rarely are these large specimens raised from spores. As large plants often represent the removal of mature plants from the natural environment, care should be taken to ascertain the origin of particular specimens. Australia and New Zealand export living trunks cut as a by-product from plantation forestry. When collected, the crown of the plant is pruned to remove the fronds, and the resulting "cutting" is shipped by container, often as far away as Europe. When unloaded, these trunks can be planted directly into potting mix and sold, often without fronds.

Successful propagation depends on the species and trunk freshness. In selecting a specimen, care should be taken to ascertain the health of the crown. Healthy plants will have a firm apex with raised new fronds waiting to uncurl. Plants that have soft crowns, are hollow, or show no signs of firm uncurling fronds should be avoided. Growth may be aided by keeping the sides of the trunk damp. It is not advised to water the top, as the apex of the crown is prone to rot.

## Propagation from Spores

Unlike most trunk cuttings, propagation from spores will provide many new plants. These are often stronger and easier to adapt to the site in which they are planted. This method of propagation requires patience, with new plants taking 3–9 months to appear and several years to mature.

## Spore Collection

Spores can be collected from sori on the underside of the fern frond. However, spore maturation varies from species to species. The presence of dark, rounded sori and sporangia is usually a good sign that spores are ready to be released from a frond (Plate 40). Immature sori will usually look green, and sori that are disrupted and broken-open indusia are good indications that spores have already been released.

Ideally, spores should be collected from plants releasing spores naturally from the sporangium. Examine the sori on the underside of the fronds and look for the presence of dust-like spores. Next, place a small piece of frond into an envelope or small paper packet and leave it to dry naturally in a cool, dry place. Damp spores lose viability, but on no account should heat be used to speed up the process. High temperatures created by artificial drying may also kill the spores. After a few days, spores and the old empty sporangia will be visible at the bottom of the packet. At this stage the spores can be separated from sporangial material by gently shaking or blowing the contents on the opened paper. Sporangia and infertile spores are slightly lighter than the fertile spores and will move first. The heavier spore material should remain as a fine powder.

## Growth

Spores may be grown in sterile culture on an agar medium in much the same way some orchid seeds are raised. However, sterile cultivation usually relies on specialist knowledge. Contamination by fungi and algae is often a problem even when the most stringent sterile techniques are used. This may be most severe when gametophytes are moved from sterile to nonsterile conditions.

In many cases, germination and growth are best achieved by simply sowing the fresh spores onto sterile, premoistened potting mix. A common mistake is to sow too many spores. This discourages good growth of individual gametophytes and encourages the growth of fungi and algae.

A humus mix with low levels of fertilizer and near neutral pH is usually best, although tree fern trunk fiber, granulated bark, and even broken terracotta are good alternatives to commercially produced mixtures and provide the uneven surface required for spore germination in some species. The seed tray may then be placed in a sealed plastic bag, with wire loops attached to hold the bag away from the surface of the mixture. At this stage, a dark period of about 2 weeks may assist spore germination in some species. The tray can then be placed into a medium-temperature, low- to medium-light environment (not direct sunlight) until germination and gametophyte development have occurred. A shade house, such as that used for the cultivation of orchids, a shaded glasshouse, or even a window ledge can provide suitable cultivation requirements. Spores will germinate best during periods of increasing day length. Planting is usually more successful in spring than winter.

## Gametophytes

Growth rate is usually species- or genus-dependent. Often, the gametophyte will take many weeks or even months to mature. The first signs of successful growth will be a slight green fuzz on the surface of the potting mixture. Unfortunately, algae will also form a green fuzz if the sample is contaminated; this will not necessarily prevent gametophyte development. However, fungal contamination (often visible as a gray or cream, concentric, hair-like growth) is much more destructive and usually results in the loss of plants. Healthy gametophytes will eventually develop into disks of thin green plant tissue.

Once the gametophytes have developed and are mature, sexual organs are produced on their undersides. These structures are either male or female. Sex at any particular stage of development of the gametophyte is determined by light and/or the temperature range in which the plant is cultivated. In most cases, however, cool nights and warmer days produce the best results. Extremes below 4°C (39°F) and above 30°C (86°F) should be avoided. Because sperm are motile, fertilization and the production of a new sporophyte plant require surface moisture. Once gametophytes are mature, occasional brief flooding of the seed tray, or spraying with an atomizer, will assist the fertilization process.

## Sporophytes

Eventually, sporophytes will appear on the gametophytes (Plate 1). However, only when these are well established can the cover be gradually opened to harden off the young plants. Development of these new plants can be retarded if they develop too close to one another. Crowding of gametophytes can result in many small plants that tend to remain male. Only large gametophytes are able to produce archegonia and subsequently bear sporophytes. Spores should always be spread evenly and in low concentrations. If clumping results, gametophytes may be thinned.

New sporophyte plants will develop fronds in 6–12 months, depending on the species and conditions of cultivation. These young plants may then be pricked off the potting mixture. This is usually best done in small clumps, and the clumps potted using a well-drained but moist mixture. Care should be taken at this stage to maintain humidity. Many species are susceptible to damage and damping-off. Clumps of sporophytes may be separated into individual plants once they are established.

## Diseases and Pests

Tree ferns cultivated at the limits of their range are most at risk to disease and pests. Such plants are usually growing slowly and may be weakened. Healthy plants, growing vigorously, are much less susceptible to disease. However, care should still be taken to minimize insect infestation or the risk from fungal attack.

### Bacterial and Fungal Diseases

Tree ferns are especially susceptible to bacterial and fungal rots of the main apical growing region. These pathogens are usually serious and may result in the death of a tree fern. Bacterial rots are usually softer than those caused by fungi.

**Crown Rots.** In many cases these infections will be discovered too late to provide treatment. Early signs include the presence of deformed fronds (see also *Rhizoctonia*) and softening within the crown. The risk of infection is increased by watering from above. Prevention is the easiest form of treatment, and care should be taken to avoid overhead watering and minimize water buildup in the crown. Newly planted trunks should be watered or misted from the side.

*Armillaria* **Root Rot.** There is no known treatment for this fungal disease, which has caused the death of tree ferns. *Dicksonia antarctica* and *D. fibrosa* are especially susceptible. The stem will contain a whitish fungal mold, and at times, mushroom-like fertile growths of the fungus may be produced at the base of the trunk. These vary in color from brown to golden.

*Rhizoctonia, Phytophthora,* **and** *Pythium.* Several fungal diseases attack tree fern roots or destroy young gametophytes. Often the symptoms, which include withering and sudden death, appear too late to effect a successful treatment. *Rhizoctonia* is a fungal infection usually caused by overwatering. This disease causes a rot at ground level. Younger plants will wither and die off. Older tree ferns produce deformed fronds or stop growing. Control measures include decreasing or carefully monitoring watering. The fungicides captan and Benlate (benomyl) have also been used as a spray treatment but can cause burning, particularly in gametophytes.

*Phytophthora* and *Pythium* are fungal diseases that infect root tips of mature plants, causing dieback, wilting, and possible plant collapse. Both fungal genera are also a problem in gametophyte cultures, where damping-off results. Again, the presence of these organisms is usually related to overwatering or poor drainage. Once established, they are difficult to control. Ridomil and Aliette are effective systemic treatments. Because these fungicides have such a specific activity, however, the fungi can readily develop resistance to them. They should only be used as a last resort and only with expert advice.

## Insect Pests

Sapsucking insects, including mealybugs, leafhoppers, scale insects, thrips, and mites, are common on many tree ferns. They often infest young growth and may cause serious frond damage and tip dieback. Some ants farm these insects for the sticky sap they produce as a by-product. Consequently, control of an ant problem will often help control the pest.

Some sapsucking insects are known to spread disease, including those caused by viruses and other related pathogens, in other plants. The passion-vine hopper (*Scolypopa australis*) is one such pest, suspected of carrying a serious pathogen (a phytoplasma), causing dieback in a number of plants. It has been suggested that the plants affected include *Cyathea medullaris* in New Zealand (Plate 73). Unusual tree fern dieback has been recorded in both New Zealand and Australia, but proof that a phytoplasma is responsible is very difficult to obtain. Whatever the causal organism, these associated diseases are very difficult to control and perhaps impossible to cure, so insect control remains a priority and perhaps the easiest healthcare step.

Insects and other animals may also cause serious damage, particularly to the fronds of a young tree fern. These include slugs, snails, caterpillars, stick insects, grasshoppers, cockroaches, and staghorn beetles. Stem-boring weevils and borers are also known to cause frond damage in some tree ferns, resulting in frond-tip dieback. This phenomenon has also been attributed to the physiological effects of wind or drought. However, the presence of an insect pest can be confirmed by the appearance of small, raised spots on the underside of the pinnule midrib. Under closer examination, these will reveal small holes where insects have hatched and escaped.

## Fungicides and Insecticides

Unfortunately, tree ferns may be damaged by the modern pesticides and fungicides that are available to treat disease and insect infestation. This is particularly true of any sprays that include oil. The wrong pesticide or fungicide may cause as much damage as the original problem. All chemical treatments should be used with care.

Manual removal of insects is recommended. This is best done in the evening or early morning. Where this form of treatment is impractical, spraying with diluted soap solutions, or a pyrethrum solution, is a suitable alternative.

There are several insecticides and fungicides that will not harm tree ferns if they are applied in diluted concentrations. These include malathion, Diazinon (a cholinesterase-inhibiting organophosphate), and carbaryl for insect infestation. Benlate (benomyl) and captan can be used to treat a wide range of fungal infections. Sulfur dust will also help control disease and is particularly useful as a preventive treatment dusted over wounds or cut stems. Copper products, including copper oxychloride, are common disease treatments and particularly useful against fungi. As these copper products are usually toxic to tree ferns, however, they should be avoided or only used as a last resort. All of these compounds should be used with appropriate safety precautions and diluted beyond the dose recommended by the manufacturer. Commercial growers may even use an eighth or a quarter of the usual dilution.

## Physiological Damage

Extreme temperature is often one of the main problems that causes a tree fern not to look its best. Frost damage (Plates 47, 86) appears as burning on fronds and may cause delayed damage to the young uncurling fronds. In some cases, all fronds can be lost, but fronds will usually grow again in spring. Low temperature (other than frost) will produce slow growth and yellowing. Sometimes, fronds will blacken and the plant will slowly wither away.

High-temperature damage results in symptoms similar to those resulting from low temperatures and are not easy to distinguish from them. High temperatures may also cause wilting and scorching. Provide shade at the hottest time of the day, and if a glasshouse is used for cultivation, increase the humidity (for example, by spraying the floor and roof with water).

Some tree ferns are able to withstand extreme events, including fire that can cause the loss of an entire head of fronds. The plant may be left as a blackened stump, but if the fire has been fast and not too hot, these plants may be capable of using stored reserves to make a full recovery. This will often occur within weeks of the initial burning (Plate 48).

Tree ferns growing outside their usual range may survive short periods of unusual temperature. Often, plants that have been damaged by low temperatures or frost will regenerate quickly in spring. However, very marginal plants may still dwindle over several successive seasons.

Water stress may take several forms, with both absence and abundance causing problems. Low soil moisture and drought will leave a tree fern with wilting fronds. Often, it is the youngest fronds that suffer first, with older ones remaining stiff. However, lack of water is not the only cause of collapse. Wilt and sudden collapse may also occur when a tree fern is overwatered for a long period, or is waterlogged, then dries out. Gardens and indoor conditions are not always ideal for cultivation. Plants are expected to grow in areas under conditions that they would not normally encounter or tolerate. It is advisable to test soil moisture regularly. An oversupply of water, especially if drainage is impeded, will eventually cause root rot, and the fern may collapse or die just as quickly as it would in prolonged drought.

Moisture content of the air will also influence how a tree fern grows. Low humidity often promotes insect infestation (particularly spider mite or thrips) and causes premature dieback and yellowing in older fronds. Fronds may become progressively smaller, and young growth may suffer tip damage. Most tree ferns grow best, and keep healthy, in conditions that provide a relative air humidity of 60–80 percent. Excessive humidity, particularly at night, may encourage weak growth, with fungal and bacterial diseases becoming more common. (For further reading see Dunk 1982, Goudey 1988, Kelly 1991, Ide et al. 1992, Mickel 1994, Chaffey 1999, and Hoshizaki and Moran 2001.)

## Landscaping

Tree ferns are increasingly used in private gardens and commercial plantings (both outdoors and indoors). Tree ferns may be used singly but often look better when used in groups. Species can be selected to suit a variety of locations and include a range of low ground-cover forms to tall specimen plants (Appendix 3). Differing trunk shapes, from thin and slender to the massive structures produced by some members of the genus *Dicksonia*, may also provide different effects. Colored hairs and scales that cover the rhizomes and leaf bases on some species may also be attractive. Some even resemble fur (for example, *Cibotium barometz*, Plate 12) and give the plants a curious half-animal look.

Most tree ferns will do best with some shelter or when planted in association with other plants, including other ferns. Tree ferns seldom look good when planted alone and in exposed situations. Plants with slender trunks are susceptible to strong winds. Although species with stronger buttress trunks (usually supported by a fibrous root mass) will survive winds, their fronds are often damaged.

Tree ferns do well in courtyards and along sheltered walls. Plants may be used as living fences with unusual results. However, they seldom do well as street plantings except in areas with warm, moist climates. Room must be provided for eventual crown breadth as well as for those plants that branch or produce massive trunks.

CHAPTER 3

# The Tree Ferns

In 1753 Carl Linnaeus, regarded as the father of the binomial system of taxonomic nomenclature, published *Species Plantarum*. Based on the ideas of Caspar Bauhin (among others) of giving two names to all living things, this work regularized the system of botanical nomenclature we use today. Each plant was given a generic and unique specific name. Plant names may be taken from any source; nevertheless, the naming is bound by rules laid down by the *International Code of Botanical Nomenclature*. Many names are descriptive, designate localities, commemorate people who discovered the plant, or honor great botanists. Linnaeus considered that the use of generic and specific names "to preserve the memory of a botanist who has deserved well of the science" a religious duty. In taxonomic circles, however, it has always been considered poor form to name a plant after one's self. Of the more than 500 accepted names of tree fern species, about 140 are named after people. Many more are named after places or are descriptive.

The publication of Linnaeus's *Species Plantarum* reflected a time of increasingly vigorous plant exploration and collection, particularly from the New World. Linnaeus included several tree fern species in the genus *Polypodium*. Today, these plants are better known as *Cibotium barometz* (from Asia), *Cnemidaria horrida* (described from Jamaica), *Cyathea arborea* (Plate 21; described from Martinique), and *Cyathea aspera* (described from Haiti).

In 1781, Linnaeus's son, Carl, described *Cyathea capensis* (as *Polypodium capense*) from material collected from the Cape of Good Hope, South Africa. By 1786, *C. affinis* (as *P. affine*) from Tahiti and *C. medullaris* (as *P. medullare*) from New Zealand had been described by Georg Forster from collections made on James Cook's second voyage to the Pacific.

Only a few years later, in 1788, the first tree fern genus *Dicksonia* was defined by Charles-Louis L'Héritier de Brutelle (1746–1800). L'Héritier was an amateur French botanist who worked principally as a magistrate. He survived the French Revolution, working for the justice department in Paris, only to be the mysteriously murdered. L'Héritier amassed a herbarium collection of about 8000 specimens. After his death, these were purchased by a famous Swiss botanist, Augustin Pyramus de Candolle. Many now survive in the herbarium at Geneva. L'Héritier's description of *Dicksonia*, published in *Sertum Anglicum* in 1788, was based on material of *D. arborescens* from St. Helena. The specimens were collected in 1771 on Cook's first voyage to the Pacific, by Joseph Banks and Daniel Solander. L'Héritier had the opportunity to observe this material, along with other, more recently collected rare plant specimens, at Kew in 1786–1787 (Stafleu and Cowan 1976–88).

L'Héritier named the genus *Dicksonia* after James Dickson (1738–1822), who was a prominent nurseryman and botanist (Mabberley 1985, Robertson 2000) perhaps best known for his work on cryptogams (lower plants including mosses and liverworts). His herbarium is still preserved in the Natural History Museum, London. Dickson's best-known work, the series *Fasciculus 1[–7] Plantarum Crytogamicarum Britanniae*, with illustrations by James Sowerby, was published 1786–1801.

*Dicksonia* was followed in 1793 by the description of one of the best-known tree fern genera, *Cyathea*, by James Edward Smith (1759–1828). Smith was a British botanist and doctor of medicine, having studied at Edinburgh and Leiden. In 1784 he purchased Linnaeus's herbarium, which included some of the tree fern specimens previously published by Linnaeus as *Polypodium*, and 4 years later established the Linnean Society, still in operation and based at Burlington House in London. Smith's description of *Cyathea* is based on *C. arborea* (Linnaeus's *P. arboreum*). He also included the first reference to *C. multiflora* from mainland Central America.

The 19th century saw a dramatic increase in the amount of plant material available for scientific study (Plates 32, 80, 90). Many of the remaining genera and families we still recognize today were described early in this period. *Sphaeropteris* was described by German botanist and horticulturist Johann Jakob Bernhardi (1774–1850) in 1801. Bernhardi used *Cyathea medullaris*, originally described by Georg Forster as *Polypodium medullare*, as the type species of the genus.

By 1810 the genus *Alsophila* had been established by Robert Brown (1773–1858). Brown (Mabberley 1985) was a friend and correspondent of James Dickson, working with him on his *fasciculi*. Brown also knew Joseph Banks, becoming his librarian and that of the Linnean Society. However, Brown is perhaps best known for his work in Australia, where he traveled extensively with Matthew Flinders. Brown's description of *Alsophila* was based on material of *A. australis* (now *Cyathea australis*) from Australia. Most of his plant collections are now housed in the herbaria of the Natural History Museum, London, or the Royal Botanic Gardens, Kew and Edinburgh.

*Cibotium* was soon added to the growing list of new genera, by German botanist Georg Friedrich Kaulfuss (1786–1830). In 1824 Kaulfuss published *Enumeratio Filicum*, a text based on the travels and collections of Ludolf Karl Adelbert von Chamisso, who served as botanist on the Russian voyage of exploration on the *Rurik* conducted by Otto von Kotzebue. Chamisso had collected some 165 ferns of which 77 were new to science. These included samples collected in 1821 from Hawaii, of the small tree fern *C. chamissoi* (Plate 13), which Kaulfuss dedicated to him. Also in this collection was *Sadleria cyatheoides* (Plates 126–128; Blechnaceae), the genus of which Kaulfuss named after the Hungarian physician and botanist Joseph Sadler.

The middle of the 19th century also saw a rise in cultivation of rare and unusual plants. Tree ferns became desirable, and plant collectors searched the world for unknown species. Jean Jules Linden (1817–1898) was one such botanical explorer, who later became director of the Jardin Royal de Zoologie et d'Horticulture in Brussels. Linden traveled widely in the Americas; his eldest son, Lucien, later shared his interests, traveling in Malesia and the Congo. The Lindens were primarily plant dealers and set up a major nursery in Luxembourg. Catalogs were issued by the nursery, often including new descriptions and illustrations. Unfortunately, many of these catalogs are now difficult to find, but the few that remain include reference to several tree ferns. By 1862 the name *Cyathea funebris* appears in one of the catalogs; this tree fern is almost certainly *C. albifrons* from New Caledonia. Jean Jules Linden was also responsible for cultivating *C. princeps* (= *Sphaeropteris horrida*) from Mexico. Sterile plants had initially been collected by Frederik Liebmann and given to Linden to grow and introduce into horticulture. Superficially, these plants resembled the genus *Cibotium* and resulted in Linden's giving the name *C. princeps* to the plant in 1866. Unbeknown to Linden, Liebmann had earlier (1849) published the name *C. horridum* for the same plant. Despite Liebmann's earlier name, this plant is still commonly known as *Cyathea princeps*. In 1970, Rolla Tryon published a new combination for this plant, *Sphaeropteris horrida*, recognizing the earlier specific name (see also Tryon 1971).

## Families

Most tree ferns are placed in the families Cyatheaceae and Dicksoniaceae. However, a few ferns from a number of unrelated families—including the

Athyriaceae, Blechnaceae, Osmundaceae, Thelypteridaceae, and even the Aspleniaceae—also acquire a short trunk. Such plants are often used in horticulture because of their relatively small size. Some of the better known species of these tree fern-like ferns are included here.

More recently, DNA fingerprints and sequences have been used to examine genetic and evolutionary relationships between different tree ferns at the molecular level. Among these studies are some that combine molecular data along with morphological information (for example, Conant et al. 1994, 1995, 1996, Hasebe et al. 1995, Stevenson and Loconte 1996, and Wolf et al. 1999). These studies support a close grouping of tree ferns of the genera *Calochlaena, Cibotium, Culcita, Dicksonia,* and *Lophosoria,* and the complex centered on *Cyathea* (including *Alsophila, Cnemidaria,* and *Sphaeropteris*). The origins and affinities of *Cystodium* and *Thyrsopteris* to the main tree fern groups are less obvious (Figure 7). Unfortunately, this same evidence suggests that some of the families currently recognized are paraphyletic, which is to say that they contain genera from different evolutionary lineages. This is particularly true of the Dicksoniaceae. For example, *Lophosoria* (sometimes placed in its own family, Lophosoriaceae) appears closely related to *Dicksonia,* within the group that also includes *Calochlaena* and *Culcita*.

The position of the genus *Cibotium,* traditionally placed in the Dicksoniaceae, may also need to be reconsidered. The origins of this genus are difficult to determine, with evidence suggesting links to both the Dicksoniaceae and Cyatheaceae. *Cibotium* may represent an older lineage, perhaps, falling between the two main groups of tree fern. A full revision of the two traditional families is long overdue.

Ferns in the family Loxsomataceae (*Loxsoma, Loxsomopsis*) and the monotypic families Hymenophyllopsidaceae (*Hymenophyllopsis*), Plagiogyriaceae (*Plagiogyria*), and Metaxyaceae (*Metaxya*) possibly should be grouped with the Cyatheaceae and Dicksoniaceae into what has been called a "tree fern clade" (Wolf et al. 1999). It is likely that all of these families share a common evolutionary origin (called a monophyletic origin). However, as few if any of these plants form true trunks and are rarely cultivated, they are not discussed further.

Unfortunately, the taxonomy within the families Cyatheaceae and Dicksoniaceae is also the subject of much debate and there is no complete, standardized list of species. In general, we may consider that the two main families together contain around nine or ten genera and more than 500 species. A list of currently accepted families and genera as treated in this text is presented in Table 2. To simplify reference, genera and species are listed alpha-

Figure 7. Tree fern phylogeny suggested by morphological and molecular data (after Conant et al. 1996, Stein et al. 1996, Wolf et al. 1999, Lewis 2001.) Cyatheaceae includes three main clades or groups: *Alsophila*, *Cyathea* (*Cnemidaria* falling within the latter), and *Sphaeropteris*. The origins of the genus *Cibotium* are less well defined, with data suggesting a three-way split with the *Cyathea* and *Dicksonia* lineages. *Lophosoria* falls between *Calochlaena–Culcita* and *Dicksonia,* and is here regarded as part of the Dicksoniaceae. The relationships of *Cystodium* and *Thyrsopteris* are unclear.

betically here. An Index, including cross-references from common names and major synonyms to the accepted scientific names, is also provided.

**TABLE 2.** Orders, families, and genera recognized in *Tree Ferns*.

| ORDER | FAMILY | GENUS | SPECIES |
|---|---|---|---|
| Osmundales | Osmundaceae | *Leptopteris* | 6 |
|  |  | *Osmunda* | 5–6 |
|  |  | *Todea* | 1–2 |
| Cyatheales | Cyatheaceae | *Cnemidaria* | 25 |
|  |  | *Cyathea* | 470+ |
|  |  | *Alsophila* clade | 230–235 |
|  |  | *Cyathea* clade | 120+ |
|  |  | *Sphaeropteris* clade | 120+ |
|  | Dicksoniaceae | *Calochlaena* | 5 |
|  |  | *Cibotium* | 10–12 |
|  |  | *Culcita* | 2 |
|  |  | *Cystodium* | 1 |
|  |  | *Dicksonia* | 20–25 |
|  |  | *Lophosoria* | 1–2 |
|  |  | *Thyrsopteris* | 1 |
| Blechnales | Blechnaceae | *Sadleria* | 5–6 |

The two main families of tree ferns—Cyatheaceae and Dicksoniaceae—are described here, followed by families that include tree fern-like plants with small trunks: Athyriaceae, Blechnaceae, Osmundaceae, and Thelypteridaceae.

## Cyatheaceae Kaulfuss 1827

Alsophilaceae C. B. Presl 1847

The Cyatheaceae is a family of terrestrial ferns (with one species, *Cyathea gracilis*, sometimes epiphytic) with tree-like trunks. A few species may have a creeping rhizome, and there are creeping variants in normally arborescent species. However, these forms are the exception. The family includes the tallest tree ferns, with trunk heights in excess of 20 m.

All Cyatheaceae have scales instead of hairs, the latter characterizing members of Dicksoniaceae. Fronds of Cyatheaceae are among the largest leaves in the plant kingdom, with those of some species reaching 3–4 m in length and a final crown width of some 6 m. Sori occur away from the margins of the pinnules and take the form of elongate or rounded receptacles. The sorus is often enclosed by a thin indusium. Spores are rounded-triangular (trilete).

Fossils attributed to the Cyatheaceae appear for the first time in late Jurassic to early Cretaceous sediments. Modern genera of the family may have an origin even as late as the Tertiary.

Traditionally, the Cyatheaceae has been regarded as the largest group of living tree ferns. More recent evidence confirms this view, but unfortunately, the exact number of species is unknown. This confusion is further increased by differences of opinion on the number of genera within the family (for example, Holttum 1963, Holttum and Edwards 1983, Tryon 1970, 1976, Conant 1983, Lellinger 1987, and Kramer 1990). Table 3 summarizes the main taxonomic treatments.

In the 19th century, species were placed in three genera, primarily depending on the form of the indusium (Bostock 1998). Species without indusia were included in *Alsophila*, those with cup-shaped indusia in *Cyathea*, and those with hooded indusia in *Hemitelia*. In time, it was recognized that this system was unnatural and that species with and without indusia could be closely related. Edwin Copeland (1908, 1947) included all Malaysian species in a single genus *Cyathea* with only minor segregates (see also Domin 1929, 1930). Unfortunately, the segregates (or minor subgroupings) were not clearly defined.

In 1925, Richard Eric Holttum (1895–1990) became acting director (then director) of the Singapore Botanic Gardens. He along with E. J. H. ("John") Corner (1906–1996) survived the Second World War under the

**TABLE 3.** Comparison of taxonomic treatments of the family Cyatheaceae, including genera, subgenera (subg.), sections (sect.), and subsections (subsect.).

| CONANT ET AL. (1996) | LELLINGER (1987) | TRYON (1970), TRYON AND TRYON (1982) | HOLTTUM AND EDWARDS (1983) |
|---|---|---|---|
| *Alsophila* clade | *Alsophila* | *Alsophila* | *Cyathea* subg. *Cyathea* sect. *Alsophila* subsect. *Alsophila* |
|  |  | *Nephelea* | subsect. *Nephelea* |
| *Cyathea* clade | *Cyathea* | *Cyathea* | sect. *Cyathea* |
|  |  | *Trichipteris* |  |
|  |  | *Sphaeropteris* subg. *Sclephropteris* |  |
|  | *Cnemidaria* | *Cnemdiaria* |  |
| *Sphaeropteris* clade | *Sphaeropteris* | *Sphaeropteris* subg. *Sphaeropteris* | *Cyathea* subg. *Sphaeropteris* |

Japanese occupation, being kept as civil internees to assist in preserving the irreplaceable botanical collections and libraries (Corner 1981, Stearn 1996b, Mabberley 2000). After the war, in 1949, Holttum became the University of Malaya's first professor of botany and was a botanist at the Royal Botanic Gardens, Kew, from 1954. He was to have a major influence on tree fern taxonomy in the 20th century (Holttum and Sen 1961, Holttum 1964, 1965a, b, 1974, 1981, Holttum and Molesworth Allen 1967). His experience, based largely in the Old World Tropics, led him initially to revert to one encompassing genus *Cyathea*. He later revised his original ideas to include two subgenera: *Cyathea* subgenus *Cyathea*, and subgenus *Sphaeropteris* (Holttum 1963, Holttum and Edwards 1983).

By the 1970s and early 1980s this view was being challenged, and six genera (partly new and partly redefined versions of Holttum's subdivisions) were circumscribed by Rolla Tryon (1970, 1976). These included *Alsophila*, *Cyathea*, *Trichipteris*, *Sphaeropteris* (with two subgenera: *Sphaeropteris* subgenus *Sphaeropteris*, and subgenus *Sclephropteris*), *Cnemidaria*, and *Nephelea*. *Nephelea* was later merged with *Alsophila* by David Conant (1983). Tryon's classification does not clearly separate genera (Holttum and Edwards 1983) and has been followed in the Americas but largely ignored in Europe and the Southern Hemisphere. Many subsequent works, including Kramer (1990) and Bostock (1998), retain a broad circumscription of *Cyathea* in the sense of Holttum, with the view that this is the only appropriate worldwide division of the family Cyatheaceae.

In 1987 Lellinger had recognized four genera: *Alsophila* (equating to Tryon's *Alsophila* combined with *Nephelea*), *Cyathea* (including Tryon's *Trichipteris* and *Sphaeropteris* subgenus *Sclephropteris*), *Cnemidaria*, and *Sphaeropteris* (equating to Tryon's *Sphaeropteris* subgenus *Sphaeropteris*). This system compares in some way with more recent molecular work that supports three major evolutionary lines within the Cyatheaceae (Conant et al. 1996); these have been called the *Alsophila* clade, the *Cyathea* clade, and the *Sphaeropteris* clade. These clades do not precisely conform to the genera recognized by Tryon or the groups used by Holttum, but they do in some way support Lellinger's view of *Alsophila* and *Sphaeropteris*. *Cnemidaria*, on the other hand, falls within *Cyathea*, making Lellinger's genus paraphyletic, which is to say a group that does not contain all descendents of the most recent common ancestor (Wiley 1981).

In 1996 Conant concluded, based on molecular and morphological evidence, that a system of three clades—*Alsophila*, *Cyathea*, and *Sphaeropteris*—is a closer reflection of evolutionary lineages within the Cyatheaceae (Conant et al. 1996). However, formal taxonomic changes have not been made. A reclassification of the family awaits further studies.

In time, these three grouping may indeed be recognized as genera in their own right. For the present, however, there are significant taxonomic problems involving name combinations and changes that must be taken into account. For the convenience of the reader, and as many of the commonly used names are still in *Cyathea*, *Tree Ferns* follows a taxonomically conservative system based on Kramer (1990). One encompassing genus *Cyathea* is recognized that includes Lellinger's *Alsophila*, *Cyathea*, and *Sphaeropteris*. *Cnemidaria* is treated as a separate genus because of the nomenclatural difficulties that must be resolved before merging it with *Cyathea* (see the introductions to *Cnemidaria* and *Cyathea* for further comment).

The varied taxonomic histories of the genera within the Cyatheaceae cause significant problems in identifying valid specific names and understanding synonyms. Despite an apparent wealth of opportunity in the creation of novel plant names, certain specific names have always been popular. The same name may appear many times in association with a variety of genera and quite different plants. These reoccurring names cause considerable confusion if genera are later combined (for example, *Trichipteris steyermarkii* is not *Cyathea steyermarkii*; see also Barrington 1978). Previously well-known names may no longer be valid. To reduce confusion, an Index is provided, and many of the more commonly used synonyms are included in the text.

**Dicksoniaceae** Bower 1908, as Dicksonieae
    Thyrsopteridaceae C. B. Presl 1847, as order Thyrsopteridaceae;
        Culcitaceae Pichi-Sermolli 1970, Lophosoriaceae Pichi-Sermolli 1970,
        Cystodiaceae J. R. Croft 1986

The Dicksoniaceae is a family of mostly terrestrial ferns but some epiphytes (for example, several species of *Cibotium*, and *Culcita coniifolia*, which may be terrestrial or epiphytic), generally but not always with rhizomes forming tree-like trunks. All Dicksoniaceae have long, tapering hairs composed of cells arranged end to end, rather than scales, the latter characteristic of Cyatheaceae. Fronds may be 1–3 m in length. Sori occur toward the margins of the pinnules and take the form of elongate or rounded receptacles. The sorus is enclosed by a thin indusium and a small reflexed lobe of the frond lamina. Spores are rounded-triangular (trilete).

The Dicksoniaceae have a long fossil record, extending into the early Jurassic or earlier. The history of the family is one of early diversity and periods of extinction. In comparison with the Cyatheaceae, the taxonomy of the Dicksoniaceae has been more stable, and seven genera are recognized here (Table 2). The largest of these is *Dicksonia* with some 20–25 species. *Dicksonia* is an ancient group with a current distribution ranging from St. Helena in the Atlantic to the Americas, the Juan Fernández Islands, other Pacific Islands, Australia, New Zealand, and Malesia. Again, because of the diversity within this genus (particularly in New Guinea), the exact number of species is unknown. *Calochlaena* has 5 recognized species, ranging from Malesia, eastern Australia, to Tasmania and the Pacific. *Cibotium* has perhaps 10–12 in America, Asia, Malesia, and principally Hawaii. *Culcita* (sometimes placed in a separate family, Culcitaceae, with *Calochlaena*) includes 2 species, one South American and the other ranging from Spain and Portugal to the Atlantic African islands. *Lophosoria* (often placed in its own family, Lophosoriaceae) is usually regarded as comprising a single species found in the Americas. However, a more recently described second species may be endemic to Costa Rica. *Cystodium* and *Thyrsopteris* are also represented by a single species each, the former distributed from Borneo to New Guinea, and the latter restricted to the Juan Fernández Islands. Although various characters, including spore morphology, suggest these latter two genera are distinctive and perhaps lie outside of the main group of dicksoniaceous ferns (Figure 7), for convenience they are here regarded as part of the Dicksoniaceae.

### **Athyriaceae** Alston 1956

The Athyriaceae is a large and diverse family (sometimes included in the Dryopteridaceae) of worldwide distribution. Their greatest diversity is in Asia. Perhaps only half of the 23 genera should continue to be recognized (Bostock 1998) as the differences between them are poorly defined (for example, *Allantodia*, *Deparia*, and *Diplazium*). *Diplazium esculentum* (Retzius) Swartz from Asia and the closely related *D. dietrichianum* (Luerssen) C. Christensen (Plate 119) from Queensland, Australia, are terrestrial ferns that may produce short trunks, to about 1 m in height. *Athyrium microphyllum* (J. Smith) Alston, in parts of Hawaii, will also produce short trunks, 24 cm or more tall and 3–4 cm in diameter. These ferns are not discussed further, however.

### **Blechnaceae** (C. B. Presl) Copeland 1947
   Blechneae C. B. Presl 1851

The Blechnaceae is a large family of ten genera or more. Family members often have strongly dimorphic fronds. The photosynthetic leaf tissue (or lamina) on fertile fronds is often reduced in size, with elongate sori often covering the lower surface of fertile pinnae. In all, spores are bilaterally symmetrical, almost bean-shaped. Only a few species are arborescent, and even fewer more than 2 m tall. The most important of these are in the genus *Sadleria*, with about six species endemic to Hawaii, almost all of which are arborescent; the species are included in the alphabetical listing.

Some other species of the family may be mentioned briefly here, including *Brainea insignis* (W. J. Hooker) J. Smith, found in Asia, the only member of the genus, and several species with trunks 1 m high or more commonly placed in the genus *Blechnum* but perhaps more appropriately split into several genera. These include *B. buchtienii* Rosenstock, *B. cycadifolia* (Colla) Sturm (Plate 3), and *B. magellanica* (Desvaux) Mettenius (Plates 7, 8), all *Lomariocycas*.

*Blechnum discolor* (G. Forster) Keyserl (Plates 4, 5) and *B. nudum* (Labillardière) Mettenius ex Luerssen (= *Lomaria nuda* (Labillardière) Willdenow) are smaller plants with relatively short trunks.

Others are more shrubby but may still have trunks as tall as 1 m. Some of these are *Blechnum brasiliense* Desvaux (compare *Gondwanopteris*); *B. fraseri* (A. Cunningham) Luerssen (= *Diploblechnum fraseri* (A. Cunningham) de Vol), of which a variant form from the Philippines produces a trunk 1–2 cm in diameter and scrambles to a height of more than 1.5 m; *B. gibbum* (Labillardière) Mettenius (Plate 6); and *B. vittatum* Brackenridge.

In general, *Blechnum* species are relatively hardy and are easy to grow under a wide range of conditions. Those producing the biggest trunks (to about 1 m) can be frost sensitive but often survive some frond damage. In the coolest regions they may be grown as container specimens and should grow well if protected from wind and given consistent moisture and good drainage.

**Marattiaceae** Berchtold & J. S. Presl 1820, as Marattiae

Angiopteridaceae Fée ex J. Bommer 1867, as Angiopterideae

Very large herbaceous ferns are common in the ancient family Marattiaceae, whose ancestors formed tree ferns in the Carboniferous period. Today, there are two living genera, *Angiopteris* (Plate 2) and *Marattia*, both with species producing large fronds, usually arising from massive, slow-creeping rhizomes. Occasionally, these stems may be semierect to just over about 50 cm in height.

Species of *Marattia* may be propagated from spores. Development is slow, however, and it may take 4 years to produce a plant approximately 5 cm high by this method. Plants are best suited to warm climates (warm temperate to tropical). They require protection from frost and need a consistent supply of moisture to do well. Plants will respond to organic fertilizer in early spring and again in fall.

## Osmundaceae Berchtold & J. S. Presl 1820

The Osmundaceae is one of the most ancient groups of ferns with fossils recognized as far back as the Permian period. Many of the extinct plants were tree fern-like. There are three extant genera, with species included in the alphabetical listing. *Leptopteris* is a Southern Hemisphere genus of about six mostly slow-growing species. All have short stems or trunks, to 1 m long. The widely distributed *Osmunda* also comprises five or six species and may produce massive trunks after many years of growth. Several species are deciduous, or at least partially so. *Todea* consists of two species of the Southern Hemisphere: *T. papuana* Hennipman from New Guinea and *T. barbara* from southern Africa through Australia to northern New Zealand. The latter species is slow-growing but may produce a massive clumping trunk as tall as 1 m, rarely 3 m. The rhizome may also be very slow-creeping and very long-lived. After many years, plants in the wild may divide to form a circular colony rather like a toadstool ring. These fern rings represent clones and may indicate great age.

## Thelypteridaceae Ching ex Pichi-Sermolli 1970

The Thelypteridaceae is a large, relatively advanced family of worldwide distribution that has a few scattered trunk-forming members. There are five genera and some 650 species. *Pneumatopteris pennigera* (G. Forster) Holttum (Plate 125) from New Zealand and Australia is a plant of the forest floor and may produce a slender trunk more than 1 m in height.

# Hybrids

Hybrids between species are often infertile, producing nonfunctional spores because of genetic mismatch. Only in rare cases, usually where parents are closely related, are fertile hybrids produced, that is, those that can reproduce themselves in the normal manner.

Tree ferns are known to hybridize, and there is evidence that some populations recognized as species may be of hybrid origin. In most cases, these are interspecific hybrids, that is, between different species of the same genus. Rare hybrids are known within the genus *Dicksonia*, including crosses between *D. fibrosa* and *D. squarrosa* in New Zealand. However, by far the majority of known hybrids occur within the Cyatheaceae.

Tryon and Tryon (1982) noted nine suspected or known hybrids within the *Alsophila* clade and ten in the *Cyathea* clade plus *Cnemidaria*. These include known crosses between *Cnemidaria horrida* and *Cyathea arborea*. The occurrence of such intergeneric hybrids weakens the argument for maintaining the two as separate genera.

Two species in the *Alsophila* clade (commonly known as *A. amintae* and *A. bryophila* because of nomenclatural problems; Appendix 1) are thought to be the parents of *Cyathea* ×*dryopteroides*. Hybrids involving these two species and *C. portoricensis* are also known to backcross with any of the three parents. Molecular studies have been important in helping to identify these plants and their relationships. In conjunction with morphological work, molecular studies may yet help us understand parental origins. Further discussion of hybrids may be found in the introductions to the genera.

## Genera and Species

### Key to Tree Ferns

1. Sori discrete and usually rounded, with or without indusia
    2. Base of the stipe with hairs but without scales, sori marginal (at edge of pinnae), covered or partially covered by lobe of the lamina . . . . . . . . . . . . . . . . . . . . . . . . . . . . . . . . . . . . . . . . . . . . . . . . . . . . . . . . . . . . . . . . . . . . . (Dicksoniaceae)
        3. Frond lamina only bipinnate . . . . . . . . . . . . . . . . . . . . . . . . . . . . . *Cystodium*
        3. Frond lamina bipinnate and dissected or more complex
            4. Axis (stem) of lamina grooved
                5. Lamina with both sterile and fertile portions more or less the same . . . . . . . . . . . . . . . . . . . . . . . . . . . . . . . . . . . . . . . . . . . . . . *Culcita*
                5. Lamina dimorphic, with fertile segment as a skeleton and strikingly different from the sterile portion . . . . . . . . . . . . *Thyrsopteris*
            4. Axis of lamina (at secondary and tertiary pinnae) ridged
                6. Indusium gradually merging with lamina; lamina green beneath and often narrowed toward the base of the frond . . . . . . . . . *Dicksonia*
                6. Indusium sharply differentiated from the lamina; lamina glaucous beneath and not narrowed toward the base of the frond . . . . *Cibotium*
    2. Base of the stipe bearing scales, or scales and hairs, with sori on lower surface of lamina but not associated with the margin of the pinnule, sori globular to cup-shaped; indusia various or absent . . . . . . . . . . (Cyatheaceae)
        7. Cells of the scale all essentially similar and the edge often toothed or even ciliate . . . . . . . . . . . . . . . . . . . . . . . . *Cyathea* (*Sphaeropteris* clade)
        7. Cells of the scale narrow near the center, surrounded by a broad margin of differently shaped cells; edge may be toothed or ciliate

  8. Scales with a prominent dark terminal seta or spine ................ *Cyathea* (*Alsophila* clade)
  8. Scales without a terminal seta, apex rounded to filamentous
   9. Spores with equatorial pores ....................... *Cnemidaria*
   9. Spores lacking large equatorial pores but granulate, spinulate, or porate .............................. *Cyathea* (*Cyathea* clade)
1. Sori aggregated, usually elongate or indiscrete when the sporangia are spread over the frond undersurface
 10. No true sori, sporangia massed on the underside of fertile pinnules ........ (Osmundaceae)
  11. Sporangia on axes usually lacking any green lamina; only the main veins are not covered; fronds may be deciduous ........... *Osmunda*
  11. Sporangia scattered on normal frond portions with green lamina and associated with veins; fronds persistent, never deciduous
   12. Fronds filmy, membranous, semitransparent, only one or two cells thick, therefore usually without stomata .......... *Leptopteris*
   12. Fronds thick, leathery, with stomata ...................... *Todea*
 10. Sporangia in complex elongate structure paralleling main vein or margin of lamina, usually with an indusium .............. (Blechnaceae)
  13. Leaves simple, pinnatifid, or simply pinnate, rarely bipinnate (only 2 species); fertile parts usually distinct from the sterile, often reduced and narrow ......................................... *Blechnum*
  13. Veins connected by arches flanking the costules in both sterile and fertile fronds; leaves pinnate and pinnatifid or bipinnate; fertile parts similar to the sterile ................................ *Sadleria*

## *Calochlaena* (Maxon) Turner & White 1988
 *Culcita* subgenus *Calochlaena* Maxon 1922
 Dicksoniaceae

William Maxon described *Calochlaena* in 1922 as a subgenus of *Culcita*. In 1988 was it raised to the level of genus by Melvin Turner and Richard White. The type species is *Calochlaena dubia*, described by Robert Brown as *Davallia dubia* in 1810 from Queensland, Australia. The name *Calochlaena* is derived from the Greek *kalos*, beautiful, and *chlaena*, cloak, in reference to the hairs that cover the rhizome. The genus is regarded as related to *Culcita*, but spores are distinct and support the recognition of a separate genus.

 *Calochlaena* is a genus of terrestrial ferns with creeping to semierect

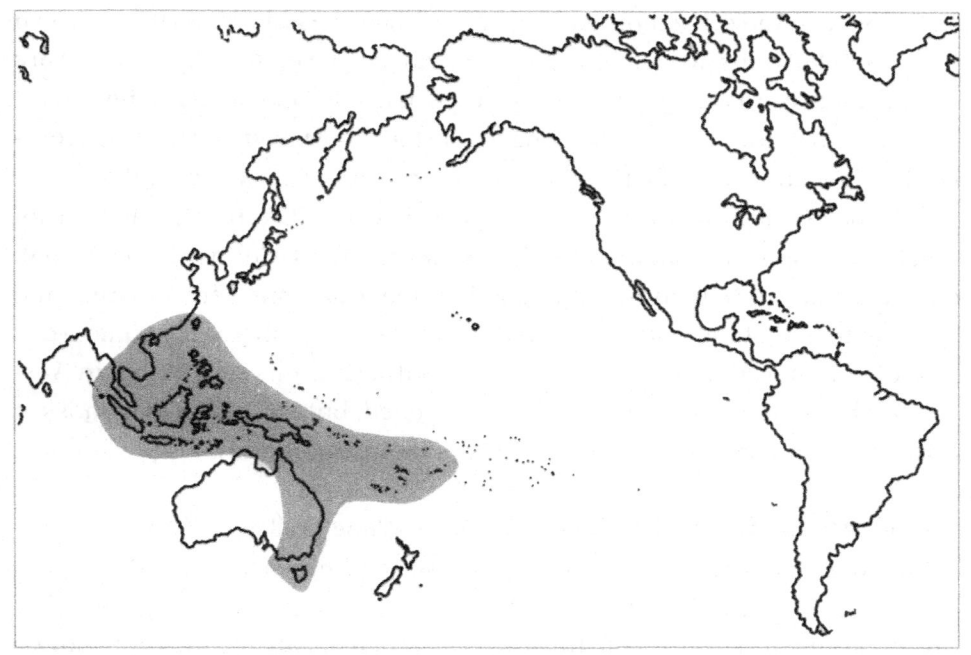

*Calochlaena,* distributed from Malesia to Polynesia and eastern Australia.

stems or rhizomes and fronds as long as 1.5 m. The rhizome seldom forms a true trunk, and *Calochlaena* can only be marginally regarded as a tree fern. The stipe is hairy, and the sori are marginal, with bivalved indusia. The sporangium is leptosporangiate, with a long stalk and a well-defined oblique structure (the annulus) situated along one edge. Spores of all species are trilete, with coarse tubercles covering the surface. Chromosome number $n =$ 55–58 for *C. dubia.*

About five species of *Calochlaena* are recorded with distributions from Malesia (Java to the Philippines and New Guinea), Melanesia, and Polynesia to eastern Australia. Plants grow in damp, open locations in tropical open forest, on hillsides and banks. Several species colonize disturbed sites such as road cuts.

### *Calochlaena dubia* (R. Brown) Turner & White 1988

*Davallia dubia* R. Brown 1810, *Culcita dubia* (R. Brown) Maxon 1922
FALSE BRACKEN, RAINBOW FERN
PLATE 9

The creeping rhizome is 1–2 cm in diameter, covered in soft silver and brown hairs. Fronds are triangular, tripinnate, yellowish green, and 1–1.5 m long. Rachis and lamina veins are sparsely hairy. The stipes are usually as long as

1.5 m, brown, and often mottled. The base of the stipe is dark and bears brown hairs. Sori have circular inner indusia, which may be membrane-like and are virtually lost by maturity. The reflexed lobe of the lamina protects their outer region. Distribution: Australia, along the eastern coast from northern Queensland to Tasmania, in open forest and common on hillsides and banks.

*Calochlaena dubia* forms large colonies. Because it is creeping, it does not reach the proportions characteristic of true tree ferns. Cultivated plants will spread rapidly in rich humus with good drainage and plentiful moisture and are able to withstand both warm and cool conditions, including some frost, provided material is obtained from the southern limits of it range in Australia. The species is not regarded as threatened, but collection of fronds for floristry is managed in Australia. Living plants are sometimes exported.

## *Calochlaena javanica* (Blume) Turner & White 1988

*Dicksonia javanica* Blume 1828, *Culcita javanica* (Blume) Maxon 1922,
   *C. copelandii* (Christ) Maxon 1922

The creeping or barely erect rhizome is as much as 50 cm long and about 6 cm in diameter. Fronds are tetra- or pentapinnate and may reach 3 m in length. Petioles are light to dark brown. The rachis is light-colored and lacks spines or scales. Hairs are present on the trunk and stipe and are orange to light brown. Sori are submarginal, one per pinnule lobe, and protected by the margin; a second inner, thin, sac-like indusium is also present. Distribution: Borneo eastward through Indonesia (including Java, hence the name *javanica*) to New Guinea, common in hill and montane forest at 1000–1600 m.

Although not common in cultivation, *Calochlaena javanica* will grow in most soils but does best in humus in open, light conditions.

## *Calochlaena straminea* (Labillardière) Turner & White 1988

*Dicksonia straminea* Labillardière 1824, *Culcita straminea* (Labillardière)
   Maxon 1922
   PLATE 10

The creeping or barely erect rhizome is as much as 50 cm long and about 6 cm in diameter. Fronds are tetra- or pentapinnate and may reach 3 m in length. Rachis and lamina veins are densely hairy beneath. Hairs are present on the trunk and stipe and are orange to light brown. Sori are submarginal, one per pinnule lobe, and protected by the margin; a larger inner sac-like indusium is also present. Distribution: East Malaysia, Taiwan, and the Philippines to New Guinea, the Solomon Islands, New Caledonia, Vanuatu, Fiji, and Samoa, in lowland forest.

Although not common in cultivation, *Calochlaena straminea* does well in most soils but best in warm areas in humus, and in open, light conditions. It is the only species of the genus listed in CITES. Overall, it is not threatened, but the exact status over much of its range is unknown. It is rare in the Philippines.

## *Calochlaena villosa* (C. Christensen) Turner & White 1988

*Culcita villosa* C. Christensen 1937

The barely erect, narrow rhizome is covered in red-brown hairs. Fronds are triangular, tri- or tetrapinnate, yellowish green, and about 1 m long. The stipe is brown and often dark toward the base, which is covered with red-brown hairs. Sori occur two or three per pinnule lobe, are circular and covered by inner indusia that are membrane-like and virtually lost by maturity. The reflexed lobe of the lamina protects the outer region. Distribution: Northern Queensland, Australia, and New Guinea and Sulawesi (Celebes), in montane forest and common on hillsides and tablelands.

*Calochlaena villosa* is a prostrate fern that usually forms clumps. The name *villosa* implies hairiness and refers to the covering of reddish brown hairs on the rhizomes and stipes. It is a montane tropical fern that does best in rich humus with good drainage and plentiful moisture. Leaves have occasionally been used in floristry.

## *Cibotium* Kaulfuss 1824

*Pinonia* Gaudichaud-Beaupré 1824

Dicksoniaceae

Georg Kaulfuss described *Cibotium* in 1824; the type species is *C. chamissoi*, described at the same time by Kaulfuss. *Pinonia*, described by Charles Gaudichaud-Beaupré later in 1824, is congeneric. The name *Cibotium* is derived from the Greek *kibotion*, a small box, in reference to the form of the sorus and indusium on the underside of the fronds, which resembles a small casket.

*Cibotium* comprises large ferns with usually prostrate or trunk-like rhizomes (to about 8 m tall) and long fronds. The rhizome often has a fluffy appearance and is covered with yellow-brown hairs. These hairs are long at the base of the stipe and often matted in appearance. Sori are marginal and bilobed. Both lobes are usually alike in texture and color, unlike *Dicksonia*, in which the lobes are dissimilar. Spores of all species are trilete. In Old World species, equatorial ridges or flanges are common; these are usually missing in American species. The spore surface is usually scabrate to granulate. Fossil spores are common in the fossil record during periods of wet climate and

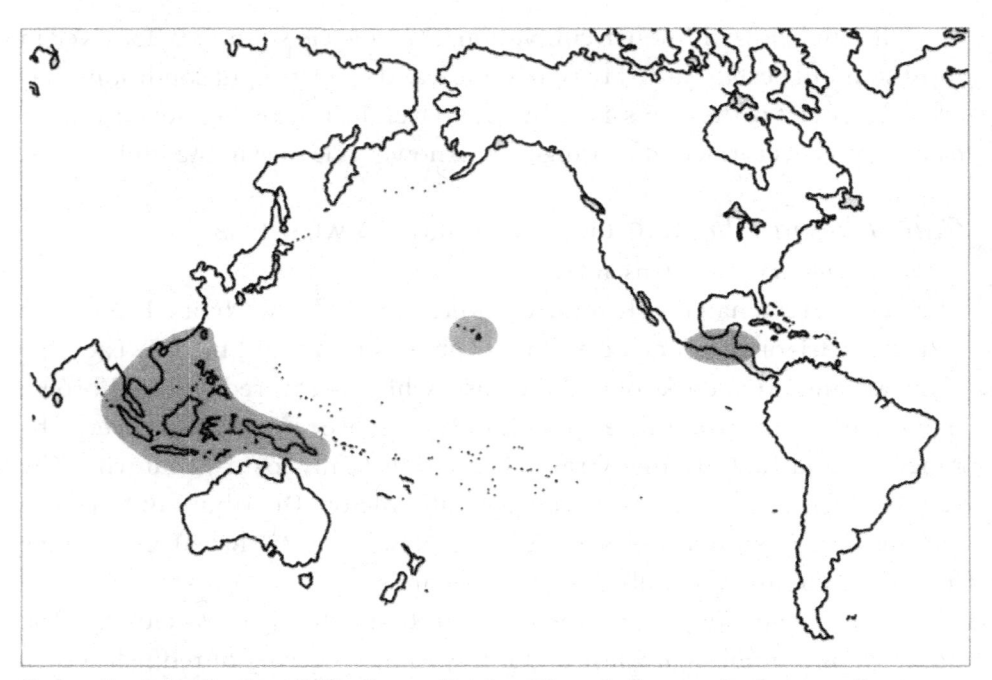

Generalized distribution of *Cibotium*, with about three to five species from southern China through Malaysia to Indonesia, four endemic to Hawaii, and two or three in Central America.

have been noted from Miocene and Quaternary sediments and peats. These *Cibotium* fossils have been regarded as an indicator of the presence of rain forest. Chromosome number $n = 68$.

Species of *Cibotium* are distributed from southern China and Taiwan to Malaysia, Indonesia, New Guinea, Pacific islands (including Hawaii), and Mexico. Plants seem to enjoy open areas in tropical hill and submontane forest at elevations of 500–2500 m, where they may form thickets. They may occur on banks and road cuts. Some species are fire resistant and will persist after land clearance.

*Cibotium* comprises 10–12 species; the nomenclature in Hawaii, where 4–5 are considered to be endemic, has been a serious source of confusion. The Hawaiian species recognized here are based on the treatment by Daniel Palmer (1994; see also Becker 1984). *Cibotium* is commonly cultivated, especially in the Tropics and as conservatory plants. Plants will grow in warm or cooler areas but do not tolerate frost well. The species will grow in most soils but do best in well-drained humus in open, light conditions, provided shelter from wind is provided.

### *Cibotium arachnoideum* (C. Christensen) Holttum 1963

*Cibotium cumingii* var. *arachnoideum* C. Christensen in
C. Christensen & Holttum 1934

The massive prostrate trunk is covered with yellow-brown hairs. Fronds are persistent and 4–5 m long; the stipe is long. The sorus has a stiff, two-lobed indusium, and sori occur marginally. Distribution: East Malaysia in lower montane forest and at 700–2100 m on Kinabalu. *Cibotium arachnoideum* occurs primarily in areas of secondary growth and survives burning, and persists on land cleared for cultivation.

*Cibotium arachnoideum* is known for its dense, massive, creeping rhizome and is only marginally a tree fern. Rhizome hairs are used as a wound dressing and to staunch blood loss. This species is not frequent in cultivation, yet within its native range it may be seen on cultivated land. It does well in most soils but best in humus. This tree fern will survive fire and persists in full sun.

### *Cibotium barometz* (Linnaeus) J. Smith 1842

*Polypodium barometz* Linnaeus 1753
GOLDEN CHICKEN FERN, SCYTHIAN LAMB,
WOOLLY FERN, BULU PUSI, PENEWAR JAMBI
PLATES 11, 12

The stout prostrate trunk may reach 1 m in height but is usually slow-creeping and covered with persistent stipe bases and long golden hairs; colonies of plants may form through the progressive growth and rotting of the trunk. Fronds are persistent, bipinnatifid to deeply tripinnatifid, more than 3 m long, yellowish green (particularly when young), and may be glaucous underneath. The stipe is as long as 1.2 m and dark brown toward the frond lamina but lighter toward the trunk; the lower regions are covered with very slender, golden or almost ginger-colored hairs. The sorus has a stiff, brown, two-lobed indusium, and sori occur marginally, with as many as five per pinnule. Distribution: China to the western Malay Peninsula, common in open forest or on road cuts and slopes in hilly and montane areas at 200–1700 m, and even prolific in disturbed sites.

*Cibotium barometz* is usually prostrate and, like *C. arachnoideum*, may only marginally be considered a tree fern. The name *barometz* is from a Tartar word meaning lamb and refers to the appearance of the woolly rhizome. This fern was considered to be half animal and half plant, and the rhizome (turned upside down, with four leaf bases) was passed off as the Scythian lamb (Figure 6). This lamb grew roots and in the 17th and 18th centuries was used as a charm to ward off evil. Plants were exported from the Malay Peninsula through China and Russia to Europe. Such charms are still sold in the Philippines, Taiwan, and Malaysia. Hairs of the rhizome and stipe may be charred or used fresh as a wound dressing and to stem the flow of blood. The leaves have also been used to ease fainting. Dried rhizome hairs have been used to stuff pillows but are known to cause lung trouble in some people. In cultivation, *C. barometz* does well in most soils but best in well-drained but moist humus in open, light conditions. Plants will grow in warm or cooler areas but do not tolerate frost well.

## *Cibotium chamissoi* Kaulfuss 1824

*Pinonia splendens* Gaudichaud-Beaupré 1824, *Cibotium splendens* (Gaudichaud-Beaupré) Krajina ex Skottsberg 1942

HAWAIIAN TREE FERN, MAN TREE FERN, HAPU'U

PLATE 13

The erect trunk reaches at least 5 m in height and about 12 cm in diameter. Some plants may be epiphytic when young. Fronds are persistent, often forming an irregular skirt about the trunk, are bi- or tripinnate, smooth, dull green, and as long as 3.5 m. Stipe bases are usually covered with woolly and golden-colored hairs. The sorus has a two-lobed indusium, and sori occur marginally in groups of as many as five or six on an edge (to ten per pinnule segment). Distribution: Hawaiian Islands in moist rain forest from 300 m to at least 1800 m.

*Cibotium chamissoi*, named after German botanist Ludolf Karl Adelbert von Chamisso (1781–1838), was described by Georg Kaulfuss in 1824 and is the type species for the genus. Later the same year, Charles Gaudichaud-Beaupré laid the basis for considerable confusion by apparently describing the same species as *Pinonia splendens*. In time, as other species (including *C. menziesii*) were recognized by William J. Hooker, the exact identity of *C. chamissoi* became confused. In 1942 this led Vladimir Krajina to interpret Hooker's *C. menziesii* incorrectly as the true *C. chamissoi*, and Hooker's view of *C. chamissoi* as Gaudichard-Beaupré's *P. splendens*, a misconception that has been perpetuated in the literature. *Cibotium chamissoi* is a popular garden tree fern and grows well in tropical areas. Plants will grow in most soils but best in well-drained humus. In general, this species is not cold hardy. It is one of several species used for starch from the trunk pith and providing hairs for padding.

## *Cibotium cumingii* Kunze 1841

*Cibotium barometz* var. *cumingii* (Kunze) C. Christensen 1905,
   *C. taiwanense* C. M. Kuo 1985

The stout prostrate trunk may be as tall as 1 m but is usually slow-creeping. Fronds are persistent, bipinnatifid to deeply tripinnatifid, and about 2 m long. The rhizome apex and young fronds are covered with reddish golden hairs. The sorus has a two-lobed indusium, and sori occur marginally, one pair at the base of each fertile segment of a pinnule. Distribution: Luzon, Mindoro, and Mindanao in the Philippines, and Taiwan, in open forest or on road cuts and slopes in hilly and montane areas.

*Cibotium cumingii* is named after botanist Hugh Cuming (1791–1865), who collected in the Americas as well as Asia.

## *Cibotium glaucum* (J. E. Smith) W. J. Hooker & Arnott 1832

*Dicksonia glauca* J. E. Smith 1808, *Cibotium st.-johnii* Krajina 1938
HAPU'U
PLATES 14, 15

The erect or partially prostrate trunk reaches at least 3 m in height and 16 cm in diameter. Frequently, there are shoots along the trunk, particularly when it is prostrate. Fronds are persistent, bi- or tripinnate, usually whitish on the underside, and may be 1–3 m long. The stipe is covered with soft, golden to reddish brown or gray hairs. The sorus has a two-lobed indusium, and sori occur marginally. Distribution: Hawaiian Islands, particularly abundant on the main island of Hawaii, growing in dry to damp forest to an elevation as high as 1800 m.

*Cibotium glaucum* may develop a stout trunk, often with offshoots. Fronds and stipes may develop a whitish blush on the underside, hence the name *glaucum*. This is a popular garden tree fern in tropical areas. It will grow in humus but may be frost sensitive. It is one of several species that provides starch from the trunk pith, and hairs for padding.

## *Cibotium menziesii* W. J. Hooker 1846

*Cibotium chamissoi* in the sense of Krajina in Skottsberg 1942, not
   *C. chamissoi* Kaulfuss 1824
HAPU
PLATE 16

The erect massive trunk reaches at least 7 m in height and 16 cm or more in diameter. Some plants may be epiphytic when young. Fronds are persistent, large, smooth, and pale underneath, sometimes with minute dots composed of tufts of hairs; the midrib may be yellowish. The stipe is usually covered with hairs or may bear warts where hairs have broken off; the hairs are dark brown, reddish, or blond, and composed of either long, straight, tubular cells or short, thick, waxy cells. The sorus has a two-lobed indusium, and sori occur marginally in groups of as many as five or six on an edge (to ten per pinnule segment). Distribution: Hawaiian Islands, on all the major islands in moist rain forest at 300–1800 m.

*Cibotium menziesii* is named after Archibald Menzies (1754–1842), botanist-physician with George Vancouver's expedition to the Hawaiian Islands. In 1942 Vladimir Krajina equated this species with *C. chamissoi*, a misconception that has been perpetuated in some texts. *Cibotium menziesii* a popular garden tree fern in tropical areas. Plants will grow in most soils but do best in well-drained humus. In general, *C. menziesii* is not cold hardy. It is one of several species that provide starch from the trunk pith, and hairs for padding.

## *Cibotium nealiae* Degener in Degener & Hatheway 1952
HAPU

The erect trunk is only about 50 cm tall and about 16 cm in diameter; in some cases, plants may be epiphytic when young. Fronds are persistent, smooth, pale underneath, and may reach 3 m in length. The stipe is dark and usually covered at the base with woolly hairs golden in color. The sorus has a two-lobed indusium, and sori occur marginally in groups of as many as five or six on an edge (to ten per pinnule segment). Distribution: Kauai in the Hawaiian Islands and rare, growing in moist rain forest at 300–1800 m or higher.

*Cibotium nealiae* is named after Hawaiian ethnobotanist Marie C. Neal (1889–1965).

## *Cibotium regale* Verschaff 1868
*Cibotium wendlandii* Mettenius ex Kuhn 1869

The erect trunk reaches at least 10 m. Fronds are persistent and large; young fronds and stipe bases are usually covered with brown hairs. The sorus has a two-lobed indusium, and sori occur marginally in groups of as many as five or six. Distribution: Chiapas, Mexico, to Guatemala, Honduras, and El Salvador, on wooded slopes and riverbanks in cloud and montane forest.

There is some confusion as to whether *Cibotium regale* and *C. wendlandii* should truly be considered the same species.

## *Cibotium schiedei* Schlechtendal & Chamisso 1830

*Dicksonia schiedei* (Schlechtendal & Chamisso) K. K. Baker 1866
MEXICAN TREE FERN
PLATES 17, 18

The erect trunk reaches at least 5 m in height. Fronds are persistent and large; young fronds and stipe bases are usually covered with brown hairs. The sorus has a two-lobed indusium, and sori occur marginally in groups of as many as five or six on an edge. Distribution: Veracruz and Oaxaca, Mexico, on wooded slopes and riverbanks in cloud and montane forest.

*Cibotium schiedei* is named after Christian Schiede (1798–1836), a German who died in Mexico and explored for plants there.

## *Cnemidaria* C. B. Presl 1836

*Hemitelia* subgenus *Cnemidaria* (C. B. Presl) C. Christensen 1906,
*Cnemidopteris* Reichenbach 1841, *Actinophlebia* C. B. Presl 1847,
*Hemistegia* C. B. Presl 1847, *Microstegnus* C. B. Presl 1847
Cyatheaceae

Carel Presl described *Cnemidaria* in 1836. The type species is *C. speciosa*, collected by Eduard Poeppig in 1829 from Pampayacu, Peru. The name *Cnemidaria* is derived from the Greek word *kneme* or *cneme*, meaning lower leg, internode, or spoke. From Carel Presl's original description it is clear he meant to imply the spokes of a wheel. As he was only able to examine fragmented dried material, it is likely that this was in reference to the anastomosing basal veins that occur in the pinnules. Robert Stolze revised the genus in 1974, including in it several newly described species and varieties. Although more recent molecular evidence suggest the plants fall within the genus *Cyathea*, no taxonomic decision has yet been made as to whether *Cnemidaria* should be absorbed into that genus.

Members of *Cnemidaria* are at best only small tree ferns, being subarborescent or only marginally arborescent with a short single stem as tall as 3.5 m and to 7 cm in diameter. Fronds are 1–3.5 m long and pinnate. Young uncurling fronds and stipe bases may be covered by scales or spines. The presence or absence of spines has been used as a diagnostic factor to distinguish between species. However, the rachis is generally smooth or in some species slightly spiny. Stipe scales have a margin of cells that are different in size and/or color from the remaining cells of the scale. The apex of the scale is usually rounded or filiform and lacks the apical cell present in *Alsophila*

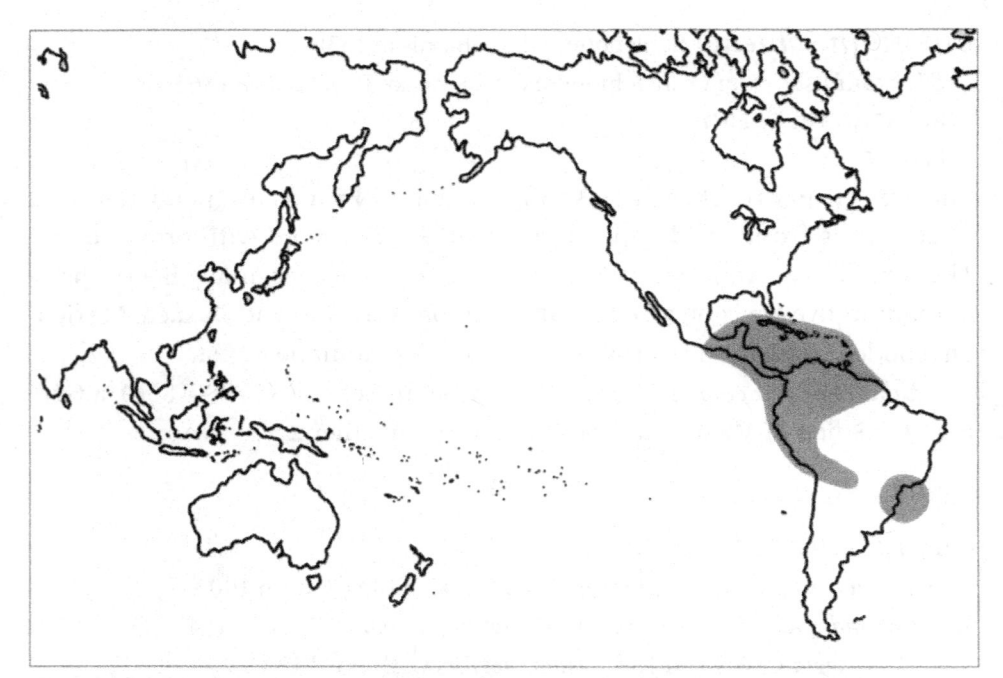

*Cnemidaria*, distributed in the New World, from islands of the Caribbean to Central and northwestern South America and southeastern Brazil.

clade of *Cyathea*. The scale margin may bear dark teeth or filiform protrusions. Sori are usually circular, and present on the underside of the frond pinnules away from the margins. They may be protected by shallow cup-like indusia. Spores are trilete and usually porate, often with three larger pores distributed regularly around the equator of the spore. Chromosome number $n = 69$.

Species of *Cnemidaria* are distributed in the New World Tropics from the Caribbean and Central America to the northern Andes, La Paz in Bolivia, and parts of southeastern Brazil. Plants grow in wet montane and cloud forests in ravines, in deep forest shade and in forest margins and clearings, on road banks, and disturbed sites. Several species aggressively colonize open or disturbed land and can survive fire. Elevations range from sea level or more typically 500–2000 m, rarely as high as 2300 m.

The exact number of species is unknown, reflecting the general lack of taxonomic knowledge in some areas of the range of *Cnemidaria*. Consequently, not all species are included here. However, best estimates suggest there are about 25. *Cnemidaria bella* may be of hybrid origin. Few species of *Cnemidaria* are commonly cultivated. Several species, however, including *C. grandifolia, C. horrida,* and *C. spectabilis,* are found in major botanical collections in the United States and Europe. Most species prefer a drained humus and will tolerate cooler conditions.

### *Cnemidaria alatissima* Stolze 1974

Plants are prostrate or have a barely erect trunk. Fronds are persistent and as long as 2 m. The rachis has an obvious wing. The stipe may have spines and is basally covered with large, whitish scales. Sori occur in a single row, and each sorus is covered by a very thin, small, brown, and almost scale-like indusium. Distribution: Peru, in cloud forest and in wet places at about 1540 m; known only from the type locality.

### *Cnemidaria amabilis* (Morton) Tryon 1970

*Hemitelia amabilis* Morton 1951

The erect trunk is 1 m high and 3–8 cm in diameter. Fronds are persistent, as long as 1 m, and have a thin green wing along the rachis. Scales on the stipe are whitish and have a small dark-pigmented region at the point of attachment. Sori are small and occur in a single row, and each sorus is covered by a yellowish brown scale-like indusium. Distribution: Northern Venezuela, in montane forest at 800–1500 m.

*Cnemidaria amabilis* may be confused with *C. mutica* but differs in having whitish scales with a minute dark region at the point of attachment. In *C. mutica*, a dark region often runs the length of the scale.

### *Cnemidaria apiculata* (W. J. Hooker & Baker) Stolze 1974

*Hemitelia apiculata* W. J. Hooker & Baker 1865, *Cyathea aristata* Domin 1930

The erect trunk is short. Fronds are persistent and as long as 1.5 m. Whitish scales with a dark brown internal region are frequent on the stipe, but spines are lacking, or small and rare. Sori are small and occur in a single row, almost marginally, and each sorus is covered by a dark brown, narrow to spoon-shaped indusium. Distribution: Only in the rain forests of Oaxaca, Mexico, at 1200–1600 m, the most northerly distribution in the genus.

### *Cnemidaria bella* (Mettenius) Tryon 1970

*Hemitelia bella* Mettenius 1856

*Cnemidaria bella* is a distinctive plant with fronds as wide as 1 m. Sori form a single row just beneath and parallel to the pinnule margin; indusia are dark brown and semicircular.

There are doubts that *Cnemidaria bella* is a true species. Original collections were from cultivated plants in the botanical gardens at Leipzig, and the species has never been found in the wild. Most spores are aborted, indicating a hybrid, possibly involving *Cyathea speciosa* and either *Cnemidaria horrida* or *C. spectabilis*.

### *Cnemidaria chocoensis* Stolze 1974

The trunk is erect. Fronds are persistent and as long as 2.5 m. Glossy dark brown scales that may have a narrow whitish margin are frequent on the stipe, but spines are lacking. Sori occur in a single row, and each sorus is covered by pale to yellowish indusium. Distribution: Colombia, in disturbed forest at 750–1650 m, the name *chocoensis* referring to the department of Chocó in western Colombia.

### *Cnemidaria choricarpa* (Maxon) Tryon 1970

*Hemitelia choricarpa* Maxon 1912, *Cyathea choricarpa* (Maxon) Domin 1929

Plants are usually prostrate or have a barely erect trunk; the rhizome may reach about 50 cm in length and as much as 2–3 cm in diameter. Fronds are pinnate and as long as 2 m. The rachis is hairy and has a narrow green wing; spines may be present. Scales on the stipe are whitish and have a dark brown internal region. Sori are rounded and occur in a single row, and each sorus is covered by a scale-like brownish indusium. Distribution: Costa Rica and Panama, with populations also reported from Colombia. Plants may be found in tropical wet forest understory to submontane forest on river and stream banks and along paths from just above sea level to 1800 m.

*Cnemidaria choricarpa* does not assume tree fern proportions but instead forms low clumps. It is apparently related to *C. mutica* and *C. decurrens*.

### *Cnemidaria cocleana* Stolze 1974

Plants are prostrate to short and erect, with a trunk as tall as 50 cm and 4–6 cm in diameter. Fronds are pinnate and as long as 1 m. The rachis lacks a wing or has only a small wing. The stipe has spines and scattered scales that are whitish and have a dark brown central region. Sori occur in a single row, and each sorus is covered by a circular yellow-brown indusium. Distribution: Costa Rica and Panama, in shaded tropical rain forest on river and stream banks, along paths, and in open sites at 500–1200 m, the name *cocleana* referring to the province of Coclé, Panama.

*Cnemidaria cocleana* is a low fern with pinnate fronds.

### *Cnemidaria consimilis* Stolze 1974

The erect trunk is as tall as 1.5 m. Fronds are persistent and as long as 2.5 m. The stipe has abundant scales and is quite spiny; the scales are whitish or have a thin, brown central strip. Sori occur in a single row, and each sorus is covered by a yellow-gray-brown indusium. Distribution: Trinidad and the Paria Peninsula, Venezuela, in forest at 600–1200 m.

### *Cnemidaria cruciata* (Desvaux) Stolze 1974

*Hemitelia cruciata* Desvaux 1827, *Cyathea leprieurii* (Kunze) Domin 1929

The trunk is short, erect, and narrow. Fronds are persistent, as long as about 2 m, and 60 cm in diameter. The rachis is spiny toward the base. The stipe also bears short spines, but scales, which have a narrow white fimbriate margin and a dark central region along their length, are sparse. Sori occur in a single row, halfway between the pinnule midvein and margin, and each sorus is covered by a pale to yellowish brown semicircular indusium. Distribution: French Guiana.

*Cnemidaria cruciata*, with overlapping pinnae, is very similar to *C. spectabilis*, in which the pinnae are more widely spread.

### *Cnemidaria decurrens* (Liebmann) Tryon 1970

*Hemitelia decurrens* Liebmann 1849, *Cyathea elegantissima* (Fée) Domin 1929, *C. guatemalensis* (Maxon) Domin 1929, *C. liebmannii* Domin 1929, *C. lucida* (Fée) Domin 1929, *C. decurrentiloba* Domin 1930

Plants are prostrate or occasionally have an erect trunk about 30 cm tall. Fronds are persistent and as long as 2.5 m. The rachis usually has a membranous wing. The stipe has spines and scales; the scales are whitish or have a brown central stripe. Sori occur in a single row, and each sorus is covered by a pale to yellow-brown indusium. Distribution: Chiapas and Oaxaca, Mexico, to Guatemala, in forest at 200–1100 m.

*Cnemidaria decurrens* varies in frond outline and a number of species were previously recognized within it. It is similar to *C. glandulosa* and may be related to *C. choricarpa* and *C. mutica*.

### *Cnemidaria ewanii* (Alston) Tryon 1970

*Cyathea ewanii* Alston 1958

Plants are prostrate or occasionally have an erect trunk about 20 cm tall. Fronds are persistent and as long as 2.5 m. Scales are whitish and have a brown central stripe. Sori occur in a single row, and each sorus is covered by a pale to yellow-brown indusium. Distribution: Colombia and Ecuador, in thickets and forest, 75–1000 m.

The name *ewanii* commemorates botanist and botanical historian Joseph A. Ewan (1909–1999). *Cnemidaria ewanii* is closely related to *C. speciosa* and may represent only a variety of that species.

### *Cnemidaria glandulosa* Stolze 1974

Plants are usually prostrate and lack a significant trunk. Fronds are small, persistent, pinnate, and less than 1.5 m long. The rachis is naked or may bear a few scattered scales. The stipe is brownish, lacks spines, but has plentiful scales that are brown and have a whitish margin. Sori occur in one or two irregular rows on either side of the midvein of fertile pinnules, and each sorus is covered by a dark brown indusium. Distribution: Panama, in montane rain forest at 1600–1800 m.

Originally known only from the type specimen, *Cnemidaria glandulosa* was collected near San Félix, Chiriquí, Panama, by Scott Mori and Jacquelyn Kallunki. It is similar to *C. decurrens*.

### *Cnemidaria grandifolia* (Willdenow) Proctor 1961

*Cyathea grandifolia* Willdenow 1810, *C. minita* Kaulfuss 1824, *C. kohautiana* (C. B. Presl) Domin 1929, *C. obtusa* (Kaulfuss) Domin 1929

Plants are largely prostrate but can have an erect trunk as tall as 1 m and about 4 cm in diameter. Fronds are pinnate and as long as 3 m. The stipe may have spines and scales; the scales may also be abundant on the rachis and are whitish and have a dark brown internal region. Sori occur in one or two rows, and each sorus is covered by a yellow to dark brown indusium. Distribution: Trinidad and Tobago to the Paraguaná Peninsula, Venezuela, at the edge of forests, on stream banks, and mountainsides at 300–1100 m.

*Cnemidaria grandifolia* includes two varieties: *grandifolia* and *obtusa* (Kaulfuss) Stolze, the latter with narrower pinnae and obtuse segments. Variety *grandifolia* extends across the Caribbean from Saba to St. Lucia, and variety *obtusa* from St. Vincent to Venezuela. Both are only marginally tree ferns.

### *Cnemidaria horrida* (Linnaeus) C. B. Presl 1836

*Polypodium horridum* Linnaeus 1753, *Cyathea horrida* (Linnaeus) J. E. Smith 1793, *C. commutata* Sprengel 1804

The erect, occasionally semiprostrate, trunk is as high as 1 m, rarely 4 m, and 4–20 cm in diameter; the apex of the trunk is covered by dark brown scales. Fronds are pinnate to almost bipinnate and as long as 3.5 m. The rachis and stipe are often spiny and have sparse scales that are whitish and have a dark brown to blackish central region. Sori are rounded and occur singly, forming a row near the pinnule margin, or several rows, and each sorus is covered by a thin, scale-like, whitish to yellow indusium. Distribution: Jamaica, Hispaniola, and Puerto Rico; Costa Rica and Panama; Venezuela, Colombia, Ecuador, and Peru. Plants range from subcoastal tropical rain forest to submontane forest, along forest margins, stream banks, and mountain areas, from near sea level to 2000 m.

The only species of the genus that is truly of tree fern stature, the wide-ranging *Cnemidaria horrida* is also one of the earliest tree ferns to have been discovered and described. Carl Linnaeus recorded it in *Species Plantarum* in 1753, based on a specimen that was apparently collected (from Jamaica?) at the end of the 17th century. *Cnemidaria horrida* may be a parent of *C. bella*.

## *Cnemidaria karsteniana* (Klotzsch) Tryon 1970

*Hemitelia karsteniana* Klotzsch 1852, *Cyathea karsteniana* (Klotzsch) Domin 1929

The erect trunk is as tall as 60 cm and 2.5 cm in diameter. Fronds are persistent, as long as 2.5 m, and have spiny stipes. Scales on the stipe have a thin whitish margin and a dark brown central region. Sori occur in a single row, and each sorus is covered by a yellowish brown indusium. Distribution: Northern Venezuela in cloud forest at 100–1600 m.

The name *karsteniana* commemorates German botanist Gustav Karsten (1817–1908), who collected in South America.

## *Cnemidaria mutica* (Christ) Tryon 1970

*Hemitelia mutica* Christ 1909, *Cyathea mutica* (Christ) Domin 1929, *C. grandis* (Maxon) Domin 1929

Plants are prostrate or have an erect trunk less than 1 m high and 3–6 cm in diameter. Fronds are as long as 1.5–3 m and vary in shape, with different degrees of dissection of the pinnules (pinnate to almost bipinnate and dissected in some varieties). The stipe is greenish yellow to brown and may bear short spines; a thin, inconspicuous wing may extend along each side of the stipe. Scales on the stipe have a narrow white margin and a dark central region along their length. Sori are small and occur in one to several rows, and each sorus is covered by a scale-like yellowish brown indusium. Distribution: Costa Rica and Panama, in wet submontane and montane forest, forest understory, and along shaded paths at 500–2200 m. One variety, *contigua*, is restricted to wet forest understory in submontane and montane forest in Costa Rica at 1200–2200 m.

Variable frond outline, and dissection and shape of the pinnules, have been used in part to discern several varieties of *Cnemidaria mutica*: *mutica*, *grandis* (Maxon) Tryon, *contigua* (Maxon) Stolze, and *chiricana* (Maxon) Stolze. *Cnemidaria mutica* may be confused with *C. amabilis* but differs in having bicolored scales, with a dark center and whitish margin; in *C. amabilis* the dark region is restricted to a minute area at the point of attachment. *Cnemidaria mutica* is apparently related to *C. choricarpa* and *C. decurrens*.

### *Cnemidaria nervosa* (Maxon) Tryon 1970
*Hemitelia nervosa* Maxon 1944

The erect trunk is as tall as 1 m. Fronds are persistent and as long as 2.5 m. Scales have a thin whitish margin and a dark brown central region. Sori occur in a single row, and each sorus is covered by a pale or yellowish indusium that may be completely circular. Distribution: Ecuador and Peru, in rain forest at 300–400 m.

### *Cnemidaria quitensis* (Domin) Tryon 1970
*Hemitelia quitensis* Domin 1929

Plants are prostrate to erect, with a trunk as high as 2 m and 4 cm in diameter. Fronds are persistent and as long as 3 m. The stipe may bear spines; scales are sparse and either pale or with a narrow white margin and a dark central region along their length. Sori occur in one or two rows, and each sorus is covered by a yellow or yellowish brown indusium. Distribution: Colombia and Ecuador, in forest at 100–1400 m, the name *quitensis* referring to Quito, Ecuador.

### *Cnemidaria roraimensis* (Domin) Tryon 1970
*Hemitelia roraimensis* Domin 1929, *Cyathea roraimensis* (Domin) Domin 1929

Plants are prostrate to erect but short. Fronds are persistent, just over 1 m long, and pinnate. Scales are absent or very sparse on the rachis and stipe. Sori occur in a single row, and each sorus is covered by a yellowish brown indusium. Distribution: Guyana along stream banks on mountainsides at 1000–1500 m, named after Mount Roraima (2810 m), where the type collection was made in 1863–1864.

*Cnemidaria roraimensis*, possibly related to *C. spectabilis*, is known from only a few incomplete collections.

### *Cnemidaria singularis* Stolze 1974

Plants are usually prostrate and lack a trunk. Fronds are persistent, just over 1 m long, and pinnate to pinnatifid. The stipe bears sparse scales, but spines are absent; the scales have a narrow white margin and a dark brown central region along their length. Sori are small and occur in a single row, and each sorus is covered by a yellowish brown scale-like indusium. Distribution: Putumayo, Colombia, known only from the type collection in wet mountain forest at 2300 m.

*Cnemidaria singularis* bears some similarities to *C. tryoniana*, which is also known only from a small region in Colombia.

## *Cnemidaria speciosa* C. B. Presl 1836

*Cyathea subincisa* (Kunze) Domin 1929

The erect trunk may be as tall as 1 m and about 4 cm in diameter. Fronds are persistent and just over 2 m long. Scales on the rachis are whitish with a brown central zone. Sori occur in a single row, and each sorus is covered by a pale or yellowish indusium. Distribution: Peru and Bolivia, at the edges of forests, along streams, and on mountainsides at 400–1900 m.

*Cnemidaria speciosa* is the type species for the genus. *Cnemidaria ewanii* is closely related and may represent only a variety of this species.

*Cnemidaria speciosa* from Peru. Tip of a pinnate frond and detail showing sori. Liz Grant, Massey University, New Zealand.

## *Cnemidaria spectabilis* (Kunze) Tryon 1970

*Hemitelia spectabilis* Kunze 1848, *Cyathea spectabilis* var. *longipinna* (Domin) Domin 1929, *C. spectabilis* var. *trinitensis* (Domin) Domin 1929, *Cnemidaria spectabilis* var. *colombiensis* Stolze 1974

The erect trunk is only as tall as 50 cm and 5 cm in diameter. Fronds are persistent, as long as about 2 m, and have pinnae as long as 40 cm and as wide as 7 cm. The rachis is spiny toward the base of the lamina. The stipe also bears spines, but scales are sparse; the scales have a narrow white and fimbriate margin and a dark central region along their length. Sori occur in a single row, and each sorus is covered by a pale to yellowish brown indusium. Distribution: Trinidad and Tobago, and the northern regions of South America, including Colombia, Venezuela, Guyana, Suriname, and French Guiana, in forest margins along stream banks and in montane forest from about 100 m to 1200 m. One variety, *colombiensis*, is restricted to wooded areas in Colombia at 70–500 m.

*Cnemidaria spectabilis* is one of the most widespread species of the genus (second only to *C. horrida*) and has two varieties: *spectabilis* and *colombiensis* Stolze. *Cnemidaria spectabilis* is similar to *C. cruciata* and possibly related to *C. roraimensis*. It may be a parent of *C. bella*.

## *Cnemidaria tryoniana* Stolze 1974

Plants are prostrate and usually lack a trunk. Fronds are persistent and as long as 1.8 m. The stipe bears scales, but spines are absent; the scales have a narrow white margin and a dark brown central region along their length or may be off-white. Sori are small and occur in a single row, and each sorus is covered by a yellowish brown scale-like indusium. Distribution: Between Valdivia and Yarumal, Colombia, at 2200 m.

*Cnemidaria tryoniana* is named after Rolla M. Tryon Jr. (1916–2001), who carried out extensive work on tropical American ferns and the tree fern family Cyatheaceae. In the mid-1970s it was still only known from the type collection made in Antioquia, Colombia, in 1942. It is similar to *C. singularis* and may be related to that species.

## *Cnemidaria uleana* (Sampaio) Tryon 1970

*Hemitelia uleana* Sampaio 1923, *Cyathea abitaguensis* (Domin) Domin 1930, *C. subarborescens* Domin 1930

Plants are prostrate or barely erect, with a trunk as tall as 50 cm and 3 cm in diameter. Fronds are persistent and as long as 2 m. Scales on the rachis have a broad white margin and a dark brown central region along their length. The stipe is usually smooth and lacks spines. Sori occur in one or two rows, and each sorus is covered by a yellow or yellowish brown indusium. Distribution: Colombia, Ecuador, Peru, and Brazil, mostly in forest and shaded mountain ravines at 580–2100 m.

The name *uleana* commemorates Ernst Heinrich Georg Ule (1854–1915), German botanist who collected in Brazil. Two varieties of *Cnemidaria uleana* are recognized: *uleana* and *abitaguensis* (Domin) Stolze. The latter has an apparently disjunct distribution in Peru and Brazil, and the former appears in Colombia and Ecuador.

## *Culcita* C. B. Presl 1836
Dicksoniaceae

Carel Presl described *Culcita* in 1836. The type species for the genus is *C. macrocarpa,* described at the same time by Presl. The name *Culcita* is Latin for pillow and may be a reference to the fluffy rhizome material used to stuff pillows on Madeira, or to the purse-like sori on the frond margins.

*Culcita* consists of terrestrial or epiphytic ferns with massive prostrate trunks or rhizomes but rarely reaching 3 m in height. Fronds are tripinnate to at least tetrapinnate and 1–3 m long, often with a groove in the rachis. Sori are marginal, and the indusia grade into the lamina tissue. Spores are rounded to globose-tetrahedral (trilete) and trilobed with a depression between the arms. Spores of *C. macrocarpa* have a spinulate surface with fine spines or rodlets, whereas those of *C. coniifolia* are distally tuberculate. Spores of both species may have a slight equatorial ridge and are strongly trilobed.

Originally considered to have as many as seven species, *Culcita* has been reduced to two, with most species now treated as *Calochlaena*. *Culcita* does well in most soils, but best in moist humus in open, light conditions. *Culcita coniifolia* is in the New World and *C. macrocarpa* in the Old World. Plants grow in open areas, on disturbed sites, and in forest clearings.

## *Culcita coniifolia* (W. J. Hooker) Maxon 1922
*Dicksonia coniifolia* W. J. Hooker 1844

The prostrate, creeping trunk is as long as 50 cm and about 6 cm in diameter. Fronds are tetra- or pentapinnate and may reach 3 m in length. The rachis is light-colored and lacks spines or scales. Hairs are present on the trunk and stipe and are orange to light brown. Petioles are light to dark brown. Sori are marginal, occur one per pinnule lobe, and each is protected by an inner indusium. Chromosome number $n = 66$. Distribution: Hispaniola, Jamaica (where it is only known from John Crow Peak) and Cuba; southern Mexico,

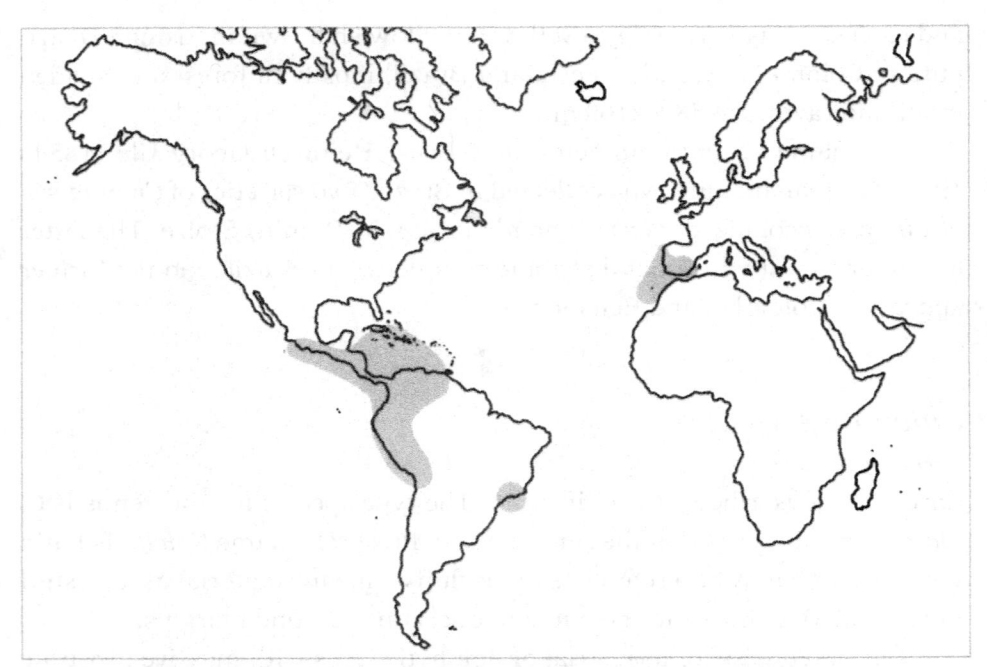

*Culcita coniifolia,* distributed in Central America, on islands of the Caribbean, and in South America, and *C. macrocarpa,* found on the Iberian Peninsula and northern Atlantic islands off the northwestern coast of Africa.

Guatemala, El Salvador, Costa Rica, and Panama; Venezuela, Guyana, French Guiana, Ecuador, Peru, Bolivia, Argentina, and southeastern Brazil. Plants are found in submontane and montane rain and cloud forest, in open locations, on steep slopes, in sheltered ravines, and on limestone at 1500–3500 m.

*Culcita coniifolia* is an epiphytic or terrestrial fern with a creeping rhizome. Although not commonly cultivated, it can be grown in most soils in open, light conditions.

### *Culcita macrocarpa* C. B. Presl 1836
The prostrate, creeping trunk is as long as 50 cm. Fronds are tetra- or pentapinnate and may reach 3 m in length. Petioles are light to dark brown. The rachis is light-colored and lacks spines or scales. Hairs are present on the trunk, stipe, and young uncurling fronds; they are long and reddish brown to light brown. Sori are submarginal, occur one per pinnule lobe, and are protected by the margin; an inner, thin, sac-like indusium is also present. Chromosome number $n = 66–68$. Distribution: Spain, Portugal, Canary Islands, Madeira, and the Azores. In Spain and Portugal, *C. macrocarpa* may be found on stream banks in oak woods at an elevation of about 350 m.

*Culcita coniifolia.*
Secondary portion of a frond and detail showing sori. Liz Grant, Massey University, New Zealand.

*Culcita macrocarpa* is regarded as endangered in Portugal. Cultivated plants will grow in most soils and do best in humus in open, light conditions. Material from the fluffy rhizome is used to stuff pillows in Madeira.

### *Cyathea* Smith 1793

*Sphaeropteris* Bernhardi 1801, *Alsophila* R. Brown 1810, *Hemitelia* R. Brown 1810, *Trichipteris* C. B. Presl 1822, *Chnoophora* Kaulfuss 1824, *Disphenia* C. B. Presl 1836, *Schizocaena* W. J. Hooker 1838, *Cormophyllum* Newman 1856, *Nephelea* Tryon 1970

Cyatheaceae

*Cyathea* is from the Greek *kyatheion*, little cup, referring to the cup-shaped sori on the underside of the fronds. The type species is *C. arborea*, originally described in 1753 as *Polypodium arboreum* by Linnaeus. *Cyathea* comprises mostly terrestrial tree ferns (*C. gracilis* may be epiphytic), usually with a single tall stem. Very rarely, the trunk may be branched or creeping. Many species develop a fibrous mass of roots at the base of the trunk.

*Cyathea* has a confusing taxonomic history (as outlined previously). In the 19th century all species without indusia were included in the genus *Alsophila*, all with cup-shaped indusia in *Cyathea*, and those with hooded indusia in *Hemitelia*. In time, it was recognized that these groupings are artificial. By 1963 Holttum was using the concept of a single genus *Cyathea* with two subgenera: *Cyathea* and *Sphaeropteris*. Tryon (1970) suggested a more complex system with six genera: *Alsophila*, *Cnemidaria*, *Cyathea*, *Nephelea*, *Sphaeropteris*, and *Trichipteris*. Unfortunately, his scheme did not always clearly separate genera. Modern work, using morphological and molecular information, suggests there are three well-defined groups of species within the supergenus *Cyathea* (Conant et al. 1996). These have been called the *Alsophila* clade, the *Sphaeropteris* clade, and the *Cyathea* clade. (The genus *Cnemidaria* is closely associated with the *Cyathea* clade and may eventually be merged into it.)

These three groupings may yet be recognized as genera in their own right and are similar to the circumscriptions used by Lellinger (1987). However, there are significant nomenclatural problems that must be taken into account, involving name combinations and sweeping changes that would be forced. For convenience, as many of the commonly used names that may have to change are still in *Cyathea;* a single encompassing genus *Cyathea* with two subgenera (*Cyathea* and *Sphaeropteris;* based on Kramer 1990) is retained here. *Cyathea* subgenus *Cyathea* includes two clades: the *Cyathea* clade and the *Alsophila* clade. The three clades are described in more detail here, and clade affinities, as indicated in the molecular work, are acknowledged and indicated for each species. The exact number of species is unknown, reflecting the general lack of taxonomic knowledge in some geographic areas. In the broadest sense, *Cyathea* is a very large genus with 470–600 species (see also Holttum 1963, 1964, 1965a, b, 1974, 1981, Holttum and Molesworth Allen 1967, Windisch 1977, 1978, Barrington 1978, Conant 1983, Holttum and Edwards 1983, Moran 1991, 1995b, 1997, and Moran and Riba 1995).

### *Cyathea* Subgenus *Cyathea*—The *Cyathea* Clade

Fronds in the *Cyathea* clade range in length from 0.25 m (usually 2–4 m, rarely as long as 6 m) and may be entire to tetrapinnate. Young uncurling fronds and stipe bases are frequently covered in scales and may have spines. Stipe scales have a margin of cells that are different in size, orientation, or shape from the rest of the cells within the scale. The apex is usually rounded or filiform and lacks the apical cell present in the *Alsophila* clade. The scale margin may bear dark teeth or filiform protrusions. Sori are circular and present on the underside of the frond pinnules away from the margins.

Spores are trilete and may be granulate, stranded, porate, or verrucate. Chromosome number $n = 69$ for the genus.

Species of the *Cyathea* clade are predominantly New World in distribution (from the Caribbean and Central America to South America and the Andes) but the subgenus also extends across the Pacific Ocean, with representatives on Cocos Island, Panama, and the Galápagos Islands, Ecuador, and when the *C. decurrens* complex is included, as far as the Austral Islands, Lord Howe Island, and New Caledonia. Members of the *Cyathea* clade are found from lowland rain forest to montane and cloud forest or occasionally savannas and grasslands in the Tropics, in ravines, forest margins, clearings, and disturbed sites. There are canopy, understory and ground-cover plants. Several species aggressively colonize open or disturbed land and may survive fire. Species range from sea level to 4200 m in the Andes, with *C. caracasana* and *C. fulva* reaching the highest elevations for species in the family Cyatheaceae.

Several hybrids have been reported involving species of the *Cyathea* clade. Many of these include members of two genera, *Cyathea* and *Cnemidaria*, which as noted may only be a specialized group within the *Cyathea*

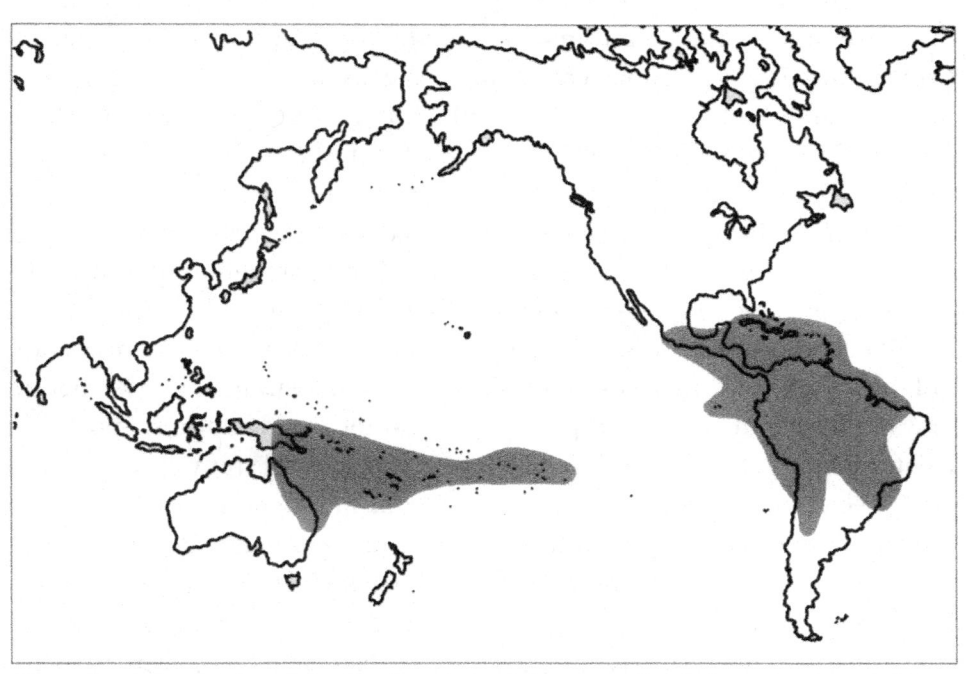

Generalized distribution of the *Cyathea* clade of the genus *Cyathea*, predominantly New World, including the Caribbean Islands, Central America, and parts of South America, but also present on many islands of the Pacific Ocean, including New Caledonia, and Lord Howe Island, Australia.

clade. Such hybrids include *Cnemidaria horrida* × *Cyathea arborea* (*Cyathea* ×*wilsonii* (W. J. Hooker) Domin), *Cnemidaria horrida* × *Cyathea parvula* (*Cyathea* ×*sessilifolia* (Jenman) Domin), *Cnemidaria grandifolia* × *Cyathea aspera*, *Cnemidaria spectabilis* × *Cyathea tenera*, *Cyathea arborea* × *C. armata* (*C.* ×*bernardii* Proctor), *Cyathea arborea* × *C. aspera* (*C.* ×*lewisii* (Morton & Proctor) Proctor), *Cyathea divergens* × *C. fulva*, and *Cyathea divergens* × *C. stipularis*. Possible hybrids between *Cyathea pungens* and species of *Cnemidaria* have also been collected. The frequency of hybrids between *Cyathea* and *Cnemidaria* further supports the merging of these two genera (Conant 1975).

### *Cyathea* Subgenus *Cyathea*—The *Alsophila* Clade

The name *Alsophila*, from the Greek *asos*, grove, and *philos*, loving, can be construed to mean grove loving or, rather, shade loving. This clade includes tree ferns usually with a single very tall stem. Rarely is the trunk branched, but it may be creeping, or as in two species (*Cyathea biformis* and *C. scandens*), scrambling or climbing. Many members develop a fibrous mass of roots at the base of the trunk, and a few species are said to produce stolons at the base of the stem, including *C. manniana* and *C. corcovadensis*.

Fronds in the *Alsophila* clade may be 0.5–5 m long and are usually finely dissected and tripinnate but may be pinnate to tetrapinnate. One species, *Cyathea sinuata*, has simple leaves. Many species have unusual small basal pinnae that form away from the main pinnules of the frond toward the base of the stipe, close to the growing apex of the tree fern. In extreme cases, these pinnules form a small nest around the growing apex. Stipe bases are frequently covered in scales and may, in some species, have spines (for example, *C. spinulosa*). Stipe scales have a margin of cells that are different in size, orientation, or shape from the rest of the cells within the scale. The apical cell is usually dark. Sori are circular and present on the underside of the frond pinnules away from the margins. Almost all have an indusium, but this structure may be missing in one or two species, or lost as the frond matures. Spores are trilete and may be ridged or have a finely granulate and spiny appearance.

Species of the *Alsophila* clade are Pantropical, extending into the southern temperate zones as far south as the subantarctic Auckland Islands. They are found in cloud or wet montane forest, on slopes or in ravines, and are low-canopy, medium-understory, or even ground-cover plants. Several species sometimes aggressively colonize open or disturbed land, forming dense thickets.

Hybrids between species of the *Alsophila* clade are common, and several have resulted in the production of viable, reproducing species. *Cyathea balano-*

*carpa* and *C. pubescens* (and *Alsophila polystichoides*, *A. setosa*, and *A. tryoniana*; Appendix 1) have apparently resulted thusly. The *C. woodwardioides* complex of some six species from the Caribbean (the other five being *C. crassa*, *C. fulgens*, *C. grevilleana*, *C. portoricensis*, and *C. tussacii*) is known to cross with *C. minor*. These hybrids often have aborted spores. Hybrids are most common in disturbed areas, either natural or the result of human activity. Among the many known hybrids are *C. hotteana* × *C. woodwardioides* (*C.* ×*confirmis* C. Christensen) from cloud forest in Haiti, *C. pubescens* (also known as *A. auneae*) × *C. tussacii* (*C.* ×*concinna* (Baker) Jenman) from Jamaica, and *C. minor* × *C. woodwardioides* (called *C.* ×*irregularis* Brause) from the Dominican Republic. *Cyathea* ×*marcescens* from Australia is apparently a cross between *C. australis* and *C. cunninghamii* (see also Conant 1975, 1983, and Conant and Cooper-Driver 1980).

The *Alsophila* clade represents one of the largest groups of commonly cultivated tree ferns. However, by far the majority of species are found only in the wild. Those that are cultivated are usually from cooler regions or the montane Tropics. The *Alsophila* clade is primarily a group of shade-loving plants. Most species enjoy rich, well-drained humus with consistent mois-

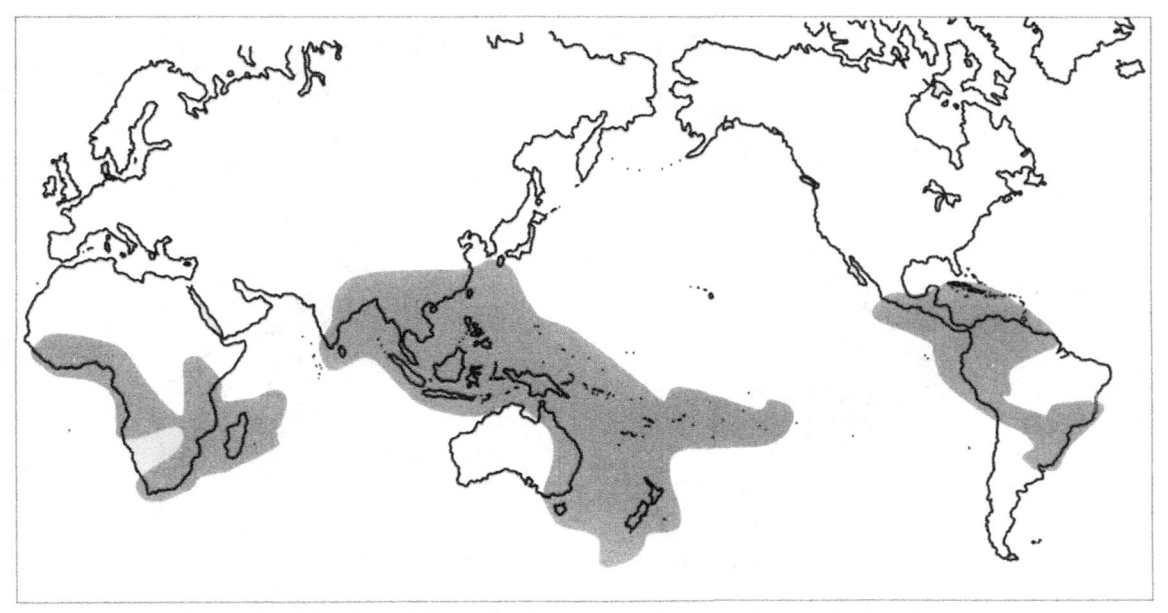

Generalized distribution of the *Alsophila* clade of the genus *Cyathea*, Pantropical and southern temperate with species in Africa, Madagascar, the Seychelles, southern and eastern India, to southern China, Malesia, the western Pacific, and Central and South America, with one species (*C. smithii*) even occurring as far south the subantarctic Auckland Islands.

ture. Some may survive frosts down to −5°C (23°F), but most will benefit from sheltered locations protected from wind and cold.

## *Cyathea* Subgenus *Sphaeropteris*—The *Sphaeropteris* Clade

The name *Sphaeropteris* is from the Greek *sphaera*, globe, and *pteris*, fern, referring to the appearance of the head of fronds. The clade contains some of the largest tree ferns, consisting of plants usually with a single tall stem. Very rarely, the trunk is creeping. Many members develop a dense fibrous mass of roots at the base of the trunk.

Fronds in the *Sphaeropteris* clade are 1–5 m long or more, usually dissected, and typically bipinnate, occasionally pinnate or tripinnate. Fronds are not generally persistent and may leave distinct rounded scars on the trunk. Young uncurling fronds and stipe bases are frequently covered by scales and may in some species (for example, *Cyathea leichhardtiana*) have spines or spine-like scales. Stipe scales are composed of cells that are generally uniform, similar in orientation, shape, size, thickness, and often color. However, the edge of the scales may bear teeth (setae) or cilia. The apical cell may be either dark or unpigmented. Sori are circular and present on the

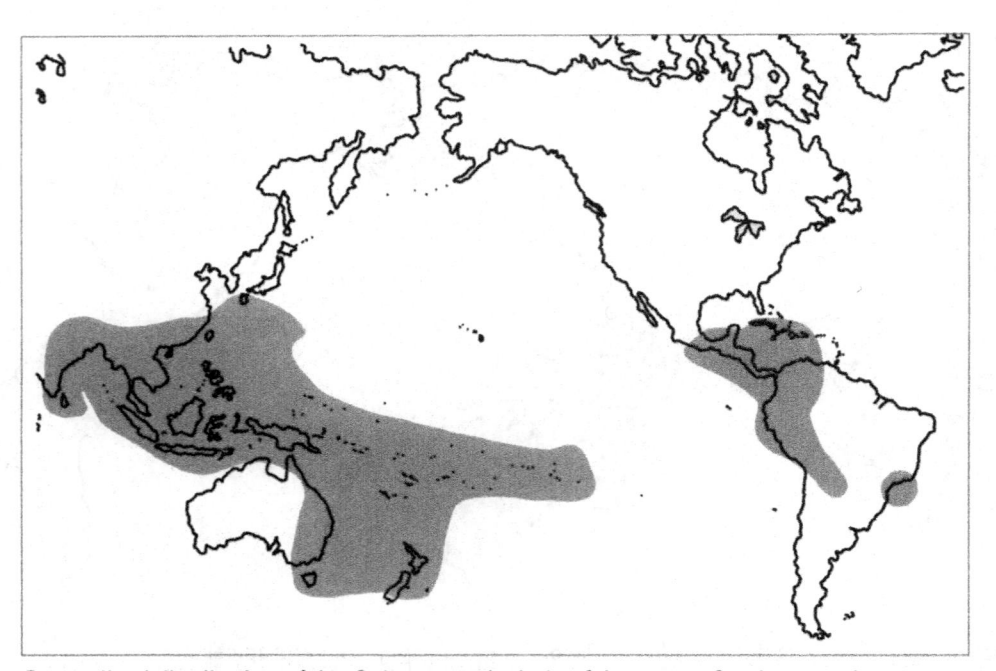

Generalized distribution of the *Sphaeropteris* clade of the genus *Cyathea*, southern temperate and almost Pantropical but absent from Africa and Madagascar, the maximum diversity occurring in Malesia, and about five species represented in the New World, including Central and South America and islands of the Caribbean.

underside of the frond pinnules away from the margins. The sorus may or may not have an indusium. Spores are trilete and have a fine or coarse spiny appearance or may be perforate.

Species of the *Sphaeropteris* clade are Pantropical and southern temperate, with maximum diversity in Malesia, but the clade appears to be absent from Africa and Madagascar. They are plants of the rain forest and tropical montane forest, of ravines, forest margins, clearings, swampy areas, and disturbed sites. They may be canopy, medium-canopy, or understory and ground-cover plants. Several species colonize open or disturbed land, forming dense thickets.

Hybrids between species of the *Sphaeropteris* clade are not commonly reported, though there are several species swarms that may involve hybridity. These include the *Cyathea hirsuta* and *C. horrida* complexes. There is also evidence that *C. binuangensis* may be of hybrid origin involving *C. integra* as one parent.

*Sphaeropteris* clade tree ferns are all large plants and require space to grow. Most also require some shelter from wind and protection from frost in cooler regions. In general, species grow in less shaded conditions than those of the *Alsophila* clade. Although plants may tolerate full sun, they still require consistent soil moisture to perform well. Given ideal conditions, plants can grow quickly and even aggressively. For example, *Cyathea cooperi* is now a recognized as a weed species in some warmer regions where it has been introduced.

## *Cyathea abbottii* Maxon 1924

*Alsophila abbottii* (Maxon) Tryon 1970

*Alsophila* clade. The erect trunk can be as tall as about 1.6 m and about 5 cm in diameter. Fronds are pinnate and may reach 1.5 m in length. The rachis is brown and has golden-brown to bicolored, (pale and brown) basal scales. Sori occur in two rows along each side of the pinnule midvein; indusia rounded, cup-like. Distribution: Hispaniola in shaded montane forest at 700–1200 m.

*Cyathea abbottii* is named after William Louis Abbott (1860–1936), collector of plants on Hispaniola. It is known to hybridize with *C. minor*.

## *Cyathea acanthophora* Holttum 1962

*Alsophila acanthophora* (Holttum) Tryon 1970

*Alsophila* clade. The erect trunk can be as tall as 5 m or higher. Fronds are bi- or tripinnate and 2–3 m long. The stipe is dark toward the base, has slender spines, and is covered with scattered scales; the scales are glossy brown and have a narrow paler margin. Sori occur near the midvein of fertile pinnules and are covered by thin, fragile, saucer-like indusia. Distribution: Kinabalu on Borneo, in montane rain forest at 1250–2000 m.

### *Cyathea aciculosa* Copeland 1936

*Sphaeropteris aciculosa* (Copeland) Tryon 1970

*Sphaeropteris* clade. The erect trunk can be as tall as 10 m. Fronds are tripinnate and about 2 m long. The stipe is dark, smooth, and covered with very small scales that are pale and have dark marginal setae. Sori lack indusia but are covered by pale overlapping scales. Distribution: Solomon Islands and Admiralty Islands in forest to about 1000 m.

*Cyathea aciculosa* is similar to *C. truncata* but differs in having larger scales covering the sori; the relationship between the two species requires further investigation.

### *Cyathea acrostichoides* (Alderwerelt van Rosenburgh) Domin 1930

*Alsophila acrostichoides* Alderwerelt van Rosenburgh 1918

*Alsophila* clade. The erect trunk is 1–3 m tall. Fronds are bipinnate and may reach 1–2 m in length. The stipe is slender and covered with spines. Scales, medium brown, are infrequent. Sori cover most of the underside of fertile pinnules; indusia are absent. Distribution: Moluccas and western New Guinea, in forest and disturbed sites at 650–1100 m.

### *Cyathea acuminata* Copeland 1952

*Alsophila acuminata* (Copeland) Tryon 1970

*Alsophila* clade. The erect trunk is 1–4 m tall or more. Fronds are bi- or tripinnate about 1 m long. The stipe is covered with scattered scales and some spines; the scales are flat and dull brown. Sori occur near the midvein of fertile pinnules and are covered by firm indusia. Distribution: Panay and Samar in the Philippines.

### *Cyathea acutidens* (Christ) Domin 1929

*Alsophila acutidens* Christ 1906

*Cyathea* clade. The erect trunk can be as tall as about 2.5 m and 5–8 cm in diameter. Fronds are bipinnate and may reach 2.5 m in length. The rachis is dark and may have yellowish hairs and scattered scales, particularly clustered toward the base; the scales have a brown central region and a yellowish to whitish margin. Sori occur on each side of the pinnule midvein and may be covered with saucer-like indusia. Distribution: Costa Rica in submontane rain forest, forest understory, and along shaded paths at 1000–1700 m.

*Cyathea acutidens* is a small tree fern with a narrow trunk and an arching crown of fronds. It is closely related to *C. multiflora* and the two may be the same species.

## *Cyathea aeneifolia* (Alderwerelt van Rosenburgh) Domin 1930

*Alsophila aeneifolia* Alderwerelt van Rosenburgh 1924,

*Sphaeropteris aeneifolia* (Alderwerelt van Rosenburgh) Tryon 1970

*Sphaeropteris* clade. The erect trunk is 4–5 m tall. Fronds are bi- or tripinnate, 2–2.5 m long, and occur in groups of 9–12 in a whorl. The rachis is short and covered with spines and warts. The stipe has dark glossy spines and is covered with scattered scales that are dark brown to nearly black. Sori occur on veins along each fertile pinnule segment; indusia are absent. Distribution: New Guinea, on forest margins and in grassland at 2800–3850 m.

*Cyathea aeneifolia* is possibly allied to *C. curranii* and *C. pilulifera*. There are several varieties of *C. aeneifolia*, including *macrophylla* Holttum, *melanacantha* (Copeland) Holttum, and *subglauca* Alderwerelt van Rosenburgh, all of which may be ecological variants.

## *Cyathea affinis* (J. R. Forster) Swartz 1801

*Polypodium affine* J. R. Forster 1786, not *Cyathea affinis* W. J. Hooker & Baker 1874 (see *C. medullaris*); *C. affinis* M. Martens & Galeotti 1842 (unable to be attributed to any species), *Alsophila tahitensis* Brackenridge 1854, *C. tahitensis* (Brackenridge) Domin 1929, *C. rapaensis* Copeland 1938

*Alsophila* clade. The erect trunk is 2–6 m tall. Fronds are bipinnate and may reach 2–3 m in length; the lowest one or two pairs of pinnae may be slightly reduced and occur toward the base of the stipe. The rachis and stipe are pale to brown or flushed with red toward the pinnule rachis. The stipe has sparse basal scales that are narrow, pale to dark, and have broad fragile edges. Sori are near the pinnule midvein and are partially or fully covered by indusia that open toward the pinnule margin. Distribution: Fiji, Samoa, Cook Islands, Austral Islands, Tahiti, and the Marquesas Islands.

*Cyathea affinis* is a variable tree fern with regard to scale and frond details. *Cyathea tahitensis*, regarded here as synonymous, may represent a separate species; the confusion over the identity of these two tree ferns requires further study. A closely related species, *C. plagiostegia*, from Fiji, has been recognized taxonomically; it differs in its smaller size and smaller indusia, and its true relationship to *C. affinis* requires further investigation. *Cyathea affinis* is related to *C. solomonensis*. Young shoots of *C. affinis* are eaten in the Marquesas Islands.

## *Cyathea agatheti* Holttum 1962

*Sphaeropteris agatheti* (Holttum) Tryon 1970

*Sphaeropteris* clade. The erect trunk is well under 1 m in height. Fronds are pinnate or bipinnate and about 1 m long or less. The stipe is dark toward the base, which is densely scaly, or slightly warty where scales have fallen; the scales are light brown and have a pale margin. Sori occur on veins of fertile pinnules; indusia are absent. Distribution: Eastern Borneo in forest on waterlogged sand at about 600 m. It is often associated with *Agathis* forest, hence the name *agatheti*.

## *Cyathea alata* (Fournier) Copeland 1931

*Alsophila alata* Fournier 1873

*Cyathea* clade. The erect trunk is 2–6 m tall and 5–10 cm in diameter, usually free of old stipes but bearing scars. Fronds are bipinnate and may reach 2–3 m in length. The rachis and stipe are brown and have basal scales and some spines; the scales are often glossy brown. Sori occur in rows along each side of the pinnule midvein and are covered by very reduced, semicircular, scale-like indusia. Distribution: Solomon Islands, New Caledonia, Fiji, and Samoa, in forest at 1000–1500 m.

*Cyathea alata* is one of a group of western Pacific species apparently related to *C. decurrens*. Members of this group have variously been attributed to *Alsophila* or *Cyathea*. Molecular evidence suggests some relationship with the latter genus, as treated here, though the relationship is by no means clear.

## *Cyathea albidosquamata* Rosenstock 1913

*Sphaeropteris albidosquamata* (Rosenstock) Tryon 1970, *Cyathea pumila* Alderwerelt van Rosenburgh 1918

*Alsophila* clade. The erect trunk is about 2 m tall. Fronds are bi- or tripinnate and 1–1.5 m long. The rachis has scales on the lower surface, and the stipe has scattered scales throughout that are glossy, pale, and have dull, fragile edges. Sori are round, occur near the fertile pinnule midvein, and have flat, saucer-like indusia. Distribution: Moluccas and New Guinea, in rain forest and montane forest at 1200–1500 m.

Richard Eric Holttum (1963) grouped *Cyathea albidosquamata* among species normally associated with the genus *Alsophila*. If that genus is recognized, a new combination would be required for *C. albidosquamata*.

### *Cyathea albifrons* Vieillard ex Fournier 1873

> *Sphaeropteris albifrons* (Vieillard ex Fournier) Tryon 1970,
> *Cyathea interjecta* Baker 1874

*Sphaeropteris* clade. The erect trunk is 7–10 m tall. Fronds are bi- or tripinnate and may reach about 3 m in length. The rachis is pale, grading to dark. The stipe is dark and scaly, or warty where scales have fallen; the scales are dark brown to nearly black. Sori occur medially along each fertile pinnule segment and are covered by pale, thin indusia. Distribution: New Caledonia in damp gully forest.

In 1862 the name *Cyathea funebris* appeared in Linden's horticultural catalogs; that material was apparently *C. albifrons*.

### *Cyathea albomarginata* R. C. Moran 1991

*Cyathea* clade. The erect trunk is about 50 cm tall. Fronds are bipinnate. The rachis has sparsely scattered scales, particularly toward the base. Petiole scales are purple-brown with a wide white margin; elsewhere, scales are ovate and golden brown. Sori are clustered on each side of the pinnule midvein and have minute, scale-like indusia. Distribution: Costa Rica and Panama, in wet forest at 2400–2800 m.

*Cyathea albomarginata* is named after the distinctive, bicolored scales and has one of the highest elevation ranges of any member of the genus.

### *Cyathea albosetacea* (Beddome) Copeland 1909

> *Alsophila albosetacea* Beddome 1876, *Sphaeropteris albosetacea*
> (Beddome) Tryon 1970

*Sphaeropteris* clade. Plants have a medium to tall, erect trunk. Fronds are bi- or tripinnate and may reach 2–3 m in length. The rachis is pale and has short spines. The stipe is pale, warty, and covered with scattered scales that are firm, glossy, and have marginal setae. Sori are plentiful on each fertile pinnule segment; indusia are apparently absent. Distribution: Camorta and Katchall in the Nicobar Islands, north of Sumatra, scattered among coral reef forest.

### *Cyathea alderwereltii* Copeland 1909

> *Alsophila alderwereltii* (Copeland) Tryon 1970, *Cyathea horridipes*
> Domin 1929, *C. spinifera* (Alderwerelt van Rosenburgh) Domin 1930

*Alsophila* clade. The erect trunk is about 4 m tall or more. Fronds are bi- or tripinnate and 1–2 m long. The stipe is spiny at the base and covered with scattered scales that are dark brown, glossy, and have a narrow paler margin. Sori occur near the fertile pinnule midvein and are covered by small, brown, scale-like indusia. Distribution: Abundant on Mount Sago, central Sumatra, in forest at 1000–1500 m.

*Cyathea alderwereltii* is named after Dutch pteridologist Cornelis Rogier Willem Carel van Alderwerelt van Rosenburgh (1863–1936), who worked extensively in the Malaysian and Indonesian region.

### *Cyathea alleniae* Holttum 1962

*Alsophila alleniae* (Holttum) Tryon 1970

*Alsophila* clade. The erect trunk is about 4 m tall and 15 cm in diameter; it may branch, producing several small crowns of fronds. Fronds are bi- or tripinnate and 1–2 m long. The stipe is spiny at the base and at least partially covered by scales that are dark brown, glossy, and have fragile edges. Sori occur near the midvein of fertile pinnules and are covered by firm, brown, scale-like indusia. Distribution: Malay Peninsula in forest margin on steep ground at about 1200 m.

*Cyathea alleniae* is named after Betty Eleanor Gosset Molesworth Allen (1913–2002), plant collector in Malaysia and Indonesia.

### *Cyathea alphonsiana* Gómez 1971

*Cyathea* clade. The erect trunk is as tall as 4–7 m and 6–10 cm in diameter. Fronds are bipinnate and may reach about 2 m in length. The petiole is yellowish and may have small raised dots. The rachis is yellowish brown to straw-colored and has yellowish hairs and scattered scales, particularly clustered toward the base; the scales are brown to yellowish brown. Sori occur each side of the pinnule midvein and may be covered with minute, flattened indusia. Distribution: Cocos Island, off the Pacific coast of Costa Rica, in dense, wet, tropical forest in the understory and in open sites, from sea level to 630 m.

*Cyathea alphonsiana* is a small tree fern with a thin trunk and a crown of fronds that may arch upward. It may bear some relationship to *C. multiflora*. The relationship between the two requires further investigation.

### *Cyathea alpicola* Domin 1930

*Alsophila alpina* Alderwerelt van Rosenburgh 1915, *Cyathea alpina* Alderwerelt van Rosenburgh 1918

*Alsophila* clade. The erect trunk is about 5 m tall or more. Fronds are bi- or tripinnate, 2–3 m long, and may persist as an irregular skirt about the trunk. The stipe is spiny and covered with a woolly layer of scales that are either dark glossy brown and have a broad paler margin and fragile edges, or small, brown, and finely fringed. Sori occur near the midvein of fertile pinnules and are covered by thin, fragile indusia. Distribution: Central Sumatra in montane rain forest at 2000–2750 m.

*Cyathea alpicola* is similar to *C. polycarpa* but differs in having spines. It may be closely allied to *C. macropoda* and *C. magnifolia*.

### *Cyathea alstonii* Tryon 1976

*Cyathea* clade. The erect trunk is short. Fronds are pinnate and about 75 cm long. Rachis and stipe scales are bullate and brown. Sori occur on each side of the pinnule midvein and may be covered with thin indusia. Distribution: Macarena Mountains, Colombia, on sandstone at 1300–1900 m, collected from Pico Renjifo.

*Cyathea alstonii* is named after Arthur Hugh Garfit Alston (1902–1958), pteridologist and collector in various areas around the world.

### *Cyathea alternans* (Wallich ex W. J. Hooker) C. B. Presl 1848

*Polypodium alternans* Wallich ex W. J. Hooker 1829, *Sphaeropteris alternans* (Wallich ex W. J. Hooker) Tryon 1970, *Cyathea sarawakensis* W. J. Hooker 1865

*Sphaeropteris* clade. The erect trunk is less than 2 m tall. Fronds are pinnate to almost bipinnate and 1–2 m long. The stipe is dark and generally smooth but has basal scales that are medium brown, firm, and glossy. Sori occur in a single row on either side of the midvein of the fertile pinnule; occasionally a second, incomplete row may be present. Indusia are present and highly variable, ranging in form from completely covering the sorus to saucer-like. Distribution: Malay Peninsula, Sumatra, and northern Borneo, in forest and near streams at 300–1300 m.

*Cyathea alternans* is a variable species, often found in association with *C. moluccana*. It may represent a hybrid swarm involving *C. alternans* and *C. moluccana*.

### *Cyathea amazonica* R. C. Moran 1995

*Cyathea* clade. The erect trunk is 2–3 m tall and 3–6 cm in diameter. Fronds are bipinnate and may reach 2.5 m in length. The underside of the lamina often has stiff whitish hairs. The rachis is tan to brown and has spines and scattered scales; the scales are lanceolate and whitish to light brown, or bicolored, with a dark brown central region and a narrow paler margin. Sori occur on each side of the pinnule midvein and may be covered with scale-like indusia. Distribution: Ecuador in tropical rain forest at 30–300 m.

*Cyathea amazonica* is similar to *C. andina*, from which it differs by the presence of whitish hairs on the underside of the lamina, and also resembles *C. pilosissima*, which differs in lacking indusia.

### *Cyathea amboinensis* (Alderwerelt van Rosenburgh) Merrill 1917

*Alsophila amboinensis* Alderwerelt van Rosenburgh 1916

*Alsophila* clade. The erect, slender trunk is 2–4 m tall. Fronds are bi- or tripinnate and 1–2 m long. The stipe is warty near the base and covered with scattered scales that are dark, glossy, and have fragile edges. Sori occur near the midvein of fertile pinnules and are covered by small, dark, scale-like indusia. Distribution: Moluccas and possibly in central and southern Sulawesi (Celebes), in swamp and forest at low elevations, the name *amboinensis* referring to Ambon or Amboina, an island in the Moluccas.

### *Cyathea andersonii* (Scott ex Beddome) Copeland 1909

*Alsophila andersonii* Scott ex Beddome 1869

*Alsophila* clade. The erect trunk is 6–10 m tall. Fronds are bi- or tripinnate and 2–3 m long. The rachis is flushed with dark purple. The stipe is dark, almost black, and has sparsely scattered scales that are lanceolate, dark, and have pale fringes. Sori occur near the midvein of fertile pinnules; indusia are absent. Distribution: India, Bhutan, and southern China, in moist valleys and montane forest at 300–1200 m.

It is likely that the name *andersonii* commemorates Thomas Anderson (1832–1870), botanist and director of the Calcutta botanical garden.

### *Cyathea andina* (Karsten) Domin 1929

*Hemitelia andina* Karsten 1857, *Cyathea boryana* (Kuhn) Domin 1929

*Cyathea* clade. The erect trunk is 1–3 m tall, rarely as tall as 8 m, and 5–8 cm in diameter. Fronds are bipinnate and may reach 2–4 m in length. The petiole is brown and has spines. The rachis is grayish brown to brown and has scattered scales that are bicolored, with a dark brown central region and a narrow paler margin. Sori occur on each side of the pinnule midvein and may be covered with scale-like indusia that split into two at maturity. Distribution: Hispaniola and Puerto Rico; Costa Rica and Panama; Colombia, Ecuador, Peru, Bolivia, Venezuela, northern Brazil, Suriname, and French Guiana. Plants grow in tropical rain forest, submontane and montane rain forest, in open sites, and on cliffs at 700–1500 m.

*Cyathea andina* is a small tree fern with a thin trunk and persistent fronds (in young plants almost to the base of the trunk). The persistence of the fronds often gives plants a scraggly appearance. The species is similar to

*C. amazonica*, differing from it by the lack of whitish hairs on the underside of the lamina, and bears some relationship to *C. weatherbyana*.

### *Cyathea aneitensis* W. J. Hooker 1865

*Alsophila aneitensis* (W. J. Hooker) Tryon 1970, *Cyathea laciniata* Copeland 1931

*Alsophila* clade. The erect trunk may be as tall as about 3 m. Fronds are bipinnate and may reach 2 m in length. The rachis and stipe are either very dark and smooth or have a few scales toward the base of the stipe; the scales are brown and narrow. Sori occur near the pinnule midvein and are covered by large, thin, fragile indusia. Distribution: Vanuatu and, possibly, New Caledonia, the name *aneitensis* referring to Aneityum, the most southerly island of Vanuatu.

*Cyathea aneitensis* is similar to *C. vieillardii* but differs in having very dark stipes and frond bases.

### *Cyathea angiensis* (Gepp) Domin 1930

*Alsophila angiensis* Gepp in Gibbs 1917, *Sphaeropteris angiensis* (Gepp) Tryon 1970

*Sphaeropteris* clade. The crown is composed of about 12 bi- or tripinnate fronds 1–2 m long in three whorls of four or five fronds each; old fronds drop immediately, leaving stipe-base scars on the trunk. Distribution: Moluccas to New Guinea, in montane forest at 600–2200 m.

*Cyathea angiensis* is similar to *C. contaminans* but much smaller.

### *Cyathea angustipinna* Holttum 1962

*Sphaeropteris angustipinna* (Holttum) Tryon 1970

*Sphaeropteris* clade. The erect trunk may be as tall as about 1 m. Fronds are pinnate and about 1 m long. The stipe is smooth and has basal scales that are pale, firm, and glossy. Sori occur in groups of two or three per group of three veins on the underside of fertile pinnules and are covered with thin, pale indusia. Distribution: Sarawak and elsewhere on Borneo, near streams in shade to 1200 m.

### *Cyathea annae* (Alderwerelt van Rosenburgh) Domin 1930

*Alsophila annae* Alderwerelt van Rosenburgh 1916

*Alsophila* clade. The erect, slender trunk may be as tall as about 3 m. Fronds are bipinnate and may reach 1–2 m in length. The final pair of pinnae are usually reduced and occur toward the base of the stipe. The stipe is dark, slender, and covered with scattered scales that are dark, glossy, and have a pale dull margin. Fertile pinnules are usually short-lobed. Sori occur two to four per pinnule lobe; indusia are absent. Distribution: Ambon in the Moluccas, in forest from sea level to about 650 m.

*Cyathea annae* was originally described from a plant cultivated at the Bogor Botanic Gardens. The name *annae* commemorates Anna Smith, wife of Johannes Jacobus Smith (1867–1947) and who apparently collected the plant on Ambon at the turn of the 20th century.

### *Cyathea apiculata* (Rosenstock) Domin 1929

*Alsophila apiculata* Rosenstock 1914, *Cyathea indrapurae* Alderwerelt van Rosenburgh 1918, *C. paleata* Copeland 1929

*Alsophila* clade. The erect trunk is about 5 m tall or more. Fronds are bi- or tripinnate and 2–3 m long. The stipe is pale, becoming dark at the base, and covered with scales that are dark and have pale fragile edges. Sori occur near the midvein of fertile pinnules and are covered by thin, very fragile indusia. Distribution: Sumatra in montane rain forest at about 1800 m.

### *Cyathea apoensis* Copeland in Emler 1910

*Alsophila apoensis* (Copeland) Tryon 1970, *Cyathea lobata* Copeland 1952

*Alsophila* clade. The erect trunk is 2–5 m tall. The rachis is dark and warty. The stipe is covered with scattered scales that are large, dark, and glossy, or small and dull brown. Sori are round, occur near the fertile pinnule midvein, and are covered by thin, brown, cup-like indusia. Distribution: Mindanao, Negros, and southern Luzon in the Philippines, in dense forest at about 1800 m, the name *apoensis* referring to Mount Apo (2954 m), the highest mountain in the Philippines, an active volcano on Mindanao.

### *Cyathea approximata* Bonaparte 1917

*Alsophila approximata* (Bonaparte) Tryon 1970

*Alsophila* clade. The erect trunk is about 2 m tall and spiny. Fronds are bipinnate, about 2 m long, and form a crown of two whorls of about seven fronds each. Scales on the stipe are dark brown and have a paler margin. Sori are round, occur near the fertile pinnule midvein, and are covered by thin, brown, cup-like indusia. Distribution: Madagascar.

### *Cyathea aramaganensis* Kanehira 1934

*Sphaeropteris aramaganensis* (Kanehira) Tryon 1970

PLATE 20

*Sphaeropteris* clade. The erect trunk is 5–10 m tall. Fronds are bi- or tripinnate and may reach about 3 m in length. The rachis is pale and has a glabrous lower surface and scattered warts. The stipe is long and has some scales that are glossy dark brown to nearly black. Sori lack indusia but may be surrounded by clusters of scales. Distribution: Mariana Islands, the name *aramaganensis* referring to the island of Alamagan or Aramagan in the northern Marianas.

### *Cyathea arborea* (Linnaeus) Smith 1793

*Polypodium arboreum* Linnaeus 1753, *Cyathea sternbergii* Pohl 1820,
C. *nigrescens* (W. J. Hooker) J. Smith 1866, in part
PLATE 21

*Cyathea* clade. The erect trunk is as tall as 10 m, rarely as tall as 15 m, and 9–15 cm in diameter. The truck lacks spines but may be covered with creamy whitish scales toward the apex, and oval frond base scars. Fronds are bipinnate, glabrous, light green, and may reach 4 m in length. The stipe is short, yellowish, warty but rarely spiny, and usually covered with creamy to dirty white scales toward the base. Sori are erect receptacles covered by saucer-like indusia. Distribution: Greater Antilles, and Lesser Antilles from Saba, St. Eustatius, and St. Kitts to Barbados and Grenada; Mexico and Central America to Venezuela. Plants grow in lowland rain forest to submontane rain forest, in moist clearings and glades and as colonizers of disturbed land, from near sea level to about 1500 m.

*Cyathea arborea* is a common tree fern, the nomenclatural type species for the genus *Cyathea*. Linnaeus described *C. arborea* in 1753 (as a *Polypodium*) based on material collected from Morne de la Calebasse, Martinique. The name *arborea* refers to the tree-like appearance of this plant, one of the first tree ferns, along with *C. aspera*, to be described in Europe. It has the same etymology as the type species for *Dicksonia* (*D. arborescens*). *Cyathea arborea* is easy to cultivate but does best in sheltered locations in rich humus with a consistent supply of moisture.

### *Cyathea archboldii* C. Christensen 1937

*Alsophila archboldii* (C. Christensen) Tryon 1970, *Cyathea bidentata*
Copeland 1942

*Alsophila* clade. The erect trunk may be as tall as about 3 m. Fronds are bipinnate and may reach 2–3 m in length. The rachis may be purplish and has short spines and scales; the scales may be pale to brown, to bicolored, brown with dark brown, fragile edges. Sori occur in two rows along each side of the pinnule midvein and are covered by firm indusia. Distribution: New Guinea and Bougainville, common in submontane rain forest at 1000–3000 m.

*Cyathea archboldii* is likely named after Richard Archbold (1907–1976).

An heir to the Standard Oil Company, Archbold became an internationally known explorer, leading several biological expeditions to Madagascar and the interior of New Guinea. *Cyathea archboldii* has been collected in New Guinea, in forest and alpine shrubbery, over a wide range of elevations. Spore material sourced from high-elevation plants may be worth cultivating for cooler climates. One variety, *horrida*, was recognized in 1963 by Richard Eric Holttum. *Cyathea archboldii* is similar to *C. foersteri* and *C. nigrolineata* but differs in frond shape (lower pinnae not as reduced) and in having longer stipes.

### *Cyathea armata* (Swartz) Domin 1930

*Polypodium armatum* Swartz 1788, ?*Alsophila strigillosa* Maxon 1922

*Cyathea* clade. The erect trunk may be as tall as 15 m and 8–15 cm in diameter. The trunk lacks spines but may be covered with whitish scales toward the apex. Fronds are bipinnate and may reach 3 m in length. The rachis is pubescent and has a few warts and sharp spines. The stipe is long, light green or glaucous, and succulent, with many spines and sharp scales; the scales are narrow and cream to dirty white with a brown patch toward their base. Sori are found in rows along the pinnule midvein; indusia are absent. Distribution: Greater Antilles in rain forest to submontane forest, on moist banks or hillsides and in clearings, at 450–1800 m.

*Cyathea armata* is a medium-sized tree fern with a large, spreading crown. The name *armata* refers to the presence of sharp spines arming the rachis. This species forms part of a complex of related tree ferns that includes *C. bicrenata*, *C. conjugata*, *C. estelae*, *C. hirsuta*, *C. nesiotica*, *C. rufa*, *C. stipularis*, *C. trichiata* and *C. tryonorum*. The tree fern known as *Alsophila strigillosa* may also be part of this complex.

### *Cyathea arthropoda* Copeland 1911

*Sphaeropteris arthropoda* (Copeland) Tryon 1970

*Sphaeropteris* clade. The erect trunk is 1–2 m tall. Fronds are pinnate and usually less than 1 m long. The stipe is covered with scattered, medium brown scales. Sori occur in one to three irregular rows on either side of the midvein of fertile pinnules; an indusium is either lacking or is narrow and ring-like at the base of each sorus. Distribution: Sarawak in lowland forest.

### *Cyathea ascendens* Domin 1930

*Alsophila rosenstockii* Brause 1920, not *Cyathea rosenstockii* Brause 1920

*Alsophila* clade. The erect trunk is 1–2 m tall. Fronds are bi- or tripinnate, may reach more than 1 m in length, and form an open crown. The stipe is covered in glossy scales with pale fragile edges. Sori occur near the midvein of fertile pinnules; indusia are absent. Distribution: Northeastern New Guinea in rain forest at 800–1000 m.

The specific name *ascendens* implies a climbing habit, but though the trunk is slim there is no evidence of a true climbing habit.

## *Cyathea aspera* (Linnaeus) Swartz 1800

*Polypodium asperum* Linnaeus 1753

*Cyathea* clade. The erect trunk is 4–6 m tall, 6–11 cm in diameter, spiny, and covered with glossy brown scales. Fronds are bipinnate, may reach 3.5 m in length, and may be partially retained, forming a skirt about the trunk. The rachis is light brown. The stipe is long, dark brown, and has warts and short spines, or may be warty only. Sori are present on pinnule vein forks; their presence may be indicated by the occurrence of pit-like depressions on the upper surface of the pinnules. The sori are covered by small scale-like indusia. Distribution: Greater Antilles in lowland rain forest to submontane rain forest, in moist clearings and glades to about 1500 m.

*Cyathea aspera* is a small tree fern with ascending fronds. This species is one of the earliest known to Europeans and was described, along with *C. arborea*, by Linnaeus in 1753 (as a *Polypodium*) based on a plant collected by Charles Plumier from Grand Cul de Sac, near Léogâne, Haiti. *Cyathea aspera* may be related to *C. gibbosa*.

## *Cyathea assimilis* W. J. Hooker 1865

*Sphaeropteris assimilis* (W. J. Hooker) Tryon 1970, *Cyathea beccariana* Cesati 1876, *C. dulitensis* Baker 1896, *C. ampla* Copeland 1911

*Sphaeropteris* clade. The erect trunk is as tall as about 2 m or higher. Fronds are pinnate or bipinnate and 1–2 m long. The stipe is medium to dark brown and finely warty and scaly near the base; the scales are brownish, glossy, and firm. Sori occur near the midvein of the fertile pinnules and are covered by thin, pale indusia. Distribution: Southern Sumatra and Borneo, in submontane and ridge forest on sandstone at 300–2000 m.

## *Cyathea atahuallpa* (Tryon) Lellinger 1984

*Sphaeropteris atahuallpa* Tryon 1972

*Cyathea* clade. Distribution: Peru. *Cyathea atahuallpa* is a rare species whose name commemorates the Inca ruler Atahuallpa (ca. 1502–1533).

### Cyathea aterrima (W. J. Hooker) Domin 1929

*Alsophila aterrima* W. J. Hooker 1866, *A. lechria* Tryon 1960,
*A. scopulina* Tryon 1960

*Cyathea* clade. The erect trunk may be as tall as about 6 m. Fronds are bipinnate to almost tripinnate and 2.5–3 m long. The stipe is warty and covered in scales, especially toward the base; the scales are narrow and light brown or straw-colored. Sori occur between the fertile pinnule midvein and pinnule margin; indusia are absent. Distribution: Venezuela, Colombia, and Peru, in forest and exposed montane areas at 700–1500 m.

*Cyathea aterrima* is a complex species with a number of synonyms and is related to *C. lockwoodiana, C. parianensis,* and *C. senilis.*

### Cyathea atropurpurea Copeland 1909

*Alsophila atropurpurea* (Copeland) C. Christensen 1913

*Alsophila* clade. The erect, slender trunk may be as tall as about 3 m. Fronds are bipinnate and may reach 1–2 m in length. The final pair of pinnae are usually reduced and occur toward the base of the stipe; these along with the stipe bases are persistent and retained about the trunk. The stipe is dark and covered with scales that are either small, dull, and brown or large, dark, and glossy. Fertile pinnules are smaller than sterile ones. Sori occur near the midvein of fertile pinnules; indusia are absent. Distribution: Luzon, Mindoro, Leyte, and Mindanao in the Philippines, in forest above 1000 m.

*Cyathea atropurpurea* is very similar to *C. ramispina,* differing in its smaller pinnae and pinnules and other frond details; the relationship between the two species requires further investigation.

### Cyathea atrospinosa Holttum 1962

*Sphaeropteris atrospinosa* (Holttum) Tryon 1970

*Sphaeropteris* clade. The erect trunk may be as tall as about 6 m. Fronds are bi- or tripinnate, occur in groups of four to six in three whorls (the top two green and living), and are 3–4 m long. The stipe has dark glossy spines about 8 mm long and is covered in scales that are pale or pale brown. Sori lack indusia. Distribution: Eastern New Guinea in montane forest, also on limestone, at 2400–2900 m.

### Cyathea atrovirens (Langsdown & Fischer) Domin 1929

*Polypodium atrovirens* Langsdown & Fischer 1810, *Cyathea fellacina*
(Domin) Domin 1930

*Cyathea* clade. The erect trunk is 1.5–6 m tall. Fronds are bipinnate and may reach 2 m or more in length. The rachis is brown to purplish and has scattered scales that are twisted and brown. Sori occur between the fertile pinnule midvein and the edge of the lamina; indusia are absent. Distribution: Argentina, Paraguay, and Brazil along the Serra do Mar, in secondary forest and scrub at 35–900 m.

*Cyathea atrovirens* is perhaps most closely related to the *C. phalerata* complex and *C. villosa*.

### *Cyathea atrox* C. Christensen 1937

*Sphaeropteris atrox* (C. Christensen) Tryon 1970

*Sphaeropteris* clade. The erect trunk is 6–7 m tall. Fronds number 20–30 in a crown, are bi- or tripinnate, and 1–2 m long. The stipe has dark glossy spines 3–5 mm long, and the base may be covered in scales that are glossy, firm, and brown. Sori occur near the midveins of the fertile pinnules; indusia are absent. Distribution: Eastern New Guinea along streams, in open grassland, drier shrubby areas, or forest margins at 2800–3600 m.

*Cyathea atrox* is a variable species. Variety *inermis* Holttum is from northeastern New Guinea and the western highlands; it differs from variety *atrox* in having very small, fringed scales on the pinnule rachis and a stipe with numerous conical warts.

### *Cyathea auriculifera* Copeland 1911

*Sphaeropteris auriculifera* (Copeland) Tryon 1970

*Sphaeropteris* clade. The erect trunk is as tall as 2–3 m. Fronds are tripinnate and may reach 2–2.5 m in length. The stipe is spiny and densely covered with scales that are pale, long or twisted, and that have paler edges. Sori occur near the midvein of each fertile pinnule and are covered with overlapping fringed scales, giving the appearance of indusia. Distribution: New Guinea and the Louisiade Archipelago, in montane forest or mossy forest transition zone, at 750–2600 m.

### *Cyathea australis* (R. Brown) Domin 1929

*Alsophila australis* R. Brown 1810, *Cyathea loddigesii* (Kunze)
   Domin 1929
ROUGH TREE FERN
PLATES 22, 23

*Alsophila* clade. The erect massive trunk is about 12 m tall, with some specimens as tall as 20 m reported from Queensland, Australia. Fronds are bi- or tripinnate and may reach 4 m in length, forming a crown that is dark green above and lighter green below. Stipe bases are often retained on the trunk and are usually covered with scales and conical blunt spines toward the base; the scales are shiny brown to bicolored (pale and brown) and often twisted. Sori are circular in outline and occur on either side of the fertile pinnule midvein. A true indusium is absent, but reduced scales may encircle the sorus. Distribution: Southeastern Queensland, New South Wales, and southern Victoria, Australia, to Tasmania and Norfolk Island, in moist shady forest, both coastal and montane, to 1200 m.

*Cyathea australis* was described (as *Alsophila*, and it is the type for that genus) by Robert Brown in 1810 from a specimen from King Island in Bass Strait, between Victoria and Tasmania. The name *australis*, southern, refers to this southerly location. (See also the discussion under *Cyathea leichhardtiana*.) *Cyathea australis* is a relatively hardy species, commonly cultivated both as a landscape specimen and in containers. It will tolerate frost and full sun (or shade in warmer regions), particularly if moisture is consistently available. Plants from Norfolk Island differ primarily in scale characteristics. They may represent a subspecies or indeed a separate species.

## *Cyathea baileyana* (Domin) Domin 1929

*Alsophila baileyana* Domin 1913
WIG TREE FERN
PLATE 24

*Alsophila* clade. The erect trunk is 4–5 m tall and about 10 cm in diameter; the upper regions may be covered in stipe bases. Offshoots may develop from the base of the trunk. The rachis and stipe are dark to darkish red, scaly, and may be warty but lack spines. Rachis and stipe scales are purplish brown to black and have a long hair-like apex. Fronds are bi- or tripinnate and 2–3 m long, occasionally as long as 7 m. The last pair of pinnae are separated from the others along the rachis and may form a clump (the wig) about the trunk apex. Sori are circular in outline and occur in one to three rows along the midvein of the pinnule; a true indusium is absent. Distribution: Northeastern Queensland, Australia, rare and growing in wet gullies and forest at 850–1200 m.

The common name "wig tree fern" refers to the pinnae that cluster about the crown of each plant. This wig is green in younger plants but may become brownish in older specimens. The name *baileyana* commemorates Australian botanist Frederick Manson Bailey (1827–1915). *Cyathea baileyana* is difficult to obtain and somewhat difficult to grow. Plants are frost sensitive and require protection from wind, sun, and dehydration.

## Cyathea balanocarpa D. C. Eaton 1860

*Alsophila balanocarpa* (D. C. Eaton) Conant 1983

*Alsophila* clade. Distribution: Cuba, Jamaica, and Hispaniola. *Cyathea balanocarpa* is apparently of hybrid origin.

## Cyathea barringtonii A. R. Smith ex Lellinger 1987

*Alsophila cordata* Klotzsch 1847, not *Cyathea cordata* (Desvaux)
   Mettenius ex Diels in Engler & Prantl 1899 (see *C. marattioides*)

*Cyathea* clade. The prostrate or leaning to erect trunk is 0.1–1 m long, occasionally as long as 2.5 m. Fronds are bipinnate and may reach 2 m in length. The rachis and stipe are almost purple and warty, and has scattered scales, especially toward the base; the scales are brown, often with a paler margin. Sori occur between the fertile pinnule midvein and the edge of the lamina; indusia are absent. Distribution: Venezuela in cloud forest at 1500–1700 m.

*Cyathea barringtonii* is named after David S. Barrington (b. 1948), pteridologist at the University of Vermont. This uncommon tree fern is allied to the *C. petiolata* complex and is very similar to *C. sagittifolia*.

## Cyathea batjanensis (Christ) Copeland 1909

*Alsophila batjanensis* Christ in Warburg 1900

*Alsophila* clade. The erect trunk is 2–3 m tall. Fronds are bi- or tripinnate and 1–2 m long. The stipe is spiny, warty, and has scattered scales that are dark brown and have fragile edges. Sori are round, occur near the fertile pinnule midvein, and are covered by small, narrow, saucer-like indusia. Distribution: Moluccas and western New Guinea, in rain forest at about 600 m, the name *batjanensis* referring to Bacan or Batjan, one of the larger islands of the Moluccas.

## Cyathea bicrenata Liebmann 1849

PLATES 25–27

*Cyathea* clade. Distribution: Mexico in humid forest at 1000–2000 m. *Cyathea bicrenata* is closely related to *C. armata* and its associated species.

## Cyathea biformis (Rosenstock) Copeland 1911

*Alsophila biformis* Rosenstock 1911

*Alsophila* clade. The climbing trunk is 1–2 cm in diameter with an apex covered in scales. Fronds are of two kinds, simple pinnate fronds, which are sterile, and bipinnate fronds, which may be fertile. The stipe is dark (almost black), smooth, and glossy but covered at the base with scales; the scales are long, very dark, and have a pale margin. Fertile pinnules are stalked and lobed. Sori occur in four pairs per pinnule lobe; indusia are absent. Distribution: Moluccas and New Guinea, against trees in mossy forest and rain forest at 850–2200 m.

*Cyathea biformis* is an unusual climbing or scrambling fern, often clinging to the supporting tree by its roots and ascending as high as 3 m. *Cyathea scandens* is similar, differing only in the shape of its fertile pinnules. These two species deserve further study and perhaps should be united.

### *Cyathea binuangensis* Alderwerelt van Rosenburgh 1920

*Sphaeropteris binuangensis* (Alderwerelt van Rosenburgh) Tryon 1970

*Sphaeropteris* clade. The erect trunk is 1–2 m tall. Fronds are pinnate and usually less than 1 m long. The stipe is densely scaly at the base; the scales are pale and thin. Sori occur about halfway between the midvein of the fertile pinnule and the edge of the lamina and are covered by thin indusia. Distribution: Luzon in the Philippines, the name *binuangensis* referring to Mount Binuang (889 m).

*Cyathea binuangensis* may be a hybrid, involving *C. integra* as one parent.

### *Cyathea bipinnata* (Tryon) R. C. Moran 1995

*Trichipteris bipinnata* Tryon 1986

*Cyathea* clade. The medium-sized trunk is erect. Fronds are bipinnate. The rachis is tan to brown and has scattered scales that are lanceolate and whitish to light brown. Sori occur on each side of the pinnule midvein and may be covered with scale-like indusia. Distribution: Northwestern Ecuador on the western slopes of the Andes at 900–1800 m.

### *Cyathea boliviana* Tryon 1976

*Cyathea* clade. The erect trunk is as tall as 15 m. Fronds are bipinnate. Stipe scales are flattish and have dark-colored apical processes. Distribution: Bolivia in montane forest at 2000–2200 m.

*Cyathea boliviana* is part of a group of related species centered on *C. straminea*.

### *Cyathea borinquena* (Maxon) Domin 1929

*Alsophila borinquena* Maxon 1925

*Cyathea* clade. The creeping to just erect trunk is about 1 m tall. Fronds are pinnate or bipinnate and may reach 2 m or more in length. The rachis is brown and has warts and scattered brown scales. Sori occur between the fertile pinnule midvein and the edge of the lamina. Veins are forked at the sori. Indusia are absent. Distribution: Puerto Rico in wet montane forest at 500–1000 m, the name *borinquena* referring to Point Borinquén, a cape at the northwestern end of the island.

*Cyathea borinquena* is possibly allied to *C. phalerata*.

### *Cyathea borneensis* Copeland 1911

*Alsophila borneensis* (Copeland) Tryon 1970, *Cyathea hemichlamydea* Copeland 1893, *C. obtusata* Rosenstock 1917

*Alsophila* clade. The erect trunk may be as tall as about 2 m or taller. Fronds are bi- to tripinnate and may reach 2–3 m in length. The stipe is spiny and warty and has scattered scales that are glossy, dark, and have narrow fragile edges. Sori are close to fertile pinnule midveins and covered by thin indusia. Distribution: Southern Thailand and Cambodia to the Malay Peninsula and Borneo, in lowland forest at 400–1100 m.

*Cyathea borneensis* is a lowland species, requiring plentiful moisture and warm temperatures.

### *Cyathea brackenridgei* Mettenius 1863

*Sphaeropteris brackenridgei* (Mettenius) Tryon 1970

*Sphaeropteris* clade. The erect trunk is as tall as 10 m. Fronds are bi- or tripinnate and 2–3 m long. The stipe is covered with scales that are either large, dark, and thickened medially, with a pale setiferous edge, or small, irregular, and dull. Sori occur halfway between the pinnule midvein and the edge of the lobe and are covered with indusia. Distribution: Solomon Islands in wet forest and beside streams.

*Cyathea brackenridgei* is named after William Dunlop Brackenridge (1810–1893), a naturalist on the U.S. Exploring Expedition of 1838–1842 commanded by Charles Wilkes. *Cyathea brackenridgei* is similar to *C. moseleyi;* the relationship between the two requires further investigation.

### *Cyathea bradei* (Windisch) Lellinger 1984

*Sphaeropteris bradei* Windisch 1973

*Cyathea* clade. The erect trunk is as tall as 5 m. Fronds are bipinnate and 1–2 m long. The stipe is scaly toward the base; the scales are dark and glossy brown, toothed or with entire edges. Sori occur near the midvein of fertile pinnules and are covered by thin, translucent, two-lobed, scale-like indusia. Distribution: Colombia on sandstone-derived soils and Peru near Iquitos, in forest at 100–1000 m.

The name *bradei* commemorates Alexandre Curt Brade (1881–1971), plant collector in Central and South America. *Cyathea bradei* is similar to *C. cyatheoides*.

## *Cyathea brevipinnata* Baker ex Bentham 1878

*Alsophila brevipinnata* (Baker ex Bentham) Tryon 1970

*Alsophila* clade. The erect trunk is as tall as about 3 m, often covered with reddish brown scales and stipe bases. Stolons may be produced at ground level. Fronds are tripinnate and may reach about 3 m in length. The stipe is brown and may be warty after scales fall; the scales are long, glossy dark brown, and have a narrow tip and fragile paler edges. Sori are attached to deeply divided fertile pinnules that may curl over the sori; indusia are firm and large. Distribution: Higher parts of Mount Gower (875 m), Lord Howe Island, Australia, in exposed situations.

*Cyathea brevipinnata* is a stunted plant with short pinnae.

## *Cyathea brevistipes* R. C. Moran 1991

*Cyathea* clade. The erect trunk is 1.5–3 m tall and about 3 cm in diameter. Fronds may reach just over 1 m in length and are bipinnate and heavily dissected to virtually tripinnate. Basal pinnules may be separated along the rachis from those of the main frond. Petioles are yellowish brown. The rachis is scaly and lacks hairs; the scales are golden brown and lanceolate to ovate. Sori occur on vein forks and are covered with globose indusia. Distribution: Ecuador in cloud forest and shrubby windswept páramos (plateaus) at 2800–3200 m.

*Cyathea brevistipes* is similar to *C. straminea*. It differs in having nonspiny petioles, narrower pinnules, and in details of scale color and shape.

## *Cyathea brooksii* Maxon 1909

*Alsophila brooksii* (Maxon) Tryon 1970

*Alsophila* clade. The prostrate trunk is about 6 cm in diameter. Fronds are pinnate or bipinnate and may reach about 2 m in length. The rachis has scales basally; the scales may be blackish with a paler margin. Sori occur in two rows, one along each side of the pinnule midvein. Distribution: Cuba, Hispaniola, and Puerto Rico, normally found on serpentine soils in shaded ravines, along streams, and on forested slopes at 250–950 m.

*Cyathea brooksii* is known to form hybrids with *C. fulgens* and *C. portoricensis*.

## *Cyathea brownii* Domin 1929

*Alsophila excelsa* R. Brown ex Endlicher 1833, *Sphaeropteris excelsa*
(R. Brown ex Endlicher) Tryon 1970
NORFOLK TREE FERN
PLATES 28, 29

*Sphaeropteris* clade. The erect trunk is 5–16 m tall, occasionally as tall as 18 m or higher; it is almost smooth and may display scars left by fallen fronds. Fronds are tripinnate and may reach 3–5 m in length. The rachis and stipe are brown and may have warty protrusions. Rachis and stipe scales are light brown, narrow, and have either marginal setae or white to brown edges. Sori occur in rows of one to ten and lack indusia but may be surrounded by a cluster of scales. Distribution: Norfolk Island, Australia, common in rain forest, near streams and gullies.

*Cyathea brownii*, named after Robert Brown (1773–1858), botanist and botanical explorer of Australia on the voyage of exploration led by Matthew Flinders, is one of the world's largest tree ferns, some with trunks reported to reach 24 m in height. If the genus *Sphaeropteris* is recognized, Brown's specific name *excelsa* takes precedence. This is a fast-growing and commonly cultivated species. Plants do best in rich, well-drained humus and will tolerate some frost though the fronds may be damaged. They also do best when given some shade during the hottest part of the day.

## *Cyathea brunei* Christ 1904

*Sphaeropteris brunei* (Christ) Tryon 1970

*Sphaeropteris* clade. The erect trunk may be as tall as about 20 m and about 20 cm in diameter. Fronds are bi- or tripinnate and may reach about 5 m in length; dead fronds may form a skirt about the trunk. The petiole is straw-colored to light brown and lacks spines. The petiole may be wholly concealed, or at least toward the base, by large scales. The rachis is straw-colored to brown and lacks hairs or scales; the scales are whitish or brown to yellowish brown, or they may be dark toward the apex and lighter basally. Sori occur in two rows along each side of the midvein of fertile pinnules and are covered with globose indusia. Distribution: Costa Rica, and more restricted in Panama and Colombia, in montane and submontane rain forest, in open sites and on riverbanks at 800–2000 m.

*Cyathea brunei* is named after Brune, who collected the type material with Carl Wercklé in Costa Rica. It is a large tree fern with a thick trunk and a large, arching crown of fronds. Dead fronds may be retained and form a complete or partial skirt about the trunk. This species is associated with a group of ferns including *C. gardneri*, *C. insignis*, *C. princeps* (= *Sphaeropteris horrida*), and *C. quindiuensis*.

### Cyathea brunnescens (Barrington) R. C. Moran 1991

*Trichipteris nigripes* var. *brunnescens* Barrington 1978, *Cyathea nigripes* var. *brunnescens* (Barrington) Lellinger 1978

*Cyathea* clade. The erect trunk is 1–6 m tall and 3–4 cm in diameter. Fronds are bipinnate, dissected, and 1.5–2 m long. The rachis is tan to light brown and has spines and scales; the scales are brown and vary from minute and linear to large and ovate. Sori occur between the pinnule midvein and the edge of the lamina; indusia are absent. Distribution: Chocó region on the Pacific coast of western Colombia, and northwestern Ecuador, in wet forest from sea level to 300 m, occasionally to 1000 m.

*Cyathea brunnescens* is part of a closely related group of tree ferns including *C. darienensis*, *C. nigripes* (as a variety of which it is also known), *C. schiedeana*, and *C. tortuosa*.

### Cyathea brunoniana (W. J. Hooker) C. B. Clarke & Baker 1888

*Alsophila brunoniana* W. J. Hooker 1844, *Sphaeropteris brunoniana* (W. J. Hooker) Tryon 1970

*Sphaeropteris* clade. The erect trunk is as tall as about 10 m. Fronds are bi- or tripinnate and may reach 2–3 m in length. The rachis and stipe are smooth, or finely warty and with basal scales that are pale brown or brown, thin, and have setiferous edges. Sori occur near the midveins of fertile pinnules and often fill the lower lamina; indusia are absent. Distribution: Northeastern Himalaya in India, and Bangladesh to Myanmar (Burma) and Vietnam.

The name *brunoniana* (brown), like that of *C. brownii*, commemorates Robert Brown (1773–1858).

### Cyathea buennermeijeri Alderwerelt van Rosenburgh 1922

*Alsophila buennermeijeri* (Alderwerelt van Rosenburgh) Tryon 1970

*Alsophila* clade. The erect trunk is about 5 m tall or more. Fronds are bi- or tripinnate and 2–3 m long. The stipe is dark, covered with spines at the base, and has many scattered scales that are dark and have pale fragile edges. Sori occur near the midvein of fertile pinnules and are covered by thin, fragile, cup-like indusia. Distribution: Natuna Islands, Indonesia, in open scrub at 600 m, a rare tree fern, known only from the summits of two low hills.

*Cyathea buennermeijeri* is named after H. A. B. Bünnemeier (b. 1890), collector of the type material from Mount Ranai, southwest of Sarawak.

## *Cyathea callosa* Christ 1906

*Alsophila callosa* (Christ) Tryon 1970

*Alsophila* clade. The erect trunk may be as tall as about 3 m or taller. Fronds are bi- or tripinnate and 1–2 m long. The stipe is spiny and covered with scattered scales that are dark and have pale fragile edges. Sori occur near the midvein of fertile pinnules and are covered by thin, pale indusia. Distribution: Luzon in the Philippines, in midmontane forest.

*Cyathea callosa* is similar to *C. spinulosa* but has fewer spines, shorter than those of *C. spinulosa*.

## *Cyathea camerooniana* W. J. Hooker 1865

*Alsophila camerooniana* (W. J. Hooker) Tryon 1970

*Alsophila* clade. The erect trunk is 2–3 m tall. Fronds are pinnate and 2–3 m long. The rachis is variable, dark to pale, with some hairs on the underside. The stipe is dark and has scales (or small warts where scales fall) throughout; the scales are glossy brown and have a thin dull edge. Sori occur at the forks of veins and are covered by thin, cup- to saucer-like indusia. Distribution: Sierra Leone, Cameroon, northern Angola, and one variety (*ugandensis*) in western Uganda, in mountain forest at 900–1200 m.

*Cyathea camerooniana* is a variable tree fern with several varieties based on minor frond and indusial differences: *camerooniana*, *aethiopica* (Welwitsch ex W. J. Hooker) Holttum, *congi* (Christ) Holttum, *currorii* Holttum, *occidentalis* Holttum, *ugandensis* Holttum, and *zenkeri* (Diels) Benl.

## *Cyathea capensis* (Linnaeus fil.) J. E. Smith 1793

*Polypodium capense* Linnaeus fil. 1781, *Alsophila capensis*
   (Linnaeus fil.) J. Smith 1842

PLATE 30

*Alsophila* clade. The erect trunk may be as tall as about 4.5 m and about 15 cm in diameter. Fronds are pinnate and may reach 2–3 m in length. The lowest pinnae may be separated from the others along the rachis and form a clump about the crown of the plant. The rachis is smooth to slightly warty and has scales that may be tan to brown or dark brown. Sori occur in two rows, one along each side of the pinnule midvein; indusia are scale-like. Distribution: *Cyathea capensis* is divided into two subspecies: Subspecies *capensis* is in the Old World Tropics, in South Africa from the Western Cape province to KwaZulu-Natal and Mpumalanga, and Swaziland, also occurring in Zimbabwe, Mozambique, Malawi, and Tanzania, in shaded moist forest along rivers and beside waterfalls at 360–1820 m. Subspecies *polypodi-*

*oides* (Swartz) Conant is in the New World Tropics, in southeastern Brazil in montane forest at 900–200 m.

*Cyathea capensis* is the only member of the Cyatheaceae reported from both the Old and New Worlds. Carl Linnaeus (the younger) originally described the species (as a *Polypodium*) in 1781, 2 years before his death. The specific name derives from the origin of his specimen, which was collected from the Cape of Good Hope, South Africa.

### *Cyathea capitata* Copeland 1917

*Sphaeropteris capitata* (Copeland) Tryon 1970

PLATE 31

*Sphaeropteris* clade. The erect trunk is 1–3 m tall. Fronds number about 12 to a crown, are pinnate, and 1–2 m long. The stipe is dark, smooth, and has basal, light brown scales. Sori occur in one or two rows on either side of the midvein of the fertile pinnules and are covered with thin, translucent indusia. Distribution: Kinabalu on Borneo, in wet ground and in forest at 1400–2100 m.

### *Cyathea caracasana* (Klotzsch) Domin 1929

*Alsophila caracasana* Klotzsch 1844, *Cyathea meridensis* Karsten 1869, *C. ocanensis* Baker 1891, *C. chimborazensis* (W. J. Hooker) Hieronymus 1906, *C. membranulosa* Christ 1907, *C. parvifolia* Sodiro 1908, *C. maxonii* Maxon 1909, *C. producta* Maxon 1922, *C. mexicana* var. *boliviensis* Rosenstock 1928, *C. sherringii* (Jenman) Domin 1929

*Cyathea* clade. The erect trunk is 2–6 m tall, occasionally as tall as 8 m, 6–15 cm in diameter, and covered at the apex by brown to dark brown scales. Fronds are bipinnate and may reach 2.5–3.5 m in length. Petioles are yellowish brown to brown and have small raised dots and brown to dark brown scales. The rachis is straw-colored and lacks hairs or scales. Sori occur on each side of the pinnule midvein and are covered with globose indusia. Distribution: Cuba, Jamaica, and Hispaniola; Costa Rica; Venezuela, Colombia, Ecuador, Peru, and Bolivia, the name *caracasana* referring to Caracas, Venezuela. Plants are found in tropical submontane and montane rain forest, in forest understory, and in openings at 1000–2800 m.

*Cyathea caracasana* is a highly complex, variable, small tree fern with a thin trunk, related to *C. dissoluta*. Several varietal names are in use, including *caracasana*, *boliviensis* (Rosenstock) Tryon, *chimborazensis* (W. J. Hooker) Tryon, *maxonii* (L. M. Underwood) Tryon, and *meridensis* (Karsten) Tryon.

### *Cyathea carrii* Holttum 1962

*Sphaeropteris carrii* (Holttum) Tryon 1970

*Sphaeropteris* clade. The erect trunk is as tall as 4–6 m. Fronds are tripinnate and may reach 1–3 m in length. The stipe is dark and smooth or densely covered with small scales and a few large scales near the base; the scales are small and dull or large, dark, and setiferous. Sori occur in groups of as many as six on each fertile pinnule and are covered with scales, giving the appearance of indusia. Distribution: Eastern New Guinea in forest at about 1500 m.

*Cyathea carrii* is named after the collector, Carr, who obtained the type material from forest at Boridi in Papua New Guinea.

### *Cyathea catillifera* Holttum 1962

*Alsophila catillifera* (Holttum) Tryon 1970

*Alsophila* clade. The erect trunk is as tall as about 1 m, 10 cm in diameter, and often branches at the base. Fronds number about six to a crown, are bi- or tripinnate, and 1–2 m long. Stipes are persistent with bases retained on the trunk; they are pale on the upper surface to dark at the base, and spiny, warty, and with scattered basal scales that are glossy dark brown and have a paler margin. Fronds may bear a pair of reduced pinnae toward the base. Sori occur near the midvein of fertile pinnules and are covered by thin, brown, saucer-like indusia. Distribution: Eastern New Guinea in montane scrub from at about 2800 m and higher, a rare tree fern known only from the type locality.

### *Cyathea caudata* (J. Smith ex W. J. Hooker) Copeland 1906

*Alsophila caudata* J. Smith ex W. J. Hooker 1841, *Cyathea brevipes* Copeland 1952, *C. arborescens* Copeland 1955

*Alsophila* clade. The erect trunk may be as tall as about 4 m or taller. Fronds are bi- or tripinnate and 1–2 m long. The stipe is warty and covered with scales that are narrow, dark, and glossy. Sori occur near the fertile pinnule midvein and are covered by firm brown indusia. Distribution: Luzon and Mindanao in the Philippines, in montane forest.

*Cyathea caudata* is very similar to the smaller *C. edanoi* and *C. heterochlamydea*. The relationship between these species requires investigation.

### *Cyathea celebica* Blume 1828

*Sphaeropteris celebica* (Blume) Tryon 1970, *Cyathea quadripinnatifida* Copeland 1942

*Sphaeropteris* clade. The erect massive trunk may be as tall as about 6 m, about 30 cm in diameter, and covered with fawn scales and persistent stipe bases. Fronds are tripinnate, occasionally tetrapinnate (particularly where fertile), and may reach 4–5 m or more in length, including the long stipe; they form a crown that is dark green above and light to whitish green below. The rachis is black-purple, with sharp spines and scattered scales, especially toward the base; the scales are straw-colored to light brown and may be fringed. The stipe is as long as 1 m, dark, and may have red-brown or purple spines. Sori occur near the midvein of fertile pinnules and are protected by cup-shaped indusia. Distribution: Northeastern Queensland, Australia, and Sulawesi (Celebes) and New Guinea, in tropical rain forest in open sites, forest margins, and near streams, from near sea level to about 1800 m, in open habitat at high elevations.

*Cyathea celebica* is a rare tree fern named after the island of Celebes (Sulawesi) in Indonesia. This species grows slowly, is frost hardy to about –5°C (23°F), and is easily cultivated in rich humus.

### *Cyathea chinensis* Copeland 1909

*Alsophila costularis* Baker 1906, *Cyathea yunnanensis* Domin 1930

*Alsophila* clade. The erect trunk is 1–2 m tall. Fronds are bipinnate and 1–2 m long. The stipe is long and warty or has short spines toward the base and scattered scales that are glossy dark brown and have fragile edges. Sori occur near the midvein of fertile pinnules and are covered with thin indusia. Distribution: Yunnan, China; Nepal to Sikkim, India; and Myanmar (Burma), Laos, and Vietnam. Plants are found in forest and montane forest at 900–1800 m.

### *Cyathea christii* Copeland 1906

*Alsophila hermannii* Tryon 1970

*Alsophila* clade. The erect trunk is about 5 m tall or more. Fronds are bi- or tripinnate and 2–3 m long. The stipe has some warts and scales; the scales are brown and narrow. Sori occur near the midvein of fertile pinnules and are covered by thin, fragile indusia. Distribution: Mindanao in the Philippines, in forest at 900–1800 m.

*Cyathea christii* is named after Swiss pteridologist Konrad Hermann Heinrich Christ (1833–1933).

### *Cyathea cicatricosa* Holttum 1964

*Alsophila cicatricosa* (Holttum) Tryon 1970

*Cyathea* clade. The erect trunk may be as tall as about 2 m and about 3 cm in diameter; it is usually free of old stipes but bears scars. Fronds are bipinnate and may reach 2 m in length. The rachis is brown and has basal scales, and the stipe is usually swollen toward its base; the scales may be brown. Sori occur in rows along each side of the pinnule midvein and may be covered by very reduced indusia. Distribution: New Caledonia in humid montane and submontane forest to 1200 m.

*Cyathea cicatricosa* is a rare, small tree fern, which for a long time was only known from the type locality on Mount Ignambi. It may form part of a group of western Pacific species apparently related to *C. decurrens*. Members of this group have variously been attributed to *Alsophila* or *Cyathea*. Molecular evidence suggests a relationship with the latter genus, as treated here, though the relationship is by no means clear.

## *Cyathea cincinnata* Brause 1920

*Alsophila cincinnata* (Brause) Tryon 1970

*Alsophila* clade. The erect trunk is short. Fronds are bi- or tripinnate and 1–1.5 m long. The stipe bears many scales that are glossy brown and have a black central band and dull edges. Sori are round, occur near the fertile pinnule midvein, and have firm, brown, cup-like indusia. Distribution: Eastern New Guinea at 1300 m or higher, known only from a few collections from the Sepik region.

## *Cyathea cinerea* Copeland in Elmer 1913

*Alsophila cinerea* (Copeland) Tryon 1970

*Alsophila* clade. The erect trunk may be as tall as about 5 m and 12 cm in diameter. Fronds are bi- or tripinnate and 1–2 m long. The stipe bears long spines and scattered scales; the scales are either narrow and pale or wide and brown. Sori occur near the midvein of fertile pinnules and are covered by brown indusia. Distribution: Mindanao in the Philippines, in forest at about 1000 m.

## *Cyathea coactilis* Holttum 1962

*Alsophila coactilis* (Holttum) Tryon 1970

*Alsophila* clade. The erect trunk is 2–3 m tall. Fronds are bi- or tripinnate, 1–2 m long, and occur in two whorls of about ten fronds each. The rachis is covered on the underside with small pale scales, and the stipe is covered with pale scales with dark, narrow, fragile edges. Sori are round, occur near the fertile pinnule midvein, and are covered by thin, cup-like indusia. Distribution: Eastern New Guinea in alpine shrubland at about 3000 m, a rare fern known only from the southern highlands of Papua New Guinea.

## *Cyathea colensoi* (J. D. Hooker) Domin 1929
*Alsophila colensoi* J. D. Hooker 1854
CREEPING TREE FERN
PLATES 32, 33

*Alsophila* clade. The trunk is usually prostrate but occasionally erect and as tall as about 1 m. Fronds are tripinnate and may reach about 1.5 m or more in length. The rachis and stipe are slender, pale brown, and have brown scales. Sori occur in two rows, one along each side of the fertile pinnule midvein; indusia are absent. Distribution: New Zealand, from the southern part of the North Island south to Stewart Island, in montane forest in damp areas, particularly near the tree line.

The name *colensoi* commemorates William Colenso (1811–1899), a missionary and well-traveled New Zealand botanist. Plants of *Cyathea colensoi* form a thicket with no sign of a trunk. This tree fern requires rich humus, a plentiful supply of moisture, and good shade. It is primarily a submontane to montane fern and although uncommon in cultivation, it could do well in cooler regions.

## *Cyathea conformis* (Tryon) Stolze 1974
*Hemitelia conformis* Tryon 1960

*Cyathea* clade. The apical pinnules and pinnae are conform (hence the name *conformis*—that is, they have the same shape, which is unusual) and articulated. Distribution: Panama and Colombia.

*Cyathea conformis* is a little-known tree fern, apparently a member of a group centered on *C. petiolata*. It is not to be confused with *C.* ×*confirmis*, which is an apparent hybrid between *C. hotteana* and *C. woodwardioides*.

## *Cyathea conjugata* (Spruce ex W. J. Hooker) Domin 1929
*Trichipteris conjugata* (Spruce ex W. J. Hooker) Tryon 1970

*Cyathea* clade. Distribution: Bolivia and Colombia, in damp forest at 650–2800 m. It forms part of the *C. armata* complex of related tree ferns.

## *Cyathea contaminans* (Wallich ex W. J. Hooker) Copeland 1909
*Alsophila contaminans* Wallich ex W. J. Hooker 1844, *Chnoophora glauca* Blume 1828, *Sphaeropteris glauca* (Blume) Tryon 1970
PLATE 34

*Sphaeropteris* clade. The erect trunk is 15–20 m tall, occasionally taller; its base is usually thickened by a root mass. Fronds are bi- or tripinnate and may reach 3–4 m or more in length. Old fronds are discarded and may leave stipe-base scars on the upper regions of trunks. The rachis is pale, spiny, and scaly, particularly when young. The stipe is glaucous, purplish toward the base, spiny, and has basal scales that are pale brown or brown, and thin. Sori occur in rows close to the pinnule midvein and lack indusia. Distribution: Throughout the Malay Peninsula and Borneo, where it is one of the most widespread species of tree ferns, also common from Java to New Guinea, in open places in forests near streams at 200–1600 m.

The common *Cyathea contaminans* is a large tree fern, allied to several species of which *C. angiensis* is probably the closest relative if it is not part of the *C. contaminans* complex itself. *Cyathea contaminans* is also allied to *C. lepifera* and *C. verrucosa*. Varietal names have been applied to populations, but the differences may be related to ecological variation. Very old plants may develop curious multibranched crowns. If the genus *Sphaeropteris* is recognized, Carl Blume's specific name *glauca* takes precedence.

## *Cyathea cooperi* (W. J. Hooker ex F. von Mueller) Domin 1929

*Alsophila cooperi* W. J. Hooker ex F. von Mueller 1866, *Sphaeropteris cooperi* (W. J. Hooker ex F. von Mueller) Tryon 1970

**SCALY TREE FERN**

**PLATES 35–37**

*Sphaeropteris* clade. The erect trunk is 10–12 m tall and about 15 cm in diameter; it is often covered in oval scars left by fallen fronds. Stipe bases do not usually persist, except in fast-growing plants. Fronds are bi- or tripinnate and may reach 4–6 m in length. The rachis and stipe are greenish to dark brown-black and may have regular wart-like protrusions. Rachis and stipe scales are either dark red or brown with a spiny margin or large and papery-white with smaller red marginal spines. Sori occur singly or in rows of as many as ten; indusia are absent. Distribution: Northeastern Queensland to New South Wales and naturalized in Western Australia, in tropical and subtropical rain forest to montane forest in open sites, near streams, and in mountain gullies from sea level to 1400 m or higher.

*Cyathea cooperi* is a medium to large, fast-growing tree fern, named after Daniel Cooper (1817–1842), curator of the Botanical Society of London in the 19th century. It is very common in cultivation, and even cultivars are available: 'Brentwood' (Plate 36) and 'Robusta' are most frequently planted in the United States. It is recognized as a weed species in many of the tropical to warm temperate regions of the world where it has been introduced. Plants do best in rich, well-drained humus and will tolerate frost though the fronds may be damaged. Once established, this fern is also tolerant of dry spells.

## Cyathea corallifera Sodiro 1883

*Cyathea aspidioides* Sodiro 1883

Cyathea clade. The erect, slender trunk is as tall as 5 m. Fronds may be as long as 5 m. Distribution: Ecuador in montane forest at 1400–2000 m.

*Cyathea corallifera* is similar to *C. divergens* and is part of a group of related species centered on *C. straminea*.

## Cyathea corcovadensis (Raddi) Domin 1929

*Polypodium corcovadense* Raddi 1819, *P. taenitis* Roth 1821,
  *Alsophila elegans* Martius 1834, not *Cyathea elegans* Heward 1838
  (see *C. grevilleana*); *C. feeana* (C. Christensen) Domin 1929,
  *C. sternbergii* Domin 1929, not *C. sternbergii* Pohl 1820 (see *C. arborea*)

Alsophila clade. The erect trunk is 30–60 cm tall. Fronds are bipinnate and may reach 2.5 m or more in length. The rachis is brown to purplish and has warts and scattered brown scales. Sori occur between the fertile pinnule midvein and the edge of the lamina, or just beside the midvein; indusia are absent. Distribution: Serra do Mar in southern Brazil, and Paraguay, in primary and secondary forest, and scrub, at 250–2100 m, the name *corcovadensis* referring to Corcovado (704 m), the peak on the southern side of the city of Rio de Janeiro.

*Cyathea corcovadensis* is a variable species, particularly with regard to pinnule shape and degree of dissection.

## Cyathea costalisora Copeland 1942

*Alsophila costalisora* (Copeland) Tryon 1970

Alsophila clade. The erect trunk is as tall as 4 m, sometimes branching near the base. Fronds are bi- or tripinnate and 1–1.5 m long. The stipe is warty, especially where scales have fallen; the scales are pale and have a dark glossy central region and a paler dull margin. Sori are round, occur near the fertile pinnule midvein, and are covered by firm, dark, cup-like indusia. Distribution: Western New Guinea on the edges of forest and in moist hollows at 1900–3225 m.

## Cyathea costaricensis (Mettenius ex Kuhn) Domin 1930

*Hemitelia costaricensis* Mettenius ex Kuhn 1869

PLATE 38

Cyathea clade. The erect trunk is 1–5 m tall and 6–10 cm in diameter. Fronds are bipinnate and may reach 2–2.5 m in length. Petioles are straw-colored and lack spines, as does the rachis. Stipe scales are white or have a thin brown central stripe. Sori occur on each side of the pinnule midvein and are covered with scale-like indusia. Distribution: Mexico to Costa Rica and Panama, in tropical rain forest and submontane forest, on grassy slopes, river canyons, and stream banks at 100–1500 m.

*Cyathea costaricensis* is a medium-sized tree fern with a large crown and arching fronds, named from the type locality, Costa Rica.

## *Cyathea costulisora* Domin 1930

*Alsophila montana* (Alderwerelt van Rosenburgh) Tryon 1970

*Alsophila* clade. The erect trunk is 1–4 m tall. Fronds are bi- or tripinnate and 1–2 m long. The stipe is covered by warts and scales; the scales are either pale and glossy or dark and flat. Sori occur near the midvein of fertile pinnules and are covered by large, firm, brown indusia. Distribution: Sumatra.

## *Cyathea crassa* Maxon 1909

not *Alsophila crassa* Karsten 1869 (named from material collected from wet, cold, montane forest at Mérida by Franz Engel in 1859—unfortunately, there are no modern collections that match this Engel material and the identity of this species remains unclear; see Barrington 1978); *A. jimeneziana* Conant 1983

*Alsophila* clade. Distribution: Hispaniola. *Cyathea crassa* is from in the Caribbean. If the genus *Alsophila* is recognized, the species name *crassa* is unavailable for this tree fern, having been used by Gustav Karsten. Recognizing this confusion, David Conant (1983) renamed it *A. jimeneziana*. *Cyathea crassa* is part of the *C. woodwardioides* complex of some six similar species from the Greater Antilles, which also includes *C. fulgens, C. grevilleana, C. portoricensis,* and *C. tussacii*.

## *Cyathea crinita* (W. J. Hooker) Copeland 1909

*Alsophila crinita* W. J. Hooker 1844, *Sphaeropteris crinita* (W. J. Hooker) Tryon 1970

*Sphaeropteris* clade. The erect trunk may be as tall as about 15 m, with numerous stipe-base scars. Fronds are bi- or tripinnate and 2–3 m long. The stipe is flushed with purple and is warty and densely scaly; the scales are long, acuminate, thin, and pale, with dark marginal setae. Sori occur near the midvein of the fertile pinnules and lack indusia. Distribution: Southern India and Sri Lanka, in forest at 1500–2100 m.

*Cyathea crinita* is similar to *C. tomentosa* of Java and *C. magna* of New Guinea; the relationship between the two species requires further study.

### *Cyathea croftii* Holttum 1981

*Alsophila* clade. The erect trunk is as tall as 3 m and usually 6 cm in diameter. Fronds are bi- or tripinnate and may reach 2–3 m in length. The rachis and stipe are slender, often light green, especially when young, and have glossy brown scales toward the base. Sori are small and occur in rows, one along each side of the pinnule midvein, and are covered with thin indusia. Distribution: Manus Island in the Admiralty Islands, in damp forest on steep slopes at about 500 m.

*Cyathea croftii* is named after pteridologist James R. Croft (b. 1951). It is an uncommon, small tree fern with a slender trunk.

### *Cyathea cucullifera* Holttum 1962

*Alsophila cucullifera* (Holttum) Tryon 1970

*Alsophila* clade. The erect trunk is 2–3 m tall. Fronds are bi- or tripinnate, may reach 2–3 m in length, and occur in two whorls of four to six fronds each. The stipe is warty and covered in scales that are large toward the base; the scales are dark, glossy, and have a narrow paler margin. Sori occur near the midvein of fertile pinnules and are covered by thin, pale brown, scale-like indusia. Distribution: Eastern New Guinea in montane forest at about 2400 m.

### *Cyathea cunninghamii* J. D. Hooker 1854

*Alsophila cunninghamii* (J. D. Hooker) Tryon 1970, ?*Cyathea stelligera* Holttum 1964

GULLY TREE FERN, SLENDER TREE FERN

FIGURE 4; PLATES 39, 40

*Alsophila* clade. The erect trunk is as tall as 20 m and usually 6–15 cm in diameter, occasionally as much as 20 cm. Fronds are tri- or tetrapinnate and may reach about 3 m or more in length. The rachis and stipe are slender, warty, black brown, and have brown scales. Sori occur along each side of the pinnule midvein; hood-like indusia are present. Distribution: Southeastern Queensland, Victoria, Tasmania, and New South Wales, Australia, and North Island, South Island, and Chatham Islands, New Zealand, in damp forest, emerging from stream gullies and riverbanks.

*Cyathea cunninghamii* is an uncommon and very tall, slow-growing tree fern with a slender trunk. It is named after Alan Cunningham (1791–1839), a botanist who traveled widely in New Zealand and Australia. New Caledonian plants known as *C. stelligera* are possibly the same species. *Cyathea cunninghamii* is known to hybridize with *C. australis* to form *C.* ×*marcescens*. In cultivation, *C. cunninghamii* requires rich humus, a plentiful supply of moisture, and importantly, protection from wind.

### *Cyathea curranii* Copeland 1909

*Sphaeropteris curranii* (Copeland) Tryon 1970

*Sphaeropteris* clade. The erect trunk may be as tall as about 3 m and about 20 cm in diameter; it is often covered in scars left by fallen fronds. Fronds are bi- or tripinnate and may reach 1–2 m in length. The stipe is pale and has warts and scales; the scales are light brown and glossy. Sori occur near the midvein of the fertile pinnules and lack indusia. Distribution: Philippines in forest edge at about 2000 m.

*Cyathea curranii* is named after botanist Hugh McCullum Curran (1875–1960), who collected in the Philippines as well as other areas. It is possibly related to *C. aeneifolia* and *C. pilulifera* of New Guinea.

### *Cyathea cuspidata* Kunze 1834

*Alsophila cuspidata* (Kunze) Conant 1983

*Alsophila* clade. The erect trunk (or multiple trunks) may be as tall as 15 m and about 10 cm in diameter, and has black spines. Fronds are bipinnate and as long as 2–3 m. The rachis and stipe are brown to dark brown and have scales that are bicolored, with a dark brown to blackish center and a pale whitish margin. Pinnule veins may have small, brown, star-shaped scales. Sori are round, with globose indusia, and form on either side of the pinnule midvein. Distribution: Mexico to Nicaragua, Costa Rica, and Panama; Colombia, Ecuador, Peru, Bolivia, Paraguay, the Amazon Basin, Brazil, and French Guiana. Plants are found in tropical rain forest up to the montane zone, in open sites, on riverbanks, and cleared pastureland from sea level to about 800 m.

*Cyathea cuspidata* is a handsome tree fern, often with multiple trunks that together form a medium-sized, feathery clump. It does best in humid warmer regions and is frost tender.

### *Cyathea cyatheoides* (Desvaux) K. U. Kramer 1978

*Hemitelia cyatheoides* Desvaux 1827, *H. multiflora* var. *sprucei* Baker 1870, *Cyathea bakeriana* Domin 1930, *C. guianensis* (Regel) Domin 1930.

*Cyathea* clade. The erect trunk is as tall as 5 m. Fronds are bipinnate and 1–2 m long. The stipe is scaly toward the base; the scales are dark, glossy, and have toothed edges. Sori occur near the midvein of fertile pinnules and are covered by thin, translucent, two-lobed, scale-like indusia. Distribution: Venezuela, Guyana, French Guiana, Suriname, and Brazil, in forest at 100–1000 m.

*Cyathea cyatheoides* is very similar to *C. hirsuta* and, to a lesser extent, *C. bradei* and *C. surinamensis*.

### *Cyathea cyclodium* (Tryon) Lellinger 1987

*Trichipteris cyclodium* Tryon 1972

*Cyathea* clade. The barely erect trunk is 5–15 cm tall. Fronds are pinnate and usually less than about 1 m long. The rachis is brown to purplish and has a few warts and scattered scales; the scales are brown with a slightly lighter margin. Sori occur in three or four rows between the fertile pinnule midvein and the edge of the lamina; indusia are absent. Distribution: Known only from the type collection from Cerro Sipapo in the Guiana Highlands of eastern Venezuela.

*Cyathea cyclodium* is apparently related to *C. demissa*.

### *Cyathea cystolepis* Sodiro 1883

*Cyathea* clade. The erect, slender trunk is as tall as about 3 m. Fronds are bipinnate and dissected, and may reach 2 m in length. The rachis and stipe are brown and have scales and basal spines; the scales are either linear and whitish or bullate and golden brown. Sori have indusia. Distribution: Ecuador in mature cloud forest at about 1550 m.

*Cyathea cystolepis* resembles *C. halonata,* differing in the presence of indusia and the absence of a halo of pinnae.

### *Cyathea darienensis* R. C. Moran 1991

*Cyathea* clade. The erect trunk is 2–3 m tall and 2–3 cm in diameter. Fronds are bipinnate and dissected and may reach 1.5 m in length. Petioles are dark brown and have short spines. The rachis and stipe are brown to purple brown and have scales and hairs. Petiole scales are brown to yellow brown and either entire or with toothed edges; elsewhere, scales are golden brown and lanceolate to ovate to bullate. Sori are borne on vein forks and occur halfway between fertile pinnule midveins and the edges of the lamina or just beneath the midvein; indusia are absent. Distribution: Panama in rain forest and cloud forest at 800–1500 m, the name *darienensis* referring to the type locality, Darién.

*Cyathea darienensis* shows some similarity to *C. brunnescens, C. nigripes, C. schiedeana,* and possibly *C. tortuosa*.

### *Cyathea dealbata* (G. Forster) Swartz 1801

*Polypodium dealbatum* G. Forster 1786, *Cyathea tricolor* Colenso 1883, *Alsophila tricolor* (Colenso) Tryon 1970

SILVER FERN, PONGA

PLATES 41–44

*Alsophila* clade. The erect trunk may be as tall as 10 m or more; a rare creeping form also occurs. Fronds are tripinnate, about 4 m long, and white-silver on the underside. The rachis and stipe are pale brown with a silver blush and have scattered scales, particularly toward the base; the scales are dark brown, often glossy and twisted. Stipe bases persist and may be seen protruding from the trunk. Sori occur on either side of the pinnule midvein; indusia are cup-like. Distribution: New Zealand, on the main islands and extending east to the Chatham Islands, in the subcanopy of drier forest, and open scrub.

*Cyathea dealbata* is a medium-sized tree fern that retains stipe bases on the trunk. The crown is dense, with an obvious silvery underside on the fronds, leading to the common name of silver fern. The species has been adopted as one of New Zealand's national emblems and is prominently used by the national sports teams. *Cyathea dealbata* resembles *C. milnei*, which differs in lacking the silvery color on the underside of the fronds. *Cyathea dealbata* does well in good, well-drained humus. Once established, it will tolerate dry conditions, provided the base of the trunk has a good layer of mulch. It will resist some frost but does best when sheltered from winds.

## *Cyathea deckenii* Kuhn 1879

*Alsophila deckenii* (Kuhn) Tryon 1970

*Alsophila* clade. The erect trunk may be as tall as 10 m. Fronds are bipinnate and as long as 2–3 m; the most basal one or two pairs of pinnae are reduced. The rachis and stipe are brown to dark brown or black-brown and have a few scales that are narrow and dark with a fragile margin of variable width. The stipe bears conical warts near the base. Sori are round, with large thin indusia. Distribution: Democratic Republic of Congo (Zaire), Tanzania, and Mozambique, in wet forest at 1350–2300 m.

*Cyathea deckenii* is named after botanist Carl (or Karl) Claus von der Decken (1833–1865).

## *Cyathea decomposita* (Karsten) Domin 1929

*Alsophila decomposita* Karsten 1869

*Cyathea* clade. The erect trunk is 1–3 m tall. Fronds are tripinnate and may reach a length of 3 m or more. The rachis is glabrous but has a few scales toward the base. The stipe is slightly warty and may be covered with a thin covering of scales. Scales are either large and glossy brown or small, pale, and fringed. Sori occur halfway between the fertile pinnule midvein and the edge of the lamina; indusia are absent. Distribution: Lake Maracaibo area of Venezuela, in wet forest and cloud forest at 1300–2800 m.

### *Cyathea decorata* (Maxon) Tryon 1976

*Hemitelia decorata* Maxon 1946

*Cyathea* clade. The erect, narrow to slender trunk may be as tall as 1 m. Fronds are bipinnate, dissected, and about 1.5 m long. Distribution: Colombia in rain forest as an understory plant, from sea level to 300 m.

*Cyathea decorata* is part of a group of species centered on *C. speciosa*.

### *Cyathea decrescens* Mettenius in Kuhn 1868

*Alsophila decrescens* (Mettenius) Tryon 1970

*Alsophila* clade. The erect trunk is 2–3 m tall, 10–12 cm in diameter, and usually has elliptical scars caused by fallen stipe bases. Fronds are bipinnate, 1–1.5 m long, and may be densely pubescent; the lower pinnules may be separated from the others and reduced. The rachis and stipe are brown and have scales that are narrow and dark brown. Sori are large and round, with fragile brown indusia. Distribution: Madagascar.

### *Cyathea decurrens* (W. J. Hooker) Copeland 1929

*Alsophila decurrens* W. J. Hooker 1844

FIGURE 4; PLATE 45

*Cyathea* clade. The erect trunk may be as tall as 5 m or more. Fronds are bi- or tripinnate and may reach 2–3 m in length. The rachis and stipe are slender and light-colored. The stipe is slightly warty and may be covered with a thin covering of scales that are either large and glossy brown or small, pale, and fringed. Sori occur in two rows, one along each side of the pinnule midvein, and are covered by small, thin indusia. Distribution: Southern New Ireland in the Bismarck Archipelago, Guadalcanal and Kolombangara in the Solomon Islands, Aneityum and Tanna in Vanuatu, Ovalau and Viti Levu in Fiji, Samoa; Rarotonga in the Cook Islands, and possibly in Australia, in damp forest at 500–2300 m.

*Cyathea decurrens* is a variable species with a very wide distribution. The various morphological forms have been given varietal or subspecific status, including variety *vaupelii* (Brause) Domin and subspecies *epaleata* Holttum. *Cyathea decurrens* is one of a group of allied western Pacific species that includes *C. alata*, *C. howeana*, and *C. robertsiana*. *Cyathea stokesii* and the lesser-known *C. cicatricosa* may also be related. Members of this group have variously been attributed to *Alsophila* or *Cyathea*. Molecular evidence suggests some relationship with the latter genus, as treated here, though the relationship is by no means clear.

### *Cyathea delgadii* Sternberg 1820

*Cyathea vestita* Martius 1822, *C. oligocarpa* Kunze 1834,
 *C. pilosa* Baker 1874, *C. trinidadensis* Brade 1936

*Cyathea* clade. The erect trunk may be as tall as 10 m and 5–15 cm in diameter. Fronds are bipinnate and may reach 3 m in length. Petioles are yellow-brown to dark brown and have spines. The rachis is also brown and has small brown scales. Sori occur on each side of the pinnule midvein and are covered with globose indusia. Distribution: Costa Rica and Panama; Venezuela, Colombia, Ecuador, Peru, Bolivia, Argentina, Paraguay, and Brazil. Plants may be found in tropical and submontane rain forest, forest understory, in open locations, and along paths, at 100 m and higher (as high as 2700 m in Peru). The name *delgadii* signifies Gancho do Generale Delgado, along the road to Caldas Novas, Brazil, where the type material was collected.

*Cyathea delgadii* is a medium-sized tree fern with a large, delicately arching crown and very slender trunk. It is part of a large group of ferns centered on *C. fulva*. In cultivation, *C. delgadii* does best in warmer areas. Plants require shelter from wind and grow best in well-drained humus with consistent moisture.

### *Cyathea deminuens* Holttum 1963

*Alsophila parvifolia* Holttum 1928, *Sphaeropteris parvifolia* (Holttum)
 Tryon 1970

*Sphaeropteris* clade. The erect trunk is less than 1 m tall. Fronds are pinnate to almost bipinnate and usually less than 1 m long. The stipe has basal scales that are pale brown and firm. Sori occur about one-third of the distance between the midvein of the fertile pinnule and the edge of the lamina; indusia are absent. Distribution: Sumatra in lowland forest.

If the genus *Sphaeropteris* is recognized, Richard Eric Holttum's specific name *parvifolia* takes precedence.

### *Cyathea demissa* (Morton) A. R. Smith ex Lellinger 1987

*Alsophila demissa* Morton 1955

*Cyathea* clade. The barely erect stem is about 30 cm tall. Fronds are bipinnate and usually less than about 1 m long. The rachis is brown to purplish and has warts and scattered scales; the scales are brown and have a slightly lighter margin. Sori occur between the fertile pinnule midvein and the edge of the lamina; indusia are absent. Distribution: Guiana Highlands of Venezuela on open, rocky slopes and in scrub forest at 1500–2100 m.

*Cyathea demissa*, with two varieties, *demissa* and *thysanolepis* (Barrington) A. R. Smith, is related to *C. cyclodium* and possibly to *C. nanna*.

## *Cyathea dichromatolepis* (Fée) Domin 1929

*Alsophila dichromatolepis* Fée 1869, *Cyathea arbuscula* (Baker) Domin 1929,
   *C. guimariensis* (Fée) Domin 1929, *C. mesocarpa* Domin 1929,
   *C. pallida* (Rosenstock) Domin 1929

*Cyathea* clade. The erect trunk is 1–4 m tall. Fronds are bipinnate and may reach 1.5 m in length. The rachis is brown and has scattered scales that are brown and have a broad, usually darker margin. Sori occur between the fertile pinnule midvein and the edge of the lamina or just beneath the midvein; indusia are absent. Distribution: Southern Brazil in wet secondary forest and coastal ranges at 800–2000 m.

The name *dichromatolepis* refers to the broad border present on the scales. *Cyathea dichromatolepis* is part of the *C. phalerata* complex of ferns.

## *Cyathea dicksonioides* Holttum 1962

*Alsophila dicksonioides* (Holttum) Tryon 1970

*Alsophila* clade. The erect trunk may be as tall as about 3 m or more and 20 cm in diameter. Fronds are bi- or tripinnate, about 1 m long, and occur in two whorls of 10–12 fronds each. The stipe is covered in scales that are glossy and have narrow, pale, fragile edges. Sori occur two to four per fertile pinnule and are covered by firm, pale, hood-like indusia. Distribution: Northeastern New Guinea, infrequent in grassland at 2600–2900 m.

*Cyathea dicksonioides* is a small tree fern with stubby trunk and irregular crown of erect bristly fronds, the inner of two whorls bending downward toward the trunk.

## *Cyathea dimorpha* (Christ) Copeland 1909

*Alsophila dimorpha* Christ 1904

*Alsophila* clade. The erect trunk is 3–4 m tall. Fronds are pinnate to bipinnate and as much as 2 m long. Fertile pinnules are reduced in size. The stipe is short and has basal scales that are narrow, glossy, dark, and have pale edges. Sori lack indusia. Distribution: Central and southeastern Sulawesi (Celebes) at 120–1700 m.

The name *dimorpha* refers to the strong difference in shape between the fertile and sterile pinnules. Sterile pinnules are larger, and the fertile narrow, reduced, and lobed.

### *Cyathea discophora* Holttum 1962

*Sphaeropteris discophora* (Holttum) Tryon 1970

*Sphaeropteris* clade. The erect trunk is medium-sized. Fronds are pinnate or bipinnate and 1–2 m long. The stipe is warty and has basal scales that are pale and have setiferous edges. Sori occur near the midvein of the fertile pinnules and are covered by brown, saucer-like indusia. Distribution: Kinabalu on Borneo, in open places in forest at about 2400 m.

### *Cyathea dissimilis* (Morton) Stolze 1974

*Hemitelia dissimilis* Morton 1951

*Cyathea* clade. The erect trunk is 0.5–3 m tall and 3–5 cm in diameter. Fronds are bipinnate and 1–2 m long. The stipe is scaly toward the base; the scales are glossy brown and have entire or, occasionally, toothed edges. Sori occur near the midvein of fertile pinnules and are covered by thin, translucent, scale-like indusia. Distribution: Venezuela and Guyana, in humid forest at 700–1600 m.

*Cyathea dissimilis* is related to *C. intramarginalis* but differs in having articulated apical pinnae.

### *Cyathea dissoluta* Baker ex Jenman 1881

*Cyathea monstrabila* Jenman 1881

*Cyathea* clade. The trunk is prostrate or short and erect, and 2–5 cm in diameter; it may have lateral off-shoots. Fronds are bipinnate and may reach 1.8 m in length. The rachis is brown and has small scales. The stipe is medium to long, brown, and has short spines and lanceolate brown scales. Sori occur in six pairs along each side of the pinnule midvein and are covered with brown, membranous, globose indusia. Distribution: Blue Mountains of Jamaica in montane rain forest at 1000–2300 m.

*Cyathea dissoluta* is a rare, small, variable tree fern that could represent a hybrid or series of hybrids related to the *C. caracasana* complex.

### *Cyathea divergens* Kunze 1834

*Cyathea firma* Kuhn 1869, *C. sartorii* Salomon 1883, *C. tuerckheimii* Maxon

*Cyathea* clade. The erect trunk may be as tall as 10 m and 6–10 cm in diameter. Fronds are bipinnate, rarely tripinnate, and may reach 3 m in length. Petioles are straw-colored to brown and have spines. The rachis is also straw-colored to yellowish brown and either smooth or with small spines. Stipe and rachis scales are bicolored, with a brown central region and whitish margin. Sori occur in two rows along each side of the pinnule midvein and are covered with globose indusia. Distribution: Mexico, Guatemala, Costa Rica, and Panama; Colombia, Ecuador, Peru, Venezuela, Guyana, Suriname, and French Guiana. Plants are found in submontane rain forest along paths and in open locations at 1000–2700 m.

*Cyathea divergens* is a highly variable, medium-sized tree fern with a large, delicately drooping crown and slender trunk. Two varieties are recognized: *divergens*, and *tuerckheimii* (Maxon) Tryon from Mexico and Guatemala. *Cyathea divergens* is part of a group centered on *C. pallescens* and is similar to *C. corallifera*. *Cyathea holdridgeana* may be a related hybrid.

## *Cyathea doctersii* Alderwerelt van Rosenburgh 1920

*Alsophila doctersii* (Alderwerelt van Rosenburgh) Tryon 1970

*Alsophila* clade. The erect trunk is 2–3 m tall. Fronds are bi- or tripinnate and may reach 2–3 m in length. The stipe is covered in scattered scales and some hairs; the scales are brown and flat. Sori occur near the midvein of fertile pinnules and are covered by thin, brown, scale-like indusia. Distribution: Sumatra in forest at 150 m.

The little-known *Cyathea doctersii* is named after botanist Willem Marius Docters van Leeuwen (1880–1960), who collected in Asia. It is similar to *C. javanica* and possibly of hybrid origin between that species and a member of the *C. latebrosa* complex.

## *Cyathea dombeyi* (Desvaux) Lellinger 1987

*Alsophila dombeyi* Desvaux 1827, *Cyathea floribunda* (Hooker & Baker) Domin 1929

*Cyathea* clade. The trunk is prostrate or leaning to erect and 0.1–2.4 m tall. Fronds are bipinnate, dissected, and may reach 2–3 m in length. The stipe is covered in brown scales (with a few to many darkened marginal cells), especially toward the base. The position of the sori may vary from almost marginal to halfway between the fertile pinnule midvein and the lamina; indusia are absent. Distribution: Eastern Andes of Peru in dense rain forest at 650–1700 m.

The name *dombeyi* commemorates Joseph Dombey (1742–1796), French botanist who accompanied Hipólito Ruiz and José Pavón on their expedition to Chile and Peru. *Cyathea dombeyi* is an extremely variable, medium-sized tree fern, possibly part of the *C. pungens* complex.

## *Cyathea dregei* Kunze 1836

*Alsophila dregei* (Kunze) Tryon 1970, *Cyathea burkei* W. J. Hooker 1844,
   *C. angolensis* Welwitsch ex W. J. Hooker 1865
   PLATES 46–48

*Alsophila* clade. The erect, stout trunk may be as tall as 5 m. Fronds are large and arching, bi- or tripinnate, and as long as 3 m; the lowest pinnae are usually reduced, and the upper surface of the frond is glabrate whereas the lower may be tomentose. The rachis and stipe are brown and have a rough surface. Stipe scales are brown. Sori occur in as many as 12 per group per pinnule. Distribution: South Africa from the Western Cape province to KwaZulu-Natal and Mpumalanga, and Swaziland; also in Lesotho, Zimbabwe, Mozambique, and Madagascar. Plants grow on stream banks, in forest margins, and grasslands, and are most frequent at 900–1800 m.

*Cyathea dregei* is named after Johann Franz Drège (1794–1881), a German plant explorer who worked in South Africa, gathering together a collection of some 200,000 specimens, representing about 8000 species. It comprises robust and variable plants with thick trunks and dense crowns of fronds. It is widely cultivated, particularly in the Southern Hemisphere, and may resist slight frosts. *Cyathea dregei* is also known to be fire resistant but does best when sheltered and grown in rich humus with a consistent supply of moisture.

## *Cyathea* ×*dryopteroides* Maxon 1925

*Alsophila* clade. *Cyathea* ×*dryopteroides* is now known to be a hybrid between *Alsophila amintae* and *A. bryophila* (see Appendix 1 for comments on both species).

## *Cyathea dudleyi* Tryon 1976

*Cyathea* clade. The erect trunk may be as tall as 2 m. Fronds are bipinnate and as long as 1.25 m. Distribution: Peru in wet, dense cloud forest at 2600–2700 m, described from plants in the Cordillera Vilcabamba.

*Cyathea dudleyi*, named after botanist Theodore Robert ("Ted") Dudley (1936–1994), is part of a group of ferns centered on *C. lechleri*.

## *Cyathea ebenina* Karsten 1856

*Cyathea* clade. The erect, narrow trunk is as tall as 3 m. Fronds are as long as 1.5 m and may have long-stalked pinnules. Distribution: Venezuela, Colombia, and Peru, in montane forest and dense cloud forest at 2100–2500 m.

*Cyathea ebenina* is part of a group of ferns centered on *C. lechleri*.

### *Cyathea edanoi* Copeland 1931

*Alsophila edanoi* (Copeland) Tryon 1970

*Alsophila* clade. The erect trunk is 1–2 m tall. Fronds are bi- or tripinnate and about 1 m long. The stipe is covered with scales that are dark, glossy, and have narrow fragile edges. Sori occur near the fertile pinnule midvein and are covered or half-covered by large, firm, brown indusia. Distribution: Luzon in the Philippines, in montane forest at 1300 m.

*Cyathea edanoi* is named after Gregorio E. Edaño (b. 1916). It is a little-known, small tree fern similar to the equally little known *C. heterochlamydea*. The relationship between these two species and *C. caudata* certainly requires investigation.

### *Cyathea elliptica* Copeland 1917

*Sphaeropteris elliptica* (Copeland) Tryon 1970, *Cyathea holttumii* Copeland 1917, *C. subbipinnata* Copeland 1917

*Sphaeropteris* clade. The erect trunk is less than 1 m tall, usually 50 cm. Fronds are pinnate and 1–2 m long. The stipe is densely scaly; the scales are glossy and medium to light brown. Sori occur about halfway between the midvein of fertile pinnules and the edge of the lamina; indusia are absent. Distribution: Kinabalu on Borneo in forest at 900–1800 m.

It is likely that *Cyathea elliptica* is simply a variant of *C. trichophora;* further investigation into the relationship between the two tree ferns is required.

### *Cyathea elmeri* Copeland 1909

*Sphaeropteris elmeri* (Copeland) Tryon 1970, *Cyathea dimorphotricha* Copeland in Elmer 1913, *C. subcomosa* Domin 1929, *Alsophila fenicis* Posthumus 1942, not *A. fenicis* (Copeland) C. Christensen 1913 (see *C. fenicis*)

*Sphaeropteris* clade. The erect trunk is 5–10 m. Fronds are bi- or tripinnate and may reach about 2 m or more in length. The lower surface of the rachis is pale and warty. The stipe has basal warts and scales that are large, tapering, thin, and medium brown. Sori occur near the midvein of fertile pinnules and lack indusia. Distribution: Philippines, Talaud Islands, and northern Sulawesi (Celebes), in forest at 500–1400 m.

*Cyathea elmeri* is named after pteridologist Adolph Daniel Edward Elmer (1870–1942).

### *Cyathea elongata* Karsten 1869

not *Alsophila elongata* W. J. Hooker 1844 (see *Cyathea poeppigii*);
*A. engelii* Tryon 1970

*Alsophila* clade. The erect trunk may be as tall as 11 m. Fronds are pinnate and may reach 2–3 m in length. The rachis and stipe are smooth to warty, brown, and have basal tan scales. Sori occur in small groups toward the base of the pinnule midvein; indusia are cup-shaped. Distribution: Venezuela and Colombia, in montane areas at 2000–3000 m.

If the genus *Alsophila* is recognized, the name *elongata* becomes unavailable, having already been used by William J. Hooker. Recognizing this confusion, Rolla Tryon proposed the use of *engelii*, after the collector Franz Engel, who gathered the type material in Venezuela.

## *Cyathea erinacea* Karsten 1857

*Alsophila erinacea* (Karsten) Conant 1983

*Alsophila* clade. The erect trunk may be as tall as 15 m and 7–10 cm in diameter, and has black spines. Fronds are bipinnate and as long as 3.5 m. The rachis and stipe are scaly and either straw-colored or brown to dark brown; the scales are bicolored, with a dark brown to blackish center and pale whitish margin, and a terminal seta. Pinnule veins have whitish scales with star-shaped setae. Sori are round, with globose indusia, and form on either side of the pinnule midvein. Distribution: Mexico, Costa Rica, and Panama; Venezuela, Colombia, Ecuador, Peru, and Bolivia. Plants are found in tropical rain forest in the understory and on riverbanks up to the montane zone at 800–2100 m.

*Cyathea erinacea* is a slim tree fern with a sparse crown of arching fronds. Plants do best in humid conditions.

## *Cyathea eriophora* Holttum 1962

*Alsophila eriophora* (Holttum) Tryon 1970

*Alsophila* clade. The erect trunk is 2–3 m tall. Fronds are bi- or tripinnate and may reach 2–3 m in length. The stipe is dark and covered in spines and scales; the scales are either small and pale or large with a dark tip. Sori occur near the midvein of fertile pinnules; indusia are absent. Distribution: Eastern New Guinea in wet ravine forest from 1400 m to about 2000 m.

## *Cyathea estelae* (Riba) Proctor 1968

*Alsophila estelae* Riba 1967

*Cyathea* clade. The erect trunk is 3–4 m tall and 3–6 cm in diameter. Fronds are bipinnate, dissected, and may reach 1.5–2 m in length. The rachis and stipe are medium brown, glabrous, and have numerous straight spines and deciduous scales toward the base; the scales are lanceolate, whitish, and have a finely fimbriate margin. Sori are medial on veins and form a cylindrical receptacle with short sterile hairs; indusia are absent. Distribution: Jamaica, known only from St. Thomas, in montane forest on slopes at 1100–1400 m.

Cyathea estelae is closely related to C. armata and associated species.

### Cyathea everta Copeland 1942

*Alsophila everta* (Copeland) Tryon 1970

*Alsophila* clade. The erect trunk may be as tall as 5 m. Fronds are numerous in the crown, bi- or tripinnate, and 1–1.5 m long. The stipe bears many spines toward the base as well as scales that are pale or dark, glossy, and have pale fringed edges. Sori are round, occur near the fertile pinnule midvein, and covered by thin, brown, cup-like indusia. Distribution: Western New Guinea in the edges of forest or in mossy forest at 1400–2800 m.

Cyathea everta is very similar to C. rigens and the two may represent the same species, in which case the name C. rigens has priority.

### Cyathea excavata Holttum 1935

*Alsophila excavata* (Holttum) Tryon 1970

*Alsophila* clade. The erect trunk is about 2 m tall or more and forms lateral shoots. Fronds are bi- or tripinnate, about 2 m long, and may be retained as a persistent skirt about the trunk. The stipe is smooth and green, and has basal scales that are dull and thin. Sori occur near the midvein of fertile pinnules and are covered by pale, thin, saucer-like indusia. Distribution: Cameron Highlands, West Malaysia, in forest, on streamsides, in clearings, and open grassy places at about 1800 m.

### Cyathea exilis Holttum 1986

*Alsophila* clade. The erect trunk is as tall as 4 m and 4–8 cm in diameter; it produces several buds, usually one at each stipe base. Fronds are bipinnate and as long as 1 m. The rachis and stipe are brown to dark brown or black-brown and have blunt spines and scales; the scales are dull brown and have terminal setae, mostly one each. Sori are round, lack indusia, and form on either side of the pinnule midvein. Distribution: Cape York Peninsula in Queensland, Australia, in vine forest on sandstone, known from only one location.

### Cyathea fadenii Holttum 1981

*Alsophila schliebenii* Reimers 1933, not *Cyathea schliebenii* Reimers 1933

*Alsophila* clade. The erect trunk may be as tall as 4 m and 3–5 cm in diameter. Fronds are bipinnate, with the most basal pair of pinnae reduced, often to veins alone. Distribution: Uluguru Mountains, Tanzania, on exposed ridges and on the upper edge of montane forest, at 1700–2100 m.

*Cyathea fadenii* was described from material collected by Robert B. Faden (b. 1942). It appears to be synonymous with *Alsophila schliebenii*.

## *Cyathea falcata* (Kuhn) Domin 1929

*Alsophila falcata* Kuhn 1869, *Cyathea kuhnii* (Hieronymus) Domin 1929

*Cyathea* clade. The erect trunk is 1–3 m tall; plants often form single-species clumps. Fronds are pinnate, dissected, and may reach 0.5–1 m in length. The rachis is glabrous or has small scales that are flattish, brown, and have a paler margin. Sori occur between the midvein of fertile pinnules and the edge of the lamina; indusia are absent. Distribution: Pacific coast of southern Colombia and associated islands, in wet forest from sea level to 1000 m.

*Cyathea falcata* is a variable species, related to the *C. petiolata* group of tree ferns.

## *Cyathea feani* E. Brown 1931

*Sphaeropteris feani* (E. Brown) Tryon 1970

*Sphaeropteris* clade. The erect trunk is 2–10 m tall or more and usually covered in scars left by fallen fronds. Fronds are tripinnate and may reach 2–6 m in length. The petiole, rachis, and stipe are greenish to black and may have blunt, very short, rough protrusions along with plentiful scales that are pale brown and often very narrow. Sori occur in pairs of two to six near the midvein of fertile pinnules and are covered with thin indusia. Distribution: Marquesas Islands in forest up to 1000 m, the name *feani* signifying the locality, Feani, of the type material.

*Cyathea feani* is very similar to *C. medullaris*, which is also present in the Marquesas Islands. Differences are minor, and the true relationship between these two tree ferns requires further investigation.

## *Cyathea felina* (Roxburgh) Morton 1974

*Polypodium felinum* Roxburgh 1844, *Sphaeropteris concinna* (Baker) Tryon 1970, *Cyathea sangirensis* (Christ) Copeland 1909

*Sphaeropteris* clade. The erect trunk may be as tall as about 8 m or more and about 20 cm in diameter. Fronds are bi- or tripinnate and may reach about 4 m in length. The rachis and stipe are pale, warty, and have scattered pale, thin scales toward the base. Sori occur in rows close to the pinnule midvein; true indusia are absent. Distribution: Northeastern Queensland, Australia, and Malaysia, Indonesia (including the Moluccas), and New Guinea, in tropical rain forest in secondary growth, in open places, and near the coast; even found in mangrove swamps on Cape York Peninsula, Australia, at sea level.

*Cyathea felina* is a rare tree fern. If the genus *Sphaeropteris* is recognized, John Gilbert Baker's specific name *concinna* takes precedence.

## *Cyathea fenicis* Copeland 1909

*Alsophila fenicis* (Copeland) C. Christensen 1913, not *A. fenicis* Posthumus 1942 (see *C. elmeri*)

*Alsophila* clade. The erect trunk is as tall as 1 m and about 6 cm in diameter. Fronds are tripinnate and as much as 1.5–2 m in length. The lowest pinnae are usually reduced. The stipe is brown to purple–dark brown and spiny, and has both long, dark brown scales and minute brown scales, or the scales may be pale. Sori are round and borne in two rows, one on either side of the pinnule midvein; indusia are very small and scale-like. Distribution: Philippines and Taiwan, in wet forest, forest margins, and on hillsides.

*Cyathea fenicis* is named after Eugenio Fénix (1883–1939), who collected the type material on the island of Batan in the Philippines. The collection was destroyed in the Manila herbarium during the Second World War.

## *Cyathea ferruginea* Christ 1907

*Alsophila ferruginea* (Christ) Tryon 1970, *Cyathea ferrugineoides* Copeland 1952

*Alsophila* clade. The erect trunk is 2–4 m tall. Fronds are bi- or tripinnate and may reach 1 m in length or more. The stipe is covered in short spines and sparse scales; the scales are dark brown and have narrow, pale, fragile edges. Sori occur near the midvein of fertile pinnules and are covered by thin, pale indusia. Distribution: Negros, Palawan, and Balabac in the Philippines, in mossy forest as high as about 1200 m.

The name *ferruginea*, rust-colored, may be from the brown scales.

## *Cyathea foersteri* Rosenstock 1912

*Alsophila foersteri* (Rosenstock) Tryon 1970

*Alsophila* clade. The erect trunk may be as tall as about 10 m. Fronds are bi- or tripinnate and 2–2.5 m long, with nine or ten composing the crown. The stipe is covered with pale scales. Sori occur near the midvein of fertile pinnules and are covered by firm, thin indusia. Distribution: Eastern New Guinea in scrub in forest margins and mossy forest at 1600–2800 m.

*Cyathea foersteri* is very similar to *C. archboldii* but differs in frond shape (the lower pinnae are reduced) and in its short stipes. *Cyathea nigrolineata* is also similar, and further study could see the two united.

## *Cyathea frigida* (Karsten) Domin 1929

*Alsophila frigida* Karsten 1859

*Cyathea* clade. The creeping to erect trunk is about 4 m tall. Fronds are bipinnate and may reach 2–2.5 m in length. The rachis is brown and warty, and has scattered, light brown scales. Sori occur along each side of the pinnule midvein, halfway between the midvein and the edge of the lamina; indusia are absent. Distribution: Eastern Cordillera de Venezuela, Colombia, and the Andes of Ecuador and eastern Peru, in cloud forest and low shrub at 2500–3500 m.

*Cyathea frigida* is variable, depending on elevation, and possibly related to *C. pauciflora*.

## *Cyathea fugax* Alderwerelt van Rosenburgh 1912

*Sphaeropteris fugax* (Alderwerelt van Rosenburgh) Tryon 1970

*Sphaeropteris* clade. The erect trunk may be as tall as about 10 m or more. Fronds are tripinnate, occur in alternate whorls of five, and may reach 3 m in length. Old fronds are lost, leaving only stipe-base scars on the trunk. The stipe has pale, thin spines and plentiful pale brown scales. Sori occur near the midvein of fertile pinnules and lack indusia. Distribution: Eastern New Guinea and offshore islands, in wet ground, secondary forest, and open places, from lowland to 1400 m.

## *Cyathea fulgens* C. Christensen 1937

*Alsophila fulgens* (C. Christensen) Conant 1983

*Alsophila* clade. Distribution: Cuba, Jamaica, and Hispaniola. *Cyathea fulgens* is part of the *C. woodwardioides* complex of six very similar species, all from the Greater Antilles in the Caribbean, which also includes *C. crassa, C. grevilleana, C. portoricensis,* and *C. tussacii*. This group of tree ferns is also known to cross with the *C. minor* complex. *Cyathea fulgens* is also known to form hybrids with *C. brooksii*.

## *Cyathea fuliginosa* (Christ) Copeland 1909

*Alsophila fuliginosa* Christ 1898, *Cyathea mindanensis* Copeland 1909,
*C. bicolor* Copeland in Elmer 1910, *C. biliranensis* Copeland 1955

*Alsophila* clade. The erect trunk may be as tall as about 5 m or more. Fronds are bi- or tripinnate and 1–3 m long. The stipe is warty and/or has short spines and many scattered scales toward the base; the scales are dark, glossy, and have fragile edges. Sori occur near the midvein of fertile pinnules and are covered by firm, dark indusia. Distribution: Luzon, Biliran, and Mindanao in the Philippines, in forest at 640–2400 m.

### *Cyathea fulva* (Martens & Galeotti) Fée 1857

*Alsophila fulva* Martens & Galeotti 1842, ?*Cyathea schanschin* Martius 1834, not *C. schanschin* Jenman 1892 (see *C. harrisii*); *C. aurea* Klotzsch 1856, *C. underwoodii* Christ 1906

*Cyathea* clade. The erect trunk may be as tall as 10 m and 6–10 cm in diameter, occasionally as much as 25 cm. Fronds are bipinnate and may reach 3.5 m in length. Petioles are straw-colored to brown and have spines. The rachis is glabrous or has small brown to dark brown scales. Sori occur in two rows along each side of the pinnule midvein and are covered with thin, ephemeral, globose indusia. Distribution: Southern Mexico, Honduras, Nicaragua, and Costa Rica; Venezuela, Colombia, and Ecuador. Plants are found in tropical and submontane rain forest and cloud forest, understory, and open locations at 800–2600 m, occasionally higher.

*Cyathea fulva* is a medium-sized tree fern with a large flattish crown. It is part of a large group of ferns that includes *C. delgadii*, *C. harrisii*, *C. furfuracea*, *C. suprastrigosa*, and *C. tenera*, and is sometimes considered synonymous with these species. *Cyathea schanschin* Martius 1834 may be synonymous with *C. fulva*, and if that is correct, then Martius's name may take precedence. The relationship between these tree ferns requires further investigation.

### *Cyathea furfuracea* Baker in W. J. Hooker & Baker 1874

*Cyathea asperula* Maxon 1913

PLATES 49, 83

*Cyathea* clade. The erect trunk may be as tall as 4 m, rarely 12 m, and about 15 cm in diameter, rarely as much as 25 cm. Fronds are bipinnate, dull green, and pale beneath, and may reach 2–3 m in length. The rachis is light brown to yellowish. The stipe is long and brown, has conical to flattened spines, and is covered in yellow-brown scales. Sori are globose and occur in three to five pairs along each side of the pinnule midvein; indusia are brown and membranous. Distribution: Greater Antilles (Cuba, Jamaica, Hispaniola, and Puerto Rico) in submontane and montane rain forest and cloud forest at 750–2200 m.

*Cyathea furfuracea* is part of a large group of ferns centered on *C. fulva*.

### *Cyathea fusca* Baker in Beccari 1886

*Sphaeropteris fusca* (Baker) Tryon 1970

*Sphaeropteris* clade. The erect trunk is 2–3 m tall. Fronds are bipinnate to almost tripinnate and about 1.5 m long. The rachis is pale and spiny beneath. The stipe is covered with scales that are thick, fleshy, and have upcurved bases. Sori occur near the pinnule midvein and are covered with pale indusia. Distribution: Eastern New Guinea in forest undergrowth.

*Cyathea fusca* is similar to *C. werneri*, differing in having hairs on the lower surface of the pinna rachis; the relationship between the two species requires further investigation.

### *Cyathea gardneri* W. J. Hooker 1844

not *Cyathea gardneri* (W. J. Hooker) Lellinger 1987 (see *Alsophila gardneri*, Appendix 1); *Sphaeropteris gardneri* (W. J. Hooker) Tryon 1970, *Cyathea incurvata* Kunze 1849

*Sphaeropteris* clade. The trunk may be as tall as about 6 m and 10–15 cm in diameter; it is often densely covered with brown scales. Fronds are bipinnate to nearly tripinnate, dark green, pale beneath, and usually about 1 m long. Sori occur in four to eight pairs per pinnule segment and are covered by papery, white, globose indusia. Distribution: Southeastern Brazil.

*Cyathea gardneri* is associated with a group of ferns that includes *C. brunei*, *C. insignis*, *C. princeps* (= *Sphaeropteris horrida*), and *C. quindiuensis*.

### *Cyathea geluensis* Rosenstock 1908

*Alsophila geluensis* (Rosenstock) Tryon 1970, *Cyathea novoguineensis* Brause 1912, *C. sepikensis* Brause 1912

*Alsophila* clade. The erect trunk is about 5 m tall or more. Fronds are bi- or tripinnate, 1–2.5 m long, and number about ten in a crown. The stipe is warty and/or has short spines and many scattered scales toward the base; the scales are pale to dark and have dull, fragile edges. Sori occur near the midvein of fertile pinnules and are covered by pale, thin indusia. Distribution: Central and eastern New Guinea and the Louisiade Archipelago, in mossy forest at 700–2000 m, the name *geluensis* likely referring to the island of Jalun or Gelun.

*Cyathea geluensis* is a variable tree fern, which may constitute a species complex. In New Guinea, plants grow at 1000–2000 m but are found at 700–900 m on the associated islands.

### *Cyathea gibbosa* (Klotzsch) Domin 1929

*Alsophila gibbosa* Klotzsch 1844, *Cyathea farinosa* (Karsten) Domin 1929

*Cyathea* clade. The erect, slender trunk is about 5 m tall. Fronds are bipinnate and may reach 1–1.5 m in length; they may be partially retained, forming a skirt about the trunk. The rachis is light brown. The stipe is long and dark brown, and has warts and short spines or is just warty. Rachis and stipe scales are glossy brown and have a lighter margin. Sori occur between the midvein and the edges of the lamina; indusia are scale-like. Distribution: Venezuela and Guyana, at 2100–2200 m.

*Cyathea gibbosa* may be related to *C. aspera*.

### *Cyathea gigantea* (Wallich ex W. J. Hooker) Holttum 1935
*Alsophila gigantea* Wallich ex W. J. Hooker 1844
PLATE 50

*Alsophila* clade. The erect trunk is as tall as about 5 m or more. Fronds are bi- or tripinnate and 2–3 m long. The rachis is long, dark or black, and rough after the fall of scales, which are dark brown, glossy, and have a narrow paler margin and fragile edges. Sori are round and lack indusia. Distribution: Northeastern India to southern India and Sri Lanka; Nepal to Myanmar (Burma), Thailand, Laos, and Vietnam, to Indonesia (central Sumatra and western Java). Plants are found in moist open areas at 600–1000 m.

*Cyathea gigantea* is very similar to *C. glabra* and appears to be part of a complex that also includes *C. podophylla* and *C. subdubia;* the relationship between these species requires further investigation. The name *gigantea* refers, in part, to the large fronds.

### *Cyathea glaberrima* Holttum 1962
*Alsophila glaberrima* (Holttum) Tryon 1970

*Alsophila* clade. The erect trunk is about 2 m tall. Fronds are bi- or tripinnate, have shallow pinnule lobes, and are 1–2 m long, forming a dense crown. The stipe is finely warty and covered with many scales that are glossy and have fragile edges. Sori occur close to the midvein of fertile pinnules and are covered by small, dark brown, scale-like indusia. Distribution: D'Entrecasteaux Islands, on the islands of Fergusson and Goodenough, in mossy forest at 900–1400 m.

### *Cyathea glabra* (Blume) Copeland 1909
*Alsophila glabra* (Blume) W. J. Hooker 1844, *Cyathea reducta* (Alderwerelt van Rosenburgh) Domin 1930

*Alsophila* clade. The erect trunk is 2–4 m tall. Fronds are bi- or tripinnate and 1–2 m long; the lowest pinnae may be very reduced. The stipe is very dark and has basal scales that are glossy, dark, and have a paler margin and fragile edges. Sori occur in groups of one to three on fertile pinnule veins; indusia are absent. Distribution: Borneo, western Java, Sumatra, and the Malay Peninsula, in lowland swamp forest and montane forest as high as 1500 m.

*Cyathea glabra* appears to be part of a complex that includes *C. gigantea*,

*C. podophylla*, and *C. subdubia;* the relationship between these species requires further investigation.

### Cyathea gleichenioides C. Christensen 1937
*Alsophila gleichenioides* (C. Christensen) Tryon 1970

*Alsophila* clade. The erect trunk is about 3 m tall and about 24 cm in diameter. Fronds are narrow and tripinnate, about 1 m long, with about 60 making a rounded crown. The stipe is warty and covered with scattered scales toward the base; the scales are either glossy brown with a paler dull margin, or small, pale, and fringed. Sori occur one or two per fertile pinnule and are covered by firm brown indusia. Distribution: New Guinea in open peaty grassland or on forest margins, often in groups, at 2800–3700 m.

*Cyathea gleichenioides* is a variable species, similar to *C. imbricata* and very similar to *C. macgregorii*, differing only in minor details of frond morphology. It is possible these variations are ecological and that *C. gleichenioides* and *C. macgregorii* should be united.

### Cyathea gracilis Griesbach 1864

*Cyathea* clade. Epiphytic or terrestrial, the erect trunk may be as tall as 60 cm, rarely 3 m, and 5–12 cm in diameter. The trunk is covered with persistent stipe bases and glossy scales that are bicolored, red-brown to dark brown with a lighter brown edge. Fronds are bipinnate and may reach 2–3 m in length. Petioles are smooth, shiny and black-brown at the base. The rachis is also smooth and brownish black. The stipe is dark purple-brown. Sori are numerous and occur each side of the pinnule midvein; indusia are brown and globose. Distribution: Jamaica; Costa Rica and Panama; Colombia and Ecuador. Plants are found in submontane rain forest and are epiphytic or grow in the understory and in open locations above about 900 m, reaching 1700 m in Colombia.

*Cyathea gracilis* is an unusual fern, which may be epiphytic and lacking an erect trunk. It is part of a group of ferns centered on *C. lechleri*.

### Cyathea gregaria (Brause) Domin 1930
*Alsophila gregaria* Brause 1920

*Alsophila* clade. The erect trunk is 4–5 m tall and about 10 cm in diameter. Fronds are bi- or tripinnate and 2–3 m long. The stipe is covered in spines but has few scales that are medium brown and have a paler margin. Sori occur near the midvein of fertile pinnules; indusia are absent. Distribution: Eastern New Guinea in lowland forest and coastal rain forest to 100 m, often forming clumps.

### *Cyathea grevilleana* Martius 1834

*Alsophila grevilleana* (Martius) Conant 1983, *Cyathea elegans* Heward 1838, *C. lindsayana* W. J. Hooker 1865

*Alsophila* clade. The erect trunk is about 7 m tall, 10–15 cm in diameter, and clothed in old stipe bases, brown scales, and blackish spines. Fronds are tripinnate, dark green, and as long as 4 m. The last pinnae may be separated, forming a clump about the trunk apex. The rachis is yellow-brown and nearly smooth. The stipe is long and dark brown, and has a few scattered spines. Sori occur in four to six pairs along the pinnule midvein and are covered with cup-like, pale brown indusia. Distribution: Jamaica in moist gullies and on wooded hills in both calcareous and noncalcareous soils at 200–1200 m.

*Cyathea grevilleana*, named after Robert Greville (1794–1866), who collected the type specimen in Jamaica in 1832, is part of the *C. woodwardioides* complex of six species from the Greater Antilles, which also includes *C. crassa*, *C. fulgens*, *C. portoricensis*, and *C. tussacii*. These plants are known to hybridize with members of the *C. minor* complex. In 1865, William J. Hooker described *C. lindsayana*, reportedly from Mount Lindsay in Queensland, Australia. As Hooker's specimen is identical with *C. grevilleana*, however, it seems more likely that this is an error and that samples have been mixed up. Hooker's *C. lindsayana* is thus also synonymous with *C. grevilleana* (see Tindale 1956).

### *Cyathea hainanensis* Ching 1959

*Sphaeropteris hainanensis* (Ching) Tryon 1970

*Sphaeropteris* clade. The erect trunk is about 5 m tall. Fronds are bi- or tripinnate and may reach about 3 m in length. The stipe is pale and smooth, and has some basal, pale brown scales. Sori lack indusia. Distribution: Hainan, China.

### *Cyathea halconensis* Christ 1908

*Alsophila halconensis* (Christ) Tryon 1970, *Cyathea mearnsii* Copeland 1909

*Alsophila* clade. The erect trunk is 2–4 m tall. Fronds are bi- or tripinnate and may reach more than 1 m in length. The stipe is covered in conical spines and scales; the scales are dark brown and have fragile edges. Sori occur near the midvein of fertile pinnules and are covered by thin, pale indusia. Distribution: Luzon and Mindoro in the Philippines, in forest at 1200–1700 m, the name *halconensis* referring to Mount Halcon (2581 m), the highest peak on Mindoro.

### *Cyathea halonata* R. C. Moran & B. Øllgaard 1998

*Cyathea* clade. The erect trunk is about 3 m tall and about 11 cm in diameter. Fronds are bipinnate, dissected, and may reach 2 m in length. Basal pinnae with expanded lamina tissue are separated from the main pinnae toward the base of the stipe and are held horizontally over the trunk. The rachis and stipe are brown and have scales and basal spines; the scales are linear and whitish, or bullate and golden brown. Sori lack indusia. Distribution: Ecuador in mature cloud forest at about 1550 m.

*Cyathea halonata* was named for its distinctive basal pinnae, which are held over the trunk, forming a halo. This species resembles *C. cystolepis*, differing in the absence of indusia and the presence the halo of pinnae.

### *Cyathea hancockii* Copeland 1909
*Alsophila denticulata* Baker 1885

*Alsophila* clade. The trunk is prostrate or short and erect. Fronds are bi- or tripinnate and as long as 1.5 m. The lowest pinnae are usually reduced. The rachis and stipe are brown to purple–dark brown, glossy, and scaly and hairy on the upper surface; the scales are brown, linear, and have rounded bases. Sori are borne in two rows, one on either side of the pinnule midvein; indusia are absent. Distribution: Ryukyu Islands, Japan, and Taiwan and Hong Kong, in forest, on stream banks, and in forest margins at about 600 m or higher.

*Cyathea hancockii*, named after William Hancock (1847–1914), a collector in Japan, China, and Southeast Asia, is occasionally cultivated. Plants may resist slight frosts but do best under shelter and in rich humus with a consistent supply of moisture.

### *Cyathea harrisii* L. M. Underwood ex Maxon 1909
*Cyathea schanschin* Jenman 1892, not *C. schanschin* Martius 1834 (see *C. fulva*)

*Cyathea* clade. The erect trunk is as tall as 3.5 m and 6–8 cm in diameter; it is covered with scales. Fronds are bipinnate, dark green, pale beneath, and may reach 2.5 m in length. The rachis is light yellow-brown to brown. The stipe is long and dark brown, and has numerous scales and spines toward the base; the scales are either glossy brown or bicolored, dark brown with a paler margin. Sori occur along each side of the pinnule midvein; indusia are globose, light brown, and membranous. Distribution: Greater Antilles (Jamaica and Hispaniola) and Lesser Antilles (Dominica), in moist forest at 2300–2500 m, often persisting after land clearance.

*Cyathea harrisii* is likely named after William H. Harris (1860–1920), who collected on Jamaica and other of the West Indies. It is part of a large group of ferns centered on *C. fulva*.

## *Cyathea haughtii* (Maxon) Tryon 1976

*Alsophila haughtii* Maxon 1944

*Cyathea* clade. The trunk is barely erect. Fronds are pinnate and may be as long as 25 cm, rarely as long as 40 cm. Distribution: Colombia on sandstone cliffs at about 1400 m.

One of the smallest ferns in the genus, *Cyathea haughtii* is part of a group of species centered on *C. speciosa*. The name *haughtii* commemorates botanist Oscar Lee Haught (1893–1975), who collected in South America.

## *Cyathea havilandii* Baker 1894

*Alsophila havilandii* (Baker) Tryon 1970, *Cyathea paleacea* Copeland 1917, *C. rigida* Copeland 1917

*Alsophila* clade. The erect trunk is about 50 cm tall or more. Fronds are narrow, erect, tripinnate, and about 1 m long. The stipe is dark, warty, and covered with scales that are medium brown and have fragile edges. Sori occur on either side of the fertile pinnule midvein and are covered by firm, dark indusia. Distribution: Kinabalu on Borneo, in ridge forest at 2400–3000 m.

*Cyathea havilandii* is named after botanist George Darby Haviland (1857–1901), who collected in Malaysia.

## *Cyathea hemiepiphytica* R. C. Moran 1995

*Cyathea* clade. The climbing, or leaning or erect, trunk may be as tall as 5 m and 3–4 cm in diameter. It is densely scaly; the scales are lanceolate with an elongated apex, and shiny dark, especially toward the base. Fronds are bipinnate, 1–1.5 m long, and usually spaced along the trunk in groups of three about 15 cm apart. Sori occur near the midvein of fertile pinnules and lack indusia. Distribution: Northwestern Ecuador on the western slopes of the Andes in humid forest at 800–1000 m.

*Cyathea hemiepiphytica* is closely related to *C. kalbreyeri* but differs in its leaning or climbing habit, which gives rise to its specific name.

## *Cyathea henryi* (Baker) Copeland 1909

*Alsophila henryi* Baker 1898

*Alsophila* clade. The erect trunk is 5–7 m tall or more. Fronds are bi- or tripinnate and 2–3 m long. The rachis is usually smooth and dark but may have a few scattered scales, as does the stipe; the scales are either small and pale with irregular fringed edges, or large and dark with a paler margin. Sori occur on minor veins; indusia are absent. Distribution: India, and Yunnan, China, in submontane and montane forest at 600–1200 m.

The name *henryi* commemorates Irish botanist Augustine Henry (1857–1930), who collected in China.

### *Cyathea heterochlamydea* Copeland 1908
*Alsophila heterochlamydea* (Copeland) Tryon 1970

*Alsophila* clade. The erect trunk may be as tall as about 4 m or more. Fronds are bi- or tripinnate and 1–2 m long. The stipe is warty and/or has short spines and is covered with scales; the scales are dark, glossy, and have a narrow pale margin. Sori occur near the midvein of fertile pinnules and are covered by firm brown indusia. Distribution: Luzon, Panay, Negros, and Mindanao in the Philippines, in montane forest.

*Cyathea heterochlamydea* is a little-known tree fern but is very similar to the smaller *C. edanoi* and possibly related to *C. caudata*.

### *Cyathea hirsuta* C. B. Presl 1822
*Cyathea* clade. Distribution: Brazil. *Cyathea hirsuta* is very similar to *C. cyatheoides* and forms part of the *C. armata* complex of tree ferns.

### *Cyathea hodgeana* Proctor 1961
*Cyathea* clade. The erect, slender trunk is 4–5 m tall and covered with brown scales. Fronds are bipinnate and may reach 1 m or slightly more in length. The rachis is light brown to brown and has numerous very small pale scales and some warts. The stipe is dark brown and has numerous scales toward the base; the scales are either large and dark brown or small and pale. Sori occur in two rows along each side of the pinnule midvein, between the vein and the edge of the lamina; their presence is usually marked by the occurrence of pit-like depressions on the upper pinnule surface. Indusia are absent. Distribution: Dominica in the Caribbean, in moist forest along rivers.

*Cyathea hodgeana* is named after botanist Walter H. Hodge (b. 1912), who collected in the West Indies as well as elsewhere in the Americas. It may be allied to *C. nigripes* and its associated group of species.

### *Cyathea holdridgeana* Nisman & L. D. Gómez 1971
*Cyathea* clade. The erect trunk may be as tall as 2 m and 6–10 cm in diameter. Fronds are bi- or tripinnate and may reach 2.5 m in length. Petioles are brown

and smooth or have small raised dots. The rachis is light brown to brown and has numerous small whitish or straw-colored scales and hairs; some bicolored scales (dark with a paler margin) may also be present. Sori occur in two rows along each side of the pinnule midvein and are covered with scale-like indusia. Distribution: Costa Rica and Panama, in submontane and montane rain forest, in understory and open locations at 2000–2800 m.

*Cyathea holdridgeana* is named after plant collector Leslie R. Holdridge (b. 1907). It is a small tree fern with a large, open, arching crown. It is possible that it is a hybrid related to *C. divergens*.

## *Cyathea hooglandii* Holttum 1962

*Alsophila hooglandii* (Holttum) Tryon 1970

*Alsophila* clade. The erect trunk may be as tall as about 3 m and about 10 cm in diameter. Fronds occur in two whorls of five to seven each, are tripinnate, and 1–2 m long. The stipe is dull and warty, or densely covered with scales that may be dark to medium brown and have a broad paler margin and fragile edges. Sori occur singly at the base of each tertiary pinnule, on the midvein, and are covered by firm, saucer-like indusia. Distribution: Western Highlands of New Guinea in mossy forest at about 3000 m.

*Cyathea hooglandii* is named after botanist Ruurd Dirk Hoogland (1922–1994), who collected on New Guinea and in Australia as well as Europe. It appears to be related to *C. microphylloides* but differs in having single sori at the base of fertile tertiary pinnules.

## *Cyathea hookeri* Thwaites 1864

*Alsophila hookeri* (Thwaites) Tryon 1970

PLATE 51

*Alsophila* clade. The erect, narrow to slender trunk may be as tall as 1–2 m. Fronds are pinnate and about 1 m long. The stipe is dark and has blunt spines and scattered scales; the scales are long, medium brown, glossy, and have fragile edges. Sori occur on the lowest one or two pairs of veins of fertile pinnules and are covered with thin indusia. Distribution: Sri Lanka in lowland forest.

*Cyathea hookeri* is named after pteridologist William Jackson Hooker (1785–1865), director of the Royal Botanic Gardens, Kew.

## *Cyathea hornei* (Baker) Copeland 1929

*Alsophila hornei* Baker 1879, *Cyathea melanoclada* Domin 1930,
*C. olivacea* (Brause) Domin 1930

*Alsophila* clade. The erect trunk is 3–4 m tall and as much as about 4 cm in diameter. Fronds are pinnate or bipinnate and as long as 2 m. The rachis and stipe are dark and have basal scales that are glossy and either dark with a paler margin or light brown and bullate. Sori almost cover the lower segments of fertile pinnules and lack indusia. Distribution: Eastern New Guinea and the Louisiade Archipelago to Fiji, in wet submontane forest, stunted forest, mossy forest, and on ridges at 400–2000 m.

The name *hornei* commemorates botanist John Horne (1835–1905), who collected on Fiji and islands of the Indian Ocean. *Cyathea hornei* is a variable species with minor differences in the division of pinnae and the presence or absence of smaller basal pinnae.

### *Cyathea horridula* Copeland 1942

*Alsophila horridula* (Copeland) Tryon 1970

*Alsophila* clade. The erect trunk may be as tall as about 3 m or more. Fronds are bi- or tripinnate and 1–2 m long. The stipe is covered with spines and scattered scales toward the base; the scales are pale and have fragile edges. Sori occur near the midvein of fertile pinnules and are covered by small, dark brown, saucer-like indusia. Distribution: Western New Guinea in montane forest at about 1700 m, a rare tree fern known only from the type locality.

### *Cyathea hotteana* C. Christensen & Ekman 1937

*Alsophila hotteana* (C. Christensen & Ekman) Tryon 1970

*Alsophila* clade. The erect trunk may be as tall as 2 m and about 8 cm in diameter. Fronds are pinnate and as long as 2 m. The rachis and stipe are brown and have brown basal scales. Sori occur in two rows, one on each side of the pinnule midvein; Indusia are shallow and plate-like, with one or two clefts at the margin. Distribution: Haiti in cloud forest at 1000–1200 m.

*Cyathea hotteana* was described from a collection made at 700 m, but forest clearance has now limited the habitat to higher elevations. This species is known to cross with *C. woodwardioides*, producing a hybrid sometimes known as *C.* ×*confirmis* C. Christensen (not to be confused with *C. conformis*).

### *Cyathea howeana* Domin 1929

*Cyathea* clade. The erect trunk may be as tall as about 8 m. Fronds are bipinnate and 2–3 m long. The rachis and stipe are dark brown and have scales and some hairs; the scales are pale and bullate. Sori are round, with red-brown globose indusia, and occur on either side of the pinnule midvein toward the base of the pinnule segment. Distribution: Lord Howe Island, Australia.

*Cyathea howeana* is one of a group of western Pacific species apparently related to *C. decurrens*. Members of this group have variously been attributed to *Alsophila* or *Cyathea*. Molecular evidence suggests a relationship with the latter genus, as treated here, though the relationship is by no means clear.

### *Cyathea humilis* Hieronymus in Engler & Prantl 1895

*Alsophila holstii* Hieronymus in Engler & Prantl 1895, not *Cyathea holstii* Hieronymus 1895 (see *C. mossambicensis*); *C. stuhlmannii* Hieronymus in Engler & Prantl 1899, *A. stuhlmannii* (Hieronymus) Tryon 1970, *C. uluguruensis* Hieronymus in Engler & Prantl 1899, *C. opizii* Domin 1929

*Alsophila* clade. The erect trunk is 2–3 m tall. Fronds are pinnate and 1–2 m long; old fronds may be retained as an irregular skirt. The rachis and stipe are light brown, with scales toward the base of the stipe; the scales are dark, glossy, and have narrow fragile edges. Sori are at the forks of veins and covered by thin, reduced indusia. Distribution: Usambara and Uluguru Mountains, Tanzania, and Kenya, in wet forest at 1100–2000 m.

The type of *Cyathea humilis*, from the Usambara Mountains in Tanzania, is almost certainly a juvenile of *C. stuhlmannii*, also described by Hieronymus. As *humilis* is the older name, it must take precedence. Variety *pycnophylla* Holttum, from the Mogodoro district of Tanzania, has been recognized; it differs in the shape of its fronds and in not retaining old fronds as a skirt. The true taxonomic status of these plants requires investigation.

### *Cyathea hunsteiniana* Brause 1920

*Alsophila brausei* Tryon 1970

*Alsophila* clade. The erect trunk may be as tall as about 1 m and about 3 cm in diameter. Fronds are bipinnate and about 1 m long. The stipe is covered with scattered scales that are dark brown with a broad paler margin and fragile edges. Sori are round, occur one or two per fertile pinnule segment, and are covered by deep, firm, cup-like indusia. Distribution: Eastern New Guinea in rain forest at 1300–2000 m.

*Cyathea hunsteiniana* is named after plant collector Carl Hunstein (1843–1888). It is very similar to *C. perpelvigeria* but lacks scales on the fronds. One variety, *acuminata* (Copeland) Brause, has been recognized. This is usually a less robust plant, growing in shady places, and may represent a simple ecological variant.

## *Cyathea hymenodes* Mettenius 1863

*Alsophila hymenodes* (Mettenius) Tryon 1970, *Cyathea korthalsii* Mettenius 1863, *C. latebrosa* var. *indusiata* Holttum 1935

*Alsophila* clade. The erect trunk may be as tall as 2–4 m. Fronds are bi- or tripinnate and 1–2 m long. The stipe is covered with scattered scales and may bear a pair of reduced pinnae toward the base; the scales are dark and have very fragile edges. Sori occur near the midvein of fertile pinnules and are covered by firm, brown, saucer-like indusia. Distribution: Malay Peninsula and Sumatra, in montane forest at 900–2000 m.

## *Cyathea imbricata* Alderwerelt van Rosenburgh 1924

*Alsophila imbricata* (Alderwerelt van Rosenburgh) Tryon 1970

*Alsophila* clade. The erect trunk is about 2 m tall. Fronds are bi- or tripinnate and usually less than 1 m long. The stipe is dark, spiny, and covered in scales when young; the scales are glossy brown and have a paler margin and fragile edges. Sori occur in groups of one to four per pinnule lobe and are covered by firm indusia. Distribution: Western New Guinea in open forest at 3240 m.

*Cyathea imbricata* is similar to *C. macgregorii* and very similar to *C. gleichenioides*, differing only in details of frond morphology. It is possible these variations are ecological and that the species should be united.

## *Cyathea impar* Tryon 1976

*Cyathea* clade. The erect, narrow trunk may be as tall as 1 m. Fronds are about 1 m long and bipinnate. Rachis and stipe scales are bicolored, brown with a pale margin. Sori are covered by scale-like indusia. Distribution: Cerro Jefe, Panama.

*Cyathea impar* is a little-known Central American species, part of a group centered on *C. petiolata*.

## *Cyathea imrayana* W. J. Hooker 1844

*Alsophila imrayana* (W. J. Hooker) Conant 1983, *Cyathea caribaea* Jenman 1898

*Alsophila* clade. The erect trunk is 8–10 m tall and 10–15 cm in diameter; it has sharp blackish spines and pale brown hairs. Fronds occur in whorls of five, are bipinnate, and 2–3 m long. The rachis and stipe are brown to dark brown and have scales that are bicolored, with a brown center and paler margin, and a terminal seta; pinnule veins have whitish scales. Sori are round, with red-brown globose indusia, and occur on either side of the pinnule midvein toward the base of the pinnule segment. Distribution: Lesser Antilles; Costa Rica and Panama; Venezuela and Ecuador. Plants are found in submontane rain forest understory and on riverbanks at 1000–2000 m.

Cyathea imrayana is named after plant collector John Imray (1811–1880). It is a tree fern with a large, spreading crown, particularly in young plants.

### Cyathea inaequalis Holttum 1962

*Sphaeropteris inaequalis* (Holttum) Tryon 1970

*Sphaeropteris* clade. The erect trunk may be as tall as 4–6 m and 5–6 cm in diameter; it is covered with leaf scars in alternate whorls. Fronds are bi- or tripinnate and 1–2 m long. The stipe is thorny and scaly toward the base; the scales are dark, glossy, thick, and fleshy toward the base. Sori occur near the midvein of fertile pinnules and are covered by thin, translucent indusia. Distribution: Western New Guinea at 700–1100 m.

### Cyathea incana Karsten 1860

*Alsophila incana* (Karsten) Conant 1983

*Alsophila* clade. Distribution: Colombia, Ecuador, Peru, Bolivia, and northern Argentina.

### Cyathea incisoserrata Copeland 1911

*Alsophila incisoserrata* (Copeland) C. Christensen 1913

*Alsophila* clade. The erect trunk is about 4 m tall and 12 cm in diameter. Fronds are bi- or tripinnate and 1–2 m long. Stipes are partly persistent and may be retained on the upper trunk; they are warty, have conical spines, and are sparsely covered by scales that are either small and fringed or bullate. Sori occur near the midvein of fertile pinnules and are covered by very small, often bilobed indusia. Distribution: Malay Peninsula and Sarawak, in forest or forest margins from the lowland to about 1250 m.

Cyathea incisoserrata is similar to *C. latebrosa*, differing in having scales throughout the length of the stipe, and in pinnule shape.

### Cyathea inquinans Christ 1896

*Alsophila inquinans* (Christ) Tryon 1970

*Alsophila* clade. The erect trunk is 2–4 m tall. Fronds are bi- or tripinnate and may reach 1 m or more in length. The stipe is covered in scales that are either large, red-brown, and thin, with narrow fragile edges, or small, with a red apical seta. Sori occur near the midvein of fertile pinnules and are covered by thin brown indusia. Distribution: Southwestern Sulawesi (Celebes) and possibly from the Moluccas, in montane forest at 2000–2800 m.

## *Cyathea insignis* D. C. Eaton 1860

*Sphaeropteris insignis* (D. C. Eaton) Tryon 1970

*Sphaeropteris* clade. The erect trunk may be as tall as about 6 m and 10–15 cm in diameter; it is often densely covered with cinnamon-colored scales. Fronds are bipinnate to nearly tripinnate, dark green above, pale beneath, and may reach about 2.5 m in length. The stipe is long, stout, and covered in cinnamon brown scales. Sori occur in four to eight pairs per fertile pinnule segment and are covered by papery, white, deep, cup-like indusia, which normally split into two halves when mature. Distribution: Cuba, Jamaica, and Hispaniola, on moist, forested hillsides and in mountainous ravines at 750–1800 m.

*Cyathea insignis* is a medium to large, fast-growing tree fern with a crown of whorled fronds. This species is associated with a group of American ferns that includes *C. brunei, C. gardneri, C. princeps* (= *Sphaeropteris horrida*), and *C. quindiuensis*.

## *Cyathea insulana* Holttum 1962

*Alsophila insulana* (Holttum) Tryon 1970

*Alsophila* clade. The erect trunk is 8–10 m tall and 14 cm in diameter. Fronds are bi- or tripinnate, about 3 m long, and form a spreading crown. The stipe is covered with thick spines and small scales; the scales are either small and pale brown, with a short fringe, or large and glossy brown, with fragile edges. Sori occur near the midvein of fertile pinnules and are covered by thin, pale indusia. Distribution: New Guinea in mossy forest and ravines at 750–1600 m, the name *insulana* referring to the island.

## *Cyathea insularum* Holttum 1962

*Sphaeropteris insularum* (Holttum) Tryon 1970

*Sphaeropteris* clade. The erect trunk may be as tall as 3–5 m and 3–6 cm in diameter; it is covered with stipe-base scars 18–25 mm in diameter and occasional dead fronds. Fronds form a dense crown, are bi- or tripinnate, and 1.5–2 m long. The stipe has abundant scales toward the base; the scales are thick, dark, and fleshy. Sori occur near the midvein of fertile pinnules and are covered by thin, pale indusia. Distribution: Four islands in the Louisiade Archipelago, in lowland forest near streams at 100–350 m, the name *insularum* referring to the islands.

## Cyathea integra J. Smith ex W. J. Hooker 1844

*Sphaeropteris integra* (J. Smith. ex W. J. Hooker) Tryon 1970,
*Cyathea arguta* Copeland 1929

*Sphaeropteris* clade. The erect trunk is 1–2 m tall. Fronds are pinnate or bipinnate and 1–2 m long. The stipe is spiny and scaly at the base; the scales are thin, pale, and may have setiferous edges. Sori occur about halfway between the midvein of the fertile pinnule and the edge of the lamina and are covered by thin indusia. Distribution: Luzon, Mindoro, Panay, Samar, Catanduanes, Basilan, Biliran, and Mindanao in the Philippines, in forest at 500–1200 m.

*Cyathea binuangensis* may be of hybrid origin, involving *C. integra* as one parent.

## Cyathea intermedia (Mettenius) Copeland 1929

*Alsophila intermedia* Mettenius 1861, *Sphaeropteris intermedia*
(Mettenius) Tryon 1970, *Cyathea francii* (Rosenstock) Domin 1929
PLATES 52, 53

*Sphaeropteris* clade. The erect trunk is 5–10 m tall. Fronds are tripinnate. The rachis and stipe are glabrescent and warty, especially beneath, and they have pale scales. Sori occur near the midvein of the pinnules and lack indusia but may be surrounded by a few scales. Distribution: New Caledonia.

## Cyathea intramarginalis (Windisch) Lellinger 1984

*Sphaeropteris intramarginalis* Windisch 1973

*Cyathea* clade. The erect, slender trunk may be as tall as 4 m. Fronds are bipinnate and 1–2 m long. The stipe is scaly toward the base; the scales are glossy dark brown to blackish and have delicately toothed edges. Sori occur on the forks of veins of fertile pinnules and are covered by thin, translucent, scale-like indusia. Distribution: Venezuela in forest at 1700–2300 m.

*Cyathea intramarginalis* is related to *C. dissimilis* but differs in having nonarticulated apical pinnae, and it is larger.

## Cyathea jamaicensis Jenman 1882

*Cyathea* clade. The erect, slender trunk is 3–4 m tall; it is usually smooth and naked below but scaly toward the apex. The scales are whitish, bicolored (whitish with pale brown toward the base), or shiny dark brown to black. Fronds are bipinnate, dissected, and may reach 1.5–2 m in length. The rachis is pale or reddish brown, and smooth. Sori are usually one or two per segment and are basal on the lowermost veins of fertile pinnules; indusia are dark brown and saucer-shaped. Distribution: Jamaica, rare.

### *Cyathea javanica* Blume 1828

*Alsophila javanica* (Blume) Tryon 1970, *Cyathea caudipinnula* Domin 1929

*Alsophila* clade. The erect trunk is about 10 m tall. Fronds are bi- or tripinnate and 2–3 m long. The stipe is spiny and has scattered scales throughout; the scales are dark and have fragile edges. Sori are round, occur near the fertile pinnule midvein, and are covered by flat, firm, saucer-like indusia. Distribution: Western Java and Sumatra, in rain forest or on riverbanks at 250–1500 m.

Carl Blume included one variety, *rigida*, in his original description of *Cyathea javanica*. Although variety *rigida* is apparently part of the *C. javanica* complex, the name has also occasionally been associated with *C. polycarpa*.

### *Cyathea junghuhniana* (Kunze) Copeland 1909

*Alsophila junghuhniana* Kunze 1848

*Alsophila* clade. The erect trunk may be as tall as about 2 m or more. Fronds are tripinnate and may reach about 3 m in length. Stipes are persistent on the trunk and are brown, spiny, and covered with scales that are glossy dark brown. Sori are near the fertile pinnule midvein, covered by thin indusia. Distribution: Southern and central Sumatra and western Java, in forest at 1000–2000 m.

The name *junghuhniana* commemorates German botanist Franz Wilhelm Junghuhn (1812–1864), who collected on Java. This species has been confused with *C. raciborskii*, from which it differs in several characteristics, including larger pinnae. *Cyathea junghuhniana* also lacks the stipe outgrowths that are present in *C. raciborskii*.

### *Cyathea kalbreyeri* (Baker) Domin 1929

*Alsophila kalbreyeri* Baker 1892

*Cyathea* clade. The erect trunk is 3.5–5 m tall and 3–4 cm in diameter. Fronds are bipinnate and 1–1.5 m long, forming a crown. Rachis and stipe scales are lanceolate with an elongated apex, and shiny dark, especially toward the base. Sori occur halfway between the midvein of fertile pinnules and the edge of the lamina, and lack indusia. Distribution: Venezuela to Bolivia on the eastern slopes of the Andes in humid forest.

*Cyathea kalbreyeri* is named after botanist Wilhelm Kalbreyer (1847–1912), who made the first collections of it from Colombia. It resembles *C. nodulifera* and is closely related to *C. hemiepiphytica* but differs in its erect habit and presence of a true crown of fronds.

## Cyathea kanehirae Holttum 1963

*Alsophila arfakensis* Gepp in Gibbs 1917

Alsophila clade. The erect trunk is 1–4 m tall. Fronds are bi- or tripinnate and 1–2 m long. The rachis is smooth. The stipe is dark and warty, and has scattered scales that are flat and brown. Sori occur near the midvein of fertile pinnules and are covered by small, cup-like indusia. Distribution: Western New Guinea in montane forest at 1600–2700 m.

Richard Eric Holttum described *Cyathea kanehirae* from montane rain forest from about 2500 m. Rolla Tryon (1970) regarded it as synonymous with *Alsophila arfakensis*, but it is possible that the two still are separate species.

## Cyathea kermadecensis W. R. B. Oliver 1910

*Alsophila kermadecensis* (W. R. B. Oliver) Tryon 1970
PLATES 54–56

Alsophila clade. The erect trunk, as tall as 20 m, is often covered with stipe-base scars. Fronds are tripinnate and as long as 4 m. The rachis and stipe are brown and have basal scales that are brown, glossy, and often twisted. Sori occur on either side of the pinnule midvein; indusia are hood-like. Distribution: Raoul Island in the Kermadec Islands, New Zealand, where it is locally common in damp (and drier) forest and scrub.

*Cyathea kermadecensis* is a tall tree fern with a slender trunk, similar to *C. cunninghamii*. Cultivated plants will survive full sun and slight frost but do best in good humus with some shade, and shelter from wind.

## Cyathea khasyana (Moore ex Kuhn) Domin 1930

*Alsophila khasyana* Moore ex Kuhn 1869, *Cyathea ornata* (Scott) Copeland 1909, *C. oldhamii* (Beddome) Domin 1930

Alsophila clade. The erect trunk is 5–7 m tall. Fronds are bi- or tripinnate and 2–3 m long. The stipe is dark and long, and has abundant scales that are dark and have broad, pale, fringed edges. Sori occur near the fertile pinnule midvein; indusia are absent. Distribution: India to Myanmar (Burma) but not Sri Lanka, in forest at 1400–1700 m, the name *khasyana* referring to the Khasi Hills, India.

## Cyathea klossii Ridley 1916

*Alsophila klossii* (Ridley) Tryon 1970

Alsophila clade. The erect trunk is 1–2 m tall and 1–2 cm in diameter. Fronds are pinnate and 0.5–1 m long. The stipe is covered with scattered scales that are dark, dull, and thick. Sori occur near the midvein of fertile pinnules and are covered by thin, pale, fragile indusia. Distribution: Western New Guinea in rain forest from the lowlands to about 750 m.

*Cyathea klossii* is named after Cecil Boden Kloss (1877–1949), who collected plants in Malaysia and nearby areas.

## *Cyathea lasiosora* (Kuhn) Domin 1929

*Alsophila lasiosora* Kuhn 1869, *A. nigra* Martius 1834, not *Cyathea nigra* Linden ex Fournet 1876 (identity cannot be determined from the limited type material); *Trichipteris nigra* (Martius) Tryon 1970

*Cyathea* clade. The erect trunk may be as tall as 6 m. Fronds are bipinnate and as long as about 3 m. The stipe is warty and has scattered scales that are either brown or bicolored, brown with a lighter margin. Sori occur between the midvein of fertile pinnules and the margin; indusia are absent. Distribution: Venezuela, Ecuador, Peru, Bolivia, northern Brazil, and the Amazon Basin, in moist lowland rain forest at 100–1000 m.

*Cyathea lasiosora* is also commonly known as *Trichipteris nigra*. When transferred to *Cyathea* the specific name *nigra* is unavailable, hence Karel Domin's use of *lasiosora*. This species seems closely allied to *C. wendlandii* and *C. schlimii*.

## *Cyathea latebrosa* (Wallich ex W. J. Hooker) Copeland 1909

*Alsophila latebrosa* Wallich ex W. J. Hooker 1844

PLATES 57–60

*Alsophila* clade. The erect trunk is 3–4 m tall. Fronds are bi- or tripinnate, about 2 m long, lighter underneath, and form a sparse feathery crown. The stipe is reddish brown, may be retained in younger plants (forming a messy skirt about the trunk), is spiny, and has some scales near the base; the scales are dark, glossy, and have fragile edges. Sori are near the midvein of the fertile pinnules and covered by small, bilobed, scale-like indusia. Distribution: Indo-China, including Cambodia and Thailand, and the Malay Peninsula to Indonesia, including Borneo and Sumatra, in forest, secondary forest, and plantations from sea level to about 1500 m.

*Cyathea latebrosa* is a common lowland tree fern. It is a variable species and part of a complex that is not fully understood. Although reported from India and Sri Lanka, those plants have thinner indusia and may rank as a separate species. Cultivated plants do best in warmer conditions and may not survive frost. Grow *Cyathea latebrosa* in rich, well-drained humus with plenty of moisture. This species is similar to *C. incisoserrata*, differing in pinnule shape and in not having scales throughout the length of the stipe.

### *Cyathea latevagens* (Baker) Domin 1929

*Alsophila latevagens* Baker 1881

*Cyathea* clade. The creeping to barely erect trunk is about 10 cm tall, often clumping. Fronds are pinnate and as long as 1–1.5 m. The stipe is warty and purplish, and has scattered scales that are brown or brown with a lighter margin. Sori are on fertile pinnules between midveins and the edge of the lamina. Veins fork at the sori. Indusia are absent. Distribution: Colombia in the upper parts of the valley of the Río Cauca, in cloud forest and persisting in cleared pasture at 1800–2000 m.

### *Cyathea latipinnula* Copeland 1911

*Alsophila latipinnula* (Copeland) Tryon 1970

*Alsophila* clade. The erect trunk is 1–2 m tall and 10 cm in diameter. Fronds are bi- or tripinnate and 1–2 m long. The stipe is spiny and covered with a few basal scales that are narrow and brown. Sori occur near the midvein of fertile pinnules and are covered by small dark indusia. Distribution: Philippines in ridge forest at about 1400 m.

### *Cyathea lechleri* Mettenius 1859

*Cyathea castanea* Baker 1874

*Cyathea* clade. The erect trunk may be as tall as 9 m. Fronds are bipinnate and 2.5 m long, occasionally as long as 6 m. The rachis is either pubescent or has scattered scales. The stipe is reddish brown, with brown scales toward the base. Distribution: Venezuela to Peru and Bolivia, in montane forest, dense cloud forest, and bamboo thickets at 800–1500 m.

*Cyathea lechleri* is variable, forming the center of a group of apparently related species that includes *C. dudleyi*, *C. ebenina*, and *C. gracilis*.

### *Cyathea ledermannii* Brause 1920

*Alsophila crassicaula* Tryon 1970

*Alsophila* clade. The erect trunk may be as tall as about 3 m. Fronds are bipinnate and may reach 2 m in length. The rachis may be purplish brown, and usually has scales at the base; the scales may be pale, to brown, to bicolored, brown with a dark margin. Sori occur along each side of the pinnule midvein and are covered by firm indusia. Distribution: New Guinea and Bougainville, common in submontane rain forest at 1000–3000 m.

*Cyathea ledermannii* is named after botanist Carl Ludwig Ledermann (1875–1958), who collected in Papua New Guinea. It has been found in New Guinea over a wide range of elevations, 1950–3000 m. Spore material sourced from high elevations may be worth cultivating for cooler climates.

## *Cyathea leichhardtiana* (F. von Mueller) Copeland 1911

*Alsophila leichhardtiana* F. von Mueller 1865, *Hemitelia australis* C. B. Presl 1851, *Sphaeropteris australis* (C. B. Presl) Tryon 1970, *A. maccarthurii* W. J. Hooker in W. J. Hooker & Baker 1866

PRICKLY TREE FERN

*Sphaeropteris* clade. The erect trunk may be as tall as 7 m and 10 cm in diameter. Fronds are bi- or tripinnate and may reach about 3 m in length. The stipe is dark and glossy, and has stiff, long, black or dark reddish, woody, sharp spines, especially toward the base. Dead stipe bases may persist and protrude from the trunk along with their associated spines. Rachis and stipe scales are pale and straw-colored, and often have a dark setiferous edge. Sori are round and occur near the midvein of the fertile pinnules; indusia are found only sometimes on young sori. Scales may occur around the base of the sorus. Distribution: Central eastern to southeastern Queensland, New South Wales, and eastern Victoria, Australia, often growing in pure stands in rain forest and southern *Nothofagus* forest on mountain slopes, near streams, and in gullies as high as 1200 m.

*Cyathea leichhardtiana* is named after the 19th-century explorer Friedrich Wilhelm Ludwig Leichhardt (1813–1848). It is a medium-sized tree fern with prickly spines, a smallish crown, and relatively dark green fronds. If the genus *Sphaeropteris* is recognized, Carel Presl's specific name *australis* has priority; this would lead to confusion with *C. australis*, also from Australia and commonly cultivated. *Cyathea leichhardtiana* is possibly less attractive as a garden specimen with its long and sometimes sharp woody spines. It is slow-growing, somewhat frost sensitive, and requires protection from sun and wind.

## *Cyathea lepidocladia* (Christ) Domin 1930

*Alsophila lepidocladia* Christ 1905

*Alsophila* clade. The erect trunk is 2–3 m tall. The crown is sparse; fronds are bipinnate and about 1.5 m long. The stipe has blunt spines and scales toward the base; the scales are glossy, dark brown, and have a paler thin margin. Sori are round, occur in groups of four or five on each fertile segment, and are protected by deep, firm, cup-like indusia. Distribution: Central and eastern New Guinea, locally common in rain forest or mossy forest at 200–1000 m.

## *Cyathea lepifera* (J. Smith ex W. J. Hooker) Copeland 1909

*Alsophila lepifera* J. Smith ex W. J. Hooker 1844, *Sphaeropteris lepifera* (J. Smith ex W. J. Hooker) Tryon 1970, *Cyathea umbrosa* Copeland 1935, *C. pteridioides* Copeland 1960

*Sphaeropteris* clade. The erect trunk may be as tall as about 6 m and 10–15 cm in diameter. Stipe bases often leave prominent oval scars. Fronds are tripinnate, dark green above, pale beneath, and may reach about 2 m in length. The rachis is pale and has darker warts. The stipe is green above, purple beneath, and may have warts and scattered scales; the scales are thin, linear, and pale, with the edges bearing setae. Sori are round and occur near the midvein of the fertile pinnules; indusia are absent. Distribution: Southern China, Taiwan, Ryukyu Islands, the Philippines, and New Guinea, in montane forest on limestone at 2400–2900 m.

*Cyathea lepifera* is a medium-sized, fast-growing tree fern with a crown of large, whorled fronds. It is apparently allied to *C. contaminans*.

### *Cyathea leucofolis* Domin 1929

*Alsophila leucolepis* Martius 1834, not *Cyathea leucolepis* Martius 1834;
*Trichipteris leucolepis* (Martius) Tryon 1970

*Cyathea* clade. The erect trunk is about 1 m tall. Fronds are bipinnate and about 2 m or more long. The rachis is brown and has scattered scales that are brown with a slightly lighter margin and a central streak. Sori occur between the fertile pinnule midvein and the edge of the lamina; indusia are absent. Distribution: Serra do Mar in Brazil, in forest at 40–1000 m.

*Cyathea leucofolis* is also commonly known as *Alsophila leucolepis* or *Trichipteris leucolepis*. When transferred to *Cyathea*, the name *leucolepis* is no longer available, hence the use of *leucofolis* suggested by Karel Domin.

### *Cyathea leucolepis* Mettenius 1863

*Sphaeropteris leucolepis* (Mettenius) Tryon 1970

*Sphaeropteris* clade. The erect, slender trunk is 3–5 m tall. Fronds are bi- or tripinnate and 2–3 m long. The stipe is covered with scales and may have warts when the scales fall; the scales are small, sometimes bullate, and pale. Sori occur halfway between the pinnule midvein and the edge of the lobe and are covered with indusia. Distribution: Vanuatu, common in wet forest at 900–1200 m.

### *Cyathea leucotricha* Christ 1905

*Sphaeropteris leucotricha* (Christ) Tryon 1970, *Cyathea cyclodonta*
    Alderwerelt van Rosenburgh 1908

*Sphaeropteris* clade. The erect trunk may be as tall as about 6 m. Fronds are tripinnate, dark green, and may reach about 2 m in length. The stipe may have many minute warts and scattered scales; the scales are dark brown and have edges bearing setae. Sori occur near the midvein of fertile pinnules and are covered with thin, pale indusia. Distribution: Borneo, scattered in wet forest as high as 700 m.

*Cyathea leucotricha* is similar to *C. strigosa* from southwestern Sulawesi (Celebes).

### *Cyathea lockwoodiana* (Windisch) Lellinger 1984

*Sphaeropteris lockwoodiana* Windisch 1976

*Cyathea* clade. The erect trunk may be as tall as about 6 m. Fronds are bipinnate to almost tripinnate and about 2.5 m long. The stipe is warty and covered in scales, especially toward the base. Scales are either bullate and whitish or narrow and light brown; bullate scales are also present on pinnule veins. Sori occur on fertile pinnules between the midvein and the pinnule margin; indusia are absent. Distribution: Panama; Venezuela and Colombia. Plants are found in forest at 25–700 m.

*Cyathea lockwoodiana* is a complex species closely related to *C. aterrima*, from which it differs in the presence of bullate scales on pinnule veins, and is similar to *C. parianensis* and *C. senilis*.

### *Cyathea loerzingii* Holttum 1962

*Alsophila loerzingii* (Holttum) Tryon 1970

*Alsophila* clade. The erect trunk may be as tall as about 3 m or more. Fronds are bi- or tripinnate and 1–2 m long. The stipe has a few warts toward the base and is covered with a few scattered scales that are glossy dark brown and have a narrow paler margin. Sori occur near the midvein of fertile pinnules and are covered by firm, brown, scale-like indusia. Distribution: Sumatra in forest at 1300–1400 m.

*Cyathea loerzingii* is named after Julius August Lörzing (1872–1945), who collected plants in Indonesia.

### *Cyathea loheri* Christ 1906

*Alsophila loheri* (Christ) Tryon 1970, *Cyathea fructuosa*
   Copeland in Elmer 1908

*Alsophila* clade. The erect trunk is 5–10 m tall and about 15 cm in diameter. Fronds are tripinnate and about 2 m long; the lowest pinnae are usually reduced. The rachis and stipe are brown to purple–dark brown and have wart-like projections and scales; the scales are lanceolate and pale brown, or minute and irregular, with fragile edges. Sori are round and borne in two rows, one on either side of the pinnule midvein; indusia are cup-like to globose and glossy brown to purplish. Distribution: Philippines, southern Taiwan, and Kinabalu on Borneo, in wet forest, forest margins, and on hillsides at 600–2500 m.

*Cyathea loheri* is named after botanist August Loher (1874–1930), who collected in the Philippines as well as Madagascar. It is very similar to *C. oinops*. If the two species were united, *C. oinops* is the older name and would take precedence.

## *Cyathea longipes* Copeland 1917

*Alsophila longipes* (Copeland) Tryon 1970

*Alsophila* clade. The erect trunk may be as tall as 2–4 m. Fronds are tripinnate and 1–2 m long. The stipe is slender, dark, and very spiny, especially toward the base where there are also scattered scales that are broad, pale, and glossy. Sori are round, borne close to the fertile pinnule midvein, and covered by thin indusia. Distribution: Kinabalu on Borneo, in ridge forest at 1250–1500 m.

## *Cyathea lunulata* (J. Forster) Copeland 1929

*Polypodium lunulatum* J. Forster 1786, *Sphaeropteris lunulata*
(J. Forster) Tryon 1970, *Cyathea naumannii* (Kuhn) Domin 1929,
*C. veitchii* (Baker) Domin 1929, *C. vitiensis* (Carruthers) Domin 1929,
*C. ponapeana* (Hosokawa) Glassman 1952

BALABALA, BALABALA BALAKA

PLATES 61–63

*Sphaeropteris* clade. The erect trunk may be as tall as 8–10 m, occasionally 20 m. Fronds are tripinnate and may reach about 6 m in length. The rachis and stipe are greenish to black and may be smooth or have fine warts, along with plentiful scales that are pale, thin, and have marginal setae. Sori occur in pairs of two to six and lack indusia but may be surrounded by a cluster of scales. Distribution: Bismarck Archipelago and Solomon Islands to Vanuatu, New Caledonia, Fiji, Tonga, Samoa, and the Caroline and Mariana Islands, in tropical and subtropical rain forest and coastal forest, from sea level to 100 m.

The common names balabala and balabala balaka are Fijian. *Cyathea lunulata* is a large tree fern, related to *C. medullaris*. Fijian plants, and possibly those of Samoa, are often recognized as *C. lunulata* subsp. *vitiensis* Carruthers in Seeman. These differ only in the type of scales on the lower pinnule veins and may not be significantly distinct.

## *Cyathea lurida* (Blume) Copeland 1901

*Chnoophora lurida* Blume 1828, *Alsophila lurida* (Blume)
W. J. Hooker 1844, *Cyathea kingii* (C. B. Clarke in Beddome)
Copeland 1909, not *C. kingii* Rosenstock 1911 (see *C. werneri*)

*Alsophila* clade. The erect trunk is 1–2 m tall. Fronds are bipinnate and 1–2 m long. The stipe is long, very dark, and rough near the base after the scales fall; the scales are dark and have a paler margin. Sori almost cover the lower surface of the fertile pinnule lobes and lack indusia. Distribution: Sumatra, Malay Peninsula, western Java, and the Philippines, in ridge forest and mossy forest at 1250–1800 m.

## *Cyathea macarthurii* (F. von Mueller) Baker 1874

*Hemitelia macarthurii* F. von Mueller 1874, not *Alsophila macarthurii*
W. J. Hooker 1866 (see *Cyathea leichhardtiana*); *C. moorei* Baker in
W. J. Hooker & Baker 1874, not *A. moorei* J. Smith 1866 (identity cannot
be determined from the poor type material); *A. ferdinandii* Tryon 1970

*Alsophila* clade. The erect trunk may be as tall as about 5 m; it may retain fronds and stipe bases or be clear, with round scars. Fronds are bipinnate and may reach 2–3 m in length. The stipe is brown and has prickly spines and scales; the scales may be long and brown. Sori occur in two rows, one along each side of the pinnule midvein, and have saucer-like indusia. Distribution: Lord Howe Island, Australia, very common in shaded moist forest along streams and in scrub from sea level to 600 m.

The name *macarthurii* commemorates botanist William MacArthur (1800–1882), who collected in Australia. *Cyathea macarthurii* has a shaggy appearance. Plants are fast-growing and may be cultivated in humus provided with consistent moisture and shelter.

## *Cyathea macgillivrayi* (Baker) Domin 1929

*Alsophila macgillivrayi* Baker 1874, *Cyathea gracillima* Copeland 1942

*Alsophila* clade. The erect trunk is about 4 m tall and has side shoots and/or basal trunks. Fronds are few, bipinnate, and may reach 1–1.5 m in length, forming a sparse crown. The stipe is dark brown toward the base, warty, and covered in scattered scales that are brown and have narrow fragile edges. Sori occur halfway between the fertile pinnule midvein and the edge of the lamina; indusia are absent, but one or two scales may occur at the base of a sorus. Distribution: New Guinea and the Louisiade Archipelago, in forest and on montane ridges as high as 2000 m, but most abundant at lower elevations, about 300 m.

### *Cyathea macgregorii* F. von Mueller 1889

*Alsophila macgregorii* (F. von Mueller) Tryon 1970

*Alsophila* clade. The erect trunk is about 3 m tall and about 24 cm in diameter. Fronds are narrow, tripinnate, about 1 m long, and occur in groups of about 60, forming a rounded crown. The stipe is warty and covered with scattered scales toward the base; the scales are either glossy brown, with a paler dull margin, or small, pale, and fringed. Sori occur in groups of four to six per pinnule lobe and are covered by firm brown indusia. Distribution: New Guinea in open peaty grassland or forest margins, often forming groups, at 3000–3700 m.

    *Cyathea macgregorii* is named after William MacGregor (1846–1919), who collected plants in New Guinea as well as other places. It is similar to *C. imbricata* and very similar to *C. gleichenioides*, differing only in details of frond morphology. It is possible these variations are ecological and that the species should be united.

### *Cyathea macrocarpa* (C. B. Presl) Domin 1929

*Hemitelia macrocarpa* C. B. Presl 1847

*Cyathea* clade. The erect trunk may be as tall as 5 m tall. Fronds are bipinnate and 1–2 m long. The stipe is warty and scaly toward the base; the scales are whitish to straw-colored and have entire or hairy edges. Sori occur at the fork of a vein, almost parallel to the margin of the pinnule, and are covered by thin, translucent, two-lobed, scale-like indusia. Distribution: Guiana Highlands of northern South America, in swamps and forests at 100–600 m.

### *Cyathea macrophylla* Domin 1930

*Hemitelia ledermannii* Brause 1920, *Sphaeropteris ledermannii*
    (Brause) Tryon 1970

*Sphaeropteris* clade. Distribution: New Guinea from sea level to about 2000 m. *Cyathea macrophylla* is a short, variable tree fern similar to *C. tripinnata* but differing in its firmer fronds and abundant small scales on the lower surface of the frond veins. If the genus *Sphaeropteris* is recognized, Guido Brause's specific name *ledermannii* takes precedence. There is one named variety, *quadripinnata* (Domin) Holttum.

### *Cyathea macropoda* Domin 1930

*Alsophila macropoda* (Domin) Tryon 1970

*Alsophila* clade. The erect trunk is about 5 m tall or more. Fronds are bi- or tripinnate and 2–3 m long. The stipe is dark at the base, armed with spines, and covered with scattered scales that are dark and have pale fragile edges. Sori occur near the midvein of fertile pinnules and are covered by thin, translucent indusia. Distribution: Central Sumatra in montane forest at 2000–2400 m.

*Cyathea macropoda* is similar to *C. alpicola*, *C. magnifolia*, and *C. polycarpa* of Sumatra.

### *Cyathea macrosora* (Baker) Domin 1929
*Alsophila macrosora* Baker 1886

*Cyathea* clade. The erect trunk is 3–5 m tall and 3–8 cm in diameter. Fronds are bipinnate and may reach 2 m in length. The rachis is light brown to brown and has numerous small whitish or straw-colored scales and hairs. The stipe is scaly toward the base. Other rachis and stipe scales are bicolored, dark brown with a paler margin. Sori occur on vein forks and are covered with thin, translucent, scale-like indusia. Distribution: Costa Rica; Colombia to Venezuela, Guyana, and Brazil. Plants are found in tropical and submontane rain forest along paths and streams at 100–2100 m.

*Cyathea macrosora* is an extremely variable species with three varieties: *macrosora* from Venezuela and Mount Roraima, *vaupensis* (Windisch) A. R. Smith in Colombia and Venezuela at 100–700 m, and *reginae* (Windisch) A. R. Smith from Colombia, Venezuela, Guyana, and Brazil.

### *Cyathea madagascarica* Bonaparte 1920

*Alsophila* clade. The trunk is short and erect. Fronds are bipinnate and about 2 m long. The rachis is grooved and has scales that are thick and dark, almost black-brown. Sori occur near the midvein of fertile pinnules and are covered by large, cup-like indusia. Distribution: Madagascar.

### *Cyathea magna* Copeland 1942
*Sphaeropteris magna* (Copeland) Tryon 1970

*Sphaeropteris* clade. The erect trunk may be as tall as 8 m. Fronds occur in groups of 8–14 in a spirally arranged crown, are bi- or tripinnate, and about 3 m long or more. The stipe is medium brown and has warts, glossy basal spines, and scales that are large, firm, and pale or medium brown, or small and brown to pale. Sori occur near the midvein of fertile pinnules and lack indusia. Distribution: New Guinea in open areas in forest or grassland at 1700–2750 m.

*Cyathea magna* is apparently allied to *C. tomentosa* of Java, differing in having narrower stipe scales and rigid pinnules, and is also similar to *C. crinita* of Sri Lanka and southern India.

## *Cyathea magnifolia* Alderwerelt van Rosenburgh 1920

*Alsophila magnifolia* (Alderwerelt van Rosenburgh) Tryon 1970

*Alsophila* clade. The erect trunk is about 5 m tall or more. Fronds are bi- or tripinnate, about 3 m long, and may persist as an irregular skirt about the trunk. The stipe is dark, spiny, and covered with a few scattered scales that are either dark glossy brown, with broad, pale, fragile edges, or small and finely fringed. Sori occur near the midvein of fertile pinnules and are covered by thin, fragile, saucer-like indusia. Distribution: Sumatra in montane rain forest at 110–2000 m.

*Cyathea magnifolia* is similar to *C. polycarpa* but differs in being larger and in having spines on the stipes. *Cyathea alpicola* and *C. macropoda* may also be allied to it.

## *Cyathea manniana* W. J. Hooker 1865

*Alsophila manniana* (W. J. Hooker) Tryon 1970, *Cyathea usambarensis* Hieronymus in Engler & Prantl 1895

PLATE 64

*Alsophila* clade. The erect trunk is about 6 m tall and covered with old fronds. Fronds are bipinnate and as long as 2–4 m. The rachis and stipe are brown and have small scales that are brown, glossy, and have fragile edges. The stipe bears black spines. Sori are round, with cup-like brown indusia. Distribution: Liberia to Zimbabwe and Mozambique, in wet forest near streams as high as 2300 m.

*Cyathea manniana*, also commonly known as *C. usambarensis*, is named after Gustav Mann (1836–1916), who collected the type specimen at an elevation of 100 m from the island of Bioko (Fernando Póo). It is a widely distributed tree fern throughout the wetter parts of Africa. Its stems may produce stolons or offshoots. Frond material has long been used as an anthelmintic (see Chapter 1, under Ethnobotany).

## *Cyathea marattioides* Willdenow in Kaulfuss 1824

*Alsophila marattioides* (Willdenow) Tryon 1970, *Cyathea cordata* (Desvaux) Mettenius ex Diels in Engler & Prantl 1899

*Alsophila* clade. The erect trunk is 3–4 m tall. Fronds are bipinnate and 2–3 m long. Rachis and trunk scales are lanceolate and bicolored, with a glossy dark brown center and paler margin. Sori occur near the midvein of fertile pinnules and are small, with fragile globose indusia. Distribution: Madagascar.

*Cyathea marattioides* is a member of a complex that also includes *C. perrieriana*, *C. serratifolia*, and *C. tsilotsilensis*.

Plate 1. Gametophytes showing emergent sporophytes. John Braggins.

Plate 2. *Angiopteris evecta* (J. R. Forster) Hoffman with a 50-cm-tall trunk. Istana Park, Singapore. Mark Large.

Plate 3. *Blechnum cycadifolia* (Colla) Sturm on a grassy slope, Juan Fernández Islands. John Engel.

Plate 4. *Blechnum discolor* (G. Forster) Keyserl in forest understory, showing the short trunk and new fronds. Mount Ruapehu, North Island of New Zealand. Mark Large.

Plate 5. *Blechnum discolor*, recently planted trunks showing the first signs of new growth. North Island of New Zealand. Mark Large.

Plate 6. *Blechnum gibbum* (Labillardière) Mettenius. Botanic Gardens, Singapore. Mark Large.

Plate 7. *Blechnum magellanica* (Desvaux) Mettenius, a group of plants all with short trunks. Alerce Costero, Chile. Martin Gardiner.

Plate 8. *Blechnum magellanica,* showing new frond growth. Alerce Mountian Lodge Forest, Chile. Martin Gardiner.

Plate 9. *Calochlaena dubia,* forming a characteristic clump above a bank. Thornleigh, Sydney, Australia. Mark Large.

Plate 10. *Calochlaena straminea* in wet forest. New Caledonia. John Braggins.

Plate 11. *Cibotium barometz*. Botanic Gardens, Singapore. Mark Large.

Plate 12. *Cibotium barometz,* showing the trunk covered in furry golden hairs. Botanic Gardens, Singapore. Mark Large.

Plate 13. *Cibotium chamissoi* in forest on Ohau, Hawaii. John Braggins.

Plate 14. Fronds of *Cibotium glaucum,* showing the whitish blush from which this tree fern gets the name *glaucum*. John Braggins.

Plate 15. *Cibotium glaucum,* detail of the erect truck covered in reddish brown hairs. John Braggins.

Plate 16. *Cibotium menziesii* in forest on Ohau, Hawaii. John Braggins.

Plate 17. *Cibotium schiedei.* Mexico. John Braggins.

Plate 18. *Cibotium schiedei,* detail of the trunk, showing offshoots or pups, which may be detached from the main plant and treated as cuttings. John Braggins.

Plate 19. *Cladophlebis* frond fossil from Jurassic deposits at Waikato, North Island of New Zealand. John Braggins.

Plate 20. *Cyathea aramaganensis*, detail of the trunk, showing glossy brown scales and greenish stipe bases. John Braggins.

Plate 21. *Cyathea arborea* on a road margin. Luquillo Mountains, Puerto Rico. Peter Bellingham.

Plate 22. *Cyathea australis* in forest. Some stipe bases have been retained, forming an irregular skirt. New South Wales, Australia. John Braggins.

Plate 23. *Cyathea australis*, detail of trunk, showing the stipe bases. John Braggins.

Plate 24. *Cyathea baileyana*, a native of northeastern Queensland, Australia (here, cultivated in a sheltered location at the Royal Botanic Gardens, Sydney). This species is frost sensitive but may be grown against a wall or under glass. Mark Large.

Plate 25. *Cyathea bicrenata*. Lowveld National Botanical Garden, Nelspruit, South Africa. John Braggins.

Plate 26. *Cyathea bicrenata,* detail of the trunk apex, showing brown scales and young frond stipes. John Braggins.

Plate 27. Maquique at Cuetzalán, Mexico, obtained from *Cyathea bicrenata*. Blanca Pérez-García.

Plate 28. *Cyathea brownii*, mature plants growing at the forest margin. Norfolk Island, Australia (with Margout Christian). John Braggins.

Plate 29. *Cyathea brownii* trunk apex with stipe bases covered in pale scales. Stipes and fronds are retained on quick-growing younger plants. John Braggins.

Plate 30. *Cyathea capensis,* detail of the lower pinnules about the apex of the plant. John Braggins.

Plate 31. *Cyathea capitata.* Mountain Garden, Kinabalu. Ewen Cameron.

Plate 32. *Cyathea colensoi*, an illustration from *The Botany of the Antarctic Voyage of H.M. Discovery Ships Erebus and Terror* (J. D. Hooker 1844–1860). Reproduced with permission of the Alexander Turnbull Library, Wellington, New Zealand.

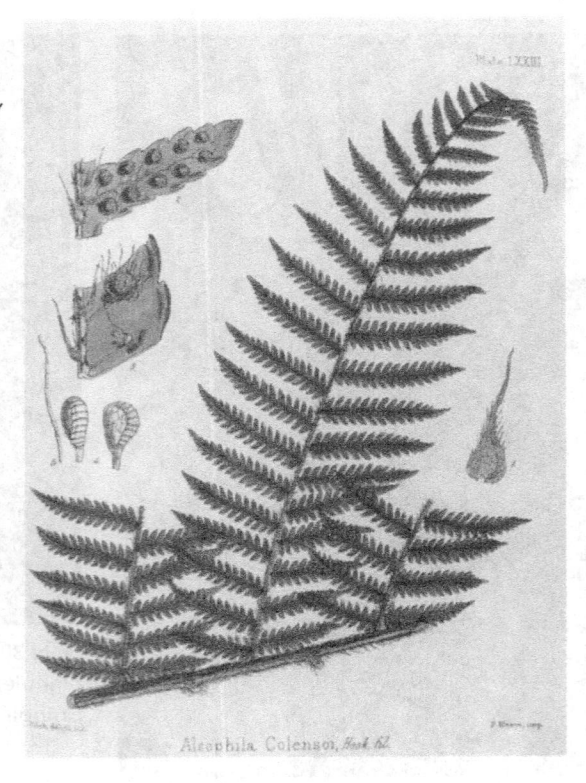

Plate 33. *Cyathea colensoi* in montane forest as part of the understory. These plants lack trunks and form large clumps or thickets. Central North Island of New Zealand. John Braggins.

Plate 34. *Cyathea contaminans,* a very common tree fern in forest throughout Malesia (here, cultivated in Hawaii). John Braggins.

Plate 35. *Cyathea cooperi*. Royal Botanic Gardens, Sydney, Australia. Mark Large.

Plate 36. *Cyathea cooperi* 'Brentwood' in Hawaii, where the species, native to Australia, is considered invasive. John Braggins.

Plate 37. *Cyathea cooperi,* detail of trunk apex. John Braggins.

Plate 38. *Cyathea costaricensis.* San Gabriel, Costa Rica. John Mickel.

Plate 39. *Cyathea cunninghamii,* one of the tallest tree ferns, often called the gully tree fern because of its tendency to grow in deep gullies, or slender tree fern in reference to its narrow trunk. Here, a mature plant is growing in rain forest, southern New South Wales, Australia. John Braggins.

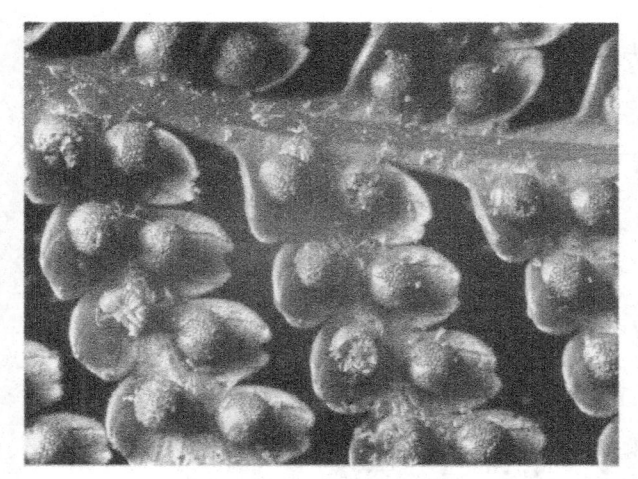

Plate 40. Underside of a frond of *Cyathea cunninghamii,* showing the mature sporangia within the sori. Spores can be collected at this stage by allowing pinnules to dry in a paper packet. John Braggins.

Plate 41. *Cyathea dealbata,* characteristic of wet forest in New Zealand where this tree fern is recognized as a national emblem and icon. Here, two plants are growing in a *Podocarpus* forest in the central North Island. John Braggins.

Plate 42. *Cyathea dealbata.* Rob Lucas.

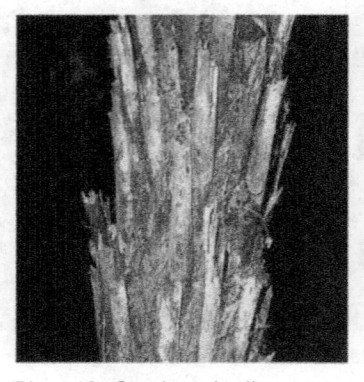

Plate 43. *Cyathea dealbata,* detail of the trunk, showing the stipe bases. John Braggins.

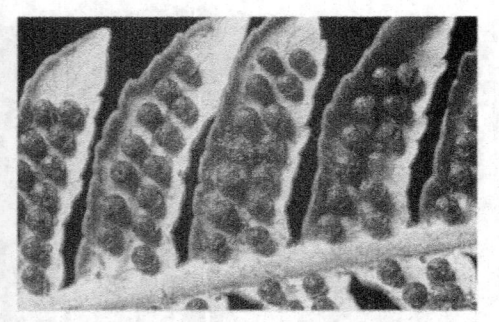

Plate 44. *Cyathea dealbata,* detail of the white underside of the frond, contrasting with the brown sori. This whitish coloration gives the fern its New Zealand common name, silver fern. John Braggins.

Plate 45. *Cyathea decurrens* in rain forest. Taipara, Rarotonga, Cook Islands. Ewen Cameron.

Plate 46. *Cyathea dregei.* Kirstenbosch National Botanical Garden, South Africa. John Braggins.

Plate 47. *Cyathea dregei,* frost damage causing frond dieback on a group of plants in a garden at Magoebaskloof, South Africa. Fanie Venter.

Plate 48. Fire damage to *Cyathea dregei*. South Africa. John Braggins.

Plate 49. *Cyathea furfuracea* (upper left) and *C. pubens* at 1650 m at the headwaters of the Clyde River, Jamaica. Peter Bellingham.

Plate 50. *Cyathea gigantea,* young plants growing on a damp bank. Sri Lanka. John Braggins.

Plate 51. *Cyathea hookeri* rising above scrub in forest understory. Sri Lanka. John Braggins.

Plate 52. *Cyathea intermedia* in rain forest. New Caledonia. John Braggins.

Plate 53. *Cyathea intermedia,* detail of the trunk, showing pale scales and stipe bases. Cultivated plant. John Braggins.

Plate 54. *Cyathea kermadecensis,* a native of Raoul Island in the Kermadec Islands. Auckland University, North Island of New Zealand. John Braggins.

Plate 55. *Cyathea kermadecensis,* detail of the trunk apex, showing stipe bases. John Braggins.

Plate 56. New roots formed on the lower trunk of *Cyathea kermadecensis.* John Braggins.

Plate 57. *Cyathea latebrosa* in the fernery, Botanic Gardens, Singapore. Mark Large.

Plate 58. *Cyathea latebrosa,* a variable species usually with a slender trunk. Here, the stipe bases have been trimmed. Botanic Gardens, Singapore. Mark Large.

Plate 59. *Cyathea latebrosa,* detail of the trunk apex, showing stipe bases and spines. Mark Large.

Plate 60. A collection of bromeliads growing on the living trunks of *Cyathea latebrosa.* Botanic Gardens, Singapore. Mark Large.

Plate 61. *Cyathea lunulata* in forest. Tonga. Ewen Cameron.

Plate 62. *Cyathea lunulata*, detail of the apex from a younger plant. Ewen Cameron.

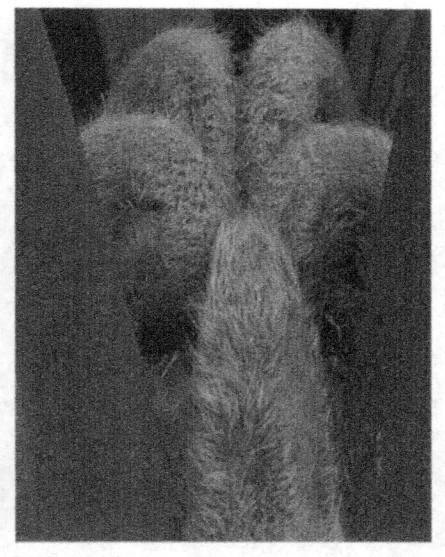

Plate 63. *Cyathea lunulata*, detail of the trunk apex and uncurling fronds covered with scales. Tanna Island, Vanuatu. Ewen Cameron.

Plate 64. *Cyathea manniana,* used as an anthelmintic. David Mabberley.

Plate 65. *Cyathea* ×*marcescens,* a hybrid found in Victoria and Tasmania, Australia (here, cultivated in New South Wales). John Braggins.

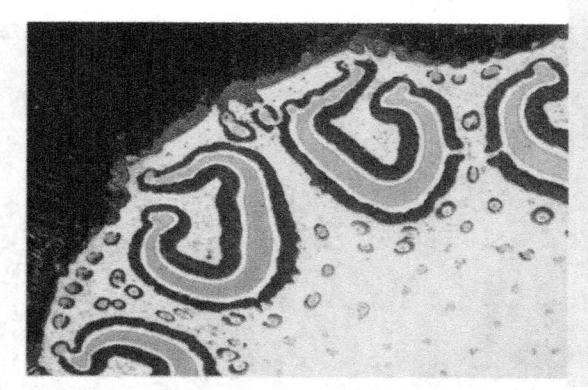

Plate 66. Section of the trunk of *Cyathea medullaris* with bands of dark sclerenchyma tissue surrounding each large vascular bundle. The small rings are vascular traces that run out to the fronds. The large white pith is composed of parenchyma cells. John Braggins.

Plate 67. Vase carved from the central stem of *Cyathea medullaris*. The dark markings are caused by bands of sclerenchyma that surround the vascular bundles and the outside of the trunk. John Braggins.

Plate 68. *Cyathea medullaris*. Kaitaia, New Zealand. John Braggins.

Plate 69. *Cyathea medullaris.* John Braggins.

Plate 70. *Cyathea medullaris,* forming a dense stand to the exclusion of other vegetation. These groves are common on disturbed sites or forest margins in New Zealand. John Braggins.

Plate 71. *Cyathea medullaris.* Rob Lucas.

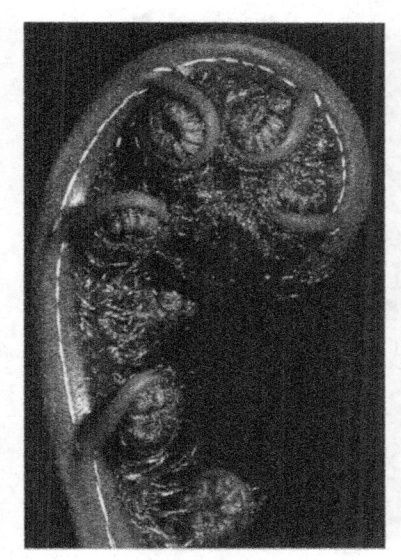

Plate 72. Uncurling frond of *Cyathea medullaris.* John Braggins.

Plate 73. Dieback in *Cyathea medullaris.* It has been suggested that this problem may be the result of a phytoplasma carried by the passionvine hopper. However, proof is difficult to obtain, and the cause is unconfirmed. John Braggins.

Plate 74. *Cyathea mexicana.* San Vito, Costa Rica. Robbin Moran.

Plate 75. *Cyathea mexicana,* young frond. John Mickel.

Plate 76. *Cyathea milnei,* a native of Raoul Island in the Kermadec Islands. Auckland University, North Island of New Zealand. John Braggins.

Plate 77. *Cyathea novae-caledoniae,* a mature plant in rain forest. Col de Amica, New Caledonia. John Braggins.

Plate 78. *Cyathea parksii* on a ridge surrounded by rain forest. Rarotonga, Cook Islands. Ewen Cameron.

Plate 79. *Cyathea parksii*, detail of trunk apex with a few dead stipe bases still attached. Ewen Cameron.

Plate 80. *Cyathea podophylla*, an illustration from *A Second Century of Ferns* (W. J. Hooker 1861).

Plate 81. *Cyathea princeps*. John Braggins.

Plate 82. *Cyathea princeps,* detail of trunk apex, showing reddish brown scales and a developing new frond. John Braggins.

Plate 83. *Cyathea pubens,* dense grove (with a single *C. furfuracea* at center right) at 1850 m, northeast of Sir John Peak, gully of the Spanish River, Jamaica. Peter Bellingham.

Plate 84. *Cyathea pubens* in the mist at 1600 m, Grand Ridge of the Blue Mountains, Jamaica. Peter Bellingham.

Plate 85. *Cyathea robertsiana.* John Braggins.

Plate 86. *Cyathea robusta,* a native of Lord Howe Island, showing frond damage after winter. Auckland University, North Island of New Zealand. John Braggins.

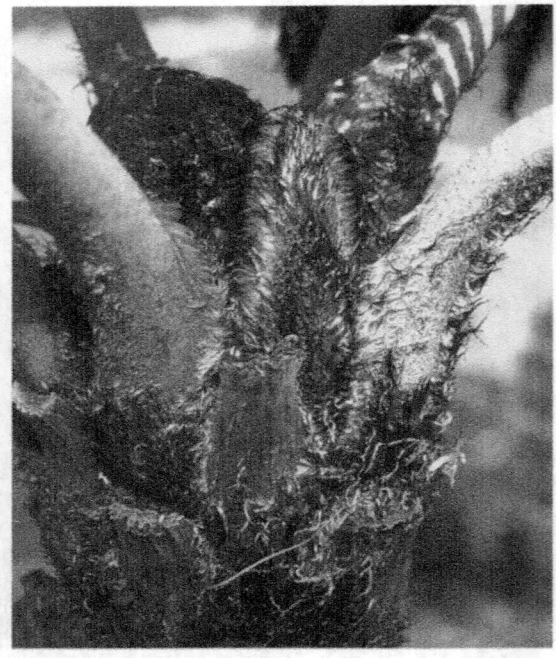

Plate 87. *Cyathea robusta,* detail of trunk apex. John Braggins.

Plate 88. *Cyathea sechellarum,* a young plant in rain forest. Mount Blanc, island of Mahé, Seychelles. Mark Large.

Plate 89. *Cyathea sinuata,* an unusual simple-leaved species, growing on the forest floor. Sri Lanka. John Braggins.

Plate 90. *Cyathea smithii,* an illustration from *The Botany of the Antarctic Voyage of H.M. Discovery Ships Erebus and Terror* (J. D. Hooker 1844–1860). Reproduced with permission of the Alexander Turnbull Library, Wellington, New Zealand.

Plate 91. *Cyathea smithii* grove. Rob Lucas.

Plate 92. *Cyathea smithii* with a skirt formed of dead stipes. New Zealand. John Braggins.

Plate 93. *Cyathea smithii* (with *Dicksonia squarrosa* visible in the foreground), showing a flush of fronds typical of spring growth, in rain forest. Haast, South Island of New Zealand. John Braggins.

Plate 94. *Cyathea smithii.* Franz Josef Glacier, South Island of New Zealand. Mark Large.

Plate 95. *Cyathea spinulosa* on a roadside. Yaku Shima, Japan. John Braggins.

Plate 96. *Cyathea tenggerensis,* a native of Indonesia (here, cultivated in South Africa). John Braggins.

Plate 97. *Cyathea tomentosissima* in scrub. New Guinea. John Braggins.

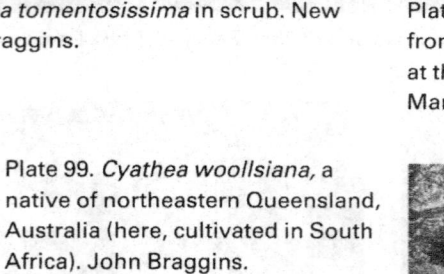

Plate 98. *Cyathea vieillardii,* a variable tree fern from New Caledonia and Vanuatu (here, cultivated at the Royal Botanic Gardens, Sydney, Australia). Mark Large.

Plate 99. *Cyathea woollsiana,* a native of northeastern Queensland, Australia (here, cultivated in South Africa). John Braggins.

Plate 100. *Dicksonia antarctica,* young plants along the road to Mount Field, Tasmania. John Braggins.

Plate 101. *Dicksonia antarctica,* detail of the trunk apex, showing many new fronds tightly curled and ready for spring growth. John Braggins.

Plate 102. *Dicksonia arborescens,* endemic to St. Helena in the Atlantic (here, cultivated at Auckland University, North Island of New Zealand). John Braggins.

Plate 103. *Dicksonia arborescens,* detail of the trunk apex. John Braggins.

Plate 104. *Dicksonia baudouini,* a native of New Caledonia (here, in a garden in Auckland, North Island of New Zealand). Mark Large.

Plate 105. *Dicksonia externa* on sea cliffs. Juan Fernández Islands, Chile. John Engel.

Plate 106. Section of the trunk of *Dicksonia fibrosa* with a wide fibrous root mantle incorporating old stipe bases and surrounding a small stem. Bands of dark sclerenchyma tissue surround interconnecting vascular bundles that in turn form a ring around a white pith of starchy parenchyma. John Braggins.

Plate 107. *Dicksonia fibrosa*. Rob Lucas.

Plate 108. *Dicksonia fibrosa,* mature plants with characteristic skirts formed from dead fronds. Taken in late winter before the spring flush of new grown, the old fronds show some frost damage. Okarito, South Island of New Zealand. John Braggins.

Plate 109. *Dicksonia lanata* in montane forest, a prostrate form suitable for cooler regions. Central North Island of New Zealand. John Braggins.

Plate 110. *Dicksonia lanata* with a slender trunk, growing in warm, moist, kauri (*Agathis australis*) forest, northern North Island, New Zealand. This erect form is difficult to grow. John Braggins.

Plate 111. *Dicksonia sellowiana.* Ecuador. Robbin Moran.

Plate 112. *Dicksonia sellowiana,* a native of Central and South America (here, cultivated in Dublin, Ireland). John Braggins.

Plate 113. *Dicksonia squarrosa,* on a stream margin, one of the most common tree ferns in New Zealand and is easy to cultivate. Plants may have an untidy appearance, with multiple trunks and an irregular skirt of dead fronds. Westland, South Island of New Zealand. John Braggins.

Plate 114. *Dicksonia squarrosa*, detail of uncurling frond and mature frond. Rob Lucas.

Plate 115. *Dicksonia squarrosa*, detail of the underside of a fertile frond, showing the sori. John Braggins.

Plate 116. Fence made from the trunks of *Dicksonia squarrosa*. Auckland, New Zealand. John Braggins.

Plate 117. *Dicksonia thyrsopteroides,* detail of the lower portion of a fertile frond. Mark Large.

Plate 118. *Dicksonia thyrsopteroides* (a native of New Caledonia, here cultivated at the Royal Botanic Gardens, Sydney, Australia), detail of the trunk apex and newly emerging fronds. Mark Large.

Plate 119. *Diplazium dietrichianum* (Luerssen) C. Christensen, a native of Queensland, Australia (here, cultivated at the Royal Botanic Gardens, Sydney). This vigorous plant forms a spreading colony. It is easy to grow in a warm garden or as a tub plant in cooler areas. Plants grow best in filtered sun and should be protected from frost. Mark Large.

Plate 120. *Leptopteris hymenophylloides* in rain forest. Unawheo, North Island of New Zealand. John Braggins.

Plate 121. *Leptopteris superba* in cool, humid forest. Fiordland, South Island of New Zealand, where rainfall can exceed 7 m per year. John Braggins.

Plate 122. *Lophosoria quadripinnata.* Valdivia, Chile. Magaly Riveros.

Plate 123. *Osmunda regalis* in woodland. John Braggins.

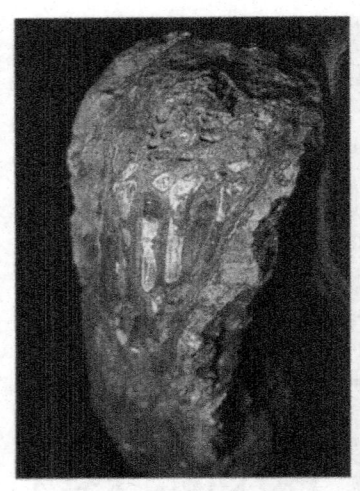

Plate 124. *Osmundacaulis* stem fossil, showing trunk apex with stipe bases, from Jurassic deposits at Waikato, North Island of New Zealand. John Braggins.

Plate 125. *Pneumatopteris pennigera* (G. Forster) Holttum in rain forest, a fern sometimes found on limestone. Mature plants may develop a slender trunk taller than 1 m. Plants are easily cultivated provided they are given protection from wind and frost. North Island of New Zealand. John Braggins.

Plate 126. *Sadleria cyatheoides* in forest. Oahu, Hawaii. John Braggins.

Plate 127. *Sadleria cyatheoides* on a lava flow. Oahu, Hawaii. John Braggins.

Plate 128. *Sadleria cyatheoides,* growing from a rock crevice. Oahu, Hawaii. John Braggins.

Plate 129. *Sadleria pallida* on a roadside bank. Oahu, Hawaii. John Braggins.

Plate 130. *Todea barbara,* showing the massive compound trunk. Royal Botanic Gardens, Sydney, Australia. Mark Large.

Plate 131. *Todea barbara,* detail of the fertile frond, showing a dense aggregation of sporangia. Spores are released when they are green. John Braggins.

## *Cyathea* ×*marcescens* N. A. Wakefield 1942

*Alsophila* ×*marcescens* (N. A. Wakefield) Tryon 1970
SKIRTED TREE FERN
PLATE 65

*Alsophila* clade. The erect trunk may be as tall as about 10 m; dead fronds often persist and hang about the trunk. Fronds are bi- or tripinnate and 3–4 m long. Rachis and trunk scales are dark brown and shiny. The stipe is thick, black, and warty. Sori occur near the midvein of fertile pinnules and are covered by thin, saucer-like indusia. Distribution: Cape Otway ranges in Victoria, and Tasmania, Australia.

*Cyathea* ×*marcescens* is a naturally occurring hybrid, apparently *C. australis* × *C. cunninghamii*, and has characteristics midway between these two species. Its spores are usually malformed and are sterile. *Cyathea* ×*marcescens* is slow-growing, sensitive to dry conditions, and requires shelter from sun and wind.

## *Cyathea marginalis* (Klotzsch) Domin 1929

*Alsophila marginalis* Klotzsch 1844

*Cyathea* clade. The erect trunk may be as tall as about 6 m. Fronds are bipinnate to almost tripinnate and about 2.5 m long. The stipe is warty and covered in scales toward the base; the scales are bullate and whitish, or narrow and light brown. Sori are about 2 mm from the margin of fertile pinnules; indusia are absent. Distribution: Guyana and Suriname, on forested slopes at 700–1100 m.

*Cyathea marginalis* is closely related to *C. sipapoensis*.

## *Cyathea marginata* (Brause) Domin 1930

*Alsophila marginata* Brause 1920, *Sphaeropteris marginata* (Brause) Tryon 1970

*Sphaeropteris* clade. The erect trunk is about 3 m tall. Fronds are bi- or tripinnate and 1.5–2 m long; one pair of reduced pinnae may occur toward the base of the stipe. The stipe is warty and has scattered scales that are thick, dark, and fleshy. Sori occur near the edge of fertile pinnules; indusia are absent. Distribution: Eastern New Guinea in montane forest at 1400–1500 m.

## *Cyathea masapilidensis* Copeland 1952

*Alsophila masapilidensis* (Copeland) Tryon 1970

*Alsophila* clade. The erect trunk may be as tall as about 3 m tall or more. Fronds are bi- or tripinnate and 1–2 m long. The stipe is slender and spiny and has a few scattered basal scales; the scales are brown and have a pale margin. Sori occur near the midvein of fertile pinnules and are covered by thin, brown, saucer-like indusia. Distribution: Luzon in the Philippines, the name *masapilidensis* referring to Mount Masapilit, Bontoc subprovince, Mountain province, on Luzon.

## *Cyathea media* Wagner 1948

*Alsophila media* (Wagner) Tryon 1970

*Alsophila* clade. The erect trunk is about 2 m tall. Fronds are tripinnate as long as 1–2 m. The stipe is dark, warty, and covered with scattered scales that are dark to medium brown and have narrow fragile edges. Sori are near the fertile pinnule midvein and covered by small scale-like indusia. Distribution: Islands northeast of New Guinea, including Manus (which includes the Admiralty Islands and adjacent islands), in forest as high as 1600 m.

## *Cyathea medullaris* (G. Forster) Swartz 1801

*Polypodium medullare* G. Forster 1786, *Sphaeropteris medullaris* (G. Forster) Bernhardi 1801, *Cyathea affinis* W. J. Hooker & Baker 1874

BLACK TREE FERN, KORAU, MAMAKU

FIGURE 4; PLATES 66–73

*Sphaeropteris* clade. The erect trunk may be as tall as about 20 m and 15–20 cm in diameter; it is often covered in scars left by fallen fronds. Fronds are tripinnate and may reach about 6 m in length. The petiole, rachis, and stipe are greenish to black and may have blunt, very short, rough protrusions along with plentiful scales that are dark brown and have a spiny margin. Sori occur in pairs of two to six and are covered with thin indusia. Distribution: Fiji and the Marquesas Islands, Tahiti, and the Austral Islands to Pitcairn Island, and New Zealand, including the Chatham Islands but not the Kermadec Islands, in tropical and subtropical rain forest and coastal forest, sometimes forming single-species stands, emergent in open sites, near streams, and in gullies from sea level to 100 m.

*Cyathea medullaris* is the type species for the genus and one of the largest tree ferns in the world. It is fast-growing, especially when young, and is commonly cultivated. Plants do best in rich, well-drained humus but require shelter and are frost sensitive.

## *Cyathea megalosora* Copeland 1917

*Sphaeropteris megalosora* (Copeland) Tryon 1970

*Sphaeropteris* clade. The erect trunk may be as tall as about 2 m or more. Fronds are pinnate or bipinnate, sometimes almost tripinnate in part, and

0.5–1 m long or more. The stipe is pale to medium brown, densely scaly, or finely warty where scales have fallen; the scales are thin and pale. Sori occur near the midvein of fertile pinnules and are covered by firm, brown, translucent indusia. Distribution: Kinabalu on Borneo, in mossy forest and on ridges at 2200–2900 m.

## *Cyathea mertensiana* (Kunze) Copeland 1909

*Alsophila mertensiana* Kunze 1848, *Sphaeropteris mertensiana* (Kunze) Tryon 1970, *Cyathea medullaris* var. *tripinnata* W. J. Hooker 1844, *A. bongardiana* Mettenius ex Baker 1868

*Sphaeropteris* clade. The erect trunk may be as tall as 2–6 m. Fronds are tripinnate and may reach about 2 m in length. The rachis is pale and has darker warts. The stipe may have warts and scattered scales; the scales are thin, bullate, and pale. Sori are round and occur near the midvein of the fertile pinnules; indusia are absent, but the sori may be partially covered by scales. Distribution: Bonin Islands, south of the main islands of Japan.

The name *mertensiana* commemorates Mertens, the collector of the type material.

## *Cyathea mesosora* Holttum 1962

*Alsophila mesosora* (Holttum) Tryon 1970

*Alsophila* clade. The erect, slender trunk may be as tall as 3 m. Fronds form a sparse crown, are bi- or tripinnate, and about 1.5 m to just over 2 m long. The stipe is dull and has abundant spines and scattered scales; the scales are thick, dark, and fleshy. Sori occur near the midvein of fertile pinnules, usually on secondary vein forks; indusia are absent. Distribution: Eastern New Guinea in forest at 1400 m to about 1800 m.

## *Cyathea metteniana* (Hance) C. Christensen 1934

*Alsophila metteniana* Hance 1868, *A. formosa* Baker 1891, *Cyathea formosana* (Baker) Copeland 1909

*Alsophila* clade. The erect trunk may be as tall as 1 m and 6–10 cm in diameter. Fronds are tripinnate and as long as 1–2.5 m long. The stipe is brown to purple-black and has scales that are long, have a broad base, and are usually bicolored, glossy brown with a paler margin. Sori are round and borne in two rows, one on either side of the pinnule midvein; indusia are absent. Distribution: China; Ryukyu Islands, Japan; and Taiwan. Plants occur in wet forest, forest margins, and on hillsides.

The name *metteniana* commemorates pteridologist Georg Heinrich Mettenius (1823–1866).

### *Cyathea mexicana* Schlechtendal & Chamisso 1830

not *Alsophila mexicana* Martius 1835 (see *Cyathea valdecrenata*);
*Hemitelia firma* Baker 1877, *A. firma* (Baker) Conant 1983

PLATES 74, 75

*Alsophila* clade. The erect trunk may be as tall as 5 m, rarely 10 m, and 5–8 cm in diameter; it has spines and occasional side shoots. Fronds are bipinnate, rarely tripinnate, and as long as 2.5 m. The rachis and stipe are straw-colored to dark brown and have some basal scales that are bicolored, with a dark brown center and pale whitish margin, and have several terminal and lateral setae. Pinnule veins have whitish scales with star-shaped setae. Sori are round, with delicate globose indusia that form on either side of the pinnule midvein. Distribution: Mexico, Guatemala, El Salvador, Honduras, Nicaragua, Costa Rica, and Panama; Ecuador. Plants are found from tropical rain forest to the montane zone in open sites, on riverbanks, and in pastureland at 900–2300 m.

*Cyathea mexicana* is a slender tree fern with an irregular crown of fronds, which have been used to arrest hemorrhage.

### *Cyathea microchlamys* Holttum 1962

*Alsophila microchlamys* (Holttum) Tryon 1970

*Alsophila* clade. The erect trunk may be as tall as about 4 m or more. Fronds are bi- or tripinnate and 1–2 m long. The stipe is finely warty, has a dark base, and is covered with basal scales that are dark, glossy, and have a paler margin. Sori occur near the midvein of fertile pinnules and are covered by scale-like indusia. Distribution: Luzon in the Philippines, in montane forest.

### *Cyathea microdonta* (Desvaux) Domin 1929

*Polypodium microdonton* Desvaux 1811

*Cyathea* clade. The erect trunk may be as tall as 6 m and 5–8 cm in diameter. Fronds are bipinnate and may reach 2.5 m or more in length. The rachis is shiny brown to purplish and glabrous, and has spines. Rachis and stipe scales are brown. Sori occur between the pinnule midvein and the edge of the lamina; indusia are absent. Distribution: Greater Antilles (Cuba, Jamaica, Hispaniola, and Puerto Rico); coastal areas in Mexico and Costa Rica; Colombia, Ecuador, Peru, Bolivia, Venezuela, Guyana, and Brazil (as far south as Rio de Janeiro). Plants are found in tropical and submontane rain forest in wet ground, around lagoons, in swamps, bogs, on riverbanks, in standing or brackish water, or in cleared pastureland, from sea level to 1700 m.

*Cyathea microdonta* is a small to medium-sized tree fern with a very wide distribution and is surprisingly uniform in its morphology. It sometimes grows in thickets and has a slim trunk and somewhat erect crown.

### *Cyathea microlepidota* Copeland 1949

*Sphaeropteris microlepidota* (Copeland) Tryon 1970

*Sphaeropteris* clade. The erect, slender trunk is 3–5 m tall. Fronds are bi- or tripinnate and 2–3 m long. The stipe is dark and covered with warts and scales; the scales are minute, pale, and fringed. Sori occur halfway between the pinnule midvein and the edge of the lobe and are covered with indusia. Distribution: Fiji in wet forest at 100–500 m.

### *Cyathea microphylla* Mettenius 1856

not *Trichipteris microphylla* (Klotzsch) Tryon 1970 (Appendix 1)

*Cyathea* clade. The erect trunk is just over 1 m tall and 1.5–2 cm in diameter. Fronds are tetrapinnate, with unusual small ultimate segments, and as long as about 75 cm. Petioles are brown and have scattered, very broad scales. Distribution: Southern Peru in submontane rain forest, in thickets, at 2100–2800 m.

*Cyathea microphylla* is a very small tree fern with small fronds and distinctively narrow ultimate segments. It is related to *C. multisegmenta*.

### *Cyathea microphylloides* Rosenstock 1913

*Alsophila microphylloides* (Rosenstock) Tryon 1970, not *A. microphylloides* Domin 1929 (see *Trichipteris microphylloides*, Appendix 1)

*Alsophila* clade. The erect trunk is 1–2 m tall. Fronds are bi- or tripinnate and about 1 m long. The rachis and stipe bear many scales that are long, crisp, and either bicolored (dark glossy central region and a whitish margin) or pale with a dull margin, and that have fragile edges. Sori are round, occur in three or four pairs per fertile pinnule segment, and are covered by small, cup-like indusia. Distribution: Eastern and central New Guinea, in forests and valleys on slopes at 1800–3000 m.

*Cyathea microphylloides* appears to be similar to *C. hooglandii*.

### *Cyathea mildbraedii* (Brause) Domin 1929

*Alsophila mildbraedii* Brause 1910

*Alsophila* clade. The erect trunk is about 4 m tall. Fronds are bipinnate and may reach 1–2 m in length. The rachis and stipe are dark. The stipe has many blunt spines and scales; the scales are either very dark and glossy, sometimes with a fragile margin, or small, brown, and bullate. Sori occur at the forks of veins and lack indusia. Distribution: Ruwenzori Mountains on the border of Uganda and the Democratic Republic of Congo (Zaire), in heath forest on ridges.

The name *mildbraedii* commemorates the botanist Gottfried Wilhelm Johannes Mildbraed (1879–1954), who made collections during a number of German expeditions to Africa. *Cyathea mildbraedii* is rare, known only from the Ruwenzori location.

### *Cyathea milnei* W. J. Hooker ex J. D. Hooker 1864

*Alsophila milnei* (W. J. Hooker ex J. D. Hooker) Tryon 1970

PLATE 76

*Alsophila* clade. The erect trunk may be as tall as 8 m; leaf bases are preserved and project from the trunk. Fronds are tripinnate and as long as 4 m; dead fronds may form a skirt around the trunk. The rachis and stipe are pale brown and have brown scales. Sori occur on either side of the pinnule midvein; indusia are cup-like. Distribution: Raoul Island in the Kermadec Islands, New Zealand, where it is common in both wet and dry forest.

*Cyathea milnei* is a medium-sized tree fern with a dense crown. It resembles *C. dealbata* but lacks the silver color on the underside of the fronds. In cultivation, *C. milnei* requires good humus but tolerates little frost and needs some shelter from wind. It will survive in full sun but does best in shade.

### *Cyathea minor* D. C. Eaton 1860

*Alsophila minor* (D. C. Eaton) Tryon 1970

*Alsophila* clade. The erect trunk may be as tall as 7 m and about 11 cm in diameter. Fronds are pinnate and as long as 2.5 m. The rachis and stipe are brown and have a few brown scales beneath. Sori occur in two rows, one on either side of the pinnule midvein; indusia are cup-like and pubescent. Distribution: Cuba and Hispaniola, in wet montane forest at 450–2500 m.

*Cyathea minor* is similar to *Alsophila bryophila* and possibly related to *A. esmeraldensis* (see Appendix 1 for comments on both species). Other hybrids with *C. abbottii* and *C. urbanii* may also occur.

### *Cyathea modesta* (Baker) Copeland 1909

*Alsophila modesta* Baker 1880

*Alsophila* clade. The erect trunk is 2–3 m tall. Fronds are bi- or tripinnate and may reach 2–3 m in length. The stipe is covered in blunt conical spines and scales; the scales are medium brown and have narrow fragile edges. Sori occur near the midvein of fertile pinnules and are covered by firm, brown, scale-like or bilobed indusia. Distribution: Sumatra in wet forest at 1800–2400 m.

### *Cyathea moluccana* R. Brown in Desvaux 1827

*Sphaeropteris moluccana* (R Brown) Tryon 1970, *Cyathea brunonis* Wallich ex W. J. Hooker 1844, *C. pinnata* Roxburgh ex C. B. Clarke 1844, *C. fuscopaleata* Copeland 1917, *C. kinabaluensis* Copeland 1917

*Sphaeropteris* clade. The erect trunk is usually about 50 cm tall. Fronds are pinnate and 1.75–3 m long. The stipe is dark, has basal scales, and may be warty when the scales fall; the scales are firm and medium brown. Sori occur in one to three rows (each row numbering four to six sori, rarely as many as ten) on either side of the midvein of fertile pinnules and are covered, particularly when young, by translucent indusia. Distribution: Malay Peninsula, central Sumatra, Borneo, southern and central Sulawesi (Celebes), and the Moluccas, in forest from near sea level to about 900 m.

*Cyathea moluccana* is often found in association with the variable *C. alternans*.

### *Cyathea moseleyi* Baker 1876

*Sphaeropteris moseleyi* (Baker) Tryon 1970

*Sphaeropteris* clade. The erect trunk is 1–3 m tall. Fronds are bi- or tripinnate and 2–3 m long. The stipe is short and has scattered scales that are dark, thickened in the middle, but not fleshy. Sori occur near the midvein of fertile pinnules and are covered with pale, thin indusia. Distribution: Admiralty Islands in the Bismarck Archipelago, in lowland forest.

*Cyathea moseleyi* is named after Henry Nottidge Moseley (1844–1890), a naturalist on the expedition of the *Challenger* in 1872–1876. It is very similar to *C. brackenridgei* of the Solomon Islands. The relationship between the two species requires investigation.

### *Cyathea mossambicensis* Baker 1891

*Alsophila mossambicensis* (Baker) Tryon 1970, *Cyathea holstii* Hieronymus in Engler & Prantl 1895

*Alsophila* clade. The erect trunk may be as tall as 1 m. Fronds are pinnate and are more than 1 m long. The rachis and stipe are dark and covered with minute warts and basal scales; the scales are glossy brown and have a paler margin. Sori occur in two rows, one on either side of the pinnule midvein; indusia are present and form deep, thin cups. Distribution: Tanzania, Mozambique, and Zimbabwe, in forest on deeply shaded stream banks at 900–1500 m.

## Cyathea mucilagina R. C. Moran 1991

*Cyathea* clade. The erect trunk may be as tall as 2 m and 4–6 cm in diameter. Fronds are bipinnate and may reach 2 m in length. Petioles are yellowish to light brown and may have wings along with spines. The rachis is straw-colored and has wings and whitish hairs. Scales are yellowish. Sori occur in two rows along each side of the pinnule midvein; indusia are absent. Distribution: Costa Rica; Ecuador and Peru. Plants are found in tropical and submontane rain forest in forest understory along stream banks and riverbanks at 600–1000 m.

*Cyathea mucilagina* is a short tree fern with upward-arching fronds and a narrow trunk. It resembles *C. pilosissima* but differs in having dull, matted, brownish white petiole scales and mucilaginous uncurling fronds (hence the name *mucilagina*). *Cyathea mucilagina* is similar to *C. multiflora, C. punctata,* and *C. schiedeana.*

## Cyathea muelleri Baker 1890

*Alsophila muelleri* (Baker) Tryon 1970, *Cyathea longipaleata* Alston 1940

*Alsophila* clade. The erect trunk may be as tall as about 10 m and 15–20 cm in diameter; trunks may be branched, forming a multitrunked stand. Fronds are erect, bi- or tripinnate, 1–1.5 m long, and occur in two whorls of 10–12 each. The stipe is spiny and covered with scales that are twisted, glossy dark brown, and have narrow fragile edges. Sori occur in about six pairs on fertile pinnule segments and are covered by firm brown indusia. Distribution: New Guinea in subalpine scrub and drier grassland at 3500–3600 m.

*Cyathea muelleri* is named after the German-born Australian botanist Ferdinand von Mueller (1825–1896), who collected on New Caledonia and in New Zealand as well as on New Guinea and in Australia. It will grow in cooler areas but may be slightly frost sensitive. It does best in humus with regular moisture. This tree fern is also suitable for cultivation in containers.

## Cyathea multiflora Smith 1793

*Cyathea austroamericana* Domin 1929, *C. columbiana* Domin 1929

*Cyathea* clade. The erect trunk is 1–5 m tall and 4–8 cm in diameter. Fronds are bipinnate and may reach 2 m in length. Petioles are brown to light brown and may have spines. The rachis may or may not have hairs and/or scales; the scales are either shiny brown to dark purplish or bicolored, dark with a whitish margin. Sori occur in two rows along each side of the pinnule midvein and are covered with scale-like indusia. Distribution: Costa Rica; Venezuela, Colombia, Ecuador, Peru, Bolivia, and Brazil. Plants are found in dense tropical and submontane rain forest in the understory, along streams and in clearings from sea level to 1600 m in Central America and as high as 2300 m in the Andes.

*Cyathea multiflora* is a small and variable tree fern with upward-arching fronds and a slim trunk. It is similar to *C. acutidens* and *C. alphonsiana*. The three species may be one. Hybrids between *C. multiflora* and *C. ursina* have been reported from Costa Rica.

### *Cyathea multisegmenta* Tryon 1976

*Cyathea* clade. The erect trunk is just over 2.5 m tall. Fronds are tetrapinnate, with unusual small ultimate segments, and about 4 m long. Petioles are brown and have scattered, very broad scales. Distribution: Southern Peru in dense cloud forest above 1800 m.

Described from a single collection, *Cyathea multisegmenta* is apparently related to *C. microphylla*.

### *Cyathea myosuroides* (Liebmann) Domin 1929

*Alsophila myosuroides* Liebmann 1849, *A. wrightii* Maxon 1920

*Cyathea* clade. The erect trunk may be as tall as about 10 m. Fronds are bipinnate and 2.5–3 m long. The stipe is covered in scales that are narrow and straw-colored to light brown. Stiff hairs may be present along the pinnule midveins. Sori lack sterile hairs about the base; indusia are absent. Distribution: Cuba and Mexico to Nicaragua, at 10–600 m.

### *Cyathea nanna* (Barrington) Lellinger 1987

*Trichipteris nanna* Barrington 1978

*Cyathea* clade. The erect trunk is about 1 m tall. Fronds are pinnate and usually less than about 50 cm long. The rachis is brown to purplish and has warts and scattered scales; the scales are brown and have a slightly lighter broad margin. Sori occur near the midvein of fertile pinnules; indusia are absent. Distribution: Mazaruni River Basin, Guyana, at about 1400 m, known from one collection from Mount Ayanganna.

*Cyathea nanna* is possibly related to *C. demissa*.

### *Cyathea negrosiana* Christ 1907

*Alsophila negrosiana* (Christ) Tryon 1970

*Alsophila* clade. The erect trunk may be as tall as about 3 m or more. Fronds are bi- or tripinnate and 1–2 m long. The stipe is warty and covered with scattered scales that are glossy and dark brown with a paler dull margin. Sori occur near the midvein of fertile pinnules and are covered by thin, brown, saucer-like indusia. Distribution: Negros in the Philippines, in montane forest at about 1000 m, first discovered on Mount Silay.

### *Cyathea nesiotica* (Maxon) Domin 1930

*Alsophila nesiotica* Maxon 1922

*Cyathea* clade. The erect trunk may be as tall as 6 m and 5–8 cm in diameter. Fronds are bipinnate and may reach 2 m in length. Petioles are straw-colored to yellow-brown and have spines or small raised dots. The rachis is straw-colored and may have hairs. Rachis and stipe scales are bicolored, with a golden brown or brown central region and paler margin. Sori occur in two rows along each side of the pinnule midvein; indusia are absent. Distribution: Cocos Island off the Pacific coast of Costa Rica, on cliffs near the coast in tropical coastal scrub or rain forest from near sea level to 100 m.

*Cyathea nesiotica* is a tall tree fern with a slender trunk and gracefully arching fronds. It is closely related to *C. armata* and its associated species.

### *Cyathea nicklesii* (Tardieu-Blot & Ballard) Tindale 1956

*Gymnosphaera nicklesii* Tardieu-Blot & Ballard 1953, *Alsophila nicklesii* (Tardieu-Blot & Ballard) Tryon 1970

*Alsophila* clade. The erect trunk is 1–4 m tall. Fronds are bipinnate and may reach a length of 1 m. The rachis is glossy black, as is the stipe. Scales are present at the base and are either brown and long or small and bullate. Sori are small, occur in two rows along each side of the pinnule midvein, and lack indusia. Distribution: Democratic Republic of Congo (Zaire) and Central African Republic, in forest and open areas.

The name *nicklesii* commemorates Maurice Nicklès (b. 1907), who collected plants in Africa.

### *Cyathea nigricans* Mettenius 1863

*Sphaeropteris nigricans* (Mettenius) Tryon 1970

*Sphaeropteris* clade. The erect trunk is medium-sized. Fronds are tripinnate. The stipe is finely warty and covered with small scales, with larger scales toward the base; the scales are pale and fringed. Sori occur almost halfway between the midvein and the edge of the pinnule and are covered with thin indusia. Distribution: Caroline Islands in moist tropical forest.

### *Cyathea nigripes* (C. Christensen) Domin 1929

*Alsophila nigripes* C. Christensen 1905

*Cyathea* clade. The erect trunk is 2–8 m tall and 6–10 cm in diameter. Fronds are bipinnate and may reach 2.5 m in length. Petioles are brown to black-brown and have small spines or raised dots. The rachis is smooth and shiny dark brown. Rachis and stipe scales are brown or dark brown. Sori occur along each side of the pinnule midvein; indusia are absent. Distribution: Costa Rica; Colombia, Ecuador, and Peru. Plants are found in submontane rain forest as understory and in open locations at 300–1200 m, occasionally as high as 1600 m.

*Cyathea nigripes* is a medium-sized plant with flattish fronds. Two varieties are often recognized: *nigripes* and *brunnescens,* the latter also recognized at specific level, as treated here (*C. brunnescens*). *Cyathea nigripes* forms part of a group of related tree ferns that includes *C. brunnescens, C. darienensis, C. phegopteroides,* and *C. tortuosa. Cyathea nigripes* may also be close to *C. hodgeana, C. schiedeana,* and *C. wendlandii,* and may be related to *C. pubens.*

### *Cyathea nigrolineata* Holttum 1962

*Alsophila nigrolineata* (Holttum) Tryon 1970

*Alsophila* clade. The erect trunk is about 10 m tall. Fronds are bi- or tripinnate, 2–3 m long, and occur in one or two whorls of five to eight each. The stipe is covered in scales that are either glossy and pale or have a narrow dark central stripe and paler fragile edges. Sori occur near the midvein of fertile pinnules and are covered with firm brown indusia. Distribution: Eastern New Guinea in forest and secondary growth at 2300–2500 m.

*Cyathea nigrolineata* is very similar to *C. foersteri,* and the two could be united; *C. archboldii* may also be allied.

### *Cyathea nigropaleata* Holttum 1962

*Alsophila nigropaleata* (Holttum) Tryon 1970

*Alsophila* clade. The erect trunk is 1–2 m tall. Fronds are bi- or tripinnate and 1–2 m long. The stipe is dark toward the base and covered with a few basal scales that are glossy, black, and have a narrow dull brown margin. Sori occur near the midvein of fertile pinnules and are covered by small, lobed, scale-like indusia. Distribution: Eastern New Guinea in forest at about 2000 m.

### *Cyathea nilgirensis* Holttum 1965b

*Alsophila nilgirensis* (Holttum) Tryon 1970

*Alsophila* clade. The erect trunk is 1–2 m tall. Fronds are bipinnate and 1–2 m long. The stipe is long and either warty or has short spines toward the base, and scattered scales that are dark and have fragile edges, or pale and bullate. Sori occur near midveins on fertile pinnules and are covered with thin indusia. Distribution: Southern India in montane forest at 1300–1800 m, the name *nilgirensis* referring to the Nilgiri Hills.

### *Cyathea nockii* Jenman 1879

*Alsophila nockii* (Jenman) Tryon 1970

*Alsophila* clade. The prostrate trunk is 10–20 cm tall and 2–4 cm in diameter; it is rough with old stipe bases. Fronds are erect and pinnate or bipinnate and may reach a length of 1.2 m. The rachis is deeply grooved and may be covered with scales that are bullate and whitish to lanceolate and brown, and that have a dark median strip. The stipe is long and dark brown. Sori occur in one to six pairs per segment on each side of the pinnule midvein; cup-like, membranous indusia are present. Distribution: Jamaica on steep forested slopes at 910–1830 m, restricted to a small region of the Blue Mountains.

*Cyathea nockii* is named after William Nock (1881–1904), who collected plants in Jamaica as well as Sri Lanka. It is a small and rare fern.

### *Cyathea nodulifera* R. C. Moran 1991

*Cyathea* clade. The erect trunk is 0.5–2 m tall and 7–12 cm in diameter. Fronds are bipinnate to almost tripinnate and may reach 3.5 m in length. Petioles are brown to shiny black-brown and have large spines. The rachis is either smooth or has scales at the base of the pinnae (spines are absent); the scales are dark brown with lighter borders or golden with finely toothed edges. Sori are red and occur in two rows along each side of the pinnule midvein; indusia are absent. Distribution: Costa Rica and Panama, in tropical and submontane rain forest in open locations at 500–1200 m.

*Cyathea nodulifera* is a small tree fern with a slender trunk and enlarged frond bases that may form trunk scars. It resembles *C. kalbreyeri*.

### *Cyathea notabilis* (Maxon) Domin 1930

*Alsophila notabilis* Maxon 1922

*Cyathea* clade. The erect trunk may be as tall as 2.5 m and about 6 cm in diameter. Fronds are bipinnate and may reach 1.5 m in length. Petioles are straw-colored and have raised dots. The rachis is also straw-colored and covered with small hairs. Rachis and trunk scales are bicolored, light brown with a paler margin. Sori contain five to ten sporangia, occur in two rows along each side of the pinnule midvein, and are covered with minute, scale-like indusia; a tuft of long paraphyses may occur at the apex of the sorus. Distribution: Cocos Island off the Pacific coast of Costa Rica, in tropical rain forest, in ravines and understory from sea level to 350 m.

*Cyathea notabilis* is a small tree fern with a slender trunk and delicately arching fronds.

## *Cyathea novae-caledoniae* (Mettenius) Copeland 1929

*Alsophila novae-caledoniae* Mettenius 1861, *Sphaeropteris novae-caledoniae* (Mettenius) Tryon 1970, *A. lepidotricha* (Fournier) Diels in Engler & Prantl 1899

PLATE 77

*Sphaeropteris* clade. The erect trunk is medium-sized to tall. Fronds are tripinnate and as long as 3 m. The stipe is pale, but dark toward the base, and covered with scales that are either small and brown or long and pale. Sori occur near the midvein of fertile pinnules and almost fill the lamina at maturity; indusia are absent, but some scales may surround the sori. Distribution: New Caledonia.

## *Cyathea obliqua* Copeland in Elmer 1911

*Sphaeropteris obliqua* (Copeland) Tryon 1970

*Sphaeropteris* clade. The erect trunk is short to medium-sized. Fronds are bipinnate to pinnate and about 1 m long. The stipe has scattered scales that are flat, light brown, bullate, and often have a short fringe. Sori are one to three on each group of veins on fertile pinnules; indusia are absent. Distribution: Sibuyan Island in the Philippines at 600 m.

*Cyathea obliqua* is a little-known and little-collected tree fern.

## *Cyathea obscura* (Scort) Copeland 1909

*Alsophila obscura* Scort in Beddome 1887, *Sphaeropteris obscura* (Scort) Tryon 1970, *Cyathea bartlettii* Domin 1929, *C. pulchra* Copeland 1929

*Sphaeropteris* clade. The erect trunk is short to medium-sized. Fronds are pinnate and 1–2 m long. The stipe is dark to medium brown and densely scaly or warty where scales have fallen, particularly toward the base; the scales are shiny, pale brown, and have setiferous edges. Sori occur on three pairs of veins about halfway between the midvein of fertile pinnules and the edge of the lamina; indusia are absent. Distribution: Malay Peninsula and Sumatra, in forest at 900–1400 m.

## *Cyathea obtusiloba* (W. J. Hooker) Domin 1929

*Alsophila obtusiloba* W. J. Hooker 1865

*Alsophila* clade. The erect trunk is 2–3 m tall. Fronds are pinnate and 1–2 m long. The stipe is dark and has scattered minute warts. Rachis and trunk scales are brown and have dark setae. Sori are small and occur at the forks of veins; indusia are small and saucer-like. Distribution: Mbini (or Río Muni) portion of Cameroon and Gabon, in forest at 900–1000 m.

### *Cyathea ogurae* (Hayata) Domin 1930

*Alsophila ogurae* Hayata 1925

*Alsophila* clade. The erect trunk is 3–4 m tall and 6–8 cm in diameter; stipe bases are retained and cover the trunk. Fronds are bi- or tripinnate and 2–2.5 m long. The stipe is either flushed with purple or is dark, nearly black, and is scaly only at the base; the scales are as long as 2 cm, glossy, medium brown, and have narrow fragile edges. Sori are borne close to the midvein of fertile pinnules (fertile veins are simple and not forked); indusia are absent. Distribution: Island of Chichi-shima in the Bonin Islands, south of the main islands of Japan, the type specimen collected from Mount Asahiyama.

The name *ogurae* commemorates botanist Yuzuru Ogura (1895–1981).

### *Cyathea oinops* Hasskarl in W. J. Hooker 1855

*Alsophila oinops* (Hasskarl) Tryon 1970

*Alsophila* clade. The erect trunk may be as tall as about 3 m or more. Fronds are bi- or tripinnate and 1–2 m long; sometimes two pinnae are reduced and occur toward the base of the stipe. The stipe is dark, warty, and covered toward the base with scales that are pale and firm. Sori occur near the midvein of fertile pinnules and are covered by firm brown indusia. Distribution: Sumatra, Java, southwestern Sulawesi (Celebes), and Lombok in the Lesser Sunda Islands, in rain forest at 2000–2500 m.

*Cyathea oinops* is similar to *C. loheri*; if the two were united, the name *oinops* would have priority.

### *Cyathea onusta* Christ 1904

*Cyathea* clade. The erect trunk may be as tall as 5 m and 5–10 cm in diameter. Fronds are bipinnate and may reach 2 m in length. Petioles are straw-colored to brown and have spines and/or raised dots. The rachis is also straw-colored to yellow-brown and covered with dark brown scales. Sori occur in two rows along each side of the pinnule midvein and are covered with delicate globose indusia. Distribution: Costa Rica and Panama, in submontane rain forest in the understory on shaded riverbanks from 850 m to about 2000 m.

*Cyathea onusta* is a small tree fern with a slender trunk and arching fronds; it is sometimes placed in synonymy under *C. fulva*.

### *Cyathea oosora* Holttum 1962

*Alsophila oosora* (Holttum) Tryon 1970, *Cyathea assimilis* Christ 1898, not *C. assimilis* W. J. Hooker 1865

*Alsophila* clade. The erect trunk is 2–4 m tall. Fronds are bi- or tripinnate and may reach 1–2 m in length. The stipe is warty toward the base and has a few scales that are narrow and brown. Sori occur near the midvein of fertile pinnules and are covered by firm, glossy brown indusia. Distribution: Kinabalu on Borneo, and northern Sulawesi (Celebes), in ridge forest at 1500–3000 m.

### *Cyathea orientalis* (Kunze) Moore 1861

*Disphenia orientalis* Kunze 1848, *Alsophila orientalis* (Kunze) Tryon 1970

*Alsophila* clade. The erect trunk is 5 m tall. Fronds are numerous in the crown, bi- or tripinnate, and 1–1.5 m long. The stipe is dark and bears many spines as well as scales; the scales are dark, glossy, and have a narrow paler margin, and basal parts of the scales may bear outgrowths. Sori are round, occur near the fertile pinnule midvein, and are covered by thin, brown, slightly constricted, cup-like indusia. Distribution: Western East Java and the Lesser Sunda Islands, including Bali, Lombok, and Flores, in montane forest at 1000–1800 m.

### *Cyathea pachyrrhachis* Copeland 1942

*Alsophila pachyrrhachis* (Copeland) Tryon 1970

*Alsophila* clade. The erect trunk may be as tall as about 7 m and 7–8 cm in diameter. Fronds are bi- or tripinnate and 1–2 m long. Stipes are deciduous, leaving scars on the trunk. The stipe is warty and covered with scattered scales that are pale or partly dark, and that have narrow fragile edges. Sori occur near the midvein of fertile pinnules and are covered by firm indusia. Distribution: Western New Guinea in rain forest, secondary forest, and mossy forest from 1000 m to about 2900 m.

### *Cyathea palaciosii* R. C. Moran 1995

*Cyathea* clade. The semierect trunk is less than 50 cm tall and 1–2 cm in diameter. Fronds are pinnate and usually less than 50 cm long. The rachis is scaly and pubescent; the scales may be either bicolored (brown with a paler margin) or golden to yellowish brown. Sori occur along each side of pinnule secondary veins and lack indusia. Distribution: Nangaritza River Valley in southern Ecuador, on limestone in cloud forest at 950–1200 m.

*Cyathea palaciosii* is named after Ecuadorian botanist Walter A. Palacios (b. 1959).

### *Cyathea paladensis* (Hieronymus) Domin 1929

*Alsophila paladensis* Hieronymus in Engler & Prantl 1900

*Cyathea* clade. The irregular, erect trunk is 3 m tall. Fronds are bipinnate and as long as 1 m. Distribution: Colombia in submontane and montane rain forest at 2300–2400 m.

### *Cyathea pallescens* (Sodiro) Domin 1929

*Alsophila pallescens* Sodiro 1883

*Cyathea* clade. The erect trunk may be as tall as 10 m and 6–10 cm in diameter. Fronds are bipinnate, rarely tripinnate, and may be exceed 4 m in length. Rachis and trunk scales range from whitish to brown or are bicolored, either brown with a paler margin or brown with pale streaks. Sori occur in two rows along each side of the pinnule midvein and are covered with globose indusia, which may open on one side. Distribution: Colombia to Bolivia, in cloud forest or montane forest at 1200–3500 m.

*Cyathea pallescens* is a highly variable species and the center of a group of ferns that includes *C. divergens* and *C. simplex*.

### *Cyathea pallidipaleata* Holttum 1962

*Alsophila pallidipaleata* (Holttum) Tryon 1970

*Alsophila* clade. The erect trunk is 2–4 m tall. Fronds are bi- or tripinnate and 1–2 m long. The stipe is brown and densely covered in scales that are pale brown, glossy, and have a dull margin. Sori are round, occur near the fertile pinnule midvein, and are covered by firm, dark, cup-like indusia. Distribution: Southwestern Sulawesi (Celebes) in montane forest at about 3000 m.

### *Cyathea papuana* (Ridley) Alderwerelt van Rosenburgh 1917

*Alsophila papuana* Ridley 1916, *Sphaeropteris papuana* (Ridley) Tryon 1970

*Sphaeropteris* clade. The erect trunk may be as tall as 2–3 m. Fronds are bi- or tripinnate and about 1.5 m long to just over 2 m. The stipe is dull and has abundant spines and scattered scales; the scales are thick, dark, and fleshy. Sori occur near the midvein of fertile pinnules and are covered by thin, translucent indusia. Distribution: Western New Guinea at 700–1100 m.

### *Cyathea parianensis* (Windisch) Lellinger 1984

*Sphaeropteris parianensis* Windisch 1976

*Cyathea* clade. The erect trunk may be as tall as about 6 m. Fronds are bipinnate to almost tripinnate and about 2.5 m long; the lamina is pubescent. The stipe is warty and covered in scales toward the base; the scales are either bullate and whitish or narrow and light brown. Sori are on fertile pinnules, between the midvein and the pinnule margin; indusia are absent. Distribution: Paria Peninsula of Venezuela, in montane forest at 600–825 m.

*Cyathea parianensis* is a rare fern related to *C. aterrima*, *C. lockwoodiana*, and *C. senilis*.

### *Cyathea parksii* Copeland 1931

*Sphaeropteris parksii* (Copeland) Tryon 1970

PLATES 78, 79

*Sphaeropteris* clade. Distribution: Cook Islands. *Cyathea parksii* is named after botanist Harold Ernest Parks (1880–1968), who collected in the South Pacific as well as other places. It is very similar to *C. medullaris*, differing only in minor details of the fertile lobes of the frond and in the absence of scales on the pinnule veins; the relationship between these two tree ferns requires further investigation.

### *Cyathea parva* Copeland 1942

not *Cyathea parva* (Maxon) Tryon 1976 (see *Alsophila parva*, Appendix 1);
*A. micra* Tryon 1970

*Alsophila* clade. The erect trunk is 1–1.5 m tall and 3–4 cm in diameter. Fronds are few, bi- or tripinnate, and about 1 m long. The stipe is covered in warts and scales; the scales are pale, or dark and glossy toward the tip, and have a dull margin. Sori are round, occur near the fertile pinnule midvein, and are covered by narrow, red, saucer-like indusia. Distribution: Western New Guinea in undergrowth of rain forest at 1700 m, a rare tree fern known from a single location.

### *Cyathea parvipinna* Holttum 1962

*Sphaeropteris parvipinna* (Holttum) Tryon 1970

*Sphaeropteris* clade. The erect trunk is about 1 m tall. Fronds are bi- or tripinnate and 1–2 m long. The stipe and basal rachis are sharply spiny and covered sparsely by scales that are brown, narrow, and fleshy toward the base. Sori occur near the midvein of fertile pinnules and are covered by thin, translucent indusia. Distribution: Eastern New Guinea on stream banks in lowland forest at about 270 m.

### *Cyathea parvula* (Jenman) Domin 1929

*Alsophila parvula* Jenman 1879, *Cyathea gracilensis* Domin 1929

*Cyathea* clade. The erect trunk may be as tall as 9 m but only 4 cm in diameter; trunks often cluster together and lack spines but may be covered with whitish scales and numerous oval stipe-base scars. Fronds are bipinnate and may reach 1.5 m in length, rarely 2 m. The stipe is light brown and has numerous short spines and scales; the scales are narrow and either pale brown to whitish or slightly bicolored, brown with a whitish margin. Sori occur in two to five pairs along each side of the pinnule midvein; indusia are pale brown, minute, and scale-like. Distribution: Greater Antilles (Cuba, Jamaica, Hispaniola, and Puerto Rico) in rain forest on wooded hillsides, in moist thickets along streams, and bordering cleared areas at 450–2000 m.

*Cyathea parvula* is a common tree fern with a sparse crown of arching fronds. It grows on both calcareous and noncalcareous soils. The trunks are narrow and were called "broom sticks" by George Jenman in his original description of the species. Plants from western Puerto Rico may bear lateral trunk branches that extend to the ground and take root.

### *Cyathea patellifera* Alderwerelt van Rosenburgh 1914

*Alsophila patellifera* (Alderwerelt van Rosenburgh) Tryon 1970

*Alsophila* clade. The erect trunk may be as tall as 2–5 m. Fronds are bi- or tripinnate and about 2 m long or more. The stipe is red-brown, dark toward the base, and covered with spines and scales, also basally; the scales are firm, medium brown, and have fragile edges. Sori occur near the midvein of fertile pinnules and are covered by firm, brown, saucer-like indusia. Distribution: Central Sumatra in montane forest at 2200–2400 m.

### *Cyathea pauciflora* (Kuhn) Lellinger 1987

*Alsophila pauciflora* Kuhn 1869

*Cyathea* clade. The erect trunk is 1–9 m tall. Fronds are bipinnate and may reach 3.5 m or more in length. The rachis is brown and has scattered brown scales. Sori occur between the midvein and the edge of the lamina and are usually confined to the base of the lobe; indusia are absent. Distribution: Andes from Aragua and Táchira, Venezuela, to Bogotá, Colombia, in cloud forest at 750–3350 m.

The name *pauciflora* may refer to the few sori, confined toward the base of pinnule lobes. *Cyathea pauciflora* is possibly related to *C. frigida*.

### *Cyathea percrassa* C. Christensen 1937

*Alsophila percrassa* (C. Christensen) Tryon 1970

*Alsophila* clade. The erect trunk is 4 m tall and 8–12 cm in diameter. Fronds number 6–12 in a crown, are bi- or tripinnate, and 1–2 m long. The rachis is covered in pale fragile scales. The stipe bears scales toward the base; the scales are rigid, twisted, and have a glossy brown central band and broad fragile edges. Sori are round, occur near the midvein of the fertile pinnule segment, and are covered by firm, shallow, cup-like indusia. Distribution: Eastern New Guinea, common in valley rain forest and mossy forest at 3000–3500 m.

### *Cyathea perpelvigera* Alderwerelt van Rosenburgh 1924

*Alsophila perpelvigera* (Alderwerelt van Rosenburgh) Tryon 1970

*Alsophila* clade. The erect trunk is 2–3 m tall and about 5 cm in diameter. Fronds are bi- or tripinnate, 1–2 m long, and occur in whorls of ten; they are partially shed and leave persistent stipe bases on the trunk. The stipe bears spines about 2 mm long and many scales that are glossy brown and that have a paler dull margin and fragile edges. Sori are round, occurring one or two (rarely three) per fertile pinnule segment, and are covered by firm cup-like indusia. Distribution: New Guinea, Moluccas, and possibly northern Sulawesi (Celebes), in rain forest in the absence of woody undergrowth at 1200–1800 m.

*Cyathea perpelvigera* is very similar to *C. hunsteniana* but has scales on the fronds.

### *Cyathea perpunctulata* (Alderwerelt van Rosenburgh) Domin 1930

*Hemitelia perpunctulata* Alderwerelt van Rosenburgh 1918,

*Alsophila perpunctulata* (Alderwerelt van Rosenburgh) Tryon 1970

*Alsophila* clade. The erect trunk may be as tall as about 4 m or more. Fronds are bi- or tripinnate and 1–2 m long. The rachis and stipe are finely warty, especially on the lower surface, and covered with basal scales that are narrow and dark. Sori occur near the fertile pinnule midvein and are covered by small, brown, scale-like indusia. Distribution: Sumatra in forest at about 650 m.

### *Cyathea perrieriana* C. Christensen 1932

*Alsophila perrieriana* (C. Christensen) Tryon 1970

*Alsophila* clade. The erect trunk is 3–4 m tall. Fronds are bipinnate and 2–3 m long. Rachis and trunk scales are bicolored, with a glossy dark brown center and paler margin, and fragile edges. Sori occur near the midvein of fertile pinnules and are covered by thick, brown indusia. Distribution: Madagascar.

*Cyathea perrieriana* is named after botanist Joseph Marie Henry Alfred Perrier de la Bâthie (1873–1958), who collected in Madagascar and Vietnam. It is a member of a complex that also includes *C. marattioides*, *C. serratifolia*, and *C. tsilotsilensis*.

### *Cyathea persquamulifera* (Alderwerelt van Rosenburgh) Domin 1930

*Alsophila persquamulifera* Alderwerelt van Rosenburgh 1920, *Sphaeropteris persquamulifera* (Alderwerelt van Rosenburgh) Tryon 1970

*Sphaeropteris* clade. The erect trunk is 3–5 m tall. Fronds are bi- or tripinnate. The rachis is warty on the underside. The stipe is covered with basal scales that are glossy, medium brown, and firm. Sori are near the midveins of the fertile pinnules and lack indusia. Distribution: Java and central Sumatra, in mountains in open places at 1500–2500 m.

### *Cyathea petiolata* (W. J. Hooker) Tryon 1976

*Hemitelia petiolata* W. J. Hooker 1844, *Cyathea panamensis* Domin 1929

*Cyathea* clade. The erect trunk may be as tall as 5 m. Fronds are bipinnate and may reach 1.5 m in length. Rachis and trunk scales are brown. Sori are minute, occur in arcs toward the outer edge of pinnule lobes, and lack indusia. Distribution: Panama; Colombia and possibly Peru. Plants are found in rain forest, on stream banks and hillsides, from near sea level to 700 m.

*Cyathea petiolata* is a medium-sized tree fern with variable frond morphology. It is the center of a complex that includes *C. barringtonii*, *C. conformis*, *C. falcata*, *C. impar*, *C. pungens*, and *C. sagittifolia*.

### *Cyathea phalaenolepis* (C. Christensen) Domin 1929

*Alsophila phalaenolepis* C. Christensen 1911

*Cyathea* clade. The creeping to barely erect trunk is about 10 cm long. Fronds are pinnate, dissected to almost bipinnate, and may reach 1.5 m in length. The rachis is hairy, brown, warty, and covered with scales that are bicolored, brown with a white margin. Sori occur between the midvein of fertile pinnules midveins and the edge of the lamina; indusia are absent. Distribution: Pacific coast of Colombia and Ecuador, in dense forest and swamps from about sea level to 300 m.

*Cyathea phalaenolepis* is a small, creeping fern, often lacking a trunk, that has pinnate fronds. It seems allied to *C. ursina* and is similar to *C. werffii*, which differs in having smaller petiole scales.

### *Cyathea phalerata* Martius 1822

*Cyathea blanchetiana* (C. B. Presl) Domin 1929, *C. iheringii* (Rosenstock) Domin 1929, *C. paulistana* (Rosenstock) Domin 1929, *C. paleolata* (Martius) Copeland 1932

*Cyathea* clade. The erect trunk is 1–10 m tall (variety *iheringii* is usually shorter, 1–2 m). Fronds are bipinnate and may reach 2–3 m in length. The rachis is brown and has scattered scales that are brown and have a margin that is often abraded. Sori occur between the midvein of the fertile pinnules and the edge of the lamina; indusia are absent. Distribution: Mato Grosso and Bahia to Rio Grande do Sul. Brazil, in secondary forest and wet scrub, especially along creek banks, at 35–1300 m.

*Cyathea phalerata* is a highly variable species that includes several varieties, including variety *iheringii* (see Barrington 1978), and is related to *C. atrovirens, C. dichromatolepis, C. villosa,* and possibly *C. borinquena.*

## *Cyathea phegopteroides* (W. J. Hooker) Domin 1929

*Alsophila phegopteroides* W. J. Hooker 1865

*Cyathea* clade. Trunk characteristics unknown. Fronds are pinnate and may reach 1 m in length or slightly more. The stipe is long, brownish purple, and has numerous scales and some spines; the scales are brown to light brown. Sori occur between the midvein of fertile pinnules and the edge of the lamina. Veins fork at the sori. Indusia are absent. Distribution: Eastern Peruvian Andes at 350 m, known only from a few collections by Richard Spruce.

The little-known *Cyathea phegopteroides* is possibly related to the wide-ranging *C. pubens* and in turn to *C. nigripes.*

## *Cyathea philippinensis* Baker 1891

*Sphaeropteris philippinensis* (Baker) Tryon 1970

*Sphaeropteris* clade. The erect trunk may be as tall as about 2 m or more. Fronds are pinnate or bipinnate and 1–2 m long. The stipe is dark and warty at the base and has scattered scales that are pale to brownish. Sori occur near the midvein of fertile pinnules and are covered by thin, translucent indusia. Distribution: Luzon and Mindoro in the Philippines, in montane forest to about 1500 m at least.

## *Cyathea physolepidota* Alston 1956

*Alsophila physolepidota* (Alston) Tryon 1970

*Alsophila* clade. The erect trunk is 2–4 m tall. Fronds are bi- or tripinnate and 1–2 m long. The stipe is very spiny and covered with very few scales that are brown and have pale fragile edges. Sori occur near the midvein of fertile pinnules and are covered by small, often bilobed indusia. Distribution: Eastern New Guinea in forest at 2200–2500 m.

## *Cyathea pilosissima* (Baker) Domin 1929

*Alsophila pilosissima* Baker 1874

*Cyathea* clade. The erect, narrow to slender trunk is 0.5–3 m tall. Fronds are bipinnate and may reach 1.5–2 m or more in length. The rachis is tan to brown and has spines and scattered scales; the scales are either blackish brown or bicolored, with a dark brown central region and a narrow reddish margin. Sori occur on each side of the pinnule midvein and lack indusia. Distribution: Panama; Colombia, Ecuador, Peru, and western Amazonia. Plants are found in tropical rain forest and along watercourses to about 800 m.

*Cyathea pilosissima* is similar to *C. amazonica* but may be distinguished by the lack of indusia; there is also some resemblance to *C. mucilagina*. The name *pilosissima* means "most pilose" or hairy.

### *Cyathea pilulifera* Copeland 1942

*Sphaeropteris pilulifera* (Copeland) Tryon 1970

*Sphaeropteris* clade. The erect trunk is 4–10 m tall. Fronds are bi- or tripinnate and 1–1.5 m long. The stipe has dark basal spines about 5 mm long and is covered in scattered pale scales. Sori occur near the midvein of the fertile pinnules and lack indusia. Distribution: Moluccas, New Guinea, and the Louisiade Archipelago, in open areas and old gardens at 1200–2800 m.

At lower elevations within its range, *Cyathea pilulifera* may become very tall; smaller plants occur at high elevations. It is possibly allied to *C. aeneifolia* from New Guinea.

### *Cyathea pinnula* (Christ) R. C. Moran 1991

*Alsophila pinnula* Christ 1901

*Cyathea* clade. The erect trunk is 0.4–2 m tall and 4–8 cm in diameter. Fronds are bipinnate to almost tripinnate and may reach 2 m in length. Petioles are grayish brown to dark brown and are either smooth or have spines. The rachis lacks scales; stipe scales are bicolored, dark brown with a paler margin, or golden, and have eroded edges. Sori occur in two rows along each side of the pinnule midvein; indusia are absent. Distribution: Nicaragua, Costa Rica, and Panama; Colombia. Plants are found in wet tropical and submontane rain forest, forest understory, and rarely in tidal forest, from sea level to 600 m, sometimes as high as 1500 m.

*Cyathea pinnula* is a short tree fern with a slender trunk that bears flattened fronds. It has often been confused with *C. wendlandii*, which differs in having smaller linear petiole scales and once-forked fertile veins.

### *Cyathea plagiostegia* Copeland 1929

*Alsophila plagiostegia* (Copeland) Tryon 1970

*Alsophila* clade. The erect trunk is 2–6 m tall. Fronds are bipinnate and may reach 2 m in length; the lowest one or two pairs of pinnae may be slightly reduced and occur toward the base of the stipe. The rachis and stipe are either pale to brown or flushed with red toward the pinnule rachis. The stipe may have sparse scales and warts and is dark toward the base; the scales are pale and have broad fragile edges. Sori are near the pinnule midvein and partially or fully covered by indusia that open toward the pinnule margin. Distribution: Fiji, Samoa, Cook Islands, Marquesas Islands, Tahiti, and Austral Islands.

*Cyathea plagiostegia* is very similar to the variable *C. affinis*, differing primarily in its smaller size and in smaller indusia; the true relationship between the two species requires further investigation.

## *Cyathea platylepis* (W. J. Hooker) Domin 1929

*Hemitelia platylepis* W. J. Hooker 1861, ?*Cyathea vilhelmii* Domin 1929

*Cyathea* clade. The erect, narrow trunk may be as tall as 1 m, rarely 3.5 m. Fronds are bipinnate to almost tripinnate (fertile pinnae are usually more dissected than sterile ones) and may reach 1.5 m in length. Rachis and trunk scales are brown. Sori occur in two rows along each side of the pinnule midvein and are covered with large, half-globose indusia. Distribution: Venezuela and Colombia, in tropical and submontane rain forest, bamboo thickets, mossy forest understory, and boggy areas from about 100 m to about 2000 m.

*Cyathea platylepis* is a short tree fern with a narrow trunk. The tree fern known as *C. vilhelmii* from Peru may be synonymous or very closely related.

## *Cyathea podophylla* (W. J. Hooker) Copeland 1909

*Alsophila podophylla* W. J. Hooker 1857

PLATE 80

*Alsophila* clade. The erect trunk may be as tall as 2 m and about 8 cm in diameter. Fronds are bipinnate and as long as 2–3 m; fronds, especially the stipes, are persistent and may form an irregular skirt about the trunk. The stipe is purple to purple-black, glossy, and covered with warts and scales; the scales are narrow, lanceolate, glossy, and dark brown. Sori are round and occur on either side of the pinnule midvein; indusia are absent. Distribution: Southern China, Taiwan, Ryukyu Islands, Vietnam, Laos, Thailand, and Cambodia, in forest by streams and in ravines at 600–1000 m.

*Cyathea podophylla* appears to be part of a complex that includes *C. gigantea*, *C. glabra*, and *C. subdubia*; the relationship between these species requires further investigation.

### *Cyathea poeppigii* (W. J. Hooker) Domin 1929

*Alsophila poeppigii* W. J. Hooker 1844, *A. elongata* W. J. Hooker 1844, *A. bakeri* Sodiro 1893, *Cyathea coriacea* (Rosenstock) Domin 1929, *C. quitensis* (C. Christensen) Domin 1929, *C. tijucensis* (Fée) Domin 1929, *C. anacampta* Alston 1958, *Sphaeropteris elongata* (W. J. Hooker) Tryon 1970

*Cyathea* clade. The erect trunk may be as tall as 10 m and 6–9 cm in diameter. Fronds are bi- or tripinnate and may reach 3 m in length. Petioles are yellowish to brown and have a few spines or raised dots. The rachis lacks spines or scales. The stipe is covered in scales, especially toward the base; the scales are either bicolored (brown with a paler margin) or narrower and straw-colored to light brown. Sori occur in two rows along each side of the pinnule midvein and sometimes have long, sterile hairs about the base; indusia are absent. Distribution: Costa Rica and Panama; Venezuela, Colombia, and Ecuador. Plants are found in tropical and submontane rain forest, in the understory, on riverbanks, and in cleared pastureland at 100–2100 m.

The name *poeppigii* commemorates German naturalist Eduard Poeppig (1798–1868), who collected in South America in 1826–1832. *Cyathea poeppigii* is a variable, tall to medium-sized tree fern with a slender trunk and large, gently arching fronds.

### *Cyathea polycarpa* Junghuhn 1845

*Alsophila polycarpa* (Junghuhn) Tryon 1970, *Cyathea crenulata* Blume 1828, *C. distans* Rosenstock 1917

*Alsophila* clade. The erect trunk is about 5 m tall or more. Fronds are bi- or tripinnate, 2–3 m long, and may persist as an irregular skirt about the trunk. The stipe is warty and covered with a woolly layer of scales that are dark, glossy, and have a paler fragile margin and basal outgrowths. Sori occur near the midvein of fertile pinnules and are covered by thin, translucent indusia. Distribution: Java, and Flores in the Lesser Sunda Islands, in montane rain forest at 1700–2700 m.

*Cyathea polycarpa* is similar to *C. alpicola* but differs in not having spines; *C. macropoda* and *C. magnifolia* from Sumatra may also be closely allied. Variety *rigida* has occasionally been associated with *C. polycarpa*, but it appears to be more properly associated with *C. javanica*.

### *Cyathea polypoda* Baker 1894

*Sphaeropteris polypoda* (Baker) Tryon 1970, *Cyathea kemberangana* Copeland 1917

*Sphaeropteris* clade. The erect trunk is usually 3 m tall and covered with stipe bases; the lower trunk may have branches. Fronds are pinnate or bipinnate and 1–2 m long. The stipe is long, pale greenish to dark, and densely scaly and warty toward the base; the scales are shiny, medium brown, and firm. Sori occur near the midvein of fertile pinnules; indusia are absent. Distribution: Malay Peninsula, Borneo, and the Philippines, in open places on ridges and summits at 600–2200 m.

### *Cyathea portoricensis* Kuhn 1869

*Alsophila portoricensis* (Kuhn) Conant 1983

*Alsophila* clade. Distribution: Puerto Rico in the Caribbean, the name *portoricensis* referring to Puerto Rico. *Cyathea portoricensis* may form hybrids with *C. brooksii*, and *Alsophila amintae* and *A. bryophila* (see Appendix 1), and is part of the *C. woodwardioides* complex of six species, all from the Greater Antilles, the other four being *C. crassa*, *C. fulgens*, *C. grevilleana*, and *C. tussacii*.

### *Cyathea praecincta* (Kunze) Domin 1929

*Alsophila praecincta* Kunze 1839, *Cyathea submarginalis* (Domin) Domin 1930

*Cyathea* clade. Trunk characteristics unknown. Fronds are bipinnate. Sori occur just beside the midvein of fertile pinnules; indusia are absent. Distribution: Coastal Bahia, Brazil.

*Cyathea praecincta* is little known, as there have been no modern collections. Rudolph Friedrich Hohenacker (1798–1874) collected the original incomplete specimens in the early 19th century. It is possible that this tree fern is part of the *C. pungens* group, but its exact status will remain a mystery until further collections are made.

### *Cyathea princeps* E. Mayer 1868

*Cibotium princeps* Linden ex J. Smith 1866, *Cyathea princeps*
  J. Smith 1866 (without description), *Cibotium horridum*
  Liebmann 1849, *Sphaeropteris horrida* (Liebmann) Tryon 1970

PALMA DE MONTAÑA, RABO DE MICO

PLATES 81, 82

*Sphaeropteris* clade. The erect trunk is 6–15 m tall and 10–40 cm in diameter; it is often densely covered with brown scales. Fronds are bipinnate to nearly tripinnate, dark green, pale beneath, and may reach 3–5 m in length. Sori occur in four to eight pairs per pinnule segment and are covered by papery, white, deep, cup-like indusia that usually split into two halves at maturity. Distribution: Southern Mexico, Guatemala, and Honduras, in moist mountain forest at 600–1800 m.

*Cyathea princeps*, also commonly known as *Sphaeropteris horrida*, was originally collected in Mexico in the early part of the 19th century by Frederik Liebmann and brought into European cultivation by Jean Jules Linden. Early sterile material was mistaken for a species of *Cibotium*, with some confusion over the specific name. It was only when Linden's plants became fertile that John Smith placed the species in *Cyathea*; Liebmann's original specific epithet, *horrida* (as *Cibotium horridum*), was overlooked. *Cyathea princeps* forms part of a complex of American species that includes *C. brunei, C. gardneri, C. insignis*, and *C. quindiuensis*.

### *Cyathea procera* Brause 1920

*Sphaeropteris procera* (Brause) Tryon 1970

*Sphaeropteris* clade. The erect trunk may be as tall as 20 m. Fronds are bi- or tripinnate, occur in whorls of six, and are 2–3.5 m long. The rachis is finely warty on the lower surface. The stipe is covered with dense bristles and is often pale, especially above the basal region; the upper stipe is warty and has an upper groove with scales that are large and dark brown, or small and paler, and that have a setiferous margin. Sori occur one to a fertile pinnule lobe and are covered with thin indusia. Distribution: New Guinea in mountain forest at 1800–2400 m.

*Cyathea procera* is apparently a higher-elevation counterpart to *C. pulcherrima*.

### *Cyathea propinqua* Mettenius 1863

*Sphaeropteris propinqua* (Mettenius) Tryon 1970

*Sphaeropteris* clade. The erect, slender trunk may be as tall as 10 m. Fronds are bi- or tripinnate and 2–3 m long. The stipe is dull, dark, and covered with minute scales, and thick fleshy scales toward the base; the scales are dull brown. Sori occur halfway between the pinnule midvein and the edge of the lobe and are covered with indusia. Distribution: Fiji in wet forest.

### *Cyathea pruinosa* Rosenstock 1913

*Alsophila pruinosa* (Rosenstock) Tryon 1970

*Alsophila* clade. The erect trunk is 5 m tall. Fronds, 10–15, occur in two loose whorls, are bi- or tripinnate, and 1–2 m long. The stipe is purplish, warty, and bears many scales that are stiff, twisted, dark brown, and have a paler margin and fragile edges. Sori are round, occur near the fertile pinnule midvein, and are covered by thin cup-like indusia. Distribution: Eastern New Guinea at the edges of forest and in grassland at 2400–3000 m.

## *Cyathea pseudomuelleri* Holttum 1962

*Alsophila pseudomuelleri* (Holttum) Tryon 1970

*Alsophila* clade. The erect trunk is about 4 m tall. Fronds are bi- or tripinnate, about 2 m long, and form a sparse erect crown. Stipes are persistent over the entire trunk. The stipe is pale, warty, and covered with basal scales that are rigid, twisted, dark brown, and have a paler narrow margin. Sori are round, occur near the fertile pinnule midvein, and are covered by firm indusia. Distribution: Western New Guinea, known only from one location in the Wilhelmina Mountains at about 3200 m.

## *Cyathea pseudonanna* (L. D. Gómez) Lellinger 1985

*Trichipteris pseudonanna* L. D. Gómez 1981

*Cyathea* clade. Plants are prostrate. Fronds are pinnate and as long as 75 cm. Petioles are brown and lack spines. The rachis has scales and hairs; the scales are bicolored, brown to black with a large white margin. Sori occur in two rows along each side of the pinnule midvein and are covered by flattened, scale-like indusia. Distribution: Costa Rica and Panama in submontane rain forest, in understory from 800 m to about 1300 m.

*Cyathea pseudonanna* is a small fern of the forest floor.

## *Cyathea pubens* Domin 1929

*Alsophila pubescens* Baker 1868, not *Cyathea pubescens* Kuhn 1869;

*Trichipteris pubescens* (Baker) Tryon 1970

PLATES 49, 83, 84

*Cyathea* clade. The erect trunk is 0.6–4 m tall and has light brown scales with a paler margin. Fronds are pinnate and 1–1.5 m long. Sori occur between the pinnule midvein and the edge of the lamina; indusia are absent. Distribution: Jamaica and possibly elsewhere in the Caribbean; Venezuela, Colombia, Peru, and Bolivia to the Guiana Highlands and eastern slopes of the Andes. Plants occur in cloud forest, montane forest, on talus slopes, and in mossy wet areas at 1200–2500 m.

*Cyathea pubens* has also been commonly known as *Trichipteris pubescens*, but when transferred to *Cyathea* the name *pubescens* is unavailable. *Cyathea pubens* is a very small but wide-ranging tree fern, perhaps related to the lesser-known *C. phegopteroides* of Peru and *C. nigripes*.

## *Cyathea pubescens* Kuhn 1869

> not *Alsophila pubescens* Baker 1868 (see *Cyathea pubens*); *A. auneae* Conant 1983

*Alsophila* clade. Distribution: Blue Mountains of Jamaica. *Cyathea pubescens* is apparently of hybrid origin; spores are aborted or absent. It is often confused with *A. bryophila* (Appendix 1), a species characteristic of mossy forest in Puerto Rico. If the genus *Alsophila* is recognized, the name *pubescens* is unavailable. Recognizing this confusion, David Conant (1983) renamed this species *A. auneae*.

## *Cyathea pulcherrima* Copeland 1942

> *Sphaeropteris pulcherrima* (Copeland) Tryon 1970

*Sphaeropteris* clade. The erect trunk is about 10 m tall and 3–5 cm in diameter; stipes fall, leaving scars on the trunk. Fronds are bi- or tripinnate and may reach 1–2 m in length. The rachis is pale and has short dark brown bristles and reddish pale hairs on the lower surface. The stipe is rigid and has dark brown bristles as long as 2 cm. Scales are small and have marginal setae. Sori occur one to a fertile pinnule lobe and are covered by pale, thin indusia. Distribution: Eastern and western New Guinea and the Admiralty Islands, in forest at 100–1100 m.

*Cyathea pulcherrima* is apparently a lower-elevation counterpart to *C. procera*.

## *Cyathea punctata* R. C. Moran & B. Øllgaard 1998

*Cyathea* clade. The erect trunk is about 50 cm tall and about 5 cm in diameter. Fronds are bipinnate, dissected, and may reach 2 m in length; the lamina is punctate (spotted with small depressions). The rachis and stipe are brown and have a few scales and basal spines; the scales are lanceolate and dark brown. Sori lack indusia. Distribution: Ecuador, restricted to the western slopes of the Andes in wet forest and on slopes at 400–500 m or higher.

Named for its lamina, which is spotted with small depressions, *Cyathea punctata* is similar to *C. mucilagina*, *C. multiflora*, and *C. schiedeana*.

## *Cyathea punctulata* (Alderwerelt van Rosenburgh) Alderwerelt van Rosenburgh 1918

> *Alsophila punctulata* Alderwerelt van Rosenburgh 1915

*Alsophila* clade. The erect trunk is about 4 m tall. Fronds are bi- or tripinnate and 1–2 m long. The stipe is dark, warty, and scaly toward the base; the scales are glossy and have fragile edges. Sori occur near the midvein of fertile pinnules and are covered by very small indusia. Distribution: Sumatra in forest at about 2400 m.

## *Cyathea pungens* (Willdenow) Domin 1929

*Polypodium pungens* Willdenow 1810, *P. procerum* Willdenow 1810, not *Cyathea procera* Brause 1920; *Trichipteris procera* (Willdenow) Tryon 1970, *C. klotzschiana* Domin 1930, *C. willdenowiana* Domin 1930

*Cyathea* clade. The trunk is prostrate or leaning to erect and 0.3–7 m tall. Fronds are bipinnate, dissected, and may reach 2–3 m in length. The stipe is covered in scales, especially toward the base; the scales are brown and have a paler margin. The position of the sori may vary from almost marginal to halfway between the fertile pinnule midvein and the lamina; indusia are absent. Distribution: Hispaniola, Puerto Rico, and the Lesser Antilles; Guiana Highlands and through the Andes to Bolivia. Plants are common in wet, shaded sites, rain forest, forest understory, and on riverbanks at 100–1400 m.

*Cyathea pungens* has also been commonly known as *Trichipteris procera*, but when transferred to *Cyathea* the name *procera* is unavailable. This is an extremely variable, medium-sized to tall tree fern allied to *C. dombeyi*, with a slender trunk and large, almost dusky fronds. Other allied species may include the *C. petiolata* complex. Possible hybrids between this species and species of *Cnemidaria* have been collected from the Dominican Republic.

## *Cyathea pycnoneura* Holttum 1962

*Alsophila pycnoneura* (Holttum) Tryon 1970

*Alsophila* clade. The erect trunk is 2–5 m tall. Fronds are bi- or tripinnate and 2–3 m long. The stipe is dark, spiny, and covered with scales that are dark and wide at the base and have a narrow paler margin. Sori are round, occur near the fertile pinnule midvein, and are covered by thin, pale cup-like indusia. Distribution: Northeastern New Guinea in *Podocarpus* forest at 2400–2500 m.

## *Cyathea quindiuensis* Karsten 1857

*Sphaeropteris quindiuensis* (Karsten) Tryon 1970, *Cyathea crassipes* Sodiro 1893, *C. bonapartii* Rosenstock 1909, *C. yungensis* C. Christensen 1926

*Sphaeropteris* clade. The erect trunk may be as tall as about 6 m and 10–15 cm in diameter; it is often densely covered with scales that are often bullate, variable in color (usually white to brown), and occasionally have toothed edges.

Fronds are bipinnate to nearly tripinnate, dark green above, pale beneath, and may reach about 2.5 m in length. Sori occur in four to eight pairs per pinnule segment and are covered with papery, white, globose indusia. Distribution: Andes of Colombia, Ecuador, Peru, and Bolivia, at 1400–2700 m, the name *quindiuensis* referring to Quindío, a department of western Colombia.

A medium to large tree fern with a large, arching crown of fronds, *Cyathea quindiuensis* is associated with a group of ferns that includes *C. brunei*, *C. gardneri*, *C. insignis*, and *C. princeps* (= *Sphaeropteris horrida*).

### *Cyathea raciborskii* Copeland 1909

*Hemitelia crenulata* Mettenius 1863, not *Cyathea crenulata* Blume 1828 (see *C. polycarpa*); *Alsophila crenulata* (Mettenius) W. J. Hooker 1864, *C. brevifoliolata* Alderwerelt van Rosenburgh 1918

*Alsophila* clade. The erect trunk may be as tall as about 2 m. Fronds are tripinnate and may reach 1–2 m in length. The stipe is warty near the base and covered with scattered scales and outgrowths; the scales are small and fringed. Sori are near the fertile pinnule midvein and covered by thin indusia. Distribution: Southern Sumatra and western Java, in forest at 1200–1600 m.

The name *raciborskii* commemorates Polish botanist Marjan Raciborski (1863–1917), who collected in Indonesia. *Cyathea raciborskii*, also known as *Alsophila crenulata*, has been confused with *C. junghuhniana*. *Cyathea raciborskii* differs in having smaller pinnae and stipe outgrowths, which are not present in *C. junghuhniana*.

### *Cyathea ramispina* (W. J. Hooker) Copeland 1909

*Alsophila ramispina* W. J. Hooker 1866, *Cyathea amaiambitensis* Domin 1930

*Alsophila* clade. The erect trunk may be as tall as about 3 m. Fronds are bipinnate and may reach 1–2 m in length. The final pair of pinnae are usually reduced and occur toward the base of the stipe; these, along with the stipe bases, are persistent and retained about the trunk. The stipe is dark and covered with scales that are either small, dull, and brown or large, dark, and glossy. Fertile pinnules are smaller than sterile ones. Sori occur near the midvein of fertile pinnules; indusia are absent. Distribution: Sarawak, and Kinabalu in Sabah, in exposed places on ridges at 1800–2500 m.

*Cyathea ramispina* is very similar to *C. atropurpurea* but differs in frond details; the relationship between the two species requires further investigation.

### *Cyathea rebeccae* (F. von Mueller) Domin 1929
*Alsophila rebeccae* F. von Mueller 1865
BLACK TREE FERN

*Alsophila* clade. The erect trunk is 3–8 m tall and as much as 10 cm in diameter; it may produce horizontal suckers at the base. Fronds are bipinnate and 2–3 m long. The rachis and stipe are dark, almost purple-black, and covered with scales, especially toward the base, or with fine warts where the scales fall; stipe bases are persistent. Scales are dark purple-brown and have a paler margin. Fertile pinnules are slightly smaller than the sterile ones. Sori occur in one or two irregular rows along the fertile pinnule midvein; indusia are absent. Distribution: Flores in the Lesser Sunda Islands, and northeastern to central Queensland Australia, in rain forest, gullies, and on ridges from sea level to 1700 m.

*Cyathea rebeccae* is a slow-growing tree fern named after Rebecca Nordt, a friend of Ferdinand von Mueller. It is an attractive species with a slender trunk, doing best in warmer regions but may be grown in containers elsewhere. It is very frost sensitive and requires protection from wind.

### *Cyathea recommutata* Copeland 1909
*Alsophila commutata* Mettenius 1863

*Alsophila* clade. The erect trunk may be as tall as about 3 m, rarely taller. Fronds are bipinnate and may reach 1–2 m in length; the lowest pair of pinnae are usually reduced and occur toward the base of the stipe. The stipe is dark and has basal scales that are dark, glossy, and have thin fragile edges. Fertile pinnules are smaller than sterile ones. Sori occur near the midvein of fertile pinnules; indusia are absent. Distribution: Malay Peninsula, central and southern Sumatra, and Borneo, in acidic peaty or sandy soils in wet forest, and in swamp forest, from sea level to 1500 m.

### *Cyathea recurvata* (Brause) Domin 1930
*Alsophila recurvata* Brause 1920

*Alsophila* clade. The erect trunk is 5 m tall. Fronds are bi- or tripinnate and 1–2 m long. The stipe is covered in scales that are medium brown and have fragile edges. Sori occur near the midvein of fertile pinnules; indusia are absent. Distribution: Northeastern New Guinea above about 850 m.

### *Cyathea rigens* Rosenstock 1913
*Alsophila rigens* (Rosenstock) Tryon 1970

*Alsophila* clade. The erect trunk is 5 m tall. Fronds are numerous in the crown, are bi- or tripinnate, and 1–2 m long. The stipe bears many spines toward the base as well as scales; the scales are either pale or dark, glossy, and have pale fragile edges. Sori are round, occur near the fertile pinnule midvein, and are covered by thin cup-like indusia. Distribution: Central and eastern New Guinea, at the edges of submontane forest, in mossy forest, and on the edges of grassland at 1570–2800 m.

*Cyathea rigens* is very similar to *C. everta*. If the two species are united, the name *rigens* has priority.

## *Cyathea robertsiana* (F. von Mueller) Domin 1929

*Alsophila robertsiana* F. von Mueller 1865
LACY TREE FERN, SLENDER TREE FERN
PLATE 85

*Cyathea* clade. The erect trunk is 5–7 m tall and occasionally as much as 10 cm in diameter though usually thinner; it bears oval stipe scars. Fronds are pinnate to tripinnate, as long as 3 m, and either form a loose crown or may occur in a lax spiral up the stem. The stipe is brown and covered with a scattering of scales that are thin and shiny brown. Sori occur, often singly on the pinnule midvein, that is, one sorus per pinnule segment lobe; indusia are small and scale-like. Distribution: Eungella Range and between the Herbert and Daintree Rivers in central and northeastern Queensland, Australia, colonizing disturbed areas and growing in mountain forests, ravines, clearings, and forest margins at 500–1500 m.

*Cyathea robertsiana* is one of a group of western Pacific species apparently related to *C. decurrens*. Members of this group have variously been attributed to *Alsophila* or *Cyathea*; molecular evidence suggests a relationship with the latter genus, as treated here, though the relationship is by no means clear. This tree fern is a colonizer of disturbed areas and clearings. It is cultivated, but plants do best in warmer regions and are very frost sensitive. More light, including some sunlight, is also a requirement. In cooler areas this species will grow in a container. The root system is often extensive and thus susceptible to drying out; it must be kept moist but not waterlogged.

## *Cyathea robinsonii* Copeland 1911

*Sphaeropteris robinsonii* (Copeland) Tryon 1970, *Cyathea pseudoalbizzia* Copeland 1929

*Sphaeropteris* clade. The erect trunk may be as tall as about 2 m or more. Fronds are pinnate or bipinnate, sometimes almost tripinnate in part, and less than 1 m long to about 1.5 m. The stipe is warty where scales have fallen;

the scales are pale to brownish and glossy. Sori occur near the midvein of fertile pinnules and are covered by firm indusia. Distribution: Luzon in the Philippines, in forest at 875–1150 m.

*Cyathea robinsonii* is named after botanist Charles Budd Robinson (1871–1913), who collected in the Philippines and North America.

### *Cyathea robusta* (C. Moore ex Watts) Holttum 1964

*Alsophila robusta* C. Moore ex Watts 1914, *Sphaeropteris robusta* (C. Moore ex Watts) Tryon 1970

PLATES 86, 87

*Sphaeropteris* clade. The erect trunk is 3–5 m tall; it is often covered in roundish scars left by fallen fronds or may retain some stipe bases. Fronds are tripinnate and may reach 4–5 m in length. The rachis and stipe are glaucous to brown, warty, and covered with plentiful scales that are large and whitish, with dark brown spiny edges, or small and pale. Sori occur in pairs and lack indusia. Distribution: Lord Howe Island, Australia, widespread but scattered in submontane areas, in rain forest to coastal forest up to 400 m.

*Cyathea robusta* is a robust, fast-growing tree fern, hence the name *robusta*. Plants are commonly cultivated and do well in humus with consistent moisture. Although frost resistant, frond damage will occur. Plants do best in sheltered situations.

### *Cyathea rosenstockii* Brause 1920

*Sphaeropteris rosenstockii* (Brause) Tryon 1970

*Sphaeropteris* clade. The erect trunk is 1–3 m tall. Fronds number six to eight in a crown, are bi- or tripinnate, and 1–2 m long. The stipe is covered with thick and fleshy scales. Sori occur near the fertile pinnule midvein and are covered with pale, thin indusia. Distribution: New Guinea in mossy forest or rain forest from 1300 m to about 1800 m.

*Cyathea rosenstockii* is named in honor of Eduard Rosenstock (1856–1928), German pteridologist.

### *Cyathea rubella* Holttum 1962

*Alsophila rubella* (Holttum) Tryon 1970

*Alsophila* clade. The erect trunk may be as tall as about 5 m. Fronds are bipinnate and may reach 2 m in length. The stipe is dark purplish brown toward the base and bears scattered slender spines and basal scales; the scales are dark and have a narrow paler margin. Sori occur either at the forks of veins on fertile pinnules or above the fork; indusia are absent. Distribution: Eastern New Guinea and the d'Entrecasteaux Islands, in dense rain forest and mossy forest at 650–900 m.

### *Cyathea rubiginosa* (Brause) Domin 1930
*Alsophila rubiginosa* Brause 1920, *A. hunsteiniana* Brause 1920,
*Cyathea albidula* Domin 1930

*Alsophila* clade. The erect trunk is about 5 m tall or more. Fronds are bi- or tripinnate and 2–3 m long. The stipe is purplish and has many small spines and scattered scales; the scales are either large and brown, with a paler margin, or small and dull brown. Sori occur on distal veins near the midvein of fertile pinnules and are covered by very thin, fragile indusia. Distribution: New Guinea in rocky open forest or in mossy forest, from 1100 m to about 2900 m.

### *Cyathea rufa* (Fée) Lellinger 1987
*Alsophila rufa* Fée 1869

*Cyathea* clade. Distribution: Brazil. *Cyathea rufa* forms part of the *C. armata* complex of related tree ferns.

### *Cyathea rufopannosa* Christ 1907
*Alsophila rufopannosa* (Christ) Tryon 1970

*Alsophila* clade. The erect trunk may be as tall as 1–2 m and about 4 cm in diameter. Fronds are bi- or tripinnate and 1–2 m long; they sometimes have a reduced pair of pinnae toward the base of the stipe. The stipe is warty toward the base and covered with scattered scales that are pale and have narrow fragile edges. Sori occur near the midvein of fertile pinnules and are covered by firm, scale-like indusia. Distribution: Philippines in montane forest at about 1200 m.

### *Cyathea ruiziana* Klotzsch 1847
*Cyathea* clade. The erect trunk is about 9 m tall; scales are large and whitish. Distribution: Central Peru in montane forest at about 2000 m. *Cyathea ruiziana* is a little-known tree fern based on material collected by Hipólito Ruiz (1754–1815) from west of Huánuco; the holotype specimen consists of a single pinna. *Cyathea ruiziana* is most likely part of a group of species centered on *C. straminea*.

### *Cyathea runensis* Alderwerelt van Rosenburgh 1908
*Sphaeropteris runensis* (Alderwerelt van Rosenburgh) Tryon 1970

*Sphaeropteris* clade. The erect trunk is 1–3 m tall. Fronds are bi- or tripinnate and 2–3 m long. The stipe is short, warty, and has scattered scales that are dull, dark, and thick but not fleshy. Sori occur near the midvein of fertile pinnules and are covered with thin indusia. Distribution: New Guinea and the Bismarck Archipelago, in lowland forest, the name *runensis* referring to Runai in the Bismarck Archipelago.

*Cyathea runensis* is very similar to *C. tripinnatifida*. The relationship between the two species requires investigation.

### *Cyathea rupestris* Maxon 1946

*Alsophila rupestris* (Maxon) Tryon 1970

*Alsophila* clade. The erect trunk is about 1.5 cm in diameter. Fronds are pinnate and about 50 cm long. The rachis and stipe are black and have plentiful scales at the base; the scales are dark, blackish, and have a paler margin. Sori occur in two simple rows on either side of the pinnule midvein and are covered by thin indusia. Distribution: Near Sarare, Colombia, at 920–1240 m, known only from the type locality.

*Cyathea rupestris* is a very small fern, perhaps the smallest member of the genus.

### *Cyathea saccata* Christ 1904

*Alsophila saccata* (Christ) Tryon 1970

*Alsophila* clade. The erect trunk is about 5 m tall or more. Fronds are bi- or tripinnate and 1–2 m long. The stipe is medium brown, has slender spines, and is covered with a few scales toward the base; the scales are either light brown or small and pale. Sori occur near the midvein of fertile pinnules and are covered by thin, translucent indusia. Distribution: Central Sulawesi (Celebes) in rain forest at 1300–1700 m.

### *Cyathea sagittifolia* (W. J. Hooker) Domin 1929

*Alsophila sagittifolia* W. J. Hooker 1866

*Cyathea* clade. The erect trunk is 1–4 m tall. Fronds are bipinnate and may reach 2–2.5 m in length. The rachis and stipe are purplish and have scattered scales that are brown and often have a paler margin. Sori occur between the fertile pinnule midvein and the edge of the lamina; true indusia are absent. Distribution: Trinidad in wet montane forest at 500–750 m.

The uncommon *Cyathea sagittifolia* is allied to *C. petiolata*.

### *Cyathea salletii* Tardieu-Blot & C. Christensen 1934

*Alsophila salletii* (Tardieu-Blot & C. Christensen) Tryon 1970

*Alsophila* clade. The erect trunk is 3–4 m tall. Fronds are bi- or tripinnate and 1–2 m long. The stipe is long and scaly at the base; the scales are either pale and have short-fringed edges or are narrow and dark. Sori are borne close to the midvein of fertile pinnules; indusia are absent. Distribution: Vietnam.

*Cyathea salletii* is named after Sallet, the French collector who gathered the type material from Bana in 1925.

### *Cyathea sarasinorum* Holttum 1963

*Sphaeropteris sarasinorum* (Holttum) Tryon 1970

*Sphaeropteris* clade. The erect trunk is 2–3 m tall. Fronds are bi- or tripinnate. The rachis is pale and has dark shiny warts, and scales. The stipe is covered with warts and basal scales. Scales are narrow and shiny brown. Sori occur near the midveins of fertile pinnules and lack indusia. Distribution: Central Sulawesi (Celebes), known from only one location.

### *Cyathea scandens* (Brause) Domin 1930

*Alsophila scandens* Brause 1920

*Alsophila* clade. The climbing trunk is 1–2 cm in diameter; its apex is covered in scales. Fronds are of two kinds, simple pinnate fronds that are sterile, and bipinnate fronds that may be fertile. Fertile pinnules slightly lobed. The stipe is dark, almost black, smooth, and glossy but covered at the base with scales that are long, very dark, and have a paler margin. Sori occur in four pairs per pinnule lobe; indusia are absent. Distribution: Eastern New Guinea against trees in mossy forest and rain forest at about 1000 m.

As the name *scandens* implies, this is an unusual climbing or scrambling fern, often clinging to the supporting tree by its roots and ascending as high as 3 m. *Cyathea scandens* is very similar to *C. biformis*, differing only in the shape of the fertile pinnules, which are slightly lobed, versus strongly lobed in *C. biformis*. It is possible that these two species should be united into one.

### *Cyathea schiedeana* (C. B. Presl) Domin 1929

*Alsophila schiedeana* C. B. Presl 1836, *Cyathea crassifolia* (Christ) Domin 1929

*Cyathea* clade. The erect trunk may be as tall as 7 m and 5–9 cm in diameter. Fronds are bipinnate and may reach 2.5 m in length. Petioles are brown to black and have spines. The rachis is brown, smooth, and shiny and has spines, scales, and hairs; the scales are either brown or bicolored, dark brown with a lighter edge. Sori occur in two rows along each side of the pinnule midvein; indusia are absent. Distribution: Mexico and Costa Rica; Colombia. Plants are found in tropical and submontane rain forest, in forest understory, or in open areas at 600–1400 m.

The name *schiedei* commemorates Christian Schiede (1798–1836), who died collecting plants in Mexico. *Cyathea schiedeana* is a medium-sized tree fern with a dark slender trunk and large, gently arching fronds. It is a variable species that bears some similarity to *C. brunnescens, C. darienensis, C. mucilagina, C. multiflora, C. nigripes, C. punctata,* and *C. squamulosa.*

## *Cyathea schlechteri* (Brause) Domin 1929

*Alsophila schlechteri* Brause 1912

*Alsophila* clade. The erect trunk is 1–3 m tall. Fronds are bi- or tripinnate and 1–2 m long. The stipe is covered by scales that are either wide and pale or narrow with a dark central band and fragile edges. Fertile pinnules are lobed and smaller than sterile ones. Sori are raised on the underside of the fertile pinnule and lack indusia. Distribution: Eastern New Guinea in montane forest at 1000 m.

The name *schlechteri* commemorates botanist Friedrich Richard Rudolf Schlechter (1872–1925), who undertook extensive collecting journeys.

## *Cyathea schliebenii* Reimers 1933

*Alsophila tanzaniana* Tryon 1970

*Alsophila* clade. The erect trunk is 4–5 m tall. Fronds are pinnate to almost bipinnate and about 1 m long. The rachis and stipe are long and scaly, particularly toward the base; the scales are dark glossy brown and have a narrow paler margin. Sori are round and covered with indusia. Distribution: Uluguru Mountains, Tanzania, in wet forest at 1800–2000 m.

*Cyathea schliebenii* is named after Hans Joachim Eberhard Schlieben (1902–1975), who collected plants in Africa and Madagascar.

## *Cyathea schlimii* (Kuhn) Domin 1929

*Alsophila schlimii* Kuhn 1869

*Cyathea* clade. The erect trunk may be as tall as about 3.5 m. Fronds are bipinnate and 3–3.5 m long. The stipe is warty and covered in brown scales toward the base. Sori are on fertile pinnules between midveins and the pinnule margin; indusia are absent. Distribution: Eastern Colombia and Venezuela, in rain forest at 500–1500 m.

The name *schlimii* commemorates Louis Joseph Schlim (1841–1852), who collected plants in South America and the West Indies. *Cyathea schlimii* is a little-known species possibly allied to *C. lasiosora* and *C. wendlandii.*

## *Cyathea sechellarum* Mettenius 1863

*Alsophila sechellarum* (Mettenius) Tryon 1970

PLATE 88

*Alsophila* clade. The erect, narrow trunk may be as tall as 4 m. Fronds are bipinnate. Distribution: Seychelles in gullies and high-elevation forest, few large plants remaining on the island of Mahé, but some regeneration is taking place.

## *Cyathea semiamplectens* Holttum 1962

*Alsophila semiamplectens* (Holttum) Tryon 1970

*Alsophila* clade. The erect trunk is 1–2 m tall. Fronds are bi- or tripinnate and 1–2 m long. The stipe is covered by scales that are narrow, with either a dark middle band and fragile edges, or pale all over. Sori occur near the midvein of fertile pinnules and are covered by thin indusia. Distribution: Northeastern New Guinea in subalpine forest and shrub at 3300–3560 m.

## *Cyathea senex* Alderwerelt van Rosenburgh 1914

*Sphaeropteris senex* (Alderwerelt van Rosenburgh) Tryon 1970

*Sphaeropteris* clade. The erect trunk may be as tall as about 2 m or more. Fronds are pinnate or bipinnate, almost tripinnate in part, and about 1 m long or more. The stipe is densely covered in scales that are pale and have dark setiferous edges. Sori occur near the midvein of fertile pinnules and are covered by firm indusia. Distribution: Central Sumatra in forest at 1500–1800 m.

## *Cyathea senilis* (Klotzsch) Domin 1929

*Alsophila senilis* Klotzsch 1847

*Cyathea* clade. The erect trunk may be as tall as about 6 m. Fronds are bipinnate to almost tripinnate and about 2.5 m long. The stipe is warty and covered in scales toward the base; the scales are bullate, whitish, and have a long brown apex. Sori are on fertile pinnules between midveins and the pinnule margin; indusia are absent. Distribution: Venezuela on forested slopes at 500–1400 m.

*Cyathea senilis* is related to *C. aterrima*, *C. lockwoodiana*, and *C. parianensis*.

## *Cyathea serratifolia* Baker 1884

*Alsophila serratifolia* (Baker) Tryon 1970, *Cyathea regularis* Baker 1899

*Alsophila* clade. The erect trunk is 3–4 m tall. Fronds are bipinnate and about 2 m long. Rachis and trunk scales are glossy and have a dark brown center and a paler margin. Sori occur near the midvein of fertile pinnules and are covered by large brown indusia. Distribution: Madagascar.

*Cyathea serratifolia* is a member of a complex that also includes *C. marattioides*, *C. perrieriana*, and *C. tsilotsilensis*.

## *Cyathea setifera* Holttum 1962

*Sphaeropteris setifera* (Holttum) Tryon 1970

*Sphaeropteris* clade. The erect trunk is short to medium-sized. Fronds are bi- or tripinnate and 1–2 m long. The stipe is covered with scales that are either thick, dark, and fleshy, with pale edges, or small and irregular. Sori occur near the edge of fertile pinnules and are covered with pale, thin indusia. Distribution: Northern Moluccas at 1000 m.

## *Cyathea setulosa* Copeland 1952

*Alsophila setulosa* (Copeland) Tryon 1970

*Alsophila* clade. The erect trunk is 2–3 m tall or more. Fronds are bi- or tripinnate and may reach 1–2 m in length. The stipe is covered in scales that are dark, glossy, and narrow. Sori occur near the midvein of fertile pinnules and are half-covered by brown indusia. Distribution: Luzon in the Philippines, in montane forest.

## *Cyathea sibuyanensis* Copeland in Elmer 1911

*Sphaeropteris sibuyanensis* (Copeland) Tryon 1970

*Sphaeropteris* clade. The erect trunk is short. Fronds are bipinnate and 0.5–1 m long or more. The rachis is warty on the lower surface and bears many scales that are pale and dull. Sori occur near the midvein of fertile pinnules and are covered by pale, translucent indusia. Distribution: Sibuyan Island in the Philippines, at about 1400 m, a little-known tree fern rarely collected and known from Mount Giting-Giting.

## *Cyathea simplex* Tryon 1976

*Cyathea* clade. The trunk is short. Fronds are bipinnate and about 1.5 m long. Distribution: Venezuela at about 1200 m.

*Cyathea simplex* is part of a group of tree ferns centered around *C. pallescens*.

## *Cyathea sinuata* W. J. Hooker & Greville 1828

*Alsophila sinuata* (W. J. Hooker & Greville) Tryon 1970

PLATE 89

*Alsophila* clade. The erect trunk is just over about 1 m tall and 1–2 cm in diameter. Fronds are simple and just over 50 cm long. The stipe is slender, dark, and covered with scales, especially when young; the scales are glossy, dark, and have pale fragile edges. Sori occur on the lowest two or three pairs of veins of fertile pinnules and are covered with thin indusia. Distribution: India and Sri Lanka, in wet lowland forest.

*Cyathea sinuata*, a small tree fern, is notable for its unusual simple fronds.

## *Cyathea sipapoensis* (Tryon) Lellinger 1984

*Sphaeropteris sipapoensis* Tryon 1972

*Cyathea* clade. The erect trunk may be as tall as about 6 m. Fronds are bipinnate to almost tripinnate and about 2.5 m long. The stipe is warty and covered in scales toward the base; the scales are bullate and whitish or narrow and light brown. Sori are close to the margin of fertile pinnules and have long, white paraphyses; indusia are absent. Distribution: Venezuela, named from the only known collection at Cerro Sipapo in the Guiana Highlands.

*Cyathea sipapoensis* is closely related to *C. marginalis*.

## *Cyathea smithii* J. D. Hooker 1854

*Alsophila smithii* (J. D. Hooker) Tryon 1970

**SOFT TREE FERN, KATOTE**

**FIGURE 4; PLATES 90–94**

*Alsophila* clade. The erect trunk may be as tall as 8 m. Fronds are tripinnate and about 2.5 m long and 1.5 m wide; the base of the frond may have occasional pinnules, forming a clump over the trunk apex. The rachis and stipe are slender, pale to dark brown, and have pale brown scales toward the base and apex. The midribs of dead fronds are retained as a prominent skirt about the trunk. Sori occur on both sides of the pinnule midvein; indusia are saucerlike. Distribution: North Island, South Island, Stewart Island, and Chatham Islands of New Zealand, and as far south as the Auckland Islands, common in montane forest and lowland forest in the southern regions of its range.

*Cyathea smithii* is named after John Smith (1798–1888). It is a medium-sized tree fern with a delicate crown, and a skirt consisting of dark brown stipe bases held around the trunk. Juvenile plants are notable for the abundance of scales on the stipes and near the apex. *Cyathea smithii* is the most southerly occurring tree fern in the world, found on the subantarctic Auckland Islands. Plants do best in cooler areas and will withstand frost provided they are given a well-drained humus with plentiful moisture and shelter from wind.

## *Cyathea solomonensis* Holttum 1964

*Alsophila solomonensis* (Holttum) Tryon 1970

*Alsophila* clade. The erect trunk may be as tall as 4 m. Fronds are bi- or tripinnate, 2–3 m long; the pinnae may be red or have some red coloration, and the lowest one or two pairs are reduced. The stipe is pale and has scales toward the base; the scales are narrow, pale to dark, and have broad fragile edges. Sori are round and partially covered by small thin indusia. Distribution: Solomon Islands in forest and on steep cliffs above streams at 500–1000 m.

*Cyathea solomonensis* is related to *C. affinis*.

## *Cyathea speciosa* Willdenow 1810

*Cyathea integrifolia* (Klotzsch) Domin 1929

*Cyathea* clade. The erect, narrow to slender trunk is 2 m tall. Fronds are bipinnate and as long as 2 m. Distribution: Venezuela and Colombia, in dense submontane rain forest and cloud forest, at 1000–1700 m.

*Cyathea speciosa* is the center of a group of species that includes *C. decorata* and *C. haughtii*. It may be a parent of *Cnemidaria bella*.

## *Cyathea spinulosa* Wallich ex W. J. Hooker 1844

*Alsophila spinulosa* (Wallich ex W. J. Hooker) Tryon 1970, *Cyathea decipiens* (Scott) C. B. Clarke & Baker 1888, *C. boninsimensis* (Christ ex Diels) Copeland 1909, *C. fauriei* (Christ) Copeland 1909, *C. taiwaniana* Nakai 1927

PLATE 95

*Alsophila* clade. The erect trunk may be as tall as 5 m and about 15 cm in diameter. Fronds are tripinnate and as long as 2–3 m. Stipes are persistent and may form an irregular skirt. The stipe is glossy, greenish, purple-black toward the base, and covered with spines and glossy brown scales. Sori are round, borne in rows, one on either side of the pinnule midvein, and covered by thin, membranous, globose indusia. Distribution: Nepal, Bhutan, central and southern India, Sri Lanka, Myanmar (Burma), southern China, Taiwan, and Japan (including Okinawa), in forest at 600–1800 m.

*Cyathea spinulosa* is similar to *C. callosa*, which has fewer and shorter spines.

## *Cyathea squamulata* (Blume) Copeland 1909

*Gymnosphaera squamulata* Blume 1828, *Sphaeropteris squamulata* (Blume) Tryon 1970, *Cyathea ridleyi* Copeland 1909, *C. glabrescens* Domin 1930, *C. xanthina* Domin 1930

*Sphaeropteris* clade. The erect trunk may be as tall as 2 m. Fronds are pinnate or bipinnate and about 1.5 m long. The stipe is densely scaly; the scales are firm and medium brown. Sori occur near the midvein of fertile pinnules; indusia are absent. Distribution: Malay Peninsula, Sumatra, Java, Borneo, and the southern Philippines, including the Sulu Archipelago, in forest from the lowlands to about 1500 m.

### *Cyathea squamulosa* (I. Losch) R. C. Moran 1991

*Hemitelia squamulosa* I. Losch 1950

*Cyathea* clade. The erect trunk may be as tall as 1.5 m and 5–8 cm in diameter. Fronds are bipinnate and may reach 2 m in length. Petioles are brown and have spines. The rachis is yellow-brown to brown. Rachis and trunk scales are long and either yellow-brown or dark brown. Sori occur in two rows along each side of the pinnule midvein and are covered with scale-like indusia. Distribution: Orosí to Tapantí, Costa Rica, and near Fortuna Dam, Panama, in wet forest, understory, and forest margins from 1300 m to about 2300 m.

*Cyathea squamulosa* is a short tree fern with a dark trunk and large, upward-arching fronds. It is related to *C. schiedeana,* differing in its stalked pinnules, larger petiole scales, and the presence of indusia.

### *Cyathea steyermarkii* Tryon 1972

not *Trichipteris steyermarkii* Tryon 1970 (see *Cyathea venezuelensis*)

*Cyathea* clade. The erect trunk may be as tall as about 1 m. Distribution: Summit of Cerro Autana (about 1200 m), Venezuela.

*Cyathea steyermarkii* is named after Julian A. Steyermark (1909–1988), botanist and prolific collector of plants, particularly in the Venezuelan Guayana, who collected the type material.

### *Cyathea stipipinnula* Holttum 1962

*Sphaeropteris stipipinnula* (Holttum) Tryon 1970

*Sphaeropteris* clade. The erect trunk is 1–2 m tall. Fronds are pinnate or bipinnate and 1–2 m long. The stipe is medium dark brown, scaly, and warty where scales have fallen; the scales are either large and shiny brown, with pale edges, or minute, pale, and fringed. Sori occur about halfway between the midvein of the fertile pinnule and the edge of the lamina, in groups of three; indusia are firm and pale. Distribution: Kinabalu on Borneo, in open places in forest at 1200–1500 m.

### *Cyathea stipularis* (Christ) Domin 1929

*Alsophila stipularis* Christ 1904

*Cyathea* clade. The erect trunk may be as tall as 15 m and 6–10 cm in diameter. Fronds are bipinnate and may reach 3 m in length. Petioles are straw-colored to yellow-brown and have spines or raised dots. The rachis is dark and spiny or may be smooth. Rachis and trunk scales are bicolored, blackish with a white margin. Sori occur in two rows along each side of the pinnule midvein; indusia are absent. Distribution: Mexico, Guatemala, Honduras,

Nicaragua, Costa Rica, and Panama, in tropical and submontane rain forest, in open areas, on riverbanks, and in cleared pastureland, at 800–2000 m.

*Cyathea stipularis* is a very tall tree fern with a dark trunk and large arching fronds. It forms part of the *C. armata* complex.

### *Cyathea stokesii* E. Brown 1931

*Alsophila stokesii* (E. Brown) Tryon 1970

*Cyathea* clade. The erect trunk may be as tall as 5 m. Fronds are pinnate and 1–2 m long. The rachis and stipe are light brown to pale and have scales toward the base of the stipe; the scales are dark, glossy brown, and have a paler margin. Sori are toward the midvein of the pinnules and covered by small thin indusia. Distribution: Rapa in the Austral Islands, French Polynesia.

*Cyathea stokesii* is named after John Francis Gray Stokes (b. 1909), who collected plants in Hawaii and the South Pacific. It is one of a group of western Pacific species apparently related to *C. decurrens*. Members of this group have variously been attributed to *Alsophila* or *Cyathea*. Molecular evidence suggests a relationship with the latter genus, as treated here, though the relationship is by no means clear.

### *Cyathea stolzei* A. R. Smith ex Lellinger 1987

*Trichipteris pinnata* Stolze 1984, not *Cyathea pinnata* Roxburgh ex
   C. B. Clarke 1844 (see *C. moluccana*)

*Cyathea* clade. The fern is trunkless. Fronds are pinnate, often glossy green, and 35 cm to 1 m long. Petioles are olive green to gray-brown and smooth. The rachis is yellow-brown and either smooth or has scales that are bicolored, glossy dark brown with a white margin. Sori occur in three to five rows; indusia are absent. Distribution: Costa Rica and Panama; Ecuador. Plants grow in tropical and submontane rain forest, in the understory, at 100–1000 m.

*Cyathea stolzei* is named after pteridologist Robert G. Stolze (b. 1927). It is a small tree fern, lacking a trunk and with simple pinnate fronds. Occasional hybrids between it and *C. ursina* have been reported from Costa Rica.

### *Cyathea straminea* Karsten 1856

*Cyathea* clade. The erect, narrow trunk is about 3 m tall. Fronds are bipinnate and heavily dissected to virtually tripinnate. Petioles are yellowish brown and somewhat spiny. The rachis is scaly and lacks hairs. Petiole scales are whitish brown to straw-colored; elsewhere, scales are straw-colored to brown and have dark peripheral or apical processes. Sori occur nearly halfway between the midvein of fertile pinnules and the edge of the lamina and are covered with globose indusia. Distribution: Colombia in montane forest at 2000–2500 m.

*Cyathea straminea* is a lesser-known tree fern with distinctive straw-colored scales. It is part of a group of species that includes *C. boliviana, C. corallifera,* and *C. ruiziana; C. brevistipes* is also similar.

### *Cyathea strigosa* Christ 1898

*Sphaeropteris strigosa* (Christ) Tryon 1970

*Sphaeropteris* clade. The erect trunk is medium-sized. Fronds are bi- or tripinnate and 2–3 m long. The rachis is pale and spiny beneath. The stipe is covered with scales that are pale and setiferous, and spines as long as 2 mm. Sori occur near the midvein of fertile pinnules and are covered with pale indusia. Distribution: Southwestern Sulawesi (Celebes), Indonesia, rare in montane and submontane forest above 2800 m.

*Cyathea strigosa* is similar to *C. leucotricha* from the lowlands of Borneo; the exact relationship between the two species probably requires further investigation.

### *Cyathea stuebelii* Hieronymus 1906

*Alsophila paucifolia* Baker in W. J. Hooker & Baker 1874

*Alsophila* clade. The short, erect trunk is about 2 cm in diameter. Fronds are pendent, simply pinnate, and as long as 1.5 m. The rachis is black and has a few scales at the base; the scales are lanceolate to ovate, blackish, and have pale margins. Sori occur in small clusters toward the base of the midvein of fertile pinnules and are covered with globose indusia. Distribution: Ecuador in montane forest at 900–1240 m, confined to cliff faces.

*Cyathea stuebelii* is named after Alphons Stübel (1835–1904), who collected plants in Ecuador and Peru. It belongs to the *C. minor* group and is very similar to the western Andean *Alsophila esmeraldensis* (Appendix 1), from which it differs in having more pendent fronds.

### *Cyathea subdubia* (Alderwerelt van Rosenburgh) Domin 1929

*Alsophila subdubia* Alderwerelt van Rosenburgh 1915, *Cyathea persquamulata* (Alderwerelt van Rosenburgh) Domin 1930

*Alsophila* clade. The erect trunk is 1–3 m tall. Fronds are bi- or tripinnate and 1–2 m long. The stipe is dark, warty near the base, and covered with scales that are dark, glossy, and have a paler margin. Sori occur in three pairs near the midvein of fertile pinnules; indusia are absent. Distribution: Central Sumatra and western Java, Indonesia, at about 1500 m.

*Cyathea subdubia* appears to be part of a complex that includes *C. gigantea*, *C. glabra*, and *C. podophylla;* the relationship between these species requires further investigation.

### *Cyathea subsessilis* Copeland 1911

*Sphaeropteris subsessilis* (Copeland) Tryon 1970

*Sphaeropteris* clade. The erect trunk is 2–3 m tall. Fronds are bi- or tripinnate and may reach just over 1 m in length. The stipe is covered with dull brown, thin scales and may have warts when the scales fall. Sori occur halfway between the midvein of fertile pinnules and the edge of the lobe and are covered with indusia. Distribution: Fiji to Samoa, in wet forest at 900–1200 m.

*Cyathea subsessilis* is very similar to *C. vaupelii*, from which it differs in its smaller size and smaller pinnules; the exact relationship between the two species probably requires further investigation.

### *Cyathea subtripinnata* Holttum 1962

*Alsophila subtripinnata* (Holttum) Tryon 1970

*Alsophila* clade. The erect trunk is 2–3 m tall. Fronds number about 18 in an unwhorled crown, are bi- or tripinnate, and 1–1.5 m long. The rachis is dull brown and finely warty. The stipe bears many scales and may be warty after scales fall; the scales are dark brown, glossy, and have fragile edges. Sori are round, occur near the fertile pinnule midvein, and are covered by firm, brown, cup-like indusia. Distribution: Eastern New Guinea at the edges of alpine shrub and grassland, at about 3000 m.

### *Cyathea subtropica* Domin 1929

*Alsophila lechleri* Mettenius 1859, not *Cyathea lechleri* Mettenius 1859;

*Trichipteris lechleri* (Mettenius) Tryon 1970

*Cyathea* clade. The erect trunk may be as tall as 12 m. Fronds are bipinnate and 1–2 m long. The stipe is purplish, warty, and scaly, especially toward the base; the scales are brown and have a wide, paler margin. Sori occur either near the midvein of fertile pinnules or between the midvein and the edge of the lamina, farther from the pinnule apex; indusia are absent. Distribution: Colombia, Ecuador, Peru, and Bolivia, from the Guiana Highlands to the eastern slopes of the Andes, in rain forest around rivers and lakes at 450–1450 m.

*Cyathea subtropica* is also commonly known as *Trichipteris lechleri*, but when moved to *Cyathea* the name *lechleri* is no longer available, hence the use of *subtropica* as proposed by Karel Domin.

### *Cyathea suluensis* Baker 1879

*Sphaeropteris suluensis* (Baker) Tryon 1970, *Cyathea sessilipinnula* Copeland 1929

*Sphaeropteris* clade. The erect trunk may be as tall as about 2 m or more. Fronds are pinnate or bipinnate and about 1 m long or longer. Rachis and trunk scales are pale and fringed. The stipe is finely spiny at the base. Sori occur near the midvein of fertile pinnules and are covered by indusia. Distribution: Philippines, the name *suluensis* referring to the Sulu Archipelago, and possibly the Moluccas, in forest at about 600 m.

### *Cyathea sumatrana* Baker 1880

*Alsophila sumatrana* (Baker) Tryon 1970, *Cyathea schizochlamys* Baker 1880

*Alsophila* clade. The erect trunk is 2–5 m tall. Fronds are bi- or tripinnate and 2–3 m long. The stipe is warty and covered with scales that are glossy, dark to medium brown, and have pale fragile edges. Sori occur near the midvein of fertile pinnules and are covered by thin, fragile indusia. Distribution: Malay Peninsula and Sumatra, in rain forest at 500–1500 m.

### *Cyathea suprastrigosa* (Christ) Maxon 1909

*Hemitelia suprastrigosa* Christ in Pitt 1901, *Cyathea conspicua* Christ 1906

*Cyathea* clade. The erect trunk may be as tall as 5 m and 10 cm in diameter. Fronds are about 1 m long. Distribution: Costa Rica in montane forest and cloud forest at 2000–3000 m.

*Cyathea suprastrigosa* is part of a group of ferns centered on *C. fulva*.

### *Cyathea surinamensis* (Miquel) Domin 1929

*Hemitelia surinamensis* Miquel 1843, *Cyathea piligera* (Hieronymus) Domin 1929, *C. superba* (Maxon) Domin 1930, *Sphaeropteris hirsuta* (Desvaux) Tryon 1970, not *C. hirsuta* C. B. Presl 1822

*Cyathea* clade. The erect trunk may be as tall as 5 m. Fronds are bipinnate and 1–2 m long. The stipe is scaly toward the base; the scales are dark and glossy, with toothed edges. Sori occur near the midvein of fertile pinnules and are covered by thin, translucent, two-lobed, scale-like indusia. Distribution: Trinidad; Venezuela, Guyana, Suriname, French Guiana, and Brazil. Plants grow in forest at 100–1000 m.

*Cyathea surinamensis* is similar to *C. cyatheoides*.

### *Cyathea tenera* (J. Smith ex W. J. Hooker) T. Moore 1861

*Alsophila tenera* J. Smith ex W. J. Hooker 1844

*Cyathea* clade. The erect trunk may be as tall as about 9 m; it is covered with spines and golden brown scales. Fronds are pinnate but deeply dissected and 2–3 m long. The rachis is brown and sparsely covered with spines. The stipe is long and brown, with a few scattered, golden brown scales near the bases. Sori occur along the midvein of fertile pinnules and are covered by globose, membranous indusia. Distribution: Greater Antilles (Cuba, Jamaica, Hispaniola, and Puerto Rico) and Lesser Antilles (Monserrat, Guadeloupe, Dominica, Martinique, St. Lucia, St. Vincent, Granada, and Trinidad), and islands off the Atlantic coast of Costa Rica, in rain forest and montane woodland in the understory and in thickets at 400–1000 m.

*Cyathea tenera* is part of a group of ferns centered on *C. fulva*.

## *Cyathea tenggerensis* (Rosenstock) Domin 1930

*Alsophila tenggerensis* Rosenstock 1917, *Sphaeropteris tenggerensis* (Rosenstock) Tryon 1970

PLATE 96

*Sphaeropteris* clade. The erect trunk is 2–3 m tall. Fronds are bi- or tripinnate. The stipe is covered with warts and basal scales; the scales are shiny brown and firm. Sori are near the midveins of the fertile pinnules and lack indusia. Distribution: Eastern Java (locally abundant in the Tengger Mountains of eastern Java, hence the specific name), southern Sulawesi (Celebes), and Flores, in open places at 1500–2300 m.

## *Cyathea tenuicaulis* Domin 1930

*Alsophila tenuis* Brause 1920

*Alsophila* clade. The erect trunk is 1–2 m tall and about 2 cm in diameter. Fronds are bi- or tripinnate and about 1 m long or less. The stipe is dull purple, warty, and covered with scattered scales that are rigid, medium brown, and have fragile edges. Sori occur near the midvein of fertile pinnules and are covered by thin, fragile indusia. Distribution: Eastern New Guinea in rain forest at 300–1500 m.

## *Cyathea ternatea* Alderwerelt van Rosenburgh 1922

*Alsophila ternatea* (Alderwerelt van Rosenburgh) Tryon 1970

*Alsophila* clade. The erect trunk is 2–3 m tall. Fronds are bi- or tripinnate and 1–2 m long. The stipe is spiny and has scattered scales that are glossy brown and have a narrow, paler, dull margin. Sori are round, occur near the fertile pinnule midvein, and are covered by small, saucer-like indusia. Distribution: Moluccas in rain forest at 600–1300 m.

### *Cyathea teysmannii* Copeland 1909

*Sphaeropteris teysmannii* (Copeland) Tryon 1970

*Sphaeropteris* clade. Distribution: Southwestern Sulawesi (Celebes) at about 1000 m.

*Cyathea teysmannii* is named after Johannes Elias Teijsmann (1809–1882), who collected plants in Malesia. It is a little-known tree fern, apparently similar to *C. tripinnata*.

### *Cyathea thomsonii* Baker 1881

*Cyathea zambesiaca* Baker 1894, *Alsophila thomsonii* (Baker) Tryon 1970

*Alsophila* clade. The erect trunk is about 2 m tall. Fronds are bipinnate and 1–2 m long. The rachis and stipe are light to dark and have scattered scales, particularly toward the base; the scales are glossy brown and have a delicate fringed edge. Sori occur about four per pinnule lobe; indusia are large and thin, forming deep cups. Distribution: Southern Tanzania, Malawi, Mozambique, Zimbabwe, Zambia, eastern Angola, and southern Democratic Republic of Congo (Zaire), in forest near streams at 600–1500 m.

*Cyathea thomsonii* is named after Joseph Thomson (1858–1895), a naturalist who made collections in Africa. It appears to be intermediate between *C. dregei* and various pinnate African species of tree ferns.

### *Cyathea tomentosa* (Blume) Zollinger & Mor in Moritzi 1846

*Chnoophora tomentosa* Blume 1828, *Sphaeropteris tomentosa* (Blume) Tryon 1970

*Sphaeropteris* clade. The erect trunk is about 15 m tall; it bears numerous stipe-base scars. Fronds are bi- or tripinnate and 2–3 m long. The stipe is densely scaly and has short spines; the scales are light brown, glossy, and firm. Sori occur near the midvein of fertile pinnules and lack indusia. Distribution: Western Java, including the hot springs on Mount Gedeh at 2200 m, and Flores, Indonesia, in ridge forest, gullies, and open swampy places.

*Cyathea tomentosa* is apparently allied to *C. magna* of New Guinea, from which it differs in its wider stipe scales and less rigid pinnules. *Cyathea crinita* of Sri Lanka and southern India may also be closely related. The relationship between these species requires further investigation.

### *Cyathea tomentosissima* Copeland 1942

*Sphaeropteris tomentosissima* (Copeland) Tryon 1970
PLATE 97

*Sphaeropteris* clade. The erect trunk is 2–3 m tall and 16 cm in diameter. Fronds number about 40 in a crown, are copper-colored, bi- or tripinnate, and reach just over 1 m in length. The rachis has pale scales on the undersurface. The stipe is light red-brown, warty, and covered with scales toward the base; the scales are twisted, shiny, firm, and brown. Sori occur one per pinnule lobe; indusia are absent. Distribution: New Guinea along streams, in open grassland, and drier shrubby areas, at 3000–3300 m.

*Cyathea tomentosissima*, a smaller tree fern, often has a scraggly appearance with an upright crown and individual fronds resembling those of the common bracken fern, *Pteridium aquilinum*. However, it is growing in popularity because of its tolerance of sunnier and drier conditions. Plants will form a trunk in 4 years, are frost resistant, and suitable for cultivation in containers.

## *Cyathea tortuosa* R. C. Moran 1991

*Cyathea* clade. The erect trunk is 1–5 m tall and 4–6 cm in diameter. Fronds are bipinnate, dissected, and 1.5–2 m long. The rachis is tan to brown, hairy, and has scattered scales that are golden brown and ovate to linear. Sori occur between the midvein of fertile pinnules and the edge of the lamina; indusia are absent. Distribution: Colombia, Ecuador, and Peru, in wet forest at 200–850 m.

The name *tortuosa* refers to the twisted whitish hairs present on the pinnule midribs of the underside of the fronds. *Cyathea tortuosa* is very similar to *C. brunnescens* but differs in details of hair and scale shape and color; there is also some similarity to *C. darienensis* and *C. nigripes*.

## *Cyathea trichiata* (Maxon) Domin 1929

*Alsophila trichiata* Maxon 1922

*Cyathea* clade. The erect trunk may be as tall as 10 m and 6–10 cm in diameter. Fronds are bipinnate and as long as 3 m; old, dead fronds may be retained, forming a skirt about the trunk. Petioles are straw-colored to yellow-brown and have spines. The rachis is straw-colored and smooth to spiny. Rachis and trunk scales are bicolored, blackish to dark brown with a white margin. Sori occur in two rows along each side of the pinnule midvein; indusia are absent. Distribution: Nicaragua, Costa Rica, and Panama; Venezuela, Colombia, and Ecuador. Plants grow in tropical and submontane rain forest, on riverbanks, in open areas, and cleared pastureland, from sea level to about 1000 m.

*Cyathea trichiata* is a medium-sized to large tree fern with large arching fronds and a skirt made up of entire dead fronds. It is closely related to *C. armata* and allied species.

### *Cyathea trichodesma* (Scort) Copeland 1909

*Alsophila trichodesma* Scort in Beddome 1887, *Sphaeropteris trichodesma* (Scort) Tryon 1970, *Cyathea burbidgei* Holttum 1954

*Sphaeropteris* clade. The erect, slender trunk is 4–5 m tall. Fronds are pinnate or bipinnate and 1–2 m long or more. The stipe is long and finely warty at the base where scales have fallen; the scales are shiny, medium brown to light brown, firm, and have setiferous edges. Sori occur near the midvein of fertile pinnules and may run together at maturity; indusia are absent. Distribution: Luzon and Mindoro in the Philippines, in montane forest to at least about 1500 m.

### *Cyathea trichophora* Copeland 1911

*Sphaeropteris trichophora* (Copeland) Tryon 1970, *Cyathea mollis* Copeland 1917, *C. ramosii* Copeland 1926

*Sphaeropteris* clade. The erect trunk is usually 50 cm tall, or at the most, less than 1 m. Fronds are pinnate and 1–2 m long. The stipe is densely scaly, particularly toward the base; the scales are shiny, medium to light brown, and have setiferous edges. Sori occur about halfway between the midvein of fertile pinnules and the edge of the lamina; indusia are absent. Distribution: Philippines, Sarawak, and Kinabalu in Sabah, in low-country forest to 1200 m.

It is likely that *Cyathea elliptica* is simply a variant of *C. trichophora;* further investigation into the relationship between the two is required.

### *Cyathea tripinnata* Copeland 1906

*Sphaeropteris tripinnata* (Copeland) Tryon 1970

*Sphaeropteris* clade. The erect trunk is 4–5 m tall. Fronds are tripinnate and 2–3 m long. The stipe is dark, sharply spiny, and densely covered with small scales; the scales are small, thin, soft, and have dark setae. Sori occur near the midvein of fertile pinnules and lack indusia but are covered by overlapping thin scales. Distribution: Moluccas, western Java, and Palau, in forest at 700 m, also in the Philippines and northern Borneo at 250–1000 m.

*Cyathea tripinnata* is similar to the little-known *C. teysmannii* and to *C. leidermannii*.

### *Cyathea tripinnatifida* Roxburgh 1844

*Sphaeropteris tripinnatifida* (Roxburgh) Tryon 1970, *Cyathea nigrospinulosa* Alderwerelt van Rosenburgh 1918

*Sphaeropteris* clade. The erect trunk is 1–3 m tall. Fronds are bi- or tripinnate and 2–3 m long. The stipe has scattered scales that are thick and fleshy toward the base. Sori occur near the midvein of fertile pinnules and are covered with thin indusia. Distribution: Moluccas, including Ambon, in lowland forest.

*Cyathea tripinnatifida* is similar to *C. runensis* from western New Guinea; the relationship between the two species requires further investigation.

### *Cyathea truncata* (Brackenridge) Copeland 1909

*Alsophila truncata* Brackenridge 1854, *Sphaeropteris truncata* (Brackenridge) Tryon 1970

*Sphaeropteris* clade. The erect trunk is about 10 m tall. Fronds are tripinnate and may reach 4–5 m in length. The rachis is dark on the underside and bears many fine warts. The stipe is dark and covered with scales, especially toward the base, and/or warts where the scales fall; the scales are thin and either pale or dark brown. Sori occur near the midvein of fertile pinnules; indusia are absent but scales may surround the sorus. Distribution: Solomon Islands to Fiji and Samoa, in rain forest to about 1300 m.

*Cyathea truncata* is similar to *C. aciculosa* but differs in its smaller scales, covering the sori; the relationship between the two species requires further investigation.

### *Cyathea tryonorum* (Riba) Lellinger 1987

*Alsophila tryonorum* Riba 1967

*Cyathea* clade. Distribution: Venezuela, Colombia, and Ecuador, in forest from sea level to 2800 m. *Cyathea tryonorum* appears to be closely related to *C. armata* and allied species.

### *Cyathea tsilotsilensis* Tardieu-Blot 1941

*Alsophila tsilotsilensis* (Tardieu-Blot) Tryon 1970

*Alsophila* clade. The erect trunk is 3–4 m tall. Fronds are bipinnate and 2–3 m long. Rachis and trunk scales are lanceolate and bicolored, with a glossy dark brown center and paler margin. Sori occur near the midvein of fertile pinnules, are small, and have fragile globose indusia. Distribution: Madagascar, the name *tsilotsilensis* referring to the type locality, Col de Tsilotsilo, northwest of Elakelaka.

*Cyathea tsilotsilensis* is a member of a complex that includes *C. marattioides*, *C. perrieriana*, and *C. serratifolia*.

### *Cyathea tussacii* Desvaux 1827

*Alsophila tussacii* (Desvaux) Conant 1983

*Alsophila* clade. The erect trunk is 8 m tall and 7–15 cm in diameter; it is rough, spiny, and covered with narrow brown scales. Fronds are tripinnate and about

3 m long. The stipe is stout, grayish, and has numerous purple-black spines and scales; the scales are narrow and brown to dark brown. Sori occur in one to three pairs on either side of the pinnule midvein; indusia are pale, membranous, and deeply cup-like. Distribution: Jamaica, where it is locally common in moist shaded ravines and mossy montane forest at 750–1700 m.

*Cyathea tussacii* was first collected by François Richard de Tussac (1751–1837) and was named by his son-in-law Auguste Desvaux. It is part of the *C. woodwardioides* complex of six species from the Greater Antilles, the other four being *C. crassa, C. fulgens, C. grevilleana,* and *C. portoricensis.*

### *Cyathea urbanii* Brause in Urban 1911

*Alsophila urbanii* (Brause) Tryon 1970

*Alsophila* clade. The prostrate trunk is about 6.5 cm in diameter. Fronds are pinnate and may reach 3 m in length; occasionally, pinnae at the base of the frond may be separated and reduced. Rachis and trunk scales are brown. Sori occur in two simple rows, one on each side of the pinnule midvein, and are covered by thin indusia. Distribution: Dominican Republic in shaded ravines along streams and in cloud forest at 800–2000 m.

*Cyathea urbanii* is named after German botanist Ignatz Urban (1848–1931). It may hybridize with *C. minor.*

### *Cyathea ursina* (Maxon) Lellinger 1987

*Alsophila ursina* Maxon 1944

*Cyathea* clade. The fern is trunkless or has a short, almost subterranean rhizome, occasionally forming clumps. Fronds are pinnate, dissected, often glossy green, and 75 cm to 1.3 m long. Petioles are brown and smooth. The rachis is brown and covered with scales that are bicolored, brown with a white margin. Sori occur between the midvein of fertile pinnules and the edge of the lamina; indusia are absent. Distribution: Belize to Costa Rica, in wet tropical rain forest as part of the understory and on stream or pond banks, from sea level to 100 m, occasionally as high as about 300 m.

*Cyathea ursina* is a small tree fern, lacking a trunk, and with pinnate fronds. It is similar to *C. phalaenolepis.* Occasional hybrids between *C. ursina* and *C. multiflora,* and *C. stolzei,* have been reported from Costa Rica.

### *Cyathea valdecrenata* Domin 1929

*Alsophila mexicana* Martius 1834, not *Cyathea mexicana* Schlechtendal & Chamisso 1930; *Trichipteris mexicana* (Martius) Tryon 1970

*Cyathea* clade. The erect trunk is about 10 m tall. Fronds are bipinnate and about 2 m long or more. The rachis is brown and has a few warts and scattered scales; the scales are either all brown or have a darker central streak. Sori occur between the midvein of fertile pinnules and the edge of the lamina. Veins fork at the sori. Indusia are absent. Distribution: Mexico to Honduras, in wet forest and cloud forest, along watercourses, at 800–3000 m.

*Cyathea valdecrenata* is commonly known as *Trichipteris mexicana*, but when transferred to *Cyathea* the name *mexicana* is unavailable, hence the use of *valdecrenata* as suggested by Karel Domin. *Cyathea valdecrenata* is possibly related to the *C. armata* complex.

## *Cyathea vandeusenii* Holttum 1962

*Alsophila vandeusenii* (Holttum) Tryon 1970

*Alsophila* clade. The erect trunk is 2–3 m tall. Fronds number about ten in a crown, are bi- or tripinnate, and about 1 m long. The lower portion of the rachis and all of the stipe are covered in scales that are pale and have a dark patch toward the base, glossy, and firm but with fragile edges. Sori are round, almost covered by scales, and protected by light brown cup-like indusia. Distribution: Northeastern New Guinea in subalpine forest margins at about 3700 m.

*Cyathea vandeusenii* is named after Mr. M. H. van Deusen, a biologist on the sixth Archbold expedition (see *C. archboldii*), who provided assistance to Leonard John Brass (1900–1971), the collector of the type material.

## *Cyathea vaupelii* Copeland 1911

*Sphaeropteris vaupelii* (Copeland) Tryon 1970, *Cyathea setchellii* Copeland 1931

*Sphaeropteris* clade. The erect trunk is 3–4 m tall. Fronds are bi- or tripinnate and may reach 1–2 m in length. The stipe is covered with scales, especially when young, and may have warts when the scales fall; the scales are thick near the base and may have setiferous edges, or small and dull brown without setiferous edges. Sori occur halfway between the midvein of fertile pinnules and the edge of the lobe and are covered with indusia. Distribution: Fiji to Samoa, in wet forest at 900–1200 m.

*Cyathea vaupelii* is named after German botanist Friedrich Johann Vaupel (1876–1927). It is very similar to *C. subsessilis*, differing in its larger size and larger pinnules; the exact relationship between the two species probably requires further investigation.

## *Cyathea venezuelensis* A. R. Smith ex Lellinger 1987

*Trichipteris steyermarkii* Tryon 1970, not *Cyathea steyermarkii* Tryon 1972

*Cyathea* clade. The erect trunk is 0.5–1 m tall. Fronds are bipinnate and may reach 1.5 m in length, rarely 2 m. The rachis and stipe are purplish and have scattered scales that are brown, usually with a lighter margin. Sori occur between the midvein of fertile pinnules and the edge of the lamina; true indusia are absent. Distribution: Summit of Cerro Autana (about 1200 m) and mountain ridges of the Paria Peninsula, Venezuela, in wet forest at 1000–1650 m.

*Cyathea venezuelensis* is a small, little-known tree fern with a short trunk. It seems closely related to *C. sagittifolia* and may be related to *C. barringtonii* and *C. pungens*.

### Cyathea verrucosa Holttum 1962

*Sphaeropteris verrucosa* (Holttum) Tryon 1970

*Sphaeropteris* clade. The erect trunk is medium-sized to tall. Fronds are bi- or tripinnate and about 3 m long. The stipe is pale and covered with warts and basal scales; the scales are pale and have setiferous edges. Sori occur one-third of the distance between the midvein of fertile pinnules and the edge of the lamina and lack indusia. Each sorus is marked by a depression on the upper surface of the pinnule. Distribution: Central Sumatra, Indonesia, in open forest at 1000–1900 m.

*Cyathea verrucosa* is closely related to *C. contaminans* but is more scaly and has a warty rather than spiny stipe.

### Cyathea vieillardii Mettenius 1861

*Alsophila vieillardii* (Mettenius) Tryon 1970, *Cyathea neocaledonica*
Compton 1923

PLATE 98

*Alsophila* clade. The erect stem is 3–4 m tall. Fronds are bi- or tripinnate and reach about 2 m in length. The rachis is pale and smooth. The stipe is short and covered at the base with scales and warts; the scales are dark, glossy, and have pale fragile edges. Sori occur almost in the middle of the pinnule lamina, between the midvein and the edge; indusia are large and thin. Distribution: New Caledonia and Vanuatu, in forest to 1400 m.

*Cyathea vieillardii* is named after botanist Eugène Vieillard (1819–1896), who collected on New Caledonia and Tahiti in 1861–1867. It is a variable species, particularly with regard to frond size and the extent of scaliness or hairiness of the lower surface of the pinnule rachis. *Cyathea vieillardii* is similar to *C. aneitensis* but has lighter stipes and frond bases.

### Cyathea villosa Willdenow 1810

*Cyathea vernicosa* (Kuhn) Domin 1929

*Cyathea* clade. The erect trunk is 1.5 m tall. Fronds are bipinnate and may reach 1–1.5 m in length. The rachis is brown, warty, and has scattered scales that are twisted and brown, often with a narrow diaphanous edge. Sori occur between the midvein of fertile pinnules and the edge of the lamina; indusia are absent. Distribution: Panama; Andes of Colombia and Bolivia, to Venezuela, and in southern Brazil. Plants grow in open areas, savannas, scrub, gullies, and pastures, at 780–1800 m.

*Cyathea villosa*, perhaps most closely related to *C. atrovirens*, often survives in poor soils and full sun. It is best known for an unusual disjunct distribution, with populations in Central and South America.

## *Cyathea vittata* Copeland 1936

*Sphaeropteris vittata* (Copeland) Tryon 1970

*Sphaeropteris* clade. The erect trunk is about 20 m tall. Fronds are tripinnate and may reach 4–5 m in length. The rachis may be pale and bear warts on the undersurface. The stipe is long and partly covered at the base by scales that are thin and pale. Sori occur near the midvein of fertile pinnules; indusia are absent, but scales may surround the sorus. Distribution: Solomon Islands, including Bougainville, in rain forest to about 800 m.

## *Cyathea walkerae* W. J. Hooker 1844

*Alsophila walkerae* (W. J. Hooker) J. Smith 1875

*Alsophila* clade. The erect trunk is medium-sized. Fronds are bi- or tripinnate and are 1–2 m long. The stipe is long and has short spines toward the base and scattered scales that are dark and have narrow fragile edges. Sori occur near the midvein of fertile pinnules and are covered with thin indusia. Distribution: Sri Lanka in montane forest at 1000–2000 m.

*Cyathea walkerae* is named after A. W. Walker, who collected in Ceylon in the 1820s to 1840s, mainly with her husband, George Warren Walker (d. 1844). It is a morphologically variable species with a named variety, *tripinnata* W. J. Hooker & Baker. It is possible that some of the variation represents a difference in species.

## *Cyathea wallacei* (Mettenius) Copeland 1909

*Alsophila wallacei* Mettenius in Kuhn 1869, *Sphaeropteris wallacei*
   (Mettenius) Tryon 1970, *Cyathea burbidgei* (Baker) Copeland 1909

*Sphaeropteris* clade. The erect trunk may be as tall as about 2 m or more. Fronds are pinnate or bipinnate, dissected, and 1–2 m long. The stipe is pale and smooth above the base and has scattered basal scales that are light brown, firm, and setiferous. Sori occur near the midvein of fertile pinnules; indusia are absent. Distribution: Borneo in lowland forest or on poor sandstone soil.

The name *wallacei* commemorates Alfred Russel Wallace (1823–1913), who collected the original specimen in 1857 on Borneo but it was later lost. A duplicate, also collected by Wallace, is in the herbarium at the Royal Botanic Gardens, Kew.

### *Cyathea weatherbyana* (Morton) Morton 1969

*Hemitelia weatherbyana* Morton 1957

*Cyathea* clade. The erect trunk may be as tall as 6 m. Fronds are bipinnate and may reach 2–4 m in length. The rachis is brown and has scattered scales that are whitish and dissected. Sori occur along each side of the midvein of fertile pinnules and may be covered with scale-like indusia. Distribution: Galápagos Islands in the fern-sedge zone, on mountain slopes at 450–800 m, the type specimen collected on Indefatigable Island.

The name *weatherbyana* commemorates pteridologist Charles Alfred Weatherby (1875–1949). *Cyathea weatherbyana* is a medium-sized tree fern, considered endemic to the Galápagos but bearing some relationship to *C. andina*.

### *Cyathea welwitschii* W. J. Hooker 1865

*Alsophila welwitschii* (W. J. Hooker) Tryon 1970

*Alsophila* clade. The erect trunk is 6 m tall. Fronds are simply pinnate and 1–2 m long. The rachis and stipe are dull and sparsely covered by small warts and scales; the scales are dark brown and glossy. Sori occur on forks of fertile pinnule veins and are covered with thin indusia that form shallow cups. Distribution: São Tomé, island west of Gabon, in forest at 900–1200 m.

*Cyathea welwitschii* is named after Friedrich Martin Joseph Welwitsch (1806–1872), an Austrian botanist specializing in the plants of Africa.

### *Cyathea wendlandii* (Mettenius ex Kuhn) Domin 1929

*Alsophila wendlandii* Mettenius ex Kuhn 1869

*Cyathea* clade. The erect trunk may be as tall as 4 m and 5–8 cm in diameter. Fronds are bipinnate and as long as 2 m. Petioles are brown to shiny black-brown and have spines. The rachis is dark brown and smooth. Rachis and trunk scales are brown. Sori are clustered toward the base of the pinnules. Veins on fertile pinnules fork only once. Indusia are absent. Distribution: Costa Rica and Panama, in tropical and submontane rain forest, in open areas and as forest understory from 400 m to about 1500 m.

The name *wendlandii* commemorates German botanist Heinrich Ludolph Wendland (1791–1869). *Cyathea wendlandii* is a tree fern with a slender trunk and large flattish fronds. It is similar to *C. lasiosora*, *C. nigripes*, *C. pinnula*, and *C. schlimii*.

## *Cyathea wengiensis* (Brause) Domin 1929

*Alsophila wengiensis* Brause 1912, *A. hieronymi* Brause 1912

*Alsophila* clade. The erect trunk is 2–3 m tall. Fronds are bi- or tripinnate and 1–2 m long. The stipe is spiny and has scattered scales that are either brown or dark and have broad dull edges. Sori are round, occur near the fertile pinnule midvein, and are covered by narrow, dark, saucer-like indusia. Distribution: Eastern New Guinea in secondary rain forest, garden regrowth, or clearings, to 600 m, the name *wengiensis* referring to Wenge, Papua New Guinea.

## *Cyathea werffii* R. C. Moran 1991

*Cyathea* clade. The erect trunk is about 2 cm in diameter. Fronds are pinnate or bipinnate. The rachis is yellow-brown and has few, if any, scales but many hairs; the scales are bullate, brown, and have whitish apices. Sori occur along each side of the midvein of fertile pinnules; indusia are absent. Distribution: Peru and Ecuador, in wet forest at 540–800 m.

*Cyathea werffii*, named after Hendrik ("Henk") van der Werff (b. 1946) of the Missouri Botanical Garden, resembles *C. phalaenolepis*, which differs in having larger petiole scales, and a hairy petiole and rachis.

## *Cyathea werneri* Rosenstock 1908

*Sphaeropteris werneri* (Rosenstock) Tryon 1970, *Cyathea kingii* Rosenstock 1911, not *C. kingii* (C. B. Clarke in Beddome) Copeland 1909 (see *C. lurida*)

*Sphaeropteris* clade. The erect trunk is 3–4 m tall. Fronds number about eight in a crown, are pinnate or bipinnate, occasionally almost tripinnate, and about 2.5 m long. The stipe has scattered scales that are pale and thin to thick toward the base. Sori occur near the midvein of fertile pinnules and are covered by thin, translucent indusia. Distribution: Southern and eastern New Guinea, in forest at 200–1100 m.

*Cyathea werneri* is named after E. Werner, who collected the type material at Damon in northeastern New Guinea. The tree fern may become fertile when very young. It is very similar to *C. fusca*, differing in the absence of hairs on the lower surface of the pinna rachis; the relationship between the two species deserves further investigation.

## *Cyathea whitmeei* Baker 1876

*Alsophila samoensis* Brackenridge 1854, *Sphaeropteris samoensis* (Brackenridge) Tryon 1970, *Cyathea wilkesiana* Domin 1930

*Sphaeropteris* clade. The erect trunk is 5–10 m tall. Fronds are tripinnate and may reach 4–5 m in length. The rachis may be suffused with dull red and may have fine warts. The stipe is long, partly covered by scales and fine warts toward the base, and may bear a pair of reduced basal pinnae; the scales are dark and dull. Sori occur near the midvein of fertile pinnules and may be incompletely covered by thin indusia. Distribution: Solomon Islands to Samoa, in open forest and hill scrub areas to about 900 m.

*Cyathea whitmeei* is named after Samuel James Whitmee (1838–1925), who collected plants on Samoa, among other places. If the genus *Sphaeropteris* is recognized, William Brackenridge's name *samoensis* (named after the islands of Samoa) takes precedence.

## *Cyathea williamsii* (Maxon) Domin 1930

*Alsophila williamsii* Maxon 1922

*Cyathea* clade. The creeping to erect, narrow trunk is 0.1–1.5 m tall. Fronds are pinnate and 1–1.5 m long. The rachis is brown and has scattered brown scales. Sori occur in one to three rows between the midvein of fertile pinnules and the edge of the lamina; indusia are absent. Distribution: Panama; Guiana Highlands of Venezuela. Plants grow in wet forest at 1350–1900 m.

*Cyathea williamsii* is known for its two disjunct populations in Panama and the Guiana Highlands. It is a variable species, particularly with regard to size.

## *Cyathea womersleyi* Holttum 1962

*Sphaeropteris womersleyi* (Holttum) Tryon 1970

*Sphaeropteris* clade. The erect trunk may be as tall as about 8 m. Fronds are semierect, number about ten in a crown, are tripinnate, and may reach about 3 m in length. The stipe is sparsely spiny and densely covered with scales that are pale, dull, soft, and have a red terminal seta. Sori are covered with overlapping fringed scales, giving the appearance of indusia. Distribution: Eastern New Guinea in rain forest at 1700–2400 m.

*Cyathea womersleyi* is named after botanist John Spencer Womersley (1920–1985), who collected in Australia and the Southwest Pacific.

## *Cyathea woodwardioides* Kaulfuss 1824

*Alsophila woodwardioides* (Kaulfuss) Conant 1983, *Cyathea nigrescens* (W. J. Hooker) J. Smith 1866, in part; *C. araneosa* Maxon 1909

*Alsophila* clade. The erect trunk is 9 m tall and 10–12 cm in diameter. Fronds are tripinnate, arching, dark green, and about 3 m long. The rachis is dark purple-brown. The stipe is stout, purple-brown, and has purple-black spines and scattered scales that are brown to glossy brown. Sori occur in one or two (rarely as many as six) pairs at the base of each pinnule segment; indusia are brown, membranous, and deeply cup-shaped. Distribution: Cuba, Jamaica, and Hispaniola, locally common in moist montane forest at 500–1800 m.

*Cyathea woodwardioides*, named after Thomas Jenkinson Woodward (1745–1820), a British botanist and gentleman after whom the fern genus *Woodwardia* (Blechnaceae) is also named, is part of a related complex of some six species from the Greater Antilles that includes *C. crassa*, *C. fulgens*, *C. grevilleana*, *C. portoricensis*, and *C. tussacii*.

## *Cyathea woollsiana* (F. von Mueller) Domin 1929

*Alsophila woollsiana* F. von Mueller 1874

PLATE 99

*Alsophila* clade. The erect, slender trunk may be as tall as 6 m, though usually much smaller, and as much as 15 cm in diameter. Fronds are bipinnate to, rarely, tripinnate and about 2.5 m long. The rachis and stipe are pale brown and covered in the lower region by warts and reddish brown, bristly scales; clumps of spines may also be present. Stipe bases persist and may be seen protruding from upper regions of the trunk. Sori occur in two simple rows, one on either side of the midvein of fertile pinnules; indusia are small, scale- to hood-like, and situated toward the interior of the pinnule. Distribution: Northeastern Queensland, Australia, in the coastal ranges between the Herbert and Bloomfield Rivers, on slopes above streams, on riverbanks, and in rain forest, to 1200 m.

The attractive *Cyathea woollsiana* commemorates clergyman, schoolteacher, and botanist William Woolls (1814–1893), who emigrated to Australia from Britain to a post at Kings School, Parramatta. Plants will grow in a wide rage of areas, including cooler regions. Once established, they will also survive dry periods. This tree fern does best in shady sites but will grow in full sun in humus provided with regular moisture. When young, *C. woollsiana* is also suitable for cultivation in containers.

## *Cyathea zakamenensis* Tardieu-Blot 1941

*Alsophila zakamenensis* (Tardieu-Blot) Tryon 1970

*Alsophila* clade. The erect trunk is 3–4 m tall and about 15 cm in diameter. Fronds are bipinnate and 2–3 m long; lower pinnae may be reduced and separated. Sori occur near the midvein of fertile pinnules and are covered by large, globose indusia. Distribution: Madagascar, the name *zakamenensis* referring to Zakamena, Bassin de l'Oribe.

## *Cyathea zamboangana* Copeland 1926

*Sphaeropteris zamboangana* (Copeland) Tryon 1970

*Sphaeropteris* clade. The medium-sized to tall, erect trunk is covered in elliptical stipe-base scars that may be about 5 cm in diameter. Fronds are pinnate or bipinnate and 1–2 m long. The stipe is dark, covered in scales, and spiny at the base; the scales are small and have densely setiferous edges. Sori occur about halfway between the midvein of fertile pinnules and the edge of the lamina; indusia are globose. Distribution: Mindanao in the Philippines, in forest at 500–800 m, the name *zamboangana* referring to the former province of Zamboanga.

## *Cystodium* J. Smith 1841

Dicksoniaceae

John Smith described *Cystodium* in 1841. There is only one species, *C. sorbifolium*, originally described as a species of *Dicksonia* by James Edward Smith in 1808, although subspecies have been recognized. *Cystodium* is usually treated as a member of the Dicksoniaceae, but study of stipe anatomy

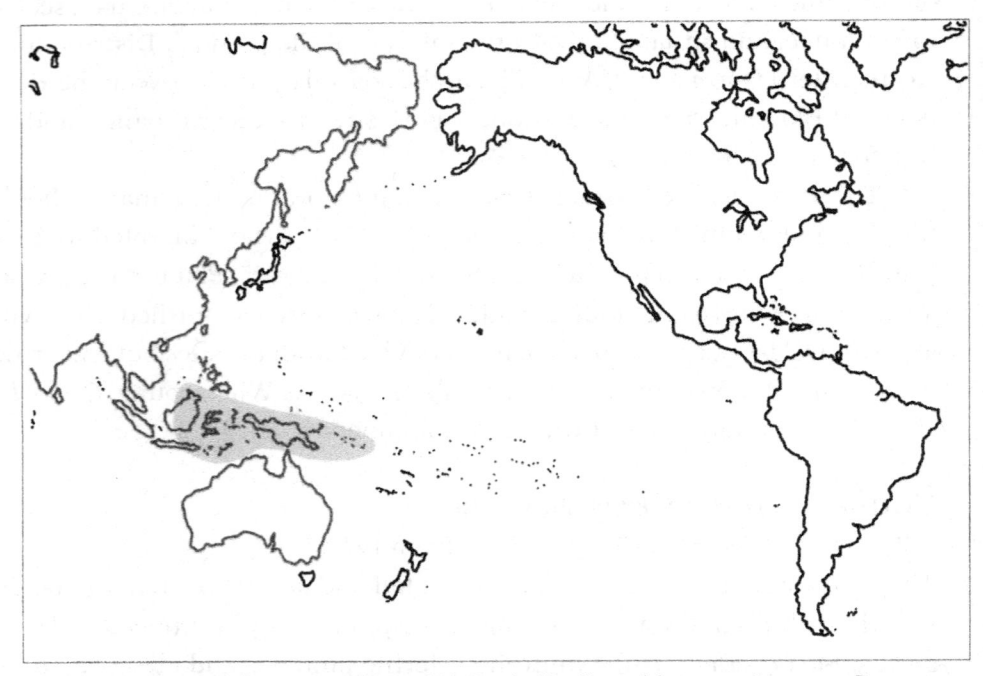

The only species of *Cystodium* (*C. sorbifolium*), distributed from northeastern Borneo to Sulawesi (Celebes), the Moluccas, New Guinea, New Britain, the Louisiade Archipelago, and the Solomon Islands.

and general morphology suggests that the genus be recognized as a distinct family (Cystodiaceae) with possible affinities to the Dennstaedtiaceae. Sporangia of *Cystodium* contain 32 rather than the 64 spores more usual for the Dicksoniaceae. Despite this difference, ongoing molecular studies still suggest an affinity with members of the Dicksoniaceae. Until these studies are completed, *Cystodium* is treated here conservatively as part of the Dicksoniaceae. Spores are rounded or globose (trilete) with granulate deposits over small and irregularly snaking ridges on the surface.

## *Cystodium sorbifolium* (Smith) J. Smith 1841

*Dicksonia sorbifolia* Smith 1808

The massive prostrate rhizome is covered with long hairs. Fronds occur in tufts, are bipinnate to almost tetrapinnate, and may reach 2.5 m in length. The stipe is grooved on its upper surface. Sori are terminal on veins and form a raised, rounded receptacle. The edge of the pinnule lobe is reflexed and forms an outer indusium. A thin inner indusium protects the sorus. Chromosome number $n$ = approximately 56 suggested by unconfirmed counts. Distribution: Paleotropical, from northeastern Borneo to Sulawesi (Celebes),

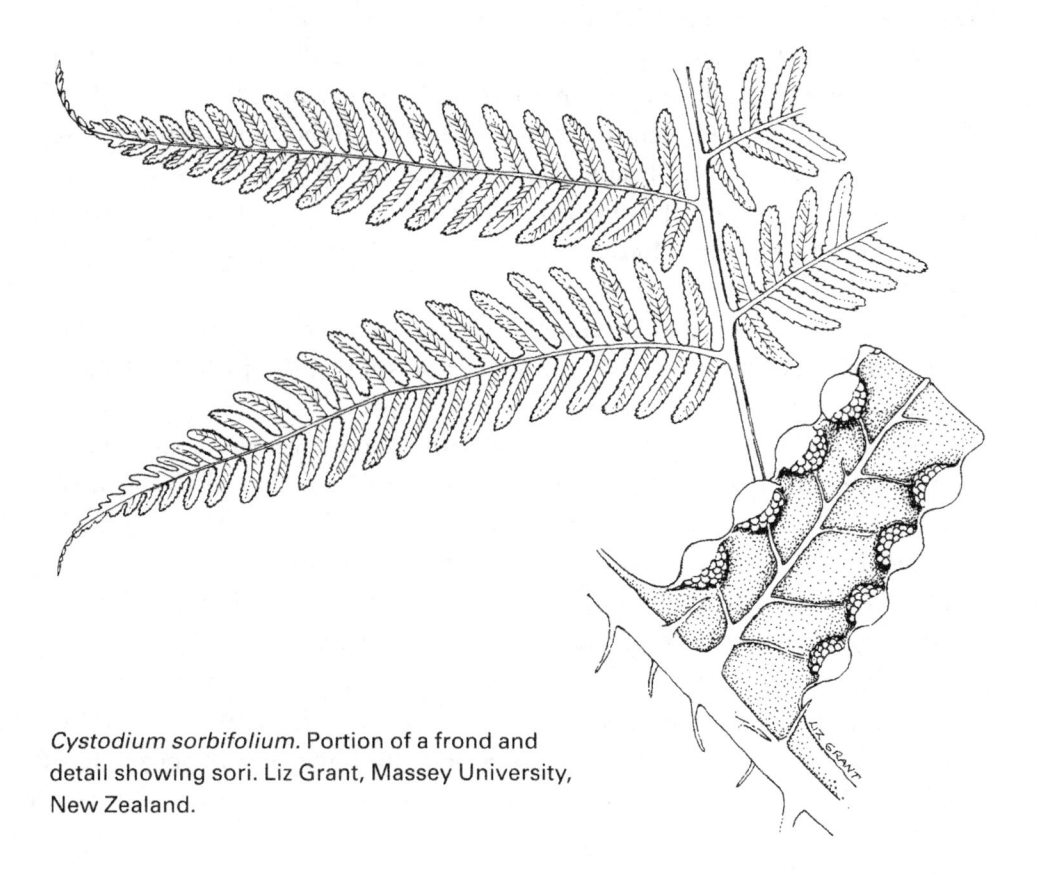

*Cystodium sorbifolium.* Portion of a frond and detail showing sori. Liz Grant, Massey University, New Zealand.

the Moluccas, New Guinea, New Britain in the Bismarck Archipelago, the Louisiade Archipelago, and the Solomon Islands, common in lowland tropical forest, on steep banks, streamsides, and ridge slopes at 50–500 m.

*Cystodium sorbifolium* subsp. *solomonensis* (J. Smith) Johns has been described from the Solomon Islands. *Cystodium sorbifolium* is not in common garden cultivation but will grow in warmer regions. Plants do best in humus and tolerate some sun. The fronds have been used in the florist industry and may be collected under managed conditions from wild populations.

## *Dicksonia* L'Héritier de Brutelle 1788
*Balantium* Kaulfuss 1824
Dicksoniaceae

Charles-Louis L'Héritier de Brutelle described the genus *Dicksonia* in 1788. Joseph Banks and Daniel Solander collected the type species, *D. arborescens*, from St. Helena in 1771 on James Cook's first voyage aboard *Endeavour;* their specimen is held in the Natural History Museum, London. *Balantium*, described by Georg Kaulfuss in 1824, is regarded as congeneric. The name *Dicksonia* honors James Dickson (see the introduction to this chapter).

*Dicksonia* has had a varied history taxonomically, with early authors confusing it with a number of genera, including *Cibotium, Culcita,* and even *Dennstaedtia*. The identification of species is difficult because features of sori and pinnae are remarkably consistent throughout the genus. Differences in hair characteristics on the stipe are clearer but not completely reliable for determination. General characteristics that distinguish species are noted in the descriptions.

*Dicksonia* is regarded as related to *Cyathea* but is considered more primitive with a fossil record (stems, pinnules, and spores) dating back at least to the Jurassic and Cretaceous periods.

*Dicksonia* tree ferns are terrestrial and have a large erect stem or rhizome. The rhizome usually forms a trunk, similar to that of *Cyathea*, that may be 10 m or more in height. Sometimes the trunk is slender, but in many species it may be quite massive (1 m or more in diameter) with the lower region covered by a thick mat of rootlets. Several are creeping and do not form an upright trunk (for example, forms of *D. lanata* from New Zealand).

Trunks of *Dicksonia*, along with the lower portion of the frond stipe, may be covered with long hairs instead of scales (such as those in *Cyathea*). Generally, stipe bases are smooth or, very occasionally, warty (as opposed to the rougher stipe bases seen in many species of *Cyathea*), but may be covered with hairs. Fronds may be as long as 4 m and are either monomorphic (all the same shape) or dimorphic (two shapes), with fertile fronds having reduced green tissue. Fertile fronds bear globular clusters of sporangia (sori) on the underside of the pinnules. The sorus forms with a characteristic two-valved cup-like indusium. The two valves are dissimilar (unlike *Cibotium*, in which the two lobes are similar) and marginal (as opposed to central in *Cyathea*), terminating the veins of the pinnules. Pinnules of both frond types may often be harsh and hard to the touch. The sporangium is leptosporangiate. Spores of all species are trilete and can be divided into three groups based on surface sculpture: smooth to granulate; covered with small irregular lumps (tuberculate); and intermediate, smooth but tuberculate. Chromosome number $n = 65$.

Species of *Dicksonia* are found on St. Helena, in tropical Central and South America, on the Juan Fernández Islands, then across the Pacific Ocean to Samoa, New Caledonia, New Guinea, Australia, and south to New Zealand, but most occur in Malesia, in montane forest. Others grow in rain forest, on the fringes of rain forest, or in protected areas within open forest. These tree ferns are a feature of montane forests in the Tropics but are prominent features of both lowland and montane forest in the Subtropics or southern temperate regions.

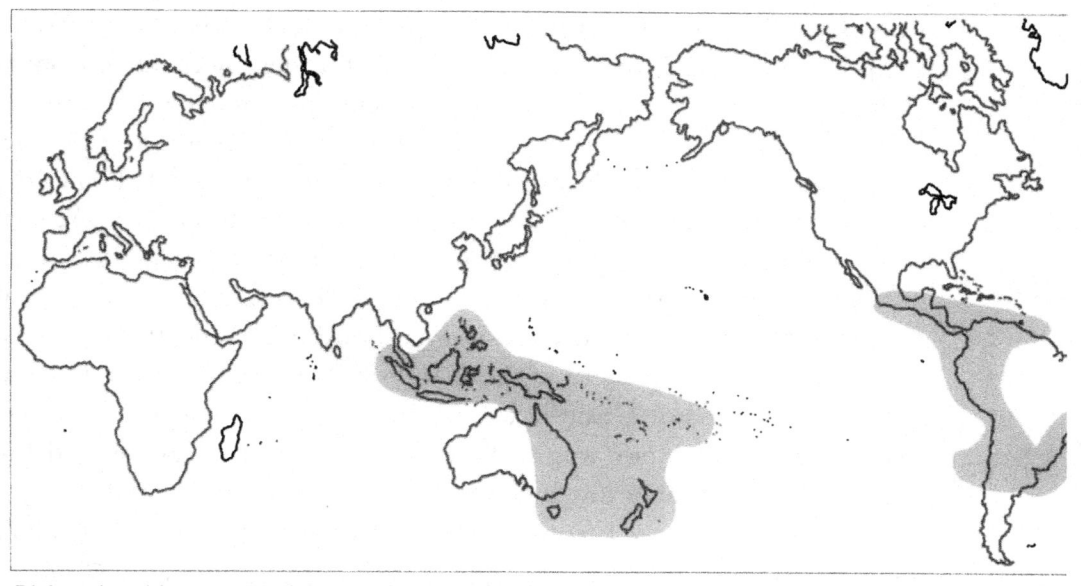

*Dicksonia,* with a scattered distribution from Malesia through Australia and New Zealand to South America, the maximum diversity occurring in New Guinea, yet with species endemic to the isolated Juan Fernández Islands in the Pacific and St. Helena in the Atlantic but apparently absent from Africa.

Best estimates suggest that *Dicksonia* comprises 20–25 species. However, the highlands of New Guinea comprise a region of particular diversity, and further study may result in the description of several additional species. Until relatively recently this area was one of the more difficult regions to explore. Studies by staff of the Royal Botanic Gardens, Kew, are underway.

Species of *Dicksonia* are popular landscape subjects, providing tree ferns that grow slower than many species of *Cyathea*. Most grow readily if provided with moisture and a rich loam. Many are excellent specimens for warmer outdoor regions (some species are able to survive light frosts) or conservatories. Because of their high humidity requirement, however, they are not ideally suited for indoor cultivation. Propagation is usually from spores, but most will readily grow from trunk cuttings, provided the apical meristem remains intact. Fronds and the trunk can be attacked by mealybugs. One of the biggest dangers in cultivation is rot of the apical meristem; overwatering the top rosette region of the rhizome usually brings this about.

## *Dicksonia antarctica* Labillardière 1807
SOFT TREE FERN, WOOLLY TREE FERN
PLATES 100, 101

The erect massive trunk is 4.5–5 m tall (occasionally reaching an exceptional 15 m), 2 m thick or more, red brown to dark brown, and usually covered in a mass of fine fibrous roots; the trunk is usually solitary, without runners, but may produce offsets. Fronds are tripinnate to almost tetrapinnate, as long as 4.5 m, mid to dark green above and paler below, and form a dense rosette atop the rhizome; fronds are borne in flushes with fertile and sterile fronds often found in alternating layers. Pinnules are linear and divided. The stipe is short, brown, and smooth to densely hairy at the base; the hairs are shed after uncoiling. Sori occur two to six per pinnule lobe and are globose, marginal, and under the hooded edges of the lobes; indusia are circular to oval. Distribution: Australia in Queensland, New South Wales (northern, central, and southern coast; northern, central, and southern tablelands and central western slopes), Victoria, South Australia (now extinct in the wild—the last surviving wild population was at Waterfall Creek, near Adelaide), and Tasmania, in high-rainfall forest, where it may form large, pure stands.

*Dicksonia antarctica* is known for its dense rhizome. Within Australia it not normally confused with other species, but it is very similar to *D. fibrosa* of New Zealand (particularly specimens of that species from the Chatham Islands) and to *D. sellowiana* of South America. Adult plants of *D. antarctica* may differ by losing old fronds from the canopy; fronds of *D. fibrosa* may be retained to form a dense skirt about the trunk.

*Dicksonia antarctica* is a popular plant for cultivation, doing well in most soils but best in humus. This tree fern is hardy in many situations (more recently being exported as cut trunks to Britain and Europe) and has even been cultivated in containers. It tolerates high light intensity to medium shade in both exposed and sheltered locations. It will tolerate light to medium frost but requires high levels of moisture or humidity in dry weather; drought is generally responsible for most losses in cultivation. In general, *D. antarctica* is easy to grow and can be transplanted with the fronds trimmed. Plants grown from spores are also successful, with sporangia maturing in the mid to late Australian summer (January–February).

The crowns of *Dicksonia antarctica* are used by the native Australian marsupial "possum" as a sleeping site. Animals and birds often eat the young uncurling fronds. The Aboriginal peoples of Australia ate the pith from the center of the trunk, which is rich in starch. The trunks, composed of a thick mass of fibrous roots, are often used as a medium on which to grow epiphytes, particularly orchids. Trunks are also used for fencing, and the central vascular material has been dried and carved to make items for the tourist industry.

## *Dicksonia arborescens* L'Héritier de Brutelle 1788
PLATES 102, 103

The erect, slender to stout trunk may be as tall as 3 m and is dark brown. Fronds are bipinnate and as long as about 1.5 m, with lower pinnae as large as 45 cm long by 20 cm wide. Pinnules are linear and divided nearly to the rachis into oblong segments; fertile pinnules are often contracted. The rachis is hairy, particularly when young, and densely covered at the base with linear reddish or golden hairs. The stipe is dark and stout. Sori occur two to six per pinnule lobe, are large, globose, marginal, and under the hooded edges of the lobes; indusia are semicircular. Distribution: St. Helena and protected by ordinance, being scheduled under the United Kingdom Forestry (Indigenous Trees and Plants) Preservation Amendment Act, 1978. Plants are common in thickets on the top of the central ridge, High Peak and Cuckhold's Point to Mount Actaeon, also occasionally in other places on the central ridge down to about 700 m. William J. Burchell, the East India Company's botanist on the island, noted it under Cason's Gate (in his unpublished journal), where it still grows, and at West Lodge Telegraph, in misty forest along ridges and in gullies.

*Dicksonia arborescens* is the type species for the genus. On St. Helena it is the dominant plant of a characteristic vegetation type found on the highest parts of the island. This tree fern thicket has a deep humus layer beneath it. Fallen tree fern trunks can sprout along their length to form new trunks. In the early 19th century, William Roxburgh recorded specimens as high as

6 m with trunks the thickness of a man's body and leaves about 2 m long. However, William J. Hooker, visiting in 1840, found most of the plants stunted and less than 1 m high, with the highest about 3 m, more like the situation today.

Spore morphology of *Dicksonia arborescens* is somewhat unusual, almost intermediate between the smooth granulate spores (for example, as seen in *D. fibrosa*) and the tuberculate spores (as seen in *D. squarrosa*). Spores of this intermediate form have been found, dating about 9 million years old (Q. Cronk, personal communication). Sterile immature tree ferns that have not yet developed a trunk are frequently found along pathsides; they may be distinguished from other ferns by the tuft of reddish or golden filiform hairs at the base of the stipe. Fertile tree ferns are occasionally found with very short trunks, the fronds scarcely off the ground. Plants of this type, first discovered by Burchell, have been recognized as variety *minor* Cronk.

*Dicksonia arborescens* is not in general cultivation, but plants have been grown from spores. Development of the gametophytes and eventual maturation of the sporophytes are slow. This tree fern does best in humus. It tolerates high light intensity to medium shade in both exposed and sheltered locations and will endure light frost. In general, it is slow-growing and does not do well if transplanted.

## *Dicksonia archboldii* Copeland 1927

The erect trunk is 4–5 m high, about 13 cm in diameter, and brown. Fronds are tripinnate and as long as about 3 m, with the widest pinnae as broad as 65 cm. The stipe is dark, stout, and covered, especially toward the base, with soft, red-brown and pale hairs. Sori occur one or two per pinnule lobe and are globose, marginal, and under the hooded edges of lobes; indusia are oblong to circular. Distribution: Wilhelmina and Arfak Mountains of western New Guinea, common on lower mountain slopes and in wet submontane forest at about 2500 m.

*Dicksonia archboldii* is likely named after Richard Archbold (1907–1976), who organized and supported biological exploration in New Guinea and Australia. It appears to be closely related to *D. sciurus* but has larger fronds and red hairs on the costae; in *D. sciurus* the hairs are pale.

## *Dicksonia baudouini* Fournier 1873

*Dicksonia deplanchei* Vieillard in Baker 1874

PLATE 104

The erect, slender trunk may be as tall as 1 m. Fronds are tripinnate and may be as long as 1.2 m. The base of the stipe bears light brown dense hairs that become progressively shorter and darker toward the base. The lamina of the fertile segments is reduced compared to the sterile portion of the frond, which is dark green, somewhat brownish above and paler on the underside. Sori are prominent on the margins. Distribution: New Caledonia, at higher elevations (restricted to the summits of the mountains), especially in the south.

Cultivated in New Zealand and Australia, *Dicksonia baudouini* does best in humus and in sheltered locations. A constant supply of moisture is essential.

## *Dicksonia berteriana* (Colla) W. J. Hooker 1844

*Davallia berteriana* Colla 1836, *Balantium berteroanum* (Colla) Kunze 1836

The erect trunk is 5 m high or more and dark brown. Fronds are bi- or tripinnate and as long as about 2 m, with lower pinnae as long as 70 cm; fertile segments often have four or five pairs of fertile lobes. The rachis is hairy, particularly when young. The stipe is dark, stout, and covered, especially toward the base, with reddish brown hairs, fine undercoat hairs, and warts. Sori occur two to six per pinnule lobe and are large, globose, marginal, and under the hooded edges of lobes; indusia are oblong to circular. Distribution: Juan Fernández Islands, Chile, in humid forest where it may form pure stands.

The name *berteriana* commemorates Italian botanist Carlo Guiseppe Bertero (1789–1831), who collected in Chile. An alternative spelling, *berteroana*, was used by Skottsberg (1953), who tried to correct the spelling based on Bertero's name.

## *Dicksonia blumei* (Kunze) Moore 1860

*Balantium blumei* Kunze 1848, *Dicksonia chrysotricha* Moore 1860

The erect trunk may be as tall as 6 m. Fronds are bi- or tripinnate and as long as about 2 m, with lower pinnae as long as 70 cm; the rachis is hairy, particularly when young. The stipe is dark and covered, especially toward the base, with reddish to dark brown hairs, fine long undercoat hairs, and warts. Sori occur two to six per pinnule lobe and are large, globose, marginal, and under the hooded edges of the lobes; indusia are oblong to circular. Distribution: Karo Plateau, Sumatra; Java, Borneo; central Sulawesi (Celebes); New Guinea; and the Philippines. Plants are common on ridges and in gullies in wet submontane and montane forest at 1500–2500 m.

The name *blumei* commemorates Carl Ludwig Blume (1796–1862), student of the flora of the Dutch Indies. *Dicksonia blumei* is similar to *D. mollis* but differs in having longer undercoat hairs on the stipe. In cultivation, *D. blumei* grows best in humus. It tolerates high light intensity to medium shade in both exposed and sheltered locations. It is a slow-growing tree fern that may show some frost tolerance.

### *Dicksonia brackenridgei* Mettenius 1861

The erect trunk may be as tall as 6 m and is dark brown. Fronds are bi- or tripinnate and as long as about 2 m, with lower pinnae as long as 70 cm; fertile segments often have four or five pairs of fertile lobes. The rachis is hairy, particularly when young. The stipe is dark, stout, and covered, especially toward the base, with brown hairs and warts. Sori occur two to six per pinnule lobe and are large, globose, marginal, and under the hooded edges of the lobes; indusia are oblong to circular. Distribution: Vanuatu to Fiji, common on ridges and in gullies in wet submontane and montane forest at 500–1500 m.

*Dicksonia brackenridgei*, like *Cyathea brackenridgei*, is named after William Dunlop Brackenridge (1810–1893), a naturalist on the U.S. Exploring Expedition.

### *Dicksonia externa* Skottsberg 1953
PLATE 105

The erect trunk may be as tall as 5 m. Fronds are bi- or tripinnate and as long as about 2 m, with lower pinnae as long as 70 cm. The rachis is hairy, particularly when young. The stipe is dark and covered, especially toward the base, with reddish brown hairs. Sori occur two to six per pinnule lobe and are globose, marginal, and under the hooded edges of the lobes; indusia are oblong to circular. Distribution: Juan Fernández Islands, Chile, in humid forest on upper slopes, where it may form extensive stands.

### *Dicksonia fibrosa* Colenso 1845
KURIPAKA, WEKI-PONGA
FIGURE 4; PLATES 106–108

The erect massive trunk may be as tall as 6 m, as thick as 2 m, red to dark brown, and is usually covered in a mass of fine roots; it is solitary, without aerial buds or runners. Fronds are tri- or tetrapinnate and persistent. They are 1–3 m long, mid to dark green above and paler below, and form a dense rosette atop the trunk. Fertile and sterile fronds can be found in alternating layers. Dead fronds, complete with dead sections of lamina, hang down and form a thick skirt about the trunk. New fronds tend to be borne in flushes. Pinnules are linear and divided to the rachis. The stipe is short, brown, and smooth to densely hairy at the base. Sori occur about six per pinnule lobe and are globose, marginal, and under the hooded edges of the lobes; indusia are circular to oval. Distribution: North Island, South Island, Stewart Island, and Chatham Islands, New Zealand, in lowland to montane forest or in semi-open country on the North Island; plants may be found in montane forest to lowland forest in the southern areas of its range, and they will also grow in open or cleared pastureland.

*Dicksonia fibrosa* is known for its dense skirt of dead fronds, which includes old pinnule material as well as stipe and rachis, and its thick rhizome. Plants from the Chatham Islands bear a strong similarity to the Australian *D. antarctica*, a possible relationship that is under investigation.

Plants do well in most soils but best in humus. *Dicksonia fibrosa* tolerates high light intensity to medium shade in both exposed and sheltered locations. It will tolerate light to medium frost. In general, this tree fern is easy to grow and can be transplanted with fronds trimmed. Plants grown from spores are also successful, with sporangia maturing in the mid to late New Zealand summer (January–February). The fibrous trunks are often used to grow epiphytes, particularly orchids, and may also be used in garden construction, such as fencing. As with *D. antarctica*, the central vascular material is turned and used to make items for the tourist industry.

## *Dicksonia grandis* Rosenstock 1908

*Dicksonia schlechteri* Brause 1912, *D. ledermannii* Brause 1920

The erect trunk may be as tall as 6 m and is dark brown. Fronds are tripinnate and 2–3 m long. The stipe is blackish and covered toward the base with soft, light brown hairs. Sori occur two to six per pinnule lobe and are globose, marginal, and under the hooded edges of the lobes; indusia are oblong to circular. Distribution: New Guinea in mixed montane and submontane forest at 1000–2500 m.

*Dicksonia schlechteri* has variously been treated as synonymous with *D. grandis* or as a separate species. Both are very similar and share parts of the same geographic range.

## *Dicksonia herbertii* W. Hill 1874

**BRISTLY TREE FERN**

The erect, or occasionally prostrate, trunk is 2–4 m tall, as thick as 15 cm, and dark brown; the upper trunk is usually covered in persistent stipe bases and coarse stiff brown to gray-brown bristly hairs that may extend up the rachis of the fronds. Fronds are bi- or tripinnate, finely divided, and pale to gray-green. Pinnules are large, linear, and divided to the rachis. Fertile pinnae are acute, and sterile pinnae obtuse. The stipe may be as long as 20 cm, finely warty, brown, and densely hairy at the base. Sori occur one per pinnule lobe and are globose, marginal, and under the hooded edges of the lobes; indusia are oval. Distribution: Northeastern Queensland, Australia, between the McLeod and Johnson Rivers, with a southern population at Eungella, in submontane or highland rain forest above 760 m.

*Dicksonia herbertii* is confined to rain forest, usually at higher elevations. Walter Hill collected the type in 1873 during his ascent of Mount Bellenden Ker, and named the species after Robert Herbert (1831–1905), the first premier of Queensland (Jones 1984). Initially confused with *D. youngiae*, *D. herbertii* may be distinguished from most other species by the large bristly hairs on the upper trunk and stipes; fronds are also duller than those of *D. youngiae*, and outgrowths from the trunk are absent. *Dicksonia herbertii* does well in most soils but best in humus. This tree fern is hardy in many sheltered situations and is often fast-growing. It tolerates high light intensity to medium shade but does not endure heavy frost very well. It may be grown in a container, provided it receives consistent moisture.

## *Dicksonia hieronymi* Brause 1920

The erect trunk is about 4 m tall or more and as thick as 10 cm or more. Fronds are sparse in the crown, tripinnate, and as long as 2 m. The rachis is dark and covered with soft brown hairs. The stipe may be as long as 30 cm, brown, and covered at the base with soft brown, matted hairs and scattered, dark brown to reddish, shiny hairs. Sori occur in three to six pairs per pinnule lobe and are globose, marginal, and under the hooded edges of the lobes; indusia are oval. Distribution: New Guinea and the Louisiade Archipelago, in mossy forest or on forest margins and ridges at 1400–3000 m.

*Dicksonia hieronymi* is named after German botanist Georg Hans Emmo Wolfgang Hieronymus (1846–1921). It is sensitive to fire. This tree fern is infrequently cultivated. It appears to do best in sheltered situations; it tolerates high light intensity to medium shade but does not abide heavy frost.

## *Dicksonia lanata* Colenso 1845

TUOKURA

PLATES 109, 110

The erect, narrow to slender trunk may be as tall as 2 m, or prostrate and creeping, with runners. Fronds are tri- or tetrapinnate, 75 cm to 2 m long, and occur in two distinct forms: sterile fronds are persistent, yellow-green to apple green above, paler below, forming a loose rosette atop the rhizome; fertile fronds stand erect above the rosette of sterile fronds. The lamina of fertile fronds is reduced and densely covered by sori below; fertile fronds are short-lived, usually dying as soon as spores are released. Pinnules are large, linear, and divided to rachis. The stipe is slender, pale brown, and smooth to densely hairy at the base. Sori occur two to six per pinnule lobe and are globose, marginal, and under the hooded edges of the lobes; indusia are oval. Distribution: New Zealand. The trunked form only occurs in northern New Zealand as an understory plant of lowland kauri (*Agathis australis*) forest at latitudes 34–37° south, usually at lower elevations. The prostrate form may be found in central and southern New Zealand, producing thickets in montane and submontane forest or in open localities at higher elevations.

Molecular evidence indicates that the trunked and prostrate forms of *Dicksonia lanata* are only marginally isolated and probably constitute subspecies. The erect form is difficult to grow, often frost sensitive, and does not respond well to transplanting. The prostrate plant is much easier to cultivate. Specimens are grown as far from New Zealand as Inverie on the western coast of Scotland and at the Logan Botanic Garden of the Royal Botanic Garden, Edinburgh. However, this form also does not transplant well. Plants grown from spores are the most successful, with sporangia maturing in the mid to late New Zealand summer (January–February). *Dicksonia lanata* does well in a light, moist soil with humus, and light to heavy shade.

### *Dicksonia lanigera* Holttum 1962

The erect trunk is 2–5 m tall and brown. Fronds are tripinnate and 1.5–2 m long, with pinnae as long as 40 cm. The stipe is covered with soft, medium brown hairs. Sori occur two to six per pinnule lobe and are globose, marginal, and under the hooded edges of the lobes; indusia are oblong to circular. Distribution: Southwestern New Guinea in submontane and montane forest at 2100–3000 m.

### *Dicksonia mollis* Holttum 1962

The erect, stout trunk may be as tall as 6 m. Fronds are bi- or tripinnate and as long as about 2 m. The stipe is dark and covered toward the base with brown hairs and fine undercoat hairs. Sori occur two to six per pinnule lobe and are globose, marginal, and under the hooded edges of the lobes; indusia are oblong to circular. Distribution: Northeastern Borneo, central Sulawesi (Celebes), and the Philippines, from Mindanao to southern Luzon, in submontane and lower montane forest at 1400–2000 m.

*Dicksonia mollis* is a stout tree fern similar in form to *D. blumei* but differing in having shorter undercoat hairs on the stipe, and tuberculate spores.

Plants from Sulawesi are smaller than those from elsewhere in its range. *Dicksonia mollis* does best in humus. It tolerates high light intensity to medium shade in both exposed and sheltered locations. This slow-growing tree fern may show some frost tolerance.

### *Dicksonia sciurus* C. Christensen 1937

The erect trunk is 4–5 m high, about 13 cm in diameter, and brown. Fronds are tripinnate and as long as about 2 m. The stipe is dark, stout, and covered, especially toward the base, with soft red-brown hairs. Sori occur one or two per lobe and are globose, marginal, and under the hooded edges of the lobes; indusia are oblong to circular. Distribution: Western New Guinea in wet submontane or montane cloud forest and in bog grassland at 1200–2500 m.

*Dicksonia sciurus* appears to be closely related to *D. archboldii* but has smaller fronds and pale hairs, rather than red hairs, on the costae.

### *Dicksonia sellowiana* W. J. Hooker 1844

*Dicksonia karsteniana* (Klotzsch) T. Moore 1860, *D. gigantea* H. Karsten 1869, *D. lobulata* Christ 1906, *D. ghiesbreghtii* Maxon 1913

PLATES 111, 112

The erect trunk may be as tall as 10 m and about 15 cm in diameter; it may be covered at the base with fibrous roots and may have a skirt of dead fronds. Fronds are tripinnate and may be as long as 3 m. Petioles are brown to straw-colored and covered with hairs, as is the rachis. The stipe is short (or long), usually persistent or semipersistent on the trunk, brown, and densely hairy at the base. Sori occur one per pinnule segment and are globose, marginal, and partially covered by the lobe margin; indusia are oval. Distribution: In its broadest sense, *Dicksonia sellowiana* is wide-ranging, from southern Mexico to Costa Rica and Panama in Central America and from Venezuela to Colombia, Bolivia, Paraguay, Uruguay, and southeastern Brazil in South America. Its usual habitat is wet woodland, submontane and montane rain forest, and cloud forest, at 1000–2000 m.

*Dicksonia sellowiana* is named after Friedrich Sello, or Sellow (1789–1831), who collected plants during the 1815–1817 expedition to Brazil by Prinz Maximilian zu Wied. *Dicksonia sellowiana* is variable (similar to *D. antarctica* and *D. fibrosa* in form), with several segregates evidently representing minor variation. These have been treated as separate species and include *D. ghiesbreghtii*, *D. gigantea*, *D. karsteniana*, and *D. lobulata* (all included here as synonymous). A further species, *D. steubelii* from Peru, is also very similar. *Dicksonia sellowiana* does best in a light, damp soil with humus, and in light to medium shade. It is not difficult to grow and may be transplanted with the fronds trimmed, but plants grown from spores are usually the most successful.

## *Dicksonia squarrosa* (G. Forster) Swartz 1802
*Trichomanes squarrosum* G. Forster 1786
ROUGH TREE FERN, WEKI
PLATES 93, 113–116

The erect, slender trunk, or multiple trunks, may be as tall as 7 m, branching from aerial buds and offsets; the trunk is covered in brown hairs and persistent black stipe bases. Fronds are tri- or tetrapinnate, 1–3 m long, dark green, paler below, and semipersistent; they form an untidy crown with a loose rosette atop the trunk. Fertile fronds usually appear only on plants exposed to ample light and occur irregularly together with sterile fronds. Pinnules are large, linear, and divided to the rachis. The rachis and stipe are medium to slender, dark black-brown, rough, and densely hairy at the base. Sori occur two to six per pinnule lobe and are globose, marginal, and under the hooded edges of the lobes; indusia are circular to oval. Distribution: Three Kings Islands, North Island, South Island, Stewart Island, and Chatham Islands, New Zealand, abundant in coastal to montane forest, often on poor or swampy soils, and particularly common on the western coast of the South Island.

*Dicksonia squarrosa* is one of the most common tree ferns in New Zealand, often surviving fire. It is usually recognizable by its ragged appearance, either as a multiheaded plant or occurring in groves (a result of its stoloniferous habit). It is easy to grow in most soils, in full sun to heavy shade, and it can be transplanted and will tolerate medium frost, but specimens look their best in sheltered locations. Plants from the western coast of South Island are usually more attractive than those from North Island populations, which tend to have a more untidy appearance. Plants may be grown from spores, with sporangia maturing mid to late in the New Zealand summer (January–February). Fibrous trunks are often used in garden construction (fencing, for example).

## *Dicksonia steubelii* Hieronymus 1906

The trunk is medium to tall, erect, and slender to stout; trunks may be covered at the base with fibrous roots and may have a skirt of dead fronds. Fronds are tripinnate and may be as long as 3 m. Petioles are brown to straw-colored and covered with hairs, as is the rachis. The stipe is short (or long) usually persistent or semipersistent on the trunk, brown, and densely hairy at base. Sori occur one per penultimate segment of larger fertile pinnules and are globose and partially covered by the lobe margin; indusia are oval. Distribution: Andes of northern Peru and Ecuador.

*Dicksonia steubelii* is named after plant collector M. A. Steubel. It is very similar to *D. sellowiana*.

## *Dicksonia thyrsopteroides* Mettenius 1861
PLATES 117, 118

The erect trunk may be as tall as 2 m and 10 cm diameter. Fronds are about 1.5 m long, tripinnate, and dissected. The sterile lamina is densely hairy on the underside along the veins. Fertile segments are the same size as the sterile but tetrapinnate, with the lamina completely absent. The base of the stipe is densely hairy. The sori appear to be on short pedicels, making the plants very distinctive; indusia are oval and cup-like. Distribution: New Caledonia, rare in the southern half of the island, and most common on the margin of the forest at 500 m and above.

*Dicksonia thyrsopteroides* is easily distinguished from other species by the extreme reduction of the fertile lamina.

## *Dicksonia youngiae* C. Moore ex Baker 1865
BRISTLY TREE FERN

The erect trunk or trunks are 2–5 m tall, 20 cm thick, and dark brown; the upper trunk is usually covered by stipe bases and coarse, stiff, reddish brown hairs, which may extend up the rachis of the fronds, and the trunk may produce offshoots and underground stolons, which eventually result in a colony. Fronds are tri- or tetrapinnate and finely divided, mid to dark green above, and paler below. Fertile and sterile fronds can be found in alternating layers. Pinnules are large, linear, and divided to the rachis. The stipe is brown and smooth to densely hairy at base. Sori occur two to six per pinnule, but one per pinnule lobe; they are globose, marginal, and under the hooded edges of the lobes. Indusia are oval. Distribution: Queensland and northern New South Wales, Australia, in rain forest in wet gullies from near sea level to 1200 m.

*Dicksonia youngiae* is confined to rain forest, usually at higher elevations. It may be distinguished from most other species by the large sori, the offshoots and characteristic clumping, and the reddish brown hairs on the upper trunk and stipes (compare with *D. herbertii;* see also Jones 1984). Plants are fast-growing, doing well in most soils but best in humus. *Dickso-*

*nia youngiae* is hardy in many sheltered situations. It tolerates high light intensity to medium shade but does not endure heavy frost very well. This tree fern may be transplanted with the fronds trimmed. Plants grown from spores are also successful, with sporangia maturing in the mid to late Australian summer (January–February).

## *Leptopteris* C. B. Presl 1846
Osmundaceae

Carel Presl described *Leptopteris* in 1846. The type species is *L. hymenophylloides*, originally described as a species of *Todea* by Achille Richard in 1832. The name *Leptopteris* is derived from the Greek *leptos*, slender, and *pteris*, fern, referring to the thin, dissected form of the lamina. Spores are globular trilete, with fine baculate-tuberculate surface ornamentation. Chromosome number $n = 22$.

The genus *Leptopteris* has a very small whole-plant fossil record, restricted to a few doubtful Miocene remnants. However, spores similar to those of *Leptopteris*, *Osmunda*, and *Todea* have been reported from the Triassic and Jurassic periods.

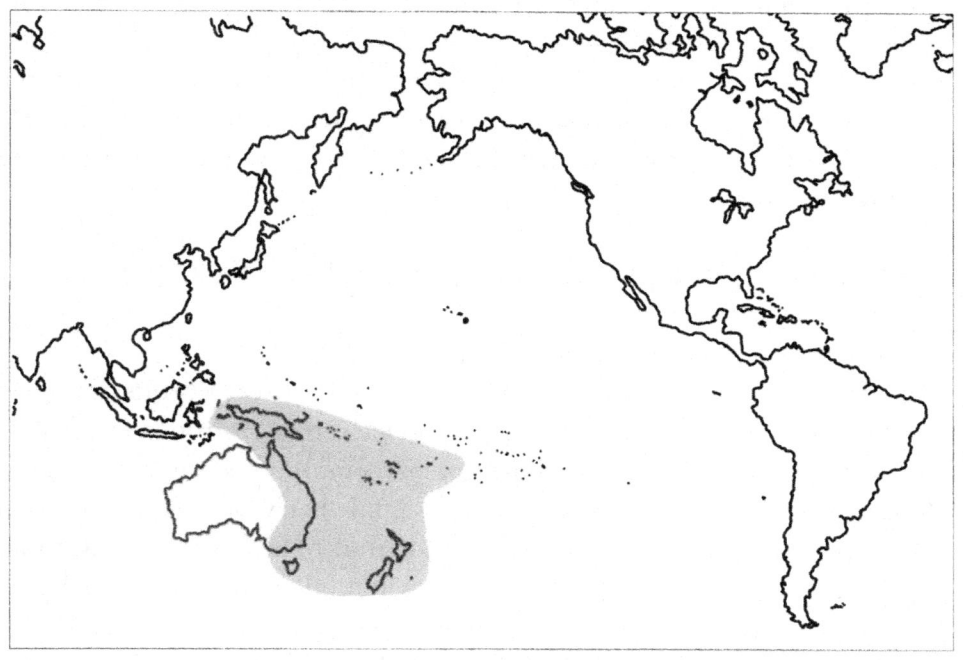

*Leptopteris*, distributed in the Southern Hemisphere from western Polynesia to Australia, New Zealand, and New Guinea.

The exact number of species is unknown because differences between members of the genus in the western Pacific—including *L. alpina* (Baker) C. Christensen of New Guinea and *L. wilkesiana* (Brackenridge) H. Christ of New Caledonia and other Pacific islands—remain unclear. In New Zealand, hybrids are common between *L. hymenophylloides* and *L. superba*. Best estimates suggest about six species with a Southern Hemisphere distribution from western Polynesia, including New Guinea, Australia, and New Zealand. Only those species that are frequently cultivated are included here; all are arborescent, albeit with short trunks.

## *Leptopteris fraseri* (W. J. Hooker & Greville) C. B. Presl 1846

*Todea fraseri* W. J. Hooker & Greville 1829

CREPE FERN

The erect trunk may be as tall as 1 m; it lacks fiber but may bear rust-colored woolly hairs, and stipe-base scars along with stipule-like outgrowths. A single crown of fronds is normally present. Fronds are light to dark green, membranous, bi- or tripinnate, and as long as 1.5 m. The stipe is smooth and not winged. Sporangia are globular and occur scattered in groups on basal pinnules and are naked; spores are released when green to yellow-green. Distribution: Northern and southern Queensland and eastern New South Wales, Australia, in humid, shaded conditions, often near streams, waterfalls, and caves, to about 1300 m.

*Leptopteris fraseri* is a delicate fern with attractive lacy fronds. It will grow in a damp, shaded spot but must be protected from wind. The relationship between this species and the Pacific members of the genus requires further investigation.

## *Leptopteris hymenophylloides* (A. Richard) C. B. Presl 1846

PLATE 120

*Todea hymenophylloides* A. Richard 1832

The erect trunk is 50 cm tall, rarely as tall as 1 m; it is fibrous and bears brown hairs and broken stipe bases. A single crown of fronds is normally present. Fronds are triangular, dark green, membranous, tripinnate, and as long as 1 m. The stipe is pale brown and slightly hairy. Sporangia are globular and occur scattered in groups on basal pinnules and are naked. Spores are released when green to yellow-green. Distribution: New Zealand, including the Chatham Islands, in lowland and montane forest, in very humid, shaded conditions, often near streams and waterfalls.

*Leptopteris hymenophylloides* is a delicate fern with attractive lacy fronds. Hybrids between it and *L. superba* are common. *Leptopteris hymenophylloides* will grow best in a damp, very shaded spot in rich humus. Plants will resist cold but must be protected from wind.

## *Leptopteris superba* (Colenso) C. B. Presl 1847

*Todea superba* Colenso 1845
CREPE FERN, PRINCE OF WALES FEATHERS,
HERUHERU, NGUTUNGUTU KIWI
PLATE 121

The erect trunk may be as tall as 1 m; it is fibrous and bears brown hairs and broken stipe bases. A single crown of fronds is normally present. Fronds are elongate, elliptic, membranous, tripinnate, almost three-dimensional in having alternate pinnule segments at right angles to the rest of the frond, and as long as 1 m. The stipe is pale brown and slightly hairy. Sporangia are globular and occur scattered in groups on basal pinnules and are naked. Spores are released when green to yellow-green. Distribution: New Zealand, including Stewart Island, in montane forest in very humid, shaded conditions.

*Leptopteris superba* is a delicate, slow-growing fern with attractive three-dimensional lacy fronds. Hybrids between it and *L. hymenophylloides* are common. *Leptopteris superba* is difficult to grow but does best in high humidity and very shaded, cool conditions in rich humus. Plants must be protected from wind.

## *Lophosoria* C. B. Presl 1847

*Trichosorus* Liebmann 1849
Dicksoniaceae

Carel Presl described *Lophosoria* in 1847. The genus was based on *L. pruinata* (Swartz) C. B. Presl, originally described as a species of *Polypodium* by Olof Peter Swartz in 1802 and now known as *L. quadripinnata*. The name *Lophosoria* comes from the Greek *lophos*, crest, referring to the crested sorus. The genus, with one or, perhaps, two species, has sometimes been placed in its own family (Lophosoriaceae).

Today, *Lophosoria* is confined to the cool, moist, montane areas of tropical America, but there is good fossil evidence suggesting that tree ferns of this type were once widespread throughout Gondwana, the Mesozoic era supercontinent that once joined the continents of the Southern Hemisphere. Spores are trilete and rounded, with a large equatorial ridge or flange; the surface is covered in coarse warts or tubercules. These characteristic spores

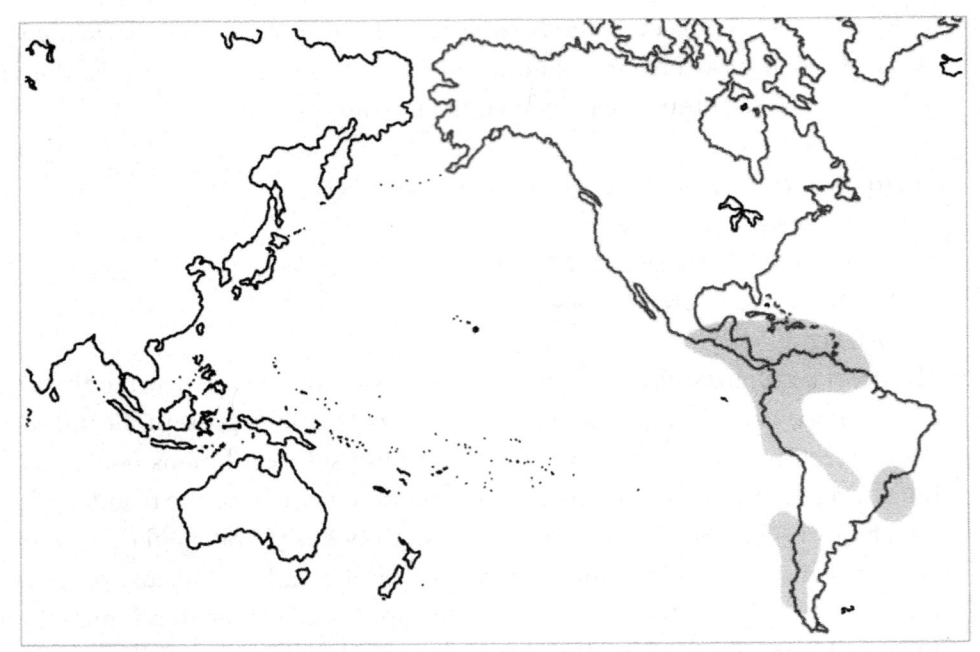

*Lophosoria*, once widely distributed but now restricted to the cooler moist regions of tropical America, from islands of the Caribbean to Central and South America as far south as Chile and the Juan Fernández Islands.

are first recorded in the fossil record from very early Cretaceous deposits located on the Antarctic Peninsula. Fossils are also known from a similar period in Australia and a little later from Patagonia, the Falkland Plateau surrounding the Falkland Islands (some having been found in cores taken from the seabed), and southwestern Africa. These tree ferns had disappeared from Australia by the end of the Cretaceous period yet had become reestablished on the continent by the mid-Eocene, when they were present as far north as southern Queensland. Ferns of this type finally became extinct in Australia for a second time in the Pliocene. *Lophosoria* did not reach New Zealand.

## *Lophosoria quadripinnata* (J. F. Gmelin) C. Christensen 1920

*Polypodium quadripinnatum* J. F. Gmelin 1791, *Lophosoria pruinata* (Swartz) C. B. Presl 1847

PLATE 122

The trunk is creeping to erect, stout, and as tall as 5 m; it is covered with long brown hairs and with many fibrous roots. Fronds form a sparse cluster, are bi- or tripinnate, sparsely to densely pubescent, and 2–3 m long or more. Sori are rounded and occur on veins of the underside of fertile pinnae; indusia are

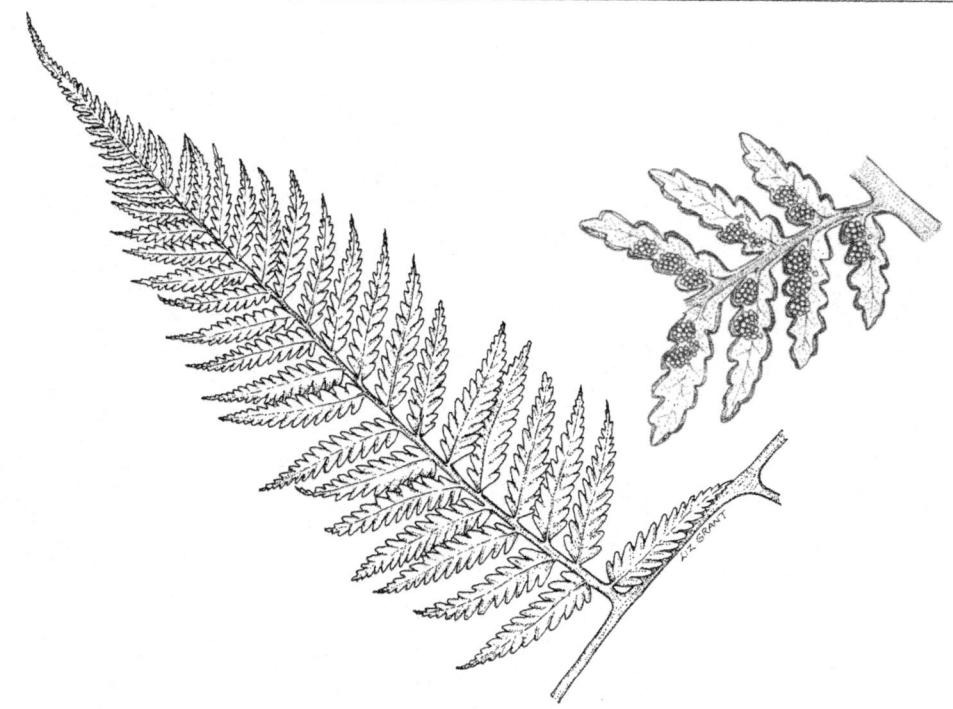

*Lophosoria quadripinnata* from Chile. Secondary portion of a frond and detail showing dehiscing sori. Liz Grant, Massey University, New Zealand.

absent. Chromosome number $n = 65$. Distribution: Greater and Lesser Antilles; Mexico to Costa Rica; Venezuela, Colombia, Ecuador, Peru, Bolivia, Brazil, southern Argentina, Chile, and the Juan Fernández Islands. Plants are found in woodland, cloud forest, montane forest, and disturbed sites, where it will survive burning, from near sea level in the south of its range or more typically at 500–3800 m.

One variety, *Lophosoria quadripinnata* var. *contracta* (Hieronymus) Tryon & Tryon, has been described from high elevation in Ecuador and Peru, and a possible additional species, *L. quesadae* A. Rojas, was described in 1996 as endemic to Costa Rica. *Lophosoria* is not commonly cultivated outside the Americas, but plants are known to grow outdoors as far north as Edinburgh, Scotland.

## *Osmunda* Linnaeus 1753
Osmundaceae

*Osmunda* was formally named by Carl Linnaeus in 1753. The type species is *O. regalis*, named at the same time by Linnaeus. The origin of the name

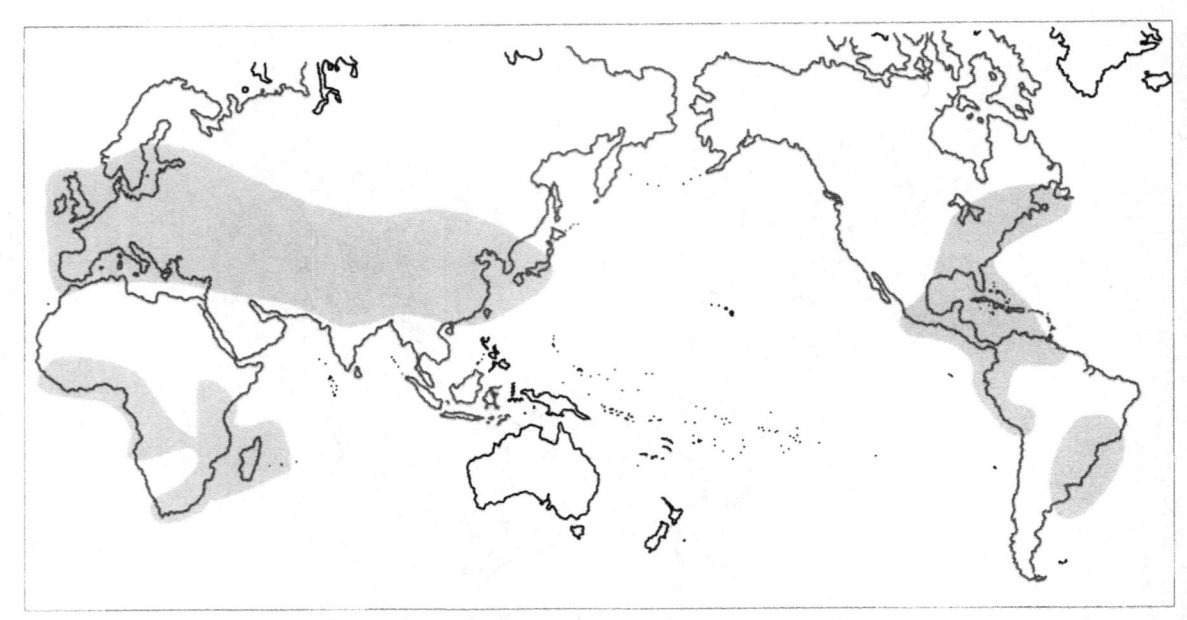

Generalized distribution of *Osmunda,* with species now naturalized in many regions of the world, Europe to Africa, Madagascar, Mauritius, Asia, and the Americas.

*Osmunda* is unknown, but it has been suggested (for example, Stearn 1996a) that the reference is to Åsmund or Osmundus (flourished 1025), a writer who helped prepare Scandinavia for Christianity. *Osmunda* is a genus of some five or six species of very wide, almost cosmopolitan distribution from temperate areas to the Tropics. It is absent from the Pacific islands and dry or very cold regions.

*Osmunda* is broadly divided into three groups sometimes regarded as different genera or subgenera: (1) *O. regalis*, *O. lancea* Thunberg, and possibly *O. claytoniana* Linnaeus, (2) *O. banksiifolia* (C. B. Presl) Kuhn and *O. javanica* Blume, and (3) *O. cinnamomea* Linnaeus. All have erect or semi-erect, trunk-like rhizomes (though *O. regalis* is most common in cultivation, with *O. cinnamomea* next, and the others rarely cultivated) and sporangia grouped in dense clusters in special fertile fronds or regions of the fronds. Spores are globular and trilete, usually with fine tubercles over the surface. Chromosome number $n = 22$.

Stem fossils have been reported from the Cainozoic period, and fossils of fertile fronds from the late Cretaceous. Fossil spores similar to those of *Osmunda*, *Leptopteris*, and *Todea* have been reported from the Triassic and Jurassic.

## *Osmunda regalis* Linnaeus 1753
ROYAL FERN

PLATE 123

The erect or semierect trunk is 1–1.5 m tall; it is fibrous and bears brown hairs and broken stipe bases. A single crown of fronds is normally present but multiple crowns are also possible. Fronds are triangular, dark green, deciduous, bipinnate, and 1–2 m long. The stipe is pale brown and slightly hairy. The upper region of the frond is often characteristically fertile, with clusters of naked sporangia densely grouped on reduced segments, completely replacing the normal lamina. Spores are released when green to yellow-brown. Distribution: Widespread, temperate Europe and the Americas, to Asia and Africa, from Zimbabwe and Sierra Leone to South Africa, Madagascar, and Mauritius, often naturalized in many temperate countries. Plants are found in open areas, on stream margins, and to elevations as high as 2000 m in warmer areas.

*Osmunda regalis* is a tough, slow-growing, deciduous fern with unusual fertile fronds. It is hardy and will grow best in cooler climates in damp to wet soils. Plants are frost resistant. Trunks have been an important source of fiber for the cultivation of orchids. In Japan, hairs from the young fronds and trunks have been mixed with wool to produce textiles.

## *Sadleria* Kaulfuss 1824
Blechnaceae

Georg Kaulfuss described *Sadleria* in 1824. The type species is *S. cyatheoides*, described at the same time by Kaulfuss, based on a collection made by Ludolf Karl Adelbert von Chamisso in Hawaii in 1821. The genus is named after the Hungarian Joseph Sadler (1791–1849), a physician and professor of botany in Budapest.

*Sadleria* consists of terrestrial, small, arborescent tree ferns with a single stem that may be as tall as 1.5 m, rarely taller. Fronds are narrow, 1–3 m long, and usually pinnate or bipinnate. The upper surface is dark green and the lower pale green, often with a white blush. Young uncurling fronds and stipe bases are frequently covered by scales. Stipe scales are golden in color and composed of cells that are generally uniform, that is, similar in orientation, shape, size, and often color. The edge of the scales may bear teeth or cilia. Sori are slit-like and run the length of the pinnae. Spores are monolete, almost bean-shaped, with an irregularly shredded perine layer. Chromosome number $n = 33$ based on a count for *S. squarrosa*.

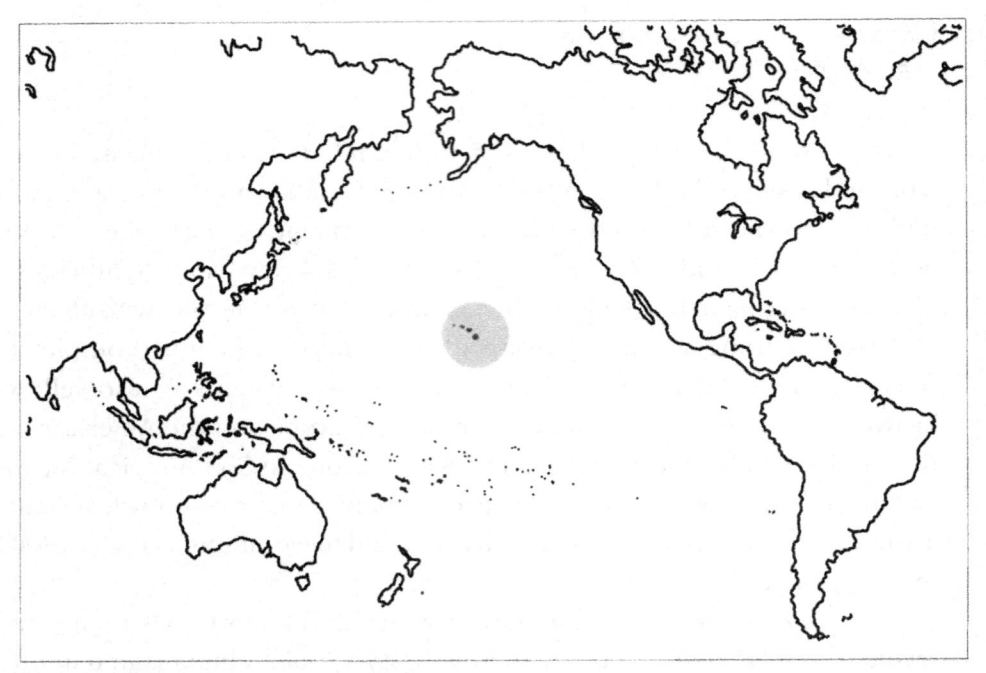

*Sadleria,* endemic to the Hawaiian Islands.

The six species of *Sadleria,* one described relatively recently, are tropical, endemic to Hawaii. The treatment here is based on the revision by Daniel Palmer (1997). The ferns usually grow in rain forest to montane forest and include low-canopy, medium-understory, and ground-cover plants. Many are important to the Hawaiians, who used them to mulch crops, trim thatched houses, and pave paths. Bark cloth was glued together with gum from these ferns, and a red dye extracted to color the cloth. Scales were also used to stuff mattresses.

### *Sadleria cyatheoides* Kaulfuss 1824
'AMA'U, 'EHU'EHU, PUA'A
PLATES 126–128

The trunk is prostrate and slender, as long as 3 m, and terminally erect to about 0.5 tall and 6–12 cm in diameter, rarely as thick as 30 cm; it may branch at or below ground level. Fronds are persistent, usually retained as a skirt about the trunk, pinnate or bipinnate, and about 30 cm long. The stipe is pale tan and has scales only at the base; the scales are soft, linear, and brown or occasionally dark with a light margin. Sori are slit-like, running parallel to the pinnule lobe midvein; they occur two per pinnule segment and are protected by indusia. Distribution: Hawaiian Islands, common in drier open or shady forest and as a colonizer of disturbed land and lava flows, from 30 m on sea cliffs to subalpine scrub at 2200 m.

The type species for the genus, *Sadleria cyatheoides* has incorrectly been ascribed to Indonesia; all members of this genus are endemic to Hawaii. *Sadleria cyatheoides* is a small tree fern with an upright crown of fronds. The prostrate section of the trunk may branch, with sections decaying; this results in a small thicket of plants. Young fronds are often salmon pink, turning dark green as they age.

## *Sadleria pallida* W. J. Hooker & Arnott 1832

*Sadleria rigida* Copeland 1916

'AMA'U'I'I

PLATE 129

The trunk is prostrate, slender, as long as 4 m, and terminally erect to about 1.5 tall and 4–10 cm in diameter; it may branch at or below ground level. Fronds are deciduous, not retained as a skirt, pinnate or bipinnate, and about 30 cm long. The stipe is pale tan and has scattered scales with the maximum aggregation toward the base; the scales are stiff, linear, and bicolored, with a dark brown central region and light brown margin. Sori are slit-like, running parallel to the pinnule lobe midvein; they occur two per pinnule segment and are protected by indusia. Distribution: Hawaiian Islands, common in closed-canopy, shady to wet forest, or in open locations on wet ridges from 30 m on sea cliffs to subalpine scrub at 2150 m.

The name *Sadleria hillebrandii* William J. Robbinson, associated with *S. pallida*, appears to have been based on several misconceptions; Daniel Palmer (1997) discusses these in detail in his revision. *Sadleria pallida* is a small tree fern with an upright crown of fronds. The prostrate section of the trunk may branch, with sections decaying; this results in a small thicket of plants. Young fronds are often salmon pink, turning dark green as they age.

## *Sadleria souleyetiana* (Gaudichaud-Beaupré) T. Moore 1857

*Blechnum souleyetianum* Gaudichaud-Beaupré 1846–1849

The trunk is prostrate, slender trunk, as long as 3 m, rarely 7 m, and terminally erect to about 1.5 tall and 3–10 cm in diameter; it may branch at or below ground level. Fronds are deciduous, not retained as a skirt, pinnate or bipinnate, and 0.3–1 m long. The stipe is tan and has scales matted at the base; the scales are thin, papery, and tan. Sori are slit-like, running parallel to the pinnule lobe midvein; they occur two per pinnule segment and are protected by indusia. Distribution: Hawaiian Islands, scattered in dry to wet forest and often locally common in open locations or in shade, at 400–1550 m.

The name *souleyetiana* has often been misspelled as *souleytiana*, but Charles Gaudichaud-Beaupré's original spelling (as a species of *Blechnum*) is *souleyetianum*. *Sadleria souleyetiana* is a small, variable tree fern with an upright crown of fronds. The prostrate section of the trunk may branch, with sections decaying. Young fronds are often salmon pink, turning dark green as they age.

### *Sadleria squarrosa* (Gaudichaud-Beaupré) T. Moore 1857

*Blechnum squarrosum* Gaudichaud-Beaupré 1854

'APULU, 'APU'U

The trunk is prostrate, narrow, and terminally erect to about 10 cm tall and 1–3 cm in diameter. Fronds are deciduous, leathery, bipinnate, and about 60 cm long. The stipe is dark and densely covered in scales that are linear and dark to red-brown. Sori are slit-like, running parallel to the pinnule lobe midvein, and protected by indusia. Distribution: Hawaiian Islands, locally common, forming colonies, on wet, heavily shaded rock faces and along streams, in mountain habitats at 400–2050 m.

*Sadleria squarrosa* is related to *S. unisora*, occupying the same habitat.

### *Sadleria unisora* (Baker) Robinson 1913

*Polypodium unisorum* Baker in W. J. Hooker & Baker 1868

The trunk is prostrate, narrow, and terminally erect to about 10 cm tall and 1–2.5 cm in diameter. Fronds are bipinnate and as long as about 30 cm. The stipe is dark brown to purple-black and has scattered scales that are linear and dark brown to dark red-brown. Sori are short and slit-like, running parallel to the pinnule lobe midvein, and protected by indusia. Distribution: Kauai in the Hawaiian Islands, on wet, heavily shaded rock faces and along streams, in mountain habitats above 400 m.

*Sadleria unisora* is related to *S. squarrosa*, occupying the same habitat, occasionally at the same locations.

### *Sadleria wagneriana* D. Palmer & T. Flynn 1997

Similar to *S. souleyetiana* but with smaller scales with ultimate segments that are obtuse and glandular, thinner stipes, and simple pinnate fronds. Distribution: Kauai in the Hawaiian Islands around 1100 m.

The name *wagneriana* commemorates pteridologists Warren Herbert ("Herb") Wagner Jr. (1920–2000) and Florence S. Wagner (b. 1919).

## *Thyrsopteris* Kunze 1835

*Panicularia* Colla 1836

Dicksoniaceae

Gustav Kunze described *Thyrsopteris* in 1835. The only species, *T. elegans*, is endemic to the Juan Fernández Islands off the Pacific coast of South America and was described at the same time by Kunze. It is sometimes placed in its own family (Thyrsopteridaceae) and even its own order (Thyrsopteridales). It has also been treated as a subfamily of the Dicksoniaceae, the family in which it is placed here. The name *Thyrsopteris*, from the Latin *thyrsus* and the Greek *pteris* (fern), implies that the leaves occur in a thyrse, a term describing a particular type of arrangement usually applied to cone-shaped indeterminate inflorescences.

Some fossil spores associated with *Thyrsopteris* have been reported from Jurassic deposits in Yorkshire, England, but their relationship is uncertain.

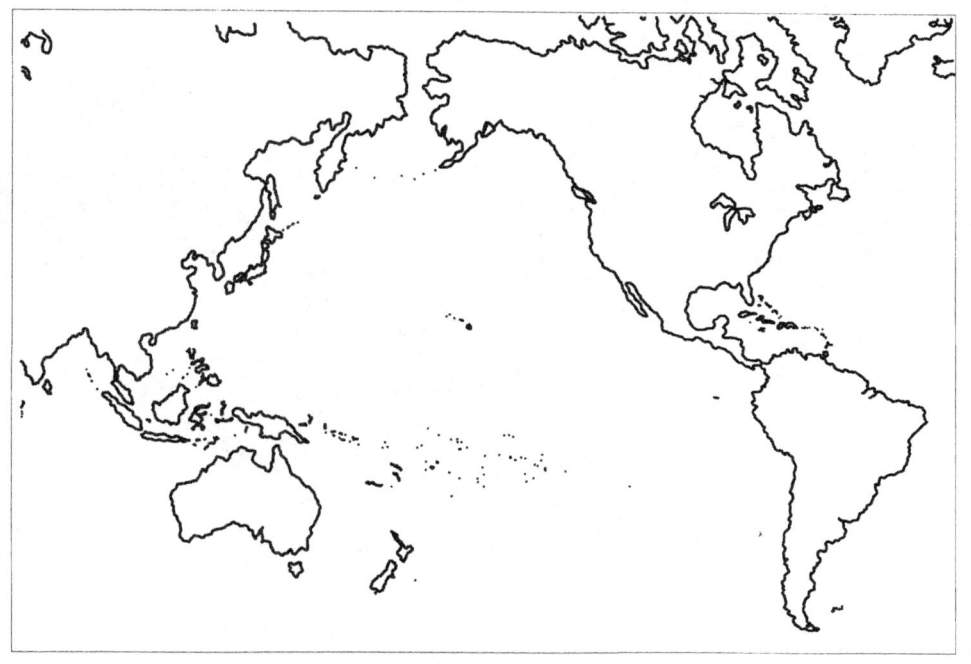

The only species of *Thyrsopteris* (*T. elegans*) is endemic to the Juan Fernández Islands off the coast of Chile.

Spores are trilete, with a fine microverrucate or papillate surface bearing a resemblance to those of *Dicksonia, Cibotium,* and *Cystodium.*

### *Thyrsopteris elegans* Kunze 1835

The trunk is creeping or semierect, massive, and as tall as 1–2 m; the trunk may bear stolons, fibrous roots, and long hairs that become matted. Fronds are partially dimorphic. Sterile fronds are tetra- or pentapinnate, 2–3.5 m long, and have complex to septapinnate fertile regions at the base of the lower pinnae; these fertile regions consist of terminal sori with virtually no lamina or very narrow regions of lamina. Chromosome number $n$ = 76–78. Distribution: Juan Fernández Islands, Chile, in woodland and heathland in upper montane forest, forming thickets on steep hill slopes and in gullies, at 500–1000 m.

*Thyrsopteris elegans.* Secondary portion of frond and detail of a basal, dehisced fertile portion. Liz Grant, Massey University, New Zealand.

*Thyrsopteris elegans* is reported to bear short stolons that form from the rhizome. In cultivation, these runners may be variously produced, and their presence apparently depends on growing conditions. This tree fern has been in limited cultivation in the United States and Chile. Plants grow best in moist but well-drained humus.

## *Todea* Willdenow ex Bernhardi 1801
Osmundaceae

Johann Bernhardi published Karl Willdenow's name *Todea* in 1801, the genus based on *T. africana* (an illegitimate name for *T. barbara*, originally described by Carl Linnaeus in 1753 as *Acrostichum barbarum*), which Willdenow described in 1802. *Todea* is named after the German botanist Heinrich Tode (1733–1797). The tree fern is widespread, from southern Africa to Australia, New Guinea, and New Zealand. *Todea* is often treated as having only a single species, *T. barbara*, but a second, *T. papuana*, was described by Elbert Hennipman from New Guinea in 1968. Both have short massive, fibrous trunks, either erect or prostrate, and sometimes multiple crowns. Sporangia are grouped in clusters on the lower parts of fronds. Spores are globular and trilete, with fine baculate-tuberculate surface ornamentation. *Todea* is rep-

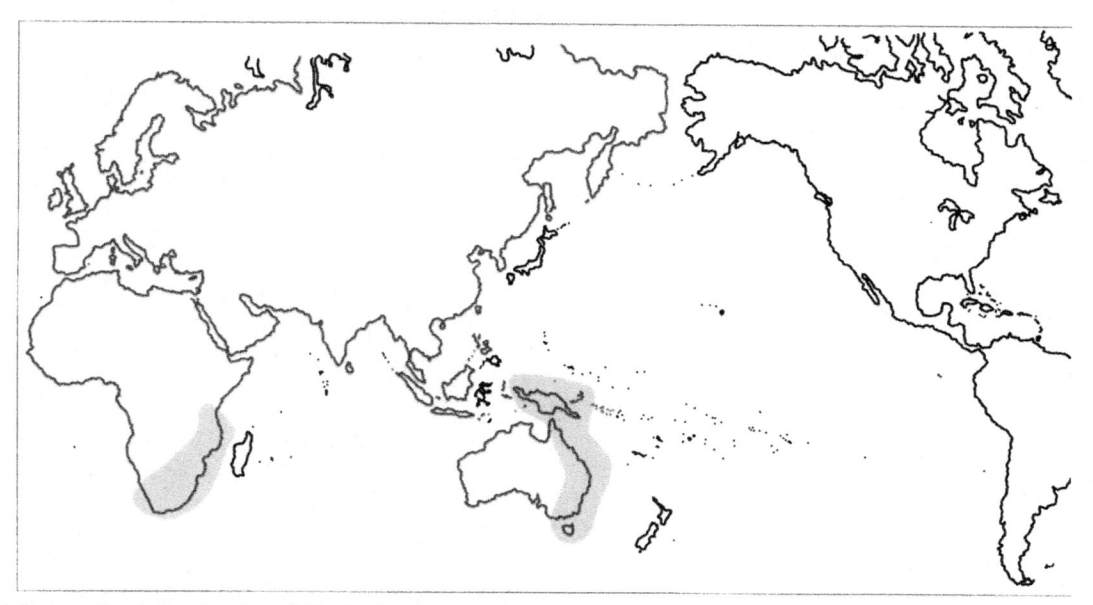

Generalized distribution of *Todea barbara*, which may be found in southern Africa and Australasia, including the northern North Island of New Zealand, with *T. papuana* endemic to New Guinea.

resented by very little (if any) whole-plant fossil material, but spores very similar to those of *Todea, Leptopteris,* and *Osmunda* have been reported from the Triassic and Jurassic periods.

### *Todea barbara* (Linnaeus) T. Moore 1857

*Acrostichum barbarum* Linnaeus 1753, *Todea africana* Willdenow 1802

PLATES 130, 131

The massive, erect trunk may be as tall as 1.5 m, rarely 3 m; it is very fibrous, covered with matted roots, and broken winged stipe bases, and it may bear numerous crowns of fronds. Fronds are bright green, pinnate or bipinnate, and as long as 2 m. The stipe is usually smooth. Sporangia occur in groups on basal pinnules and are naked on the veins. Spores are released when yellow-green or reddish green. Chromosome number $n = 22$. Distribution: Southern Africa, Australia (Queensland, New South Wales, Victoria, Tasmania and rare in South Australia), and northern North Island, New Zealand, in open locations, scrub, dark gullies, rock crevices, shaded wet areas in rain forest and forest clearings, swamps, and on stream banks.

The largest plants of *Todea barbara* grow in shaded areas. Trunks may be as much as 3 m in diameter but are almost composite, with many crowns of long fronds. This tree fern is slow-growing, long-lived, and excellent for cultivation in containers in warmer areas, or easily grown in cooler areas with some protection. It is frost tolerant but can be damaged. Spores are green and short-lived, losing freshness very quickly.

# APPENDIX 1

# Tree Ferns That Require Further Study

The following species are listed here because of the nomenclatural problems that would ensue if they were formally included in the genus *Cyathea* (see the introduction to that genus for further discussion).

### *Alsophila amintae* Conant 1983

*Alsophila* clade. The erect trunk may be as tall as about 1.3 m and about 5 cm in diameter. Fronds are pinnate and may reach 1.6 m in length. The rachis may be purplish brown and has scales, usually on the underside; the scales are golden brown to bicolored (pale with darker margins). Sori occur along each side of the pinnule midvein; indusia are cup-like. Distribution: Puerto Rico in shaded areas and cloud forest at 1000–1200 m.

*Alsophila amintae* is known to form hybrids with *A. bryophila*, producing a plant commonly known as *Cyathea* ×*dryopteroides*, and with *C. portoricensis*.

### *Alsophila bryophila* Tryon 1972

*Alsophila* clade. The erect trunk may be as tall as about 7 m and about 10 cm in diameter. Fronds are pinnate or bipinnate and may reach about 2 m in length. The underside of the rachis is pubescent and has occasional scales toward the base; the scales may be brown to bicolored (pale with brown margins). Sori occur along each side of the pinnule midvein and have scale-like indusia. Distribution: Puerto Rico in the understory in wet montane and mossy forest, from about 750 m to 1200 m.

*Alsophila bryophila* is also commonly but erroneously called *Cyathea pubescens*. It is characteristic of mossy forest, hence the name *bryophila*, "bryophyte loving." Plants may be cultivated if given cool and consistently moist conditions but are susceptible to insect damage. This tree fern is slow-growing, with a recorded trunk growth rate of about 5 cm per year; it has been suggested that plants may live in excess of 150 years. *Alsophila bryophila* is similar to *C. brooksii*, *C. hotteana*, and *C. minor* and may form hybrids with *A. amintae* (for example, plants known as *C.* ×*dryopteroides*) and *C. portoricensis*.

### *Alsophila esmeraldensis* R. C. Moran 1995

*Alsophila* clade. The erect trunk is about 80 cm tall and about 3 cm in diameter. Fronds are erect or spreading, simply pinnate or bipinnate basally, and as long as 2.5 m. The rachis is dark brown to blackish and has a few scales that are linear, whitish with a central brown region, and with edges and apexes with dark setae. Sori are protected by cup-like indusia. Distribution: Western Andes of Ecuador, on the sides of rocky streambeds at 500–1000 m, the name *esmeraldensis* referring to the province of Esmeralda.

*Alsophila esmeraldensis* belongs to the *Cyathea minor* group and is very similar to the eastern Andean *C. stuebelii*, from which it differs in its more erect fronds. The two may represent sister species.

### *Alsophila gardneri* W. J. Hooker 1844

*Cyathea gardneri* (W. J. Hooker) Lellinger 1987, not *C. gardneri* W. J. Hooker 1844; *C. mexiae* Copeland 1932

*Cyathea* clade. The erect trunk is 1–4 m tall. Fronds are bipinnate and may reach 3 m or more in length. The rachis is brown and has scattered brown scales. Sori occur between the fertile pinnule midvein and the edge of the lamina; indusia are absent. Distribution: Mato Grosso, Rio de Janeiro, São Paulo, and Minas Gerais, Brazil, in secondary forest and drainage ditches at 700–1000 m.

*Alsophila gardneri* is a variable species similar to *Cyathea phalerata*.

### *Alsophila parva* Maxon 1944

*Cyathea parva* (Maxon) Tryon 1976, not *C. parva* Copeland 1942

*Cyathea* clade. The erect trunk is only a few centimeters tall. Fronds are bipinnate, dissected, and as long as about 75 cm. The rachis is often broadly winged. Sori are covered by small indusia. Distribution: Colombia in rain forest, in the understory, from sea level to about 90 m.

*Alsophila parva* is part of a group of species centered on *Cyathea speciosa*. There is considerable confusion over the use of *parva* as a species name, *C. parva* (in the *Alsophila* clade) having already been used by Edwin Copeland.

### *Alsophila polystichoides* Christ 1896

*Nephelea polystichoides* (Christ) Tryon 1970

*Alsophila* clade. The erect trunk is 1–3 m tall, occasionally as tall as 5 m, and

5–8 cm in diameter; it has black spines and occasional side shoots. Fronds are tripinnate and 2–3 m long. The rachis and stipe are straw-colored to brown or reddish brown and have scales that are bicolored (dark brown center and whitish margin), and several apical and lateral setae. Petiole spines are present. Sori are round, with globose indusia, and occur on either side of the pinnule midvein. Distribution: Costa Rica and Panama, in tropical rain forest and submontane forest, in understory and on riverbanks, at 700–2000 m.

*Alsophila polystichoides* is a small tree fern with a thin trunk that may form a rough clump with an open crown. It is of possible hybrid origin, involving *A. salvinii* and *Cyathea mexicana* (also known as *A. firma*) as parents.

## *Alsophila salvinii* W. J. Hooker in W. J. Hooker & Baker 1866
*Alsophila munchii* Christ 1905

*Alsophila* clade. The erect trunk is about 9 m tall. Fronds are tripinnate to, rarely, tetrapinnate and about 2.5 m long; the base of the frond may have as many as 15 pairs of reduced pinnae that form a loose clump over the trunk apex. The rachis and stipe are black, warty, and have plentiful brown scales at the base. Sori occur in two simple rows on either side of the pinnule midvein; indusia are absent. Distribution: Southern Mexico, Guatemala, and Honduras, in cloud forest at 910–2600 m.

*Alsophila salvinii* is named after Osbert Salvin (1835–1898), coeditor of *Biologia Centrali-Americana* and botanist who collected in Central America and the West Indies.

## *Alsophila setosa* Kaulfuss 1824

*Alsophila* clade. Distribution: Southeastern Brazil and Argentina. *Alsophila setosa* may be of hybrid origin.

## *Alsophila tryoniana* (Gastony) Conant 1983
*Nephelea tryoniana* Gastony 1973

*Alsophila* clade. Distribution: Guatemala, Honduras, and Nicaragua. The name *tryoniana* commemorates pteridologist Rolla M. Tryon Jr. (1916–2001). *Alsophila tryoniana* is of possible hybrid origin, involving *A. salvinii* and *Cyathea mexicana* (also known as *A. firma*) as parents.

## *Sphaeropteris cuatrecasassi* Tryon 1971

*Sphaeropteris* clade. The erect trunk is about 3 m tall and 15–20 cm in diameter. Fronds are bipinnate and as long as 2.5 m. Distribution: Colombia at 2200–2300 m.

*Sphaeropteris cuatrecasassi* is named after botanist José Cuatrecasas (1903–1996). It is very similar to *Cyathea brunei* but differs in having distinctive reddish squamulae beneath large scales. It forms part of a group of ferns associated with *C. princeps* (= *Sphaeropteris horrida*).

## *Trichipteris microphylla* (Klotzsch) Tryon 1970

*Alsophila microphylla* Klotzsch 1844, not *Cyathea microphylla* Mettenius 1856; *A. squamata* Klotzsch 1844, *A. microphylloides* Domin 1929, not *A. microphylloides* (Rosenstock) Tryon 1970 (see *C. microphylloides*)

*Cyathea* clade. The erect trunk is 0.5–3 m tall. Fronds are bipinnate and 2–2.5 m long. Rachis and stipe scales are bullate, brown, and have whitish apices. Sori occur between the midvein of fertile pinnules and the edge of the lamina; indusia are absent. Distribution: Northern Colombia and coastal ranges in Venezuela, and possibly in Trinidad, in forest at 1800–3000 m.

The placement of *Trichipteris microphylla* in *Cyathea* presents a nomenclatural problem. An alternative name, *C. microphylloides*, proposed by Karel Domin is unavailable because of prior use of the epithet by Eduard Rosenstock. The original name, *microphylla*, is also unavailable in *Cyathea*, having been used by Georg Mettenius.

# APPENDIX 2

# Tree Ferns by Geographic Region

## Africa and Madagascar
*Cyathea approximata.* Madagascar
*Cyathea camerooniana.* Angola, Cameroon, Sierra Leone, Uganda
*Cyathea capensis.* Malawi, Mozambique, South Africa, Tanzania, Zimbabwe
*Cyathea deckenii.* Mozambique, Tanzania, Democratic Republic of Congo (Zaire)
*Cyathea decrescens.* Madagascar
*Cyathea dregei.* Madagascar, Mozambique, Sierra Leone, South Africa, Zimbabwe
*Cyathea fadenii.* Tanzania
*Cyathea madagascarica.* Madagascar
*Cyathea manniana.* Liberia, Mozambique, Zimbabwe
*Cyathea marattioides.* Madagascar
*Cyathea mildbraedii.* Ruwenzori mountains (Uganda and Democratic Republic of Congo [Zaire])
*Cyathea mossambicensis.* Mozambique, Tanzania, Zimbabwe
*Cyathea nicklesii.* Central African Republic, Democratic Republic of Congo (Zaire)
*Cyathea obtusiloba.* Cameroon, Gabon
*Cyathea perrieriana.* Madagascar
*Cyathea schliebenii.* Tanzania
*Cyathea serratifolia.* Madagascar
*Cyathea thomsonii.* Angola, Malawi, Mozambique, Tanzania, Democratic Republic of Congo (Zaire), Zambia, Zimbabwe
*Cyathea tsilotsilensis.* Madagascar
*Cyathea welwitschii.* São Tomé
*Cyathea zakamenensis.* Madagascar
*Todea barbara.* South Africa

## Atlantic Ocean and Europe
*Culcita macrocarpa.* Azores, Canary Islands, Madeira, Portugal, Spain
*Dicksonia arborescens.* St. Helena

## Australia and Pacific Ocean
*Calochlaena dubia.* Australia
*Calochlaena straminea.* Fiji, New Caledonia, Samoa, Vanuatu
*Calochlaena villosa.* Australia
*Cibotium chamissoi.* Hawaii
*Cibotium glaucum.* Hawaii
*Cibotium menziesii.* Hawaii
*Cibotium nealiae.* Hawaii
*Cyathea affinis.* Austral Islands, Cook Islands, Fiji, Marquesas Islands, Samoa, Tahiti
*Cyathea alata.* Fiji, New Caledonia, Samoa
*Cyathea albifrons.* New Caledonia
*Cyathea aneitensis.* New Caledonia, Vanuatu

*Cyathea aramaganensis.* Mariana Islands
*Cyathea australis.* Australia
*Cyathea baileyana.* Australia
*Cyathea brevipinnata.* Lord Howe Island
*Cyathea brownii.* Norfolk Island
*Cyathea celebica.* Australia
*Cyathea cicatricosa.* New Caledonia
*Cyathea colensoi.* New Zealand
*Cyathea cooperi.* Australia
*Cyathea cunninghamii.* Australia, New Zealand
*Cyathea dealbata.* New Zealand
*Cyathea decurrens.* Cook Islands, Fiji, Samoa, Vanuatu
*Cyathea feani.* Marquesas Islands
*Cyathea felina.* Australia
*Cyathea hornei.* Fiji to the Louisiade Archipelago
*Cyathea howeana.* Lord Howe Island
*Cyathea intermedia.* New Caledonia
*Cyathea kermadecensis.* Kermadec Islands
*Cyathea leichhardtiana.* Australia
*Cyathea leucolepis.* Vanuatu
*Cyathea lunulata.* Fiji, Caroline Islands, Mariana Islands, New Caledonia, Samoa, Tonga, Vanuatu
*Cyathea macarthurii.* Lord Howe Island
*Cyathea ×marcescens.* Australia
*Cyathea medullaris.* Austral Islands, Fiji, Marquesas Islands, New Zealand, Pitcairn Island, Tahiti
*Cyathea microlepidota.* Fiji
*Cyathea milnei.* Kermadec Islands
*Cyathea nigricans.* Caroline Islands
*Cyathea novae-caledoniae.* New Caledonia
*Cyathea parksii.* Cook Islands
*Cyathea plagiostegia.* Austral Islands, Cook Islands, Fiji, Marquesas Islands, Samoa, Tahiti
*Cyathea propinqua.* Fiji
*Cyathea rebeccae.* Australia
*Cyathea robertsiana.* Australia
*Cyathea robusta.* Lord Howe Island

*Cyathea smithii.* New Zealand to as far south as the Auckland Islands
*Cyathea stokesii.* Austral Islands
*Cyathea subsessilis.* Samoa to Solomon Islands, including Fiji
*Cyathea truncata.* Fiji to Samoa
*Cyathea vaupelii.* Fiji to Samoa
*Cyathea vieillardii.* New Caledonia, Vanuatu
*Cyathea whitmeei.* Samoa to Solomon Islands, including Fiji
*Cyathea woollsiana.* Australia
*Dicksonia antarctica.* Australia
*Dicksonia baudouini.* New Caledonia
*Dicksonia brackenridgei.* Fiji to Vanuatu
*Dicksonia fibrosa.* New Zealand
*Dicksonia herbertii.* Australia
*Dicksonia lanata.* New Zealand
*Dicksonia squarrosa.* New Zealand
*Dicksonia thyrsopteroides.* New Caledonia
*Dicksonia youngiae.* Australia
*Leptopteris fraseri.* Australia
*Leptopteris hymenophylloides.* New Zealand
*Leptopteris superba.* New Zealand
*Sadleria cyatheoides.* Hawaii
*Sadleria pallida.* Hawaii
*Sadleria souleyetiana.* Hawaii
*Sadleria squarrosa.* Hawaii
*Sadleria unisora.* Hawaii
*Sadleria wagneriana.* Hawaii
*Todea barbara.* Australia, northern New Zealand

## Asia, Including India

*Calochlaena straminea.* Taiwan
*Cibotium barometz.* China to Indo-China
*Cyathea andersonii.* Bhutan, China, India
*Cyathea borneensis.* Cambodia, Thailand
*Cyathea brunoniana.* Bangladesh, Myanmar (Burma), India, Vietnam
*Cyathea chinensis.* Myanmar (Burma), China, India, Laos, Vietnam
*Cyathea crinita.* India, Sri Lanka

*Cyathea fenicis.* Taiwan
*Cyathea gigantea.* Myanmar (Burma), India, Laos, Nepal, Sri Lanka, Thailand, Vietnam
*Cyathea hancockii.* Ryukyu Islands, Taiwan, Hong Kong
*Cyathea henryi.* India, Yunnan in China
*Cyathea hookeri.* Sri Lanka
*Cyathea khasyana.* Myanmar (Burma) to India
*Cyathea latebrosa.* Indo-China, including Cambodia and Thailand
*Cyathea lepifera.* Ryukyu Islands, southern China, Taiwan
*Cyathea loheri.* Southern Taiwan
*Cyathea mertensiana.* Bonin Islands
*Cyathea metteniana.* China, Japan, Taiwan
*Cyathea nilgirensis.* Southern India
*Cyathea ogurae.* Chichi-shima, Bonin Islands
*Cyathea podophylla.* Cambodia, China, Laos, Ryukyu Islands, Taiwan, Thailand, Vietnam
*Cyathea salletii.* Vietnam
*Cyathea sechellarum.* Seychelles
*Cyathea sinuata.* India, Sri Lanka
*Cyathea spinulosa.* Myanmar (Burma), China, eastern Himalaya, India, Japan, Sri Lanka, Taiwan
*Cyathea walkerae.* Sri Lanka

## Malesia

*Calochlaena javanica.* Borneo, Indonesia
*Calochlaena straminea.* Malaysia, New Guinea, Philippines, Solomon Islands
*Calochlaena villosa.* Sulawesi (Celebes), New Guinea
*Cibotium arachnoideum.* Borneo, Malaysia
*Cibotium barometz.* Malay Peninsula
*Cibotium cumingii.* Philippines
*Cyathea acanthophora.* Kinabalu, Borneo
*Cyathea aciculosa.* Solomon Islands
*Cyathea acrostichoides.* Moluccas, New Guinea
*Cyathea acuminata.* Philippines
*Cyathea aeneifolia.* New Guinea
*Cyathea agatheti.* Borneo
*Cyathea alata.* Solomon Islands
*Cyathea alderwereltii.* Central Sumatra
*Cyathea alleniae.* Malay Peninsula
*Cyathea alpicola.* Central Sumatra
*Cyathea alternans.* Borneo, Malay Peninsula, Sarawak, Sumatra
*Cyathea amboinensis.* Sulawesi (Celebes), Moluccas
*Cyathea angiensis.* Moluccas to New Guinea
*Cyathea angustipinna.* Borneo, Sarawak
*Cyathea annae.* Moluccas
*Cyathea apiculata.* Sumatra
*Cyathea apoensis.* Philippines
*Cyathea archboldii.* Bougainville, New Guinea
*Cyathea arthropoda.* Sarawak
*Cyathea ascendens.* New Guinea
*Cyathea ascendens.* New Guinea
*Cyathea assimilis.* Borneo, Sumatra
*Cyathea atropurpurea.* Philippines
*Cyathea atrospinosa.* New Guinea
*Cyathea atrox.* New Guinea
*Cyathea auriculifera.* Louisiade Archipelago, New Guinea
*Cyathea batjanensis.* Moluccas, New Guinea
*Cyathea biformis.* Moluccas, New Guinea
*Cyathea binuangensis.* Philippines
*Cyathea borneensis.* Borneo, Malay Peninsula
*Cyathea brackenridgei.* Solomon Islands
*Cyathea buennermeijeri.* Indonesia, Natuna Islands
*Cyathea callosa.* Philippines
*Cyathea capitata.* Borneo
*Cyathea carrii.* New Guinea
*Cyathea catillifera.* New Guinea
*Cyathea caudata.* Philippines

*Cyathea celebica.* Sulawesi (Celebes), New Guinea
*Cyathea christii.* Philippines
*Cyathea cincinnata.* New Guinea
*Cyathea cinerea.* Philippines
*Cyathea coactilis.* New Guinea
*Cyathea contaminans.* Borneo, Java, Malay Peninsula, Sumatra
*Cyathea contaminans.* Indonesia, Malaysia, New Guinea
*Cyathea costalisora.* New Guinea
*Cyathea costulisora.* Sumatra
*Cyathea cucullifera.* New Guinea
*Cyathea curranii.* Philippines
*Cyathea decurrens.* New Ireland, Bismarck Archipelago; Solomon Islands
*Cyathea deminuens.* Sumatra
*Cyathea dicksonioides.* New Guinea
*Cyathea dimorpha.* Sulawesi (Celebes)
*Cyathea discophora.* Kinabalu, Borneo
*Cyathea doctersii.* Sumatra
*Cyathea edanoi.* Philippines
*Cyathea elliptica.* Kinabalu, Borneo
*Cyathea elmeri.* Sulawesi (Celebes), Philippines
*Cyathea eriophora.* New Guinea
*Cyathea everta.* New Guinea
*Cyathea excavata.* Malay Peninsula
*Cyathea felina.* Indonesia, Malaysia, New Guinea
*Cyathea fenicis.* Philippines
*Cyathea ferruginea.* Philippines
*Cyathea foersteri.* New Guinea
*Cyathea fugax.* New Guinea
*Cyathea fuliginosa.* Philippines
*Cyathea fusca.* New Guinea
*Cyathea geluensis.* Louisiade Archipelago, New Guinea
*Cyathea gigantea.* Java, Sumatra
*Cyathea glaberrima.* D'Entrecasteaux Islands
*Cyathea gleichenioides.* New Guinea
*Cyathea gregaria.* New Guinea
*Cyathea halconensis.* Philippines
*Cyathea havilandii.* Kinabalu, Borneo

*Cyathea heterochlamydea.* Philippines
*Cyathea hooglandii.* New Guinea
*Cyathea hornei.* Louisiade Archipelago, New Guinea
*Cyathea horridula.* New Guinea
*Cyathea hunsteiniana.* New Guinea
*Cyathea hymenodes.* Malay Peninsula, Sumatra
*Cyathea imbricata.* New Guinea
*Cyathea inaequalis.* New Guinea
*Cyathea incisoserrata.* Malay Peninsula, Sarawak
*Cyathea inquinans.* Sulawesi (Celebes)
*Cyathea insulana.* New Guinea
*Cyathea insularum.* Louisiade Archipelago
*Cyathea integra.* Philippines
*Cyathea javanica.* Java, Sumatra
*Cyathea junghuhniana.* Java, Sumatra
*Cyathea kanehirae* New Guinea
*Cyathea klossii.* New Guinea
*Cyathea latebrosa.* Borneo, Indonesia, Malay Peninsula
*Cyathea latipinnula.* Philippines
*Cyathea ledermannii.* Bougainville, New Guinea
*Cyathea lepidocladia.* New Guinea
*Cyathea lepifera.* New Guinea, Philippines
*Cyathea leucotricha.* Borneo
*Cyathea loerzingii.* Sumatra
*Cyathea loheri.* Kinabalu, Borneo; Philippines
*Cyathea longipes.* Kinabalu, Borneo
*Cyathea lunulata.* Solomon Islands
*Cyathea lurida.* Java, Malay Peninsula, Philippines, Sumatra
*Cyathea macgillivrayi.* Louisiade Archipelago, New Guinea
*Cyathea macgregorii.* New Guinea
*Cyathea macrophylla.* New Guinea
*Cyathea macropoda.* Sumatra
*Cyathea magna.* New Guinea
*Cyathea magnifolia.* Sumatra
*Cyathea marginata.* New Guinea

*Cyathea masapilidensis.* Philippines
*Cyathea media.* Islands northeast of New Guinea, including Manus (Admiralty Islands and adjacent islands)
*Cyathea megalosora.* Kinabalu, Borneo
*Cyathea mesosora.* New Guinea
*Cyathea microchlamys.* Philippines
*Cyathea microphylloides.* New Guinea
*Cyathea modesta.* Sumatra
*Cyathea moluccana.* Borneo, Sulawesi (Celebes), Malay Peninsula, Moluccas, Sumatra
*Cyathea moseleyi.* Admiralty Islands
*Cyathea muelleri.* New Guinea
*Cyathea negrosiana.* Philippines
*Cyathea nigrolineata.* New Guinea
*Cyathea nigropaleata.* New Guinea
*Cyathea obliqua.* Philippines
*Cyathea obscura.* Malay Peninsula, Sumatra
*Cyathea oinops.* Sulawesi (Celebes), Java, Lesser Sunda Islands, Sumatra
*Cyathea oosora.* Kinabalu, Borneo; Sulawesi (Celebes)
*Cyathea orientalis.* Java, Lesser Sunda Islands
*Cyathea pachyrrhachis.* New Guinea
*Cyathea pallidipaleata.* Sulawesi (Celebes)
*Cyathea papuana.* New Guinea
*Cyathea parva.* New Guinea
*Cyathea parvipinna.* New Guinea
*Cyathea patellifera.* Sumatra
*Cyathea percrassa.* New Guinea
*Cyathea perpelvigera.* Moluccas, New Guinea
*Cyathea perpunctulata.* Sumatra
*Cyathea persquamulifera.* Java, Sumatra
*Cyathea philippinensis.* Philippines
*Cyathea physolepidota.* New Guinea
*Cyathea pilulifera.* Louisiade Archipelago, New Guinea
*Cyathea polycarpa.* Flores, Java
*Cyathea polypoda.* Borneo, Malay Peninsula, Philippines
*Cyathea procera.* New Guinea

*Cyathea pruinosa.* New Guinea
*Cyathea pseudomuelleri.* New Guinea
*Cyathea pulcherrima.* Admiralty Islands, New Guinea
*Cyathea punctulata.* Sumatra
*Cyathea pycnoneura.* New Guinea
*Cyathea raciborskii.* Java, Sumatra
*Cyathea ramispina.* Kinabalu, Borneo; Sarawak
*Cyathea rebeccae.* Flores
*Cyathea recommutata.* Borneo, Malay Peninsula, Sumatra
*Cyathea recurvata.* New Guinea
*Cyathea rigens.* New Guinea
*Cyathea robinsonii.* Philippines
*Cyathea rubella.* D'Entrecasteaux Islands, New Guinea
*Cyathea rubiginosa.* New Guinea
*Cyathea rufopannosa.* Philippines
*Cyathea runensis.* Bismarck Archipelago, New Guinea
*Cyathea saccata.* Sulawesi (Celebes)
*Cyathea sarasinorum.* Sulawesi (Celebes)
*Cyathea scandens.* New Guinea
*Cyathea schlechteri.* New Guinea
*Cyathea semiamplectens.* New Guinea
*Cyathea senex.* Sumatra
*Cyathea setifera.* Moluccas
*Cyathea setulosa.* Philippines
*Cyathea sibuyanensis.* Philippines
*Cyathea solomonensis.* Solomon Islands
*Cyathea squamulata.* Borneo, Java, Malay Peninsula, Sulu Archipelago, Philippines
*Cyathea stipipinnula.* Kinabalu, Borneo
*Cyathea strigosa.* Sulawesi (Celebes)
*Cyathea subdubia.* Java, Sumatra
*Cyathea subtripinnata.* New Guinea
*Cyathea suluensis.* Philippines
*Cyathea sumatrana.* Malay Peninsula, Sumatra
*Cyathea tenggerensis.* Sulawesi (Celebes), Flores, Java
*Cyathea tenuicaulis.* New Guinea
*Cyathea ternatea.* Moluccas

*Cyathea teysmannii.* Sulawesi (Celebes)
*Cyathea tomentosa.* Flores, Java
*Cyathea tomentosissima.* New Guinea
*Cyathea trichodesma.* Philippines
*Cyathea trichophora.* Kinabalu, Borneo; Philippines, Sarawak
*Cyathea tripinnata.* Borneo, Java, Philippines, Palau
*Cyathea tripinnatifida.* Moluccas, including Ambon
*Cyathea truncata.* Solomon Islands
*Cyathea vandeusenii.* New Guinea
*Cyathea verrucosa.* Sumatra
*Cyathea vittata.* Bougainville, Solomon Islands
*Cyathea wallacei.* Borneo
*Cyathea wengiensis.* New Guinea
*Cyathea werneri.* New Guinea
*Cyathea whitmeei.* Solomon Islands
*Cyathea womersleyi.* New Guinea
*Cyathea zamboangana.* Philippines
*Cystodium sorbifolium.* Borneo, Indonesia, Louisiade Archipelago, New Guinea, New Britain, Solomon Islands
*Dicksonia archboldii.* New Guinea
*Dicksonia blumei.* Sumatra, Java, Borneo, Sulawesi (Celebes), New Guinea, Philippines
*Dicksonia grandis.* New Guinea
*Dicksonia hieronymi.* New Guinea, Louisiade Archipelago
*Dicksonia lanigera.* New Guinea
*Dicksonia mollis.* Borneo, Sulawesi (Celebes), Philippines
*Dicksonia sciurus.* New Guinea

## Caribbean

*Alsophila amintae.* Puerto Rico (Appendix 1)
*Alsophila bryophila.* Puerto Rico (Appendix 1)
*Cnemidaria consimilis.* Trinidad
*Cnemidaria grandifolia.* Trinidad and Tobago
*Cnemidaria horrida.* Hispaniola, Jamaica, Puerto Rico
*Cnemidaria spectabilis.* Trinidad and Tobago
*Cyathea abbottii.* Hispaniola
*Cyathea andina.* Hispaniola, Puerto Rico
*Cyathea arborea.* Lesser Antilles
*Cyathea armata.* Greater Antilles
*Cyathea aspera.* Greater Antilles
*Cyathea balanocarpa.* Cuba, Jamaica, Hispaniola
*Cyathea borinquena.* Puerto Rico
*Cyathea brooksii.* Cuba, Hispaniola, Puerto Rico
*Cyathea crassa.* Hispaniola
*Cyathea dissoluta.* Jamaica
*Cyathea estelae.* Jamaica
*Cyathea fulgens.* Cuba, Jamaica, Hispaniola
*Cyathea furfuracea.* Greater Antilles
*Cyathea gracilis.* Jamaica
*Cyathea grevilleana.* Jamaica
*Cyathea harrisii.* Hispaniola, Jamaica, Dominica
*Cyathea hodgeana.* Dominica
*Cyathea hotteana.* Haiti
*Cyathea imrayana.* Lesser Antilles
*Cyathea insignis.* Cuba, Hispaniola, Jamaica
*Cyathea jamaicensis.* Jamaica
*Cyathea microdonta.* Greater Antilles
*Cyathea minor.* Hispaniola
*Cyathea myosuroides.* Cuba
*Cyathea nockii.* Jamaica
*Cyathea parvula.* Greater Antilles
*Cyathea portoricensis.* Puerto Rico
*Cyathea pubescens.* Jamaica
*Cyathea pungens.* Hispaniola, Puerto Rico, Lesser Antilles
*Cyathea sagittifolia.* Trinidad
*Cyathea surinamensis.* Trinidad
*Cyathea tenera.* Greater and Lesser Antilles
*Cyathea tussacii.* Jamaica

*Cyathea urbanii.* Dominican Republic
*Cyathea woodwardioides.* Jamaica
*Lophosoria quadripinnata.* Greater and Lesser Antilles

## Central America

*Alsophila polystichoides.* Costa Rica, Panama (Appendix 1)
*Alsophila salvinii.* Southern Mexico, Guatemala, Honduras (Appendix 1)
*Alsophila tryoniana.* Guatemala, Honduras, Nicaragua (Appendix 1)
*Cibotium regale.* Mexico, Guatemala, Honduras, El Salvador
*Cibotium schiedei.* Mexico
*Cnemidaria apiculata.* Mexico
*Cnemidaria choricarpa.* Costa Rica, Panama
*Cnemidaria cocleana.* Costa Rica, Panama
*Cnemidaria decurrens.* Mexico, Guatemala
*Cnemidaria glandulosa.* Panama
*Cnemidaria horrida.* Costa Rica, Panama
*Cnemidaria mutica.* Costa Rica, Panama
*Culcita coniifolia.* Mexico, Guatemala, El Salvador, Costa Rica, Panama
*Cyathea acutidens.* Costa Rica
*Cyathea albomarginata.* Costa Rica, Panama
*Cyathea alphonsiana.* Cocos Island, Costa Rica
*Cyathea andina.* Costa Rica, Panama
*Cyathea arborea.* Mexico, Central America
*Cyathea bicrenata.* Mexico
*Cyathea brunei.* Costa Rica, Panama
*Cyathea caracasana.* Costa Rica
*Cyathea conformis.* Panama
*Cyathea costaricensis.* Mexico to Costa Rica, Panama
*Cyathea cuspidata.* Mexico to Nicaragua, Costa Rica, and Panama
*Cyathea darienensis.* Panama
*Cyathea delgadii.* Costa Rica, Panama

*Cyathea divergens.* Mexico, Guatemala, Costa Rica, Panama
*Cyathea erinacea.* Mexico, Costa Rica, Panama
*Cyathea fulva.* Mexico, Honduras, Nicaragua, Costa Rica
*Cyathea gracilis.* Costa Rica, Panama
*Cyathea holdridgeana.* Costa Rica, Panama
*Cyathea impar.* Panama
*Cyathea imrayana.* Costa Rica, Panama
*Cyathea lockwoodiana.* Panama
*Cyathea macrosora.* Costa Rica
*Cyathea mexicana.* Mexico, Guatemala, El Salvador, Honduras, Nicaragua, Costa Rica, and Panama
*Cyathea microdonta.* Mexico, Costa Rica
*Cyathea mucilagina.* Costa Rica
*Cyathea multiflora.* Costa Rica
*Cyathea myosuroides.* Mexico to Nicaragua
*Cyathea nesiotica.* Cocos Island, Costa Rica
*Cyathea nigripes.* Costa Rica
*Cyathea nodulifera.* Costa Rica, Panama
*Cyathea notabilis.* Cocos Island, Costa Rica
*Cyathea onusta.* Costa Rica, Panama
*Cyathea petiolata.* Panama
*Cyathea pilosissima.* Panama
*Cyathea pinnula.* Nicaragua, Costa Rica, Panama
*Cyathea poeppigii.* Costa Rica, Panama
*Cyathea princeps* (= *Sphaeropteris horrida*). Mexico, Guatemala, Honduras
*Cyathea pseudonanna.* Costa Rica, Panama
*Cyathea schiedeana.* Mexico, Costa Rica
*Cyathea squamulosa.* Costa Rica, Panama
*Cyathea stipularis.* Mexico, Guatemala, Honduras, Nicaragua, Costa Rica, Panama
*Cyathea stolzei.* Costa Rica, Panama

*Cyathea suprastrigosa.* Costa Rica
*Cyathea tenera.* Islands off Costa Rica
*Cyathea trichiata.* Nicaragua, Costa Rica, Panama
*Cyathea ursina.* Belize to Costa Rica
*Cyathea valdecrenata.* Mexico to Honduras
*Cyathea villosa.* Panama
*Cyathea wendlandii.* Costa Rica, Panama
*Cyathea williamsii.* Panama
*Dicksonia sellowiana.* Mexico, Costa Rica, Panama
*Lophosoria quadripinnata.* Mexico to Costa Rica

## South America

*Alsophila esmeraldensis.* Ecuador (Appendix 1)
*Alsophila gardneri.* Brazil (Appendix 1)
*Alsophila parva.* Colombia (Appendix 1)
*Alsophila setosa.* Brazil, Argentina (Appendix 1)
*Cnemidaria alatissima.* Peru
*Cnemidaria amabilis.* Venezuela
*Cnemidaria chocoensis.* Colombia
*Cnemidaria choricarpa.* Colombia?
*Cnemidaria consimilis.* Venezuela
*Cnemidaria cruciata.* French Guiana
*Cnemidaria ewanii.* Colombia, Ecuador
*Cnemidaria grandifolia.* Venezuela
*Cnemidaria horrida.* Venezuela, Colombia, Ecuador, Peru
*Cnemidaria karsteniana.* Venezuela
*Cnemidaria nervosa.* Ecuador, Peru
*Cnemidaria quitensis.* Colombia, Ecuador
*Cnemidaria roraimensis.* Guiana
*Cnemidaria singularis.* Colombia
*Cnemidaria speciosa.* Bolivia to Peru
*Cnemidaria spectabilis.* Colombia, Venezuela, Guyana, Suriname, French Guiana
*Cnemidaria tryoniana.* Colombia
*Cnemidaria uleana.* Colombia, Ecuador, Peru, Brazil
*Culcita coniifolia.* Venezuela, Guyana, French Guiana, Ecuador, Peru, Bolivia, Argentina, Brazil
*Cyathea alstonii.* Colombia
*Cyathea amazonica.* Ecuador
*Cyathea andina.* Colombia, Ecuador, Peru, Bolivia, Venezuela, Brazil, Suriname, French Guiana
*Cyathea arborea.* Venezuela
*Cyathea atahuallpa.* Peru
*Cyathea aterrima.* Colombia, Peru
*Cyathea atrovirens.* Argentina, Paraguay, Brazil
*Cyathea barringtonii.* Venezuela
*Cyathea bipinnata.* Ecuador
*Cyathea boliviana.* Bolivia
*Cyathea bradei.* Colombia
*Cyathea brevistipes.* Ecuador
*Cyathea brunei.* Colombia
*Cyathea brunnescens.* Colombia, Ecuador
*Cyathea capensis.* Brazil
*Cyathea caracasana.* Venezuela, Colombia, Ecuador, Peru, Bolivia
*Cyathea conformis.* Colombia
*Cyathea conjugata.* Colombia, Bolivia
*Cyathea corallifera.* Ecuador
*Cyathea corcovadensis.* Brazil
*Cyathea cuspidata.* French Guiana, Colombia, Ecuador, Peru, Brazil, Bolivia, Paraguay
*Cyathea cyatheoides.* Venezuela, Guyana, French Guiana, Suriname, Brazil
*Cyathea cyclodium.* Venezuela
*Cyathea cystolepis.* Ecuador
*Cyathea decomposita.* Venezuela
*Cyathea decorata.* Colombia
*Cyathea delgadii.* Venezuela, Colombia, Ecuador, Peru, Bolivia, Argentina, Paraguay, Brazil
*Cyathea demissa.* Venezuela
*Cyathea dichromatolepis.* Brazil
*Cyathea dissimilis.* Venezuela, Guyana
*Cyathea divergens.* Colombia, Ecuador, Peru, Venezuela, Guyana, Suriname, French Guiana
*Cyathea dombeyi.* Peru

*Cyathea dudleyi*. Peru
*Cyathea ebenina*. Venezuela, Colombia, Peru
*Cyathea elongata*. Venezuela, Colombia
*Cyathea erinacea*. Venezuela, Colombia, Ecuador, Peru, Bolivia
*Cyathea falcata*. Colombia
*Cyathea frigida*. Venezuela, Colombia, Ecuador, Peru
*Cyathea fulva*. Venezuela, Colombia, Ecuador
*Cyathea gardneri*. Brazil
*Cyathea gibbosa*. Venezuela, Guyana
*Cyathea gracilis*. Colombia, Ecuador
*Cyathea halonata*. Ecuador
*Cyathea haughtii*. Colombia
*Cyathea hemiepiphytica*. Ecuador
*Cyathea hirsuta*. Brazil
*Cyathea imrayana*. Venezuela, Ecuador
*Cyathea incana*. Colombia, Ecuador, Peru, Bolivia, Argentina
*Cyathea intramarginalis*. Venezuela
*Cyathea kalbreyeri*. Venezuela to Bolivia
*Cyathea lasiosora*. Venezuela, Ecuador, Peru, Bolivia, Brazil
*Cyathea latevagens*. Colombia
*Cyathea lechleri*. Venezuela to Peru and Bolivia
*Cyathea leucofolis*. Brazil
*Cyathea lockwoodiana*. Venezuela, Colombia
*Cyathea macrocarpa*. Venezuela, Guyana, Suriname, French Guiana, Brazil
*Cyathea macrosora*. Colombia, Venezuela, Guyana, Brazil
*Cyathea marginalis*. Guyana, Suriname
*Cyathea mexicana*. Ecuador
*Cyathea microdonta*. Colombia, Ecuador, Peru, Bolivia, Venezuela, Guyana, Brazil
*Cyathea microphylla*. Peru
*Cyathea mucilagina*. Ecuador, Peru
*Cyathea multiflora*. Venezuela, Colombia, Ecuador, Peru, Bolivia, Brazil
*Cyathea multisegmenta*. Peru

*Cyathea nanna*. Guyana
*Cyathea nigripes*. Colombia, Ecuador, Peru
*Cyathea palaciosii*. Ecuador
*Cyathea paladensis*. Colombia
*Cyathea pallescens*. Colombia to Bolivia
*Cyathea parianensis*. Venezuela
*Cyathea pauciflora*. Venezuela, Colombia
*Cyathea petiolata*. Colombia, Peru?
*Cyathea phalaenolepis*. Colombia, Ecuador
*Cyathea phalerata*. Brazil
*Cyathea phegopteroides*. Peru
*Cyathea pilosissima*. Colombia, Ecuador, Peru, Brazil
*Cyathea pinnula*. Colombia
*Cyathea platylepis*. Venezuela, Colombia
*Cyathea poeppigii*. Venezuela, Colombia, Ecuador
*Cyathea praecincta*. Brazil
*Cyathea pubens*. Venezuela, Colombia, Peru, Bolivia, Brazil, Guyana, Suriname, French Guinea
*Cyathea punctata*. Ecuador
*Cyathea pungens*. Bolivia, Brazil, Guyana, Suriname, French Guinea
*Cyathea quindiuensis*. Colombia, Ecuador, Peru, Bolivia
*Cyathea rufa*. Brazil
*Cyathea ruiziana*. Peru
*Cyathea rupestris*. Colombia
*Cyathea schiedeana*. Colombia
*Cyathea schlimii*. Venezuela, Colombia
*Cyathea senilis*. Venezuela
*Cyathea simplex*. Venezuela
*Cyathea sipapoensis*. Venezuela
*Cyathea speciosa*. Venezuela, Colombia
*Cyathea steyermarkii*. Venezuela
*Cyathea stolzei*. Ecuador
*Cyathea straminea*. Colombia
*Cyathea stuebelii*. Ecuador
*Cyathea subtropica*. Colombia, Ecuador, Peru, Bolivia
*Cyathea surinamensis*. Venezuela, Guyana, Suriname, French Guiana, Brazil

*Cyathea tortuosa.* Colombia, Ecuador, Peru
*Cyathea trichiata.* Venezuela, Colombia, Ecuador
*Cyathea tryonorum.* Venezuela, Colombia, Ecuador
*Cyathea venezuelensis.* Venezuela
*Cyathea villosa.* Colombia, Bolivia, Venezuela, Brazil
*Cyathea weatherbyana.* Galápagos Islands
*Cyathea werffii.* Ecuador, Peru
*Cyathea williamsii.* Venezuela
*Dicksonia berteriana.* Juan Fernández Islands
*Dicksonia externa.* Juan Fernández Islands
*Dicksonia sellowiana.* Venezuela, Colombia, Brazil, Bolivia, Paraguay, Uruguay
*Dicksonia steubelii.* Ecuador, Peru
*Lophosoria quadripinnata.* Venezuela, Colombia, Ecuador, Peru, Bolivia, Brazil, Argentina, Chile, Juan Fernández Islands
*Sphaeropteris cuatrecasassi.* Colombia (Appendix 1)
*Thyrsopteris elegans.* Juan Fernández Islands
*Trichipteris microphylla.* Colombia, Venezuela (Appendix 1)

# APPENDIX 3

# Tree Ferns for Gardens

Cold climates are marginal for most tree ferns and none of the plants is truly hardy. Many tree ferns inhabit a wide geographic range, however, and plants sourced from higher elevations or from the coolest limits of their ranges can be more tolerant of cold weather. Warm, moist climates suit many tree ferns, including many that naturally grow in a cooler climate. Cool-dwelling species do best in shaded areas in a garden or at higher elevations. See also Tryon and Tryon (1959), Hoshizaki (1964), Dunk (1982), Graf (1985), Duncan and Isaac (1986), Rickard (1987), Brownsey and Smith-Dodsworth (1989), Jones and Clemesha (1989), Andrews (1990), Benzona (1994), Chin (1997), van der Mast and Hobbs (1998), and Hoshizaki and Moran (2001).

| SPECIES | APPROXIMATE HEIGHT (M) | ORIGIN |
|---|---|---|
| *Cool moist conditions; will survive occasional snow and frosts of –5°C (23°F) or lower, doing best at higher elevations if grown in the Tropics* | | |
| Cyathea australis | 12+ | Australia |
| Cyathea colensoi | prostrate to 1 m | New Zealand |
| Cyathea dregei | 5 | Africa |
| Cyathea smithii | 8 | New Zealand |
| Dicksonia antarctica | 5, rarely to 15 | Australia |
| Dicksonia fibrosa | 6 | New Zealand |
| Dicksonia squarrosa | 7 | New Zealand |
| *Cool moist conditions; will survive some frost to about –3°C (26°F)* | | |
| Cyathea celebica | 6 | Australia, New Guinea, Sulawesi (Celebes) |
| Cyathea cooperi | 10–12 | Australia |
| Cyathea dealbata | 10+ | New Zealand |
| Cyathea tomentosissima | 2–3 | New Guinea |
| Cyathea woollsiana | <6 | Australia |
| Dicksonia brackenridgei | <6 | Fiji, Vanuatu |
| Dicksonia herbertii | 2–4 | Australia |
| Dicksonia mollis | <6 | Malaysia, Philippines |
| Dicksonia sellowiana | 3–10 | Central and South America |
| Dicksonia youngiae | 2–4 | Australia |

# APPENDIX 3  Tree Ferns for Gardens

| SPECIES | APPROXIMATE HEIGHT (M) | ORIGIN |
|---|---|---|

Cool moist conditions; may survive occasional frost, particularly if plants are mature; some protection required

| Species | Height | Origin |
|---|---|---|
| *Cyathea atrox* | 6–7 | New Guinea |
| *Cyathea brownii* | 5–16, rarely 18+ | Norfolk Island |
| *Cyathea caracasana* | 2–6 | Central and South America |
| *Cyathea cunninghamii* | 20 | New Zealand |
| *Cyathea fulva* | 10 | Central and South America |
| *Cyathea gleichenioides* | 3 | New Guinea |
| *Cyathea leichhardtiana* | 7 | Australia |
| *Cyathea macarthurii* | 5 | Australia |
| *Cyathea macgregorii* | 3 | New Guinea |
| *Cyathea medullaris* | 20 | New Zealand |
| *Cyathea mexicana* | 5–10 | Central and South America |
| *Cyathea milnei* | 8 | New Zealand |
| *Cyathea muelleri* | 10 | New Guinea |
| *Cyathea robusta* | 3–5 | Lord Howe Island |

Moist conditions, usually frost sensitive; some will survive full sun in wet areas, doing best when given shelter in drier areas

| Species | Height | Origin |
|---|---|---|
| *Cibotium chamissoi* | 5 | Hawaii |
| *Cibotium glaucum* | 3 | Hawaii |
| *Cibotium menziesii* | 7 | Hawaii |
| *Cibotium regale* | 10 | Mexico, Central America |
| *Cibotium schiedei* | 5 | Mexico |
| *Cyathea affinis* | 2–6 | Tahiti, Fiji? |
| *Cyathea albifrons* | 7–10 | New Caledonia |
| *Cyathea arborea* | 10–15+ | West Indies, Central and South America |
| *Cyathea baileyana* | 4–5 | Australia |
| *Cyathea brevipinnata* | 0.5–3 | Lord Howe Island |
| *Cyathea contaminans* | 15–20 | Malesia |
| *Cyathea capensis* | 4.5 | South Africa |
| *Cyathea deckenii* | 10 | Africa |
| *Cyathea felina* | 8+ | Australia, Malesia |
| *Cyathea gigantea* | 5+ | India, Vietnam |
| *Cyathea hornei* | 3–4 | Fiji, New Guinea |
| *Cyathea howeana* | 2–8 | Lord Howe Island |
| *Cyathea lepifera* | <6 | New Guinea, Asia |
| *Cyathea loheri* | 5+ | Taiwan, Philippines, Borneo |
| *Cyathea manniana* | 6 | Africa |
| *Cyathea ×marcescens* | 10 | Australia |
| *Cyathea microlepidota* | 3–5 | Fiji |
| *Cyathea propinqua* | 10 | Fiji |
| *Cyathea rebeccae* | 6–8 | Australia, Indonesia |
| *Cyathea robertsiana* | 5–7 | Australia |
| *Cyathea spinulosa* | 4–5 | China |
| *Cyathea truncata* | 10 | Fiji, Samoa, Solomon Islands |
| *Cyathea vieillardii* | 3–4 | New Caledonia, Vanuatu |
| *Cyathea whitmeei* | 5–10 | Samoa, Solomon Islands |

# Conversion Tables

| CM | INCHES |
|---|---|
| 0.1 | 0.04 |
| 0.2 | 0.08 |
| 0.3 | 0.12 |
| 0.4 | 0.16 |
| 0.5 | 0.20 |
| 0.6 | 0.24 |
| 0.7 | 0.28 |
| 0.8 | 0.31 |
| 0.9 | 0.35 |
| 1 | 0.4 |
| 2 | 0.8 |
| 3 | 1.2 |
| 4 | 1.6 |
| 5 | 2.0 |
| 6 | 2.4 |
| 7 | 2.8 |
| 8 | 3.1 |
| 9 | 3.5 |
| 10 | 4 |
| 20 | 8 |
| 30 | 12 |
| 40 | 16 |
| 50 | 20 |
| 60 | 24 |
| 70 | 28 |
| 80 | 31 |
| 90 | 35 |
| 100 | 39 |

| M | FEET |
|---|---|
| 1 | 3.3 |
| 2 | 6.6 |
| 3 | 9.8 |
| 4 | 13 |
| 5 | 16 |
| 6 | 20 |
| 7 | 23 |
| 8 | 26 |
| 9 | 30 |
| 10 | 33 |
| 20 | 66 |
| 30 | 98 |
| 40 | 130 |
| 50 | 160 |
| 60 | 200 |
| 70 | 230 |
| 80 | 260 |
| 90 | 300 |
| 100 | 330 |
| 200 | 660 |
| 300 | 980 |
| 400 | 1,310 |
| 500 | 1,640 |
| 600 | 1,970 |
| 700 | 2,300 |
| 800 | 2,620 |
| 900 | 2,950 |
| 1,000 | 3,280 |
| 2,000 | 6,560 |
| 3,000 | 9,840 |
| 4,000 | 13,120 |
| 5,000 | 16,400 |

# Glossary

**acuminate** tapering to a long fine point, the sides concave
**annulus** (plural, annuli) incomplete ring of thick-walled cells that form a band around the head of the fern sporangium, forming part of the dehiscence mechanism
**aphlebiae** "without veins" and originally used to describe a condition in fossils; the term is also commonly, albeit perhaps incorrectly, used to describe the situation in tree ferns where the lowest pair or pairs of frond pinnules are reduced and finely divided
**archegonium** (plural, archegonia) female sex organ, containing the egg, and found on the underside of a gametophyte
**baculate** rod-like
**bipinnate** frond divided twice, the divisions usually called pinnae (bipinnatifid, incompletely so divided)
**bullate** with a puckered or blistered surface
**Cainozoic** geologic time era (also known as the Cenozoic) beginning at the boundary of the Cretaceous and Tertiary periods (65 million years ago) and encompassing the Tertiary and the Quaternary periods (about 10,000 years ago)
**calcareous** with deposits of calcium carbonate (lime)
**Carboniferous** geologic time period from 360 million to 286 million years ago; part of the Paleozoic era
**caudex** (plural, caudices) rhizome or nonwoody portion of the trunk of a tree fern
**center of diversity** center of maximum diversity; usually with the maximum number of species or genera
**ciliate** fringed with fine hairs, usually marginally
**circinate vernation** coiled, with the growing apex innermost; the situation seen in the uncurling of young fronds
**clade** a group descended from a single ancestor; see monophyletic
**clone** genetically identical to the parent
**cortex** region of a stem or trunk immediately beneath the epidermis
**costa** (plural, costae) midrib of a pinnule
**costate** with a prominent midrib

**costule** small ridge
**Cretaceous** geologic time period from 144 million to 65 million years ago; part of the Mesozoic era
**deciduous** shedding leaves or fronds annually
**Devonian** geologic time period from 408 million to 360 million years ago; part of the Paleozoic era
**dictyostele** stem structure characterized by rings of vascular bundles (each of xylem surrounded by phloem) that connect to form a network of strands
**dimorphic** in two forms or shapes
**diploid** with two basic sets of chromosomes in the nucleus; see haploid
**endemic** restricted to a particular region
**Eocene** geologic time epoch from 65 million to 56 million years ago; the beginning of the Tertiary period
**epidermis** outer layer of cells, providing a skin over all of the inner structures of a plant
**erect** upright
**family** taxonomic group of closely related genera; the name generally bearing the suffix -aceae
**filamentous** thread-like
**filiform** very slender and thread-like
**filmy** thin and membranous, almost translucent
**fimbriate** with branching filaments
**frond** fern leaf, including the stipe, rachis, and lamina; sporangia are often borne on the underside
**gametophyte** an independent, reduced plant, also known in ferns as the prothallus, that produces eggs and sperm; the gametophyte has half the chromosome complement of the sporophyte
**genus** (plural, genera) taxonomic group of closely related species or sometimes a single species not closely related to any other
**glabrate** smooth and devoid of hairs or scales
**glaucous** covered with a bluish green or whitish blush
**globose** rounded
**granulate** with small granular deposits
**grooved** with a narrow channel running along the stem
**hair** outgrowth from the epidermis, consisting of a single row of cells; hairs may be branched or simple
**haploid** with one set of chromosomes in the nucleus; see diploid
**indusium** (plural, indusia) thin outgrowth of tissue covering the sorus; it may shrivel at maturity
**inflorescence** general term for a grouping of flowers in a particular form
**Jurassic** geologic time period from 208 million to 144 million years ago; part of the Mesozoic era
**KT boundary** (about 65 million years ago) between the Cretaceous and Tertiary periods, coinciding with the extinction of the dinosaurs (KT rather than CT to distin-

guish the Cretaceous from the earlier Carboniferous); the boundary is marked by an iridium layer, indicative of a major meteoritic impact, and is found in many sedimentary deposits around the world

**laesura** (plural, laesurae) line of dehiscence on a fern spore, brought about by contact with the other daughter cells after meiosis

**lamina** leafy part of the frond

**lanceolate** lance-shaped, longer than wide and tapering gradually to the apex, and more rapidly to the base

**leathery** tough, thick, and opaque

**leptosporangium** (plural, leptosporangia) sporangium with an annulus; each leptosporangium originates from a single initial cell and has a wall one cell layer thick

**lignin** polymer found in secondarily thickened plant walls, containing phenolic derivatives of phenylpropane

**Malesia** geographic term for the area comprising Indonesia, Malaysia, Brunei, the Philippines, Singapore, Timor, and eastern New Guinea

**meiosis** process of cell division, also known as reduction division, that results in a tetrad of cells, each nucleus with half the chromosome complement of the original mother cell nucleus

**membranous** thin and delicate, translucent

**meristem** area of active cell division and growth at the growing tip of a root or shoot; there, new cells are produced by mitosis

**Mesozoic** geologic time era from 248 million to 65 million years ago; encompassing the Triassic, Jurassic, and Cretaceous periods

**mitosis** simple cell division in which each daughter nucleus (and cell) contains the same number of chromosomes as the mother cell

**monolete** spores usually bean-shaped, with a single line of dehiscence called a laesura

**monomorphic** in one form or shape

**monophyletic** of a group of species descended from a single ancestor, including all species descended from that ancestor

**montane** high-elevation forest immediately below the subalpine zone

**Miocene** geologic time epoch from 24 million to 5 million years ago; part of the Tertiary period

**morphology** the shape and structure of an organism

**Neotropics** Tropics of the New World

**order** taxonomic group of closely related families; the name usually bearing the suffix -ales

**offshoot** a new growth, occurring on the truck or at the base of a plant; these may be removed and treated like cuttings

**palea** (plural, paleae) see scale

**Paleotropics** Tropics of the Old World

**Paleozoic** geologic time era from before the beginning of life on Earth to 248 million years ago; ending with the Devonian, Carboniferous, and Permian periods

**Pantropical** in the Tropics of both the Old and New Worlds

**papillate** with small pimple-like protruberances
**paraphyletic** of a group of species that includes a common ancestor and only some of its descendents
**paraphyses** sterile hairs
**parenchyma** tissue composed of large, thin-walled (cellulose) cells
**pedicel** stalk
**pentapinnate** frond divided five times
**Permian** geologic time period from 286 million to 248 million years ago; falling at the end of the Paleozoic era
**perine** outer, often ornamented wall layer in fern spores
**petiole** stem attached to the pinnule and leading to the rachis
**phloem** vascular tissue composed of sugar-conducting cells
**photosynthesis** photochemical process by which plants use sunlight to fix and convert atmospheric carbon dioxide into complex carbohydrates
**pinna** (plural, pinnae) segment of a divided lamina; pinnae may be primary, secondary, tertiary, etc., depending on how many times the frond is divided; final divisions are usually termed pinnules
**pinnate** a once-divided frond in which the lamina is divided to the rachis, with the parts arranged on either side of the rachis like a feather
**pinnatifid** of a lamina almost divided to the petiole or rachis, but the division incomplete
**pinnule** ultimate divisions of the lamina; see pinna
**pith** tissue in the center of a stem or root, usually consisting of thin-walled parenchyma cells
**Pliocene** geologic time epoch from 5 million to 1.8 million years ago; ending the Tertiary period
**porate** with pores
**pup** outgrowth of the trunk or rhizome, usually producing a growing apex; see offshoot
**Quaternary** geologic time period from 1.8 million years ago to the present; falling at the end of the Cainozoic era
**rachis** frond stem that extends through the lamina from the apex to the lowermost pinnae
**rhizoid** small hair-like growth from the rhizome; usually involved in absorption
**rhizome** stem to which fronds are attached; the rhizome may be erect, tufted, creeping, or underground
**ridged** with a narrow raised strip along the length of the stem
**scabrate** with fine dust-like deposits
**scale** a dry membranous outgrowth consisting of a plate of cells
**sclerenchyma** tissue consisting of cells such as fibers that are thickened with lignin; providing support or protection
**septapinnate** frond divided seven times
**seta** (plural, setae) small bristle-like outgrowth
**setiferous** bearing setae

**skirt** aggregation of dead fronds or stipes that are persistent and hang down from the crown about the trunk

**sorus** (plural, sori) cluster of sporangia on the margin or underside of a fertile frond; a sorus may be protected by an indusium, and sorus shape is often characteristic of fern genera

**speciation** biological process by which new species arise

**species** (plural, species) may be defined as taxonomic group or a population of closely related individuals sharing common features; species are generally reproductively isolated from other groups, but individuals of a species may interbreed to produce new fertile individuals

**spinulate** with fine, tapering, rod-like projections

**sporangium** (plural, sporangia) small sac or package in which spores are produced

**spore** microscopic asexual reproductive structure produced by the sporophyte through the process of meiosis; a spore is the dispersal phase of an independent gametophyte and does not contain an embryo

**sporophyte** a plant that reproduces by the production of spores; the main plant we recognize as a fern (see gametophyte)

**sporopollenin** a compound of carotenoids and carotenoid esters that is incorporated into the spore wall; sporopollenin is highly resistant to processes of decay and chemical erosion

**squamulae** small scales composed of only a few cells; squamulae are usually found on the surface of the petiole, and occasionally, the rachis

**stipe** frond stem occurring below the lamina and joining it to the rhizome or trunk

**stipule** scale-like or leaf-like appendage on either side of the base of a leaf petiole or frond stipe

**stolon** slender, lateral, creeping stem growing form the main rhizome, rooting at the nodes, and usually forming small plantlets either at the nodes or at its apex

**stoloniferous** producing stolons

**stoma** (plural, stomata) pores in the epidermis through which gas exchange can take place; stomata are protected by two guard cells that open or close depending on atmospheric humidity or water availability

**subgenus** taxonomic group of closely related species, forming an assemblage within a genus

**subspecies** (abbreviation, subsp.) taxonomic group of closely related individuals forming a group within a species

**Tertiary** geologic time period from 65 million to 1.6 million years ago; falling at the beginning of the Cainozoic era

**tetrapinnate** frond divided four times

**thyrse** usually used to describe a particular type of aggregation of flowers (inflorescence); a cone-shaped, indeterminate, branched inflorescence

**tomentose** with hairs

**transpiration** the movement of gases and water vapor during the process of photosynthesis

**tripinnate** frond divided three times (tripinnatifid, incompletely so divided)

**Triassic** geologic time period from 248 million to 208 million years ago; falling at the beginning of the Mesozoic era

**trilete** tetrahedral or rounded spore bearing three laesurae

**tuberculate** with small irregular lumps

**type** in botanical nomenclature a plant name is attached to a particular specimen, thereby always identifying that particular name with that specimen; this is known as a type specimen

**variety** (abbreviation, var.) taxonomic group of closely related individuals forming a group within a species

**vein** a strand of conducting tissue (xylem and phloem) in a leaf

**verrucate** with a wart-like elevation

**xylem** vascular tissue composed of tube-like water transport cells that are usually lignified

**zygote** the immediate cell product of fusion of the sperm and egg nuclei; the zygote develops into a new sporophyte, which is temporarily parasitic on the gametophyte

# Bibilography

Adams, D. C. 1977. Ciné analysis of the medullary bundle system in *Cyathea fulva*. American Fern Journal 67: 73–80.

Adams, O. L. G. 1945. Maori medicinal plants. Auckland Botanical Society Bulletin 2.

Andrews, S. B. 1990. Ferns of Queensland: a Handbook to the Ferns and Fern Allies. Queensland Department of Primary Industries, Brisbane.

Andrews, H. N., and E. M. Kerns. 1947. The Idaho tempskyas and associated fossil plants. Annals of the Missouri Botanical Garden 34: 119–186.

Ashton, J. 1890. Curious Creatures in Zoology. J. C. Nimmo, London.

Barrington, D. S. 1978. A revision of the genus *Trichipteris*. Contributions from the Gray Herbarium, Harvard University, 208: 3–93.

Becker, R. 1984. The identification of Hawaiian tree ferns of the genus *Cibotium*. American Fern Journal 74: 97–100.

Bell, P. R. 1992. Green Plants: Their Origin and Diversity. Dioscorides Press (Timber Press), Portland, Oregon, and Cambridge University Press, Cambridge.

Bell, T. W. 1890. Medical notes on New Zealand. New Zealand Medical Journal 3: 65–83, 129–145.

Benzona, N. C., F. D. Rauch, and R. Y. Iwata. 1994. Tree Ferns for Hawai'i Gardens. Research Extension Series / Hawaii Institute of Tropical Agriculture and Human Resources 144: 1–13.

Best, R. 1986. Tree ferns for English conditions. Pteridologist 1(3): 131–132.

Bostock, P. D. 1998. Cyatheaceae, pp. 193–205 in P. M. McCarthy, editor, Flora of Australia, Vol. 48, Ferns, Gymnosperms and Allied Groups. ABRS / CSIRO, Melbourne.

Brooker, S. G., R. C. Cambie, and R. C. Cooper. 1981. New Zealand Medicinal Plants. Heinemann, Auckland.

Brownsey, P. J., and J. C. Smith-Dodsworth. 1989. New Zealand Ferns and Allied Plants. David Bateman, Auckland.

Burkill, I. H. 1935. A Dictionary of the Economic Products of the Malay Peninsula. Crown Agents for the Colonies, London.

Cambie, R. C., and J. Ash. 1994. Fijian Medicinal Plants. CSIRO, Canberra.

Cambie, R. C., and A. A. Brewis. 1997. Anti-Fertility Plants of the Pacific. CSIRO, Canberra.

Chaffey, C. H. 1999. Australian Ferns: Growing Them Successfully. Kangaroo Press, Sydney.

Chin Wee Yeow. 1997. Ferns of the Tropics. Times Editions, Singapore, and Timber Press, Portland, Oregon.

Collinson, M. E. 1996. What use are fossil ferns? Pp. 349–394 in J. M. Camus, M. Gibby, and R. J. Johns, editors, Pteridology in Perspective. Royal Botanic Gardens, Kew.

Conant, D. S. 1975. Hybrids in the American Cyatheaceae. Rhodora 77: 441–455.

Conant, D. S. 1983. A revision of the genus *Alsophila* (Cyatheaceae) in the Americas. Journal of the Arnold Arboretum 64: 333–382.

Conant, D. S., and G. Cooper-Driver. 1980. Autogamous allohomoploidy in *Alsophila* and *Nephelea* (Cyatheaceae). American Journal of Botany 67: 1269–1288.

Conant, D. S., D. B. Stein, A. E. C. Valinski, P. Sundarsanam, and M. E. Ahearn. 1994. Phylogenetic implications of chloroplast DNA variation in the Cyatheaceae 1. Systematic Botany 19: 60–72.

Conant, D. S., L. A. Raubeson, and D. B. Stein. 1995. The relationships of Papuasian Cyatheaceae to New World tree ferns. American Fern Journal 85(4): 328–340.

Conant, D. S., L. A. Raubeson, D. K. Attwood, S. Perera, E. A. Zimmer, J. A. Sweere, and D. B. Stein. 1996. Phylogenetic and evolutionary implications of combined analysis of DNA and morphology in the Cyatheaceae, pp. 231–248 in J. M. Camus, M. Gibby, and R. J. Johns, editors, Pteridology in Perspective. Royal Botanic Gardens, Kew.

Copeland, E. B. 1908. New species of *Cyathea*. Philippine Journal of Science 3: 353–357.

Copeland, E. B. 1947. *Cyathea*, pp. 94–99 in Genera Filicum. Cramer, Braunschweig.

Corner, E. J. H. 1981. The Marquis: a Tale of Syonan-to. Heinemann Asia, Singapore.

Domin, K. 1929. Pteridophyta. Nákladem České Akademie ved a Umení, Prague.

Domin, K. 1930. The species of the genus *Cyathea* J. E. Smith. Acta Botanica Bohemica 9: 85–174.

Duncan, B. D., and G. Isaac. 1986. Ferns and Allied Plants of Victoria, Tasmania and South Australia. Melbourne University Press, Melbourne.

Dunk, G. 1982. Ferns for the Home and Garden. Angus and Robertson, Sydney.

Esau, K. 1977. Anatomy of Seed Plants. John Wiley and Sons, New York.

Fahn, A. 1982. Plant Anatomy. Pergamon, Oxford.

Gastony, G. J. 1973. A revision of the fern genus *Nephelea*. Contributions from the Gray Herbarium, Harvard University, 203: 81–148.

Gastony, G. J. 1979. Spore morphology in the Cyatheaceae: 3. The genus *Trichipteris*. American Journal of Botany 66: 1238–1260.

Gastony, G. J., and R. M. Tryon. 1976. Spore morphology in the Cyatheaceae: 2. The genera *Lophosoria, Metaxya, Sphaeropteris, Alsophila,* and *Nephelea*. American Journal of Botany 63: 738–758.

Godwin, H. 1932. Anatomy of the stele of *Cyathea medullaris* Sw. New Phytologist 31: 254–264.

Goebel, K. 1930. Pteridophyten, pp. 643–1378 in Organographie der Pflanzen, Dritte Auflage, Bd. 2. Gustav Fischer, Jena.

Goudey, C. J. 1988. A Handbook of Ferns for Australia and New Zealand. Lothian, Melbourne.

Goy, D. A. 1943. The tree ferns of Queensland. Queensland Naturalist 12: 40–46.

Graf, A. B. 1985. Tropica. Roehrs, East Rutherford, New Jersey.

Hasebe, M., P. G. Wolf, K. M. Pryer, K. Ueda, M. Ito, R. Sano, G. J. Gastony, J. Yokoyama, J. R. Manhart, N. Murakami, E. H. Crane, C. H. Haufler, and W. D. Hauk. 1995. Fern phylogeny based on *rbc*L nucleotide sequences. American Fern Journal 85: 134–181.

Hill, R. S., and G. J. Jordan. 1998. The fossil record of ferns and fern allies in Australia, pp. 37–46 in P. M. McCarthy, editor, Flora of Australia, Vol. 48, Ferns, Gymnosperms and Allied Groups. ABRS / CSIRO, Melbourne.

Holttum, R. E. 1963. Flora Malesiana, Series II, Pteridophyta 1(2): 65–176.

Holttum, R. E. 1964. The tree ferns of the genus *Cyathea* in Australasia and the Pacific. Blumea 12: 241–274.

Holttum, R. E. 1965a. Tree ferns of the genus *Cyathea* in Java. Reinwardtia 7: 5–8.

Holttum, R. E. 1965b. Tree ferns of the genus *Cyathea* in Asia (excluding Malaysia). Kew Bulletin 19: 463–487.

Holttum, R. E. 1974. The tree-ferns of the genus *Cyathea* in Borneo. Gardens' Bulletin Singapore 27: 167–182.

Holttum, R. E. 1981. The tree-ferns of Africa. Kew Bulletin 36: 463–482.

Holttum, R. E., and P. J. Edwards. 1983. The tree ferns of Mount Roraima and neighbouring areas of the Guayana Highlands with comments on the family Cyatheaceae. Kew Bulletin 38: 155–188.

Holttum, R. E., and B. Molesworth Allen. 1967. The tree ferns of Malaya. Gardens' Bulletin Singapore 22: 41–51.

Holttum, R. E., and U. Sen 1961. Morphology and classification of tree ferns. Phytomorphology 11: 406–420.

Hooker, J. D. 1844–1860. The Botany of the Antarctic Voyage of H.M. Discovery Ships *Erebus* and *Terror* in the Years 1839–1843. Reeve, London.

Hooker, W. J. 1861. A Second Century of Ferns; Being Figures with Brief Descriptions of One Hundred New, or Rare, or Imperfectly Known Species of Ferns; from Various Parts of the World. Pamplin, London.

Hoshizaki, B. J. 1964. Cultivated tree ferns of the genus *Cibotium* (Dicksoniaceae). Baileya 12: 137–146.

Hoshizaki, B. J., and R. C. Moran, 2001. Fern Grower's Manual, Revised and Expanded Edition. Timber Press, Portland, Oregon.

Ide, J. M., A. C. Jermy, and A. M. Paul. 1992. Fern Horticulture: Past, Present and Future Perspectives. Intercept, Andover, United Kingdom.

Jones, D. L. 1984. *Dicksonia herbertii* W. Hill and *D. youngiae* C. Moore ex Baker are different species. ASBS [Australian Systematic Botany Society] Newsletter 39: 20–21.

Jones, D. L. 1987. Encyclopaedia of Ferns. Thomas C. Lothian, Melbourne, and Timber Press, Portland, Oregon.

Jones, D. L., and S. C. Clemesha. 1989. Australian Ferns and Fern Allies, Third Edition. Currawong Press, Chatswood, New South Wales.

Kelly, J. 1991. Ferns in Your Garden. Souvenir Press, London.

Kramer, K. U. 1990. Cyatheaceae, in K. Kubitzki, editor, The Families and Genera of Vascular Plants, Vol. 1, Pteridophytes and Gymnosperms. Springer-Verlag, New York.

Kunkel G. 1965. Catalogue of the pteridophytes of the Juan Fernández Islands (Chile). Nova Hedwigia 9: 245–284.

Lantz, T. C., G. W. Rothwell, and R. A. Stockey. 1999. *Conantiopteris shuchmanii*, gen. et sp. nov., and the role of fossils in resolving the phylogeny of the Cyatheaceae s.l. Journal of Plant Research 112: 361–381.

Large, M. F., and J. E. Braggins. 1991. A spore atlas of New Zealand ferns and fern allies. New Zealand Journal of Botany 29(Supplement): 1–168.

Lee, H. 1887. The Vegetable Lamb of Tartary: a Curious Fable of the Cotton Plant, to Which Is Added a Sketch of the History of Cotton and the Cotton Trade. S. Low, Marston, Searle & Rivington, London.

Lellinger, D. B. 1987. The disposition of *Trichopteris* (Cyatheaceae). American Fern Journal 77: 90–94.

Lellinger, D. B. 1989. The ferns and fern-allies of Costa Rica, Panama and the Chocó. Part 1 (Psilotaceae through Dicksoniaceae). Pteridologia 2A: 1–364.

Lewis, R. L. 2001. Studies on New Zealand Tree-Ferns. M.Sc. Thesis, Massey University, Palmerston North, New Zealand.

Liew, F. S., and S. C. Wang. 1976. The tree fern family Cyatheaceae and its allied species found in Taiwan. Taiwania 21: 251–267.

Lucansky, T. W. 1974. Comparative studies of the nodal and vascular anatomy in the Neotropical Cyatheaceae, II. Squamate genera. American Journal of Botany 61: 472–480.

Lucansky, T. W., and R. A. White. 1974. Comparative studies of the nodal and vascular anatomy in the Neotropical Cyatheaceae, III. Nodal and petiole patterns: summary and conclusions. American Journal of Botany 61: 818–828.

Mabberley, D. J. 1985. Jupiter Botanicus: Robert Brown of the British Museum. J. Cramer, Braunschweig, and British Museum (Natural History), London.

Mabberley, D. J. 1997. The Plant-Book: a Portable Dictionary of the Vascular Plants, Second Edition. Cambridge University Press, Cambridge.

Mabberley, D. J. 2000. A tropical botanist finally vindicated. Gardens' Bulletin Singapore 52: 1–4.

Martius, C. F. P. 1828–1834. Icones Plantarum Cryptogamicarum . . . Brasiliam. . . . Munich.

Mickel, J. T. 1994. Ferns for American Gardens. Macmillan, New York; reprinted with updates in 2003 by Timber Press, Portland, Oregon.

Mickel, J. T., and J. M. Beitel. 1988. Pteridophyte Flora of Oaxaca, Mexico. Memoirs of the New York Botanical Garden 46: 1–568.

Moran, R. C. 1991. Eight new species of tree ferns (*Cyathea*, Cyatheaceae) from the American Tropics and three new combinations. Novon 1: 88–104.

Moran, R. C. 1994. Pteridophytes as trees. Fiddlehead Forum 21: 10–13.

Moran, R. C. 1995a. The importance of mountains to pteridophytes, with emphasis on Neotropical montane forests, pp. 359–363 in S. P. Churchill et al., editors, Biodiversity and Conservation of Neotropical Montane Forests. New York Botanical Garden, Bronx.

Moran, R. C. 1995b. Five new species and two new combinations of ferns (Polypodiopsida) from Ecuador. Nordic Journal of Botany 15: 49–58.

Moran, R. C. 1997. New species of ferns (Polypodiopsida) from Ecuador. Nordic Journal of Botany 18: 431–439.

Moran, R. C., and R. Riba, editors. 1995. Pteridofitas in Flora Mesoamericana, Vol. 1, Psilotaceae à Salviniaceae. Missouri Botanical Garden Press, St. Louis; Universidad Nacional Autónoma de México; and Natural History Museum, London.

Nelson, R. E., and E. M. Hornibrook. 1962. Commercial uses and volume of Hawaiian tree fern. Pacific Southwest Forest and Range Experiment Station, Berkeley, California, Technical Paper 73.

Neyland, M. G. 1986. Conservation and management of tree ferns in Tasmania. Technical Report (Tasmania National Parks and Wildlife Service, Wildlife Division) 86/1.

Ogura, Y. 1927. Comparative anatomy of Japanese Cyatheaceae. Journal of the Faculty of Science, University of Tokyo, Botany, 1: 141–350.

Oldfield, S. 1995. International Trade in Tree-Ferns and Evaluation on the Application of CITES. World Conservation Monitoring Centre, Cambridge.

Orbell, M. 1996. The Natural World of the Maori, Second Edition. Bateman, Auckland.

Page, C. N., and P. J. Brownsey. 1986. Tree-fern skirts: a defence against climbers and large epiphytes. Journal of Ecology 74: 787–796.

Palmer, D. D. 1994. The Hawaiian species of *Cibotium*. American Fern Journal 84: 73–85.

Palmer, D. D. 1997. A revision of the genus *Sadleria* (Blechnaceae). Pacific Science 51: 288–305.

Proctor, G. R. 1977. Pteridophyta in R. A. Howard, editor, Flora of the Lesser Antilles, Vol. 2. Arnold Arboretum, Harvard University, Jamaica Plain, Massachusetts.

Proctor, G. R. 1985. Ferns of Jamaica. British Museum (Natural History), London.

Rickard, M. 1987. Tree-ferns out-of-doors in the British Isles. Pteridologist 1(4): 182–185.

Robertson, F. W. 2000. Early Scottish Gardeners and Their Plants 1650–1750. Tuckwell Press, Phantassie, East Linton, Scotland.

Seiler, R. L. 1981. Leaf turnover rate and natural history of the central American tree fern *Alsophila salvinii*. American Fern Journal 71: 75–81.

Seiler, R. L. 1995. Verification of estimated growth rates in the tree fern *Alsophila salvinii*. American Fern Journal 85: 96–97.

Skottsberg, C. 1953. The vegetation of the Juan Fernández Islands, pp. 795–960 from The Natural History of Juan Fernández and Easter Island, Vol. 2. Almqvist & Wiksells, Uppsala.

Stafleu, F. A., and R. S. Cowan. 1976–1988. Taxonomic Literature, Second Edition, Vols. 1–7. Bohn, Scheltema & Holkema, Utrecht.

Stearn, W. T. 1996a. Stearn's Dictionary of Plant Names for Gardeners. Cassell, London, and Timber Press, Portland, Oregon.

Stearn W. T. 1996b. A short account of the life of Richard Eric Holttum (1895–1990) tropical botanist and religious thinker, pp. 3–11 in J. M. Camus, M. Gibby, and R. J. Johns, editors, Pteridology in Perspective. Royal Botanic Gardens, Kew.

Stein, D. B., D. S. Conant, and A. E. C. Valinski. 1996. The implications of chloroplast DNA restriction site variation on the classification and phylogeny of the Cyatheaceae, pp. 235–254 in J. M. Camus, M. Gibby, and R. J. Johns, editors, Pteridology in Perspective. Royal Botanic Gardens, Kew.

Stevenson, D. W., and H. Loconte. 1996. Ordinal and familial relationships of pteridophyte genera, pp. 435–467 in J. M. Camus, M. Gibby, and R. J. Johns, editors, Pteridology in Perspective. Royal Botanic Gardens, Kew.

Stolze, R. G. 1974. A taxonomic revision of the genus *Cnemidaria*. Fieldiana (Botany) 37: 1–98.

Tanner, E. U. J. 1983. Leaf demography and growth of the tree fern *Cyathea pubescens*. Mett. ex Kuhn in Jamaica. Botanical Journal of the Linnean Society 87: 213–227.

Tardieu-Blot, M. L. 1941. Sur les aphlebiae des Cyathéacées Malgaches. Bulletin de la Société Botanique de France 88: 522–531.

Tidwell, W. D., and S. R. Ash. 1994. A review of selected Triassic to early Cretaceous ferns. Journal of Plant Research 107: 417–442.

Tidwell, W. D., and N. Herbert. 1992. Species of the Cretaceous tree fern *Tempskya* from Utah. International Journal of Plant Science 153: 513–528.

Tidwell, W. D., and H. Nishida. 1993. A new fossilized tree fern stem, *Nishidacaulis burgii* gen. et sp. nov., from Nebraska–South Dakota, USA. Review of Paleobotany and Palynology 78: 55–67.

Tindale, M. D. 1956. The Cyatheaceae of Australia. Contributions from the New South Wales National Herbarium 2: 327–361.

Tryon, R. M. 1970. The classification of the Cyatheaceae. Contributions from the Gray Herbarium, Harvard University, 200: 1–53.

Tryon, R. M. 1971. The American tree ferns allied to *Sphaeropteris horrida*. Rhodora 73: 1–19.

Tryon R. M. 1972. Taxonomic fern notes VI: new species of American Cyatheaceae. Rhodora 74: 441–450.

Tryon, R. M. 1976. A revision of the genus *Cyathea*. Contributions from the Gray Herbarium, Harvard University, 206: 19–101.

Tryon, A. F., and L. J. Feldman. 1975. Tree fern indusia: studies of development and diversity. Canadian Journal of Botany 53: 2260–2273.

Tryon, R. M., and Gastony, G. J. 1975. The biogeography of endemism in the Cyatheaceae. Fern Gazette 11: 73–79.

Tryon, A. F., and B. Lugardon. 1990. Spores of the Pteridophyta. Springer-Verlag, New York.

Tryon, R. M., and A. F. Tryon. 1959. Observations on cultivated tree ferns: the hardy species of tree fern (Dicksoniaceae and Cyatheaceae). American Fern Journal 49: 129–142.

Tryon, R. M., and A. F. Tryon. 1982. Ferns and Allied Plants with Special Reference to Tropical America. Springer-Verlag, New York.

Voeller, B. R. 1966. Crozier uncoiling of ferns. Rockefeller University Review 4: 4019.

Van der Mast, S., and J. Hobbs. 1998. Ferns for New Zealand Gardens. Godwit, Auckland.

White, R. A., and Turner, M. D. 1988. *Calochlaena*, a new genus of dicksonioid ferns. American Fern Journal 78: 86–95.

Wiley, E. O. 1981. Phylogenetics: the Theory and Practice of Phylogenetic Systematics. Wiley-Liss, New York.

Windisch, P. G. 1977. Synopsis of the genus *Sphaeropteris* with a revision of the Neotropical exindusiate species. Botanische Jahrbücher für Systematik, Pflanzengeschichte und Pflanzengeographie 98: 176–198.

Windisch, P. G. 1978. The botany of the Guayana Highland: 10. *Sphaeropteris* (Cyatheaceae): the systematics of the group of *Sphaeropteris hirsuta*. Memoirs of the New York Botanical Garden 29: 1–22.

Wolf, P. G., S. D. Sipes, M. R. White, M. L. Martines, K. M. Pryer, A. R. Smith, and K. Ueda. 1999. Phylogenetic relationships of enigmatic fern families Hymenophyllopsidaceae and Lophosoriaceae: evidence from *rbc*L nucleotide sequences. Plant Systematics and Evolution 219: 263–270.

# Index

*Acrostichum barbarum*, see *Todea barbara*
*Actinophlebia*, see *Cnemidaria*
*Allantodia*, 56
*Alsophila*, 48, 50, 51; see also *Cyathea*
*Alsophila abbottii*, see *Cyathea abbottii*
*Alsophila acanthophora*, see *Cyathea acanthophora*
*Alsophila acrostichoides*, see *Cyathea acrostichoides*
*Alsophila acuminata*, see *Cyathea acuminata*
*Alsophila acutidens*, see *Cyathea acutidens*
*Alsophila aeneifolia*, see *Cyathea aeneifolia*
*Alsophila alata*, see *Cyathea alata*
*Alsophila albosetacea*, see *Cyathea albosetacea*
*Alsophila alderwereltii*, see *Cyathea alderwereltii*
*Alsophila alleniae*, see *Cyathea alleniae*
*Alsophila alpina*, see *Cyathea alpicola*
*Alsophila amboinensis*, see *Cyathea amboinensis*
*Alsophila amintae*, 59, 127, 245, 309, 310
*Alsophila andersonii*, see *Cyathea andersonii*
*Alsophila aneitensis*, see *Cyathea aneitensis*
*Alsophila angiensis*, see *Cyathea angiensis*
*Alsophila annae*, see *Cyathea annae*
*Alsophila apiculata*, see *Cyathea apiculata*
*Alsophila apoensis*, see *Cyathea apoensis*
*Alsophila approximata*, see *Cyathea approximata*
*Alsophila archboldii*, see *Cyathea archboldii*
*Alsophila arfakensis*, see *Cyathea kanehirae*
*Alsophila aterrima*, see *Cyathea aterrima*
*Alsophila atropurpurea*, see *Cyathea atropurpurea*
*Alsophila auneae*, see *Cyathea pubescens*
*Alsophila australis*, see *Cyathea australis*
*Alsophila baileyana*, see *Cyathea baileyana*
*Alsophila bakeri*, see *Cyathea poeppigii*
*Alsophila balanocarpa*, see *Cyathea balanocarpa*
*Alsophila batjanensis*, see *Cyathea batjanensis*
*Alsophila biformis*, see *Cyathea biformis*
*Alsophila bongardiana*, see *Cyathea mertensiana*
*Alsophila borinquena*, see *Cyathea borinquena*
*Alsophila borneensis*, see *Cyathea borneensis*
*Alsophila brausei*, see *Cyathea hunsteiniana*
*Alsophila brevipinnata*, see *Cyathea brevipinnata*
*Alsophila brooksii*, see *Cyathea brooksii*
*Alsophila brunoniana*, see *Cyathea brunnescens*
*Alsophila bryophila*, 19, 59, 127, 226, 245, 248, 309
*Alsophila buennermeijeri*, see *Cyathea buennermeijeri*

## Index

*Alsophila callosa*, see *Cyathea callosa*
*Alsophila camerooniana*, see *Cyathea camerooniana*
*Alsophila capensis*, see *Cyathea capensis*
*Alsophila caracasana*, see *Cyathea caracasana*
*Alsophila catillifera*, see *Cyathea catillifera*
*Alsophila caudata*, see *Cyathea caudata*
*Alsophila cicatricosa*, see *Cyathea cicatricosa*
*Alsophila cincinnata*, see *Cyathea cincinnata*
*Alsophila cinerea*, see *Cyathea cinerea*
*Alsophila coactilis*, see *Cyathea coactilis*
*Alsophila colensoi*, see *Cyathea colensoi*
*Alsophila commutata*, see *Cyathea recommutata*
*Alsophila contaminans*, see *Cyathea contaminans*
*Alsophila cooperi*, see *Cyathea cooperi*
*Alsophila cordata*, see *Cyathea barringtonii*
*Alsophila costalisora*, see *Cyathea costalisora*
*Alsophila costularis*, see *Cyathea chinensis*
*Alsophila crassa*, see under *Cyathea crassa*
*Alsophila crassicaula*, see *Cyathea ledermannii*
*Alsophila crenulata*, see *Cyathea raciborskii*
*Alsophila crinita*, see *Cyathea crinita*
*Alsophila cucullifera*, see *Cyathea cucullifera*
*Alsophila cunninghamii*, see *Cyathea cunninghamii*
*Alsophila cuspidata*, see *Cyathea cuspidata*
*Alsophila deckenii*, see *Cyathea deckenii*
*Alsophila decomposita*, see *Cyathea decomposita*
*Alsophila decrescens*, see *Cyathea decrescens*
*Alsophila decurrens*, see *Cyathea decurrens*
*Alsophila demissa*, see *Cyathea demissa*
*Alsophila denticulata*, see *Cyathea hancockii*
*Alsophila dichromatolepis*, see *Cyathea dichromatolepis*
*Alsophila dicksonioides*, see *Cyathea dicksonioides*
*Alsophila dimorpha*, see *Cyathea dimorpha*
*Alsophila doctersii*, see *Cyathea doctersii*
*Alsophila dombeyi*, see *Cyathea dombeyi*
*Alsophila dregei*, see *Cyathea dregei*
*Alsophila edanoi*, see *Cyathea edanoi*
*Alsophila elegans*, see *Cyathea corcovadensis*
*Alsophila elongata*, see *Cyathea poeppigii*
*Alsophila engelii*, see *Cyathea elongata*
*Alsophila erinacea*, see *Cyathea erinacea*
*Alsophila eriophora*, see *Cyathea eriophora*
*Alsophila esmeraldensis*, 226, 264, 310
*Alsophila estelae*, see *Cyathea estelae*
*Alsophila everta*, see *Cyathea everta*
*Alsophila excavata*, see *Cyathea excavata*
*Alsophila excelsa*, see *Cyathea brownii*
*Alsophila falcata*, see *Cyathea falcata*
*Alsophila fenicis* (Copeland) C. Christensen, see *Cyathea fenicis*
*Alsophila fenicis* Posthumus, see *Cyathea elmeri*
*Alsophila ferdinandii*, see *Cyathea macarthurii*
*Alsophila ferruginea*, see *Cyathea ferruinea*
*Alsophila firma*, see *Cyathea mexicana*
*Alsophila foersteri*, see *Cyathea foersteri*
*Alsophila formosa*, see *Cyathea metteniana*
*Alsophila frigida*, see *Cyathea frigida*
*Alsophila fulgens*, see *Cyathea fulgens*
*Alsophila fuliginosa*, see *Cyathea fuliginosa*
*Alsophila fulva*, see *Cyathea fulva*
*Alsophila gardneri*, 310
*Alsophila geluensis*, see *Cyathea geluensis*
*Alsophila gibbosa*, see *Cyathea gibbosa*
*Alsophila gigantea*, see *Cyathea gigantea*
*Alsophila glaberrima*, see *Cyathea glaberrima*
*Alsophila glabra*, see *Cyathea glabra*
*Alsophila gleichenioides*, see *Cyathea gleichenioides*
*Alsophila gregaria*, see *Cyathea gregaria*
*Alsophila grevilleana*, see *Cyathea grevilleana*

# Index

*Alsophila halconensis*, see *Cyathea halconensis*
*Alsophila haughtii*, see *Cyathea haughtii*
*Alsophila havilandii*, see *Cyathea havilandii*
*Alsophila henryi*, see *Cyathea henryi*
*Alsophila hermannii*, see *Cyathea christii*
*Alsophila heterochlamydea*, see *Cyathea heterochlamydea*
*Alsophila hieronymi*, see *Cyathea wengiensis*
*Alsophila holstii*, see *Cyathea humilis*
*Alsophila hooglandii*, see *Cyathea hooglandii*
*Alsophila hookeri*, see *Cyathea hookeri*
*Alsophila hornei*, see *Cyathea hornei*
*Alsophila horridula*, see *Cyathea horridula*
*Alsophila hotteana*, see *Cyathea hotteana*
*Alsophila hunsteiniana*, see *Cyathea rubiginosa*
*Alsophila hymenodes*, see *Cyathea hymenodes*
*Alsophila imbricata*, see *Cyathea imbricata*
*Alsophila imrayana*, see *Cyathea imrayana*
*Alsophila incana*, see *Cyathea incana*
*Alsophila incisoserrata*, see *Cyathea incisoserrata*
*Alsophila inquinans*, see *Cyathea inquinans*
*Alsophila insulana*, see *Cyathea insulana*
*Alsophila intermedia*, see *Cyathea intermedia*
*Alsophila javanica*, see *Cyathea javanica*
*Alsophila jimeneziana*, see *Cyathea crassa*
*Alsophila junghuhniana*, see *Cyathea junghuhniana*
*Alsophila kalbreyeri*, see *Cyathea kalbreyeri*
*Alsophila kermadecensis*, see *Cyathea kermadecensis*
*Alsophila khasyana*, see *Cyathea khasyana*
*Alsophila klossii*, see *Cyathea klossii*
*Alsophila lasiosora*, see *Cyathea lasiosora*
*Alsophila latebrosa*, see *Cyathea latebrosa*
*Alsophila latevagens*, see *Cyathea latevagens*
*Alsophila latipinnula*, see *Cyathea latipinnula*
*Alsophila lechleri*, see *Cyathea subtropica*
*Alsophila lechria*, see *Cyathea aterrima*
*Alsophila leichhardtiana*, see *Cyathea leichhardtiana*
*Alsophila lepidocladia*, see *Cyathea lepidocladia*
*Alsophila lepidotricha*, see *Cyathea novaecaledoniae*
*Alsophila lepifera*, see *Cyathea lepifera*
*Alsophila leucolepis*, see *Cyathea leucofolis*
*Alsophila loerzingii*, see *Cyathea loerzingii*
*Alsophila loheri*, see *Cyathea loheri*
*Alsophila longipes*, see *Cyathea longipes*
*Alsophila lurida*, see *Cyathea lurida*
*Alsophila maccarthurii*, see *Cyathea leichhardtiana*
*Alsophila macgillivrayi*, see *Cyathea macgillivrayi*
*Alsophila macgregorii*, see *Cyathea macgregorii*
*Alsophila macropoda*, see *Cyathea macropoda*
*Alsophila macrosora*, see *Cyathea macrosora*
*Alsophila magnifolia*, see *Cyathea magnifolia*
*Alsophila manniana*, see *Cyathea manniana*
*Alsophila marattioides*, see *Cyathea marattioides*
*Alsophila ×marcescens*, see *Cyathea ×marcescens*
*Alsophila marginalis*, see *Cyathea marginalis*
*Alsophila marginata*, see *Cyathea marginata*
*Alsophila masapilidensis*, see *Cyathea masapilidensis*
*Alsophila media*, see *Cyathea media*
*Alsophila mertensiana*, see *Cyathea mertensiana*
*Alsophila mesosora*, see *Cyathea mesosora*
*Alsophila metteniana*, see *Cyathea metteniana*
*Alsophila mexicana*, see *Cyathea valdecrenata*
*Alsophila micra*, see *Cyathea parva*

*Alsophila microchlamys*, see *Cyathea microchlamys*
*Alsophila microphylla*, see *Trichipteris microphylla*
*Alsophila microphylloides* Domin, see *Trichipteris microphylla*
*Alsophila microphylloides* (Rosenstock) Tryon, see *Cyathea microphylloides*
*Alsophila mildbraedii*, see *Cyathea mildbraedii*
*Alsophila milnei*, see *Cyathea milnei*
*Alsophila minor*, see *Cyathea minor*
*Alsophila modesta*, see *Cyathea modesta*
*Alsophila montana*, see *Cyathea costulisora*
*Alsophila moorei*, see under *Cyathea macarthurii*
*Alsophila mossambicensis*, see *Cyathea mossambicensis*
*Alsophila muelleri*, see *Cyathea muelleri*
*Alsophila munchii*, see *A. salvinii*
*Alsophila myosuroides*, see *Cyathea myosuroides*
*Alsophila negrosiana*, see *Cyathea negrosiana*
*Alsophila nesiotica*, see *Cyathea nesiotica*
*Alsophila nicklesii*, see *Cyathea nicklesii*
*Alsophila nigripes*, see *Cyathea nigripes*
*Alsophila nigrolineata*, see *Cyathea nigrolineata*
*Alsophila nigropaleata*, see *Cyathea nigropaleata*
*Alsophila nilgirensis*, see *Cyathea nilgirensis*
*Alsophila nockii*, see *Cyathea nockii*
*Alsophila notabilis*, see *Cyathea notabilis*
*Alsophila novae-caledoniae*, see *Cyathea novae-caledoniae*
*Alsophila obscura*, see *Cyathea obscura*
*Alsophila obtusiloba*, see *Cyathea obtusiloba*
*Alsophila ogurae*, see *Cyathea ogurae*
*Alsophila oinops*, see *Cyathea oinops*
*Alsophila oosora*, see *Cyathea oosora*
*Alsophila orientalis*, see *Cyathea orientalis*
*Alsophila pachyrrhachis*, see *Cyathea pachyrrhachis*
*Alsophila paladensis*, see *Cyathea paladensis*
*Alsophila pallescens*, see *Cyathea pallescens*
*Alsophila pallidipaleata*, see *Cyathea pallidipaleata*
*Alsophila papuana*, see *Cyathea papuana*
*Alsophila parva*, 310
*Alsophila parvifolia*, see *Cyathea deminuens*
*Alsophila parvula*, see *Cyathea parvula*
*Alsophila patellifera*, see *Cyathea patellifera*
*Alsophila pauciflora*, see *Cyathea pauciflora*
*Alsophila paucifolia*, see *Cyathea stuebelii*
*Alsophila percrassa*, see *Cyathea percrassa*
*Alsophila perpelvigera*, see *Cyathea perpelvigera*
*Alsophila perpunctulata*, see *Cyathea perpunctulata*
*Alsophila perrieriana*, see *Cyathea perrieriana*
*Alsophila persquamulifera*, see *Cyathea persquamulifera*
*Alsophila phalaenolepis*, see *Cyathea phalaenolepis*
*Alsophila phegopteroides*, see *Cyathea phegopteroides*
*Alsophila physolepidota*, see *Cyathea physolepidota*
*Alsophila pilosissima*, see *Cyathea pilosissima*
*Alsophila pinnula*, see *Cyathea pinnula*
*Alsophila plagiostegia*, see *Cyathea plagiostegia*
*Alsophila podophylla*, see *Cyathea podophylla*
*Alsophila poeppigii*, see *Cyathea poeppigii*
*Alsophila polycarpa*, see *Cyathea polycarpa*
*Alsophila polystichoides*, 85, 310
*Alsophila portoricensis*, see *Cyathea portoricensis*
*Alsophila praecincta*, see *Cyathea praecincta*
*Alsophila pruinosa*, see *Cyathea pruinosa*

*Alsophila pseudomuelleri*, see *Cyathea pseudomuelleri*
*Alsophila pubescens*, see *Cyathea pubens*
*Alsophila punctulata*, see *Cyathea punctulata*
*Alsophila pycnoneura*, see *Cyathea pycnoneura*
*Alsophila ramispina*, see *Cyathea ramispina*
*Alsophila rebeccae*, see *Cyathea rebeccae*
*Alsophila recurvata*, see *Cyathea recurvata*
*Alsophila rigens*, see *Cyathea rigens*
*Alsophila robertsiana*, see *Cyathea robertsiana*
*Alsophila robusta*, see *Cyathea robusta*
*Alsophila rosenstockii*, see *Cyathea ascendens*
*Alsophila rubella*, see *Cyathea rubella*
*Alsophila rubiginosa*, see *Cyathea rubiginosa*
*Alsophila rufa*, see *Cyathea rufa*
*Alsophila rufopannosa*, see *Cyathea rufopannosa*
*Alsophila rupestris*, see *Cyathea rupestris*
*Alsophila saccata*, see *Cyathea saccata*
*Alsophila sagittifolia*, see *Cyathea sagittifolia*
*Alsophila salletii*, see *Cyathea salletii*
*Alsophila salvinii*, 311
*Alsophila samoensis*, see *Cyathea whitmeei*
*Alsophila scandens*, see *Cyathea scandens*
*Alsophila schiedeana*, see *Cyathea schiedeana*
*Alsophila schlechteri*, see *Cyathea schlechteri*
*Alsophila schliebenii*, see *Cyathea fadenii*
*Alsophila schlimii*, see *Cyathea schlimii*
*Alsophila scopulina*, see *Cyathea aterrima*
*Alsophila sechellarum*, see *Cyathea sechellarum*
*Alsophila semiamplectens*, see *Cyathea semiamplectens*
*Alsophila senilis*, see *Cyathea senilis*
*Alsophila serratifolia*, see *Cyathea serratifolia*
*Alsophila setosa*, 85, 311

*Alsophila setulosa*, see *Cyathea setulosa*
*Alsophila sinuata*, see *Cyathea sinuata*
*Alsophila smithii*, see *Cyathea smithii*
*Alsophila solomonensis*, see *Cyathea solomonensis*
*Alsophila spinulosa*, see *Cyathea spinulosa*
*Alsophila squamata*, see *Trichipteris microphylla*
*Alsophila stipularis*, see *Cyathea stipularis*
*Alsophila stokesii*, see *Cyathea stokesii*
*Alsophila strigillosa*, see *Cyathea armata*
*Alsophila stuhlmannii*, see *Cyathea humilis*
*Alsophila subdubia*, see *Cyathea subdubia*
*Alsophila subtripinnata*, see *Cyathea subtripinnata*
*Alsophila sumatrana*, see *Cyathea sumatrana*
*Alsophila tahitensis*, see *Cyathea affinis*
*Alsophila tanzaniana*, see *Cyathea schliebenii*
*Alsophila tenera*, see *Cyathea tenera*
*Alsophila tenggerensis*, see *Cyathea tenggerensis*
*Alsophila tenuis*, see *Cyathea tenuicaulis*
*Alsophila ternatea*, see *Cyathea ternatea*
*Alsophila thomsonii*, see *Cyathea thomsonii*
*Alsophila trichiata*, see *Cyathea trichiata*
*Alsophila trichodesma*, see *Cyathea trichodesma*
*Alsophila tricolor*, see *Cyathea dealbata*
*Alsophila truncata*, see *Cyathea truncata*
*Alsophila tryoniana*, 85, 311
*Alsophila tryonorum*, see *Cyathea tryonorum*
*Alsophila tsilotsilensis*, see *Cyathea tsilotsilensis*
*Alsophila tussacii*, see *Cyathea tussacii*
*Alsophila urbanii*, see *Cyathea urbanii*
*Alsophila ursina*, see *Cyathea ursina*
*Alsophila vandeusenii*, see *Cyathea vandeusenii*
*Alsophila vieillardii*, see *Cyathea vieillardii*
*Alsophila walkerae*, see *Cyathea walkerae*
*Alsophila wallacei*, see *Cyathea wallacei*
*Alsophila welwitschii*, see *Cyathea welwitschii*

## Index

*Alsophila wendlandii*, see *Cyathea wendlandii*
*Alsophila wengiensis*, see *Cyathea wengiensis*
*Alsophila williamsii*, see *Cyathea williamsii*
*Alsophila woodwardioides*, see *Cyathea woodwardioides*
*Alsophila woollsiana*, see *Cyathea woollsiana*
*Alsophila wrightii*, see *Cyathea myosuroides*
*Alsophila zakamenensis*, see *Cyathea zakamenensis*
Alsophilaceae, see Cyatheaceae
*Alsophilocaulis*, 25
'ama'u, see *Sadleria cyatheoides*
'ama'u'i'i, see *Sadleria pallida*
Angiopteridaceae, see Marattiaceae
*Angiopteris*, 26, 57
*Angiopteris evecta*, 161
aphlebiae, 21
'apulu, see *Sadleria squarrosa*
'apu'u, see *Sadleria squarrosa*
*Armillaria*, 42
Aspleniaceae, 50
Athyriaceae, 50, 56
*Athyrium microphyllum*, 56
balabala (balaka), see *Cyathea lunulata*
*Balantium*, see *Dicksonia*
*Balantium berteroanum*, see *Dicksonia berteriana*
*Balantium blumei*, see *Dicksonia blumei*
Banks, Joseph, 11, 48
barometz, the, see *Cibotium barometz*
Bauhin, Caspar, 47
Bernhardi, Johann Jakob, 48
black tree fern, see *Cyathea medullaris*, *C. rebeccae*
Blechnaceae, 15, 50, 52, 56, 60, 301
Blechnales, 52
Blechneae, see Blechnaceae
*Blechnum*, 57, 60
*Blechnum brasiliense*, 57
*Blechnum buchtienii*, 57
*Blechnum cycadifolia*, 57, 161
*Blechnum discolor*, 57, 162

*Blechnum fraseri*, 57
*Blechnum gibbum*, 57, 163
*Blechnum magellanica*, 57, 164
*Blechnum nudum*, 57
*Blechnum souleyetianum*, see *Sadleria souleyetiana*
*Blechnum squarrosum*, see *Sadleria squarrosa*
*Blechnum vittatum*, 57
bracken, false, see *Calochlaena dubia*
*Brainea insignis*, 57
bristly tree fern, see *Dicksonia herbertii*, *D. youngiae*
Brown, Robert, 48
Bull, William, 34
bulu pusi, see *Cibotium barometz*
*Calochlaena*, 25, 50, 51, 52, 60, 79
*Calochlaena dubia*, 60, 61, 165
*Calochlaena javanica*, 62
*Calochlaena straminea*, 62, 165
*Calochlaena villosa*, 63
caudex, 17, 18
Chamisso, Ludolf Karl Adelbert von, 49, 66
*Chnoophora*, see *Cyathea*
*Chnoophora glauca*, see *Cyathea contaminans*
*Chnoophora lurida*, see *Cyathea lurida*
*Chnoophora tomentosa*, see *Cyathea tomentosa*
*Cibotiocaulis*, 25
*Cibotium*, 31, 32, 49, 50, 51, 52, 59, 63, 282, 306
*Cibotium arachnoideum*, 32, 65
*Cibotium barometz*, 30, 32, 33, 45, 47, 65, 166, 167
  var. *cumingii*, see *C. cumingii*
*Cibotium chamissoi* Kaulfuss, 49, 63, 66, 68, 167
*Cibotium chamissoi* in the sense of Krajina in Skottsberg, see *C. menziesii*
*Cibotium cumingii*, 67
  var. *arachnoideum*, see *C. arachnoideum*
*Cibotium glaucum*, 39, 67, 167, 168
*Cibotium horridum*, see *Cyathea princeps*
*Cibotium menziesii*, 66, 67, 168

*Cibotium nealiae*, 68
*Cibotium princeps*, see *Cyathea princeps*
*Cibotium regale*, 68
*Cibotium st.-johnii*, see *C. glaucum*
*Cibotium schiedei*, 69, 169
*Cibotium splendens*, see *C. chamissoi*
*Cibotium taiwanense*, see *C. cumingii*
*Cibotium wendlandii*, see *C. regale*
CITES (Convention on International Trade in Endangered Species), 28, 63
*Cladophlebis*, 28, 169
*Cnemidaria*, 25, 50, 51, 52, 69, 82, 249
*Cnemidaria alatissima*, 71
*Cnemidaria amabilis*, 71, 75
*Cnemidaria apiculata*, 71
*Cnemidaria bella*, 70, 71, 75, 78, 261
*Cnemidaria chocoensis*, 72
*Cnemidaria choricarpa*, 72, 73, 76
*Cnemidaria coclcana*, 72
*Cnemidaria consimilis*, 72
*Cnemidaria cruciata*, 73, 78
*Cnemidaria decurrens*, 72, 73, 74, 76
*Cnemidaria ewanii*, 73, 77
*Cnemidaria glandulosa*, 73, 74
*Cnemidaria grandifolia*, 70, 74, 84
    var. *grandifolia*, 74
    var. *obtusa*, 74
*Cnemidaria horrida*, 47, 59, 70, 72, 74, 78, 84
*Cnemidaria karsteniana*, 75
*Cnemidaria mutica*, 71, 72, 73, 75
    var. *chiricana*, 75
    var. *contigua*, 75
    var. *grandis*, 75
    var. *mutica*, 75
*Cnemidaria nervosa*, 76
*Cnemidaria quitensis*, 76
*Cnemidaria roraimensis*, 76, 78
*Cnemidaria singularis*, 76, 78
*Cnemidaria speciosa*, 69, 73, 77
*Cnemidaria spectabilis*, 70, 72, 73, 76, 78, 84
    var. *colombiensis*, 78
    var. *spectabilis*, 78
*Cnemidaria tryoniana*, 77, 78
*Cnemidaria uleana*, 78
    var. *abitaguensis*, 79
    var. *uleana*, 79
*Cnemidopteris*, see *Cnemidaria*
Conant, David, 54
*Conantiopteris*, 25
*Coniopteris*, 25
Cook, James, 11, 47
*Cormophyllum*, see *Cyathea*
Corner, E. J. H. (John), 53
creeping tree fern, see *Cyathea colensoi*
crepe fern, see *Leptopteris fraseri*, *L. superba*
*Culcita*, 30, 50, 51, 52, 59, 60, 79, 282
*Culcita* subg. *Calochlaena*, see *Calochlaena*
*Culcita coniifolia*, 79, 81
*Culcita copelandii*, see *Calochlaena javanica*
*Culcita dubia*, see *Calochlaena dubia*
*Culcita javanica*, see *Calochlaena javanica*
*Culcita macrocarpa*, 30, 79, 80
*Culcita straminea*, see *Calochlaena straminea*
*Culcita villosa*, see *Calochlaena villosa*
Culcitaceae, see Dicksoniaceae
*Cyathea*, 25, 50, 51, 52, 59, 81, 282
*Cyathea abbottii*, 87, 226
*Cyathea abitaguensis*, see *Cnemidaria uleana*
*Cyathea acanthophora*, 87
*Cyathea aciculosa*, 88, 271
*Cyathea acrostichoides*, 88
*Cyathea acuminata*, 88
*Cyathea acutidens*, 88, 229
*Cyathea aeneifolia*, 89, 119, 242
    var. *macrophylla*, 89
    var. *melanacantha*, 89
    var. *subglauca*, 89
*Cyathea affinis* (J. R. Forster) Swartz, 47, 89, 243, 261
*Cyathea affinis* W. J. Hooker & Baker, see *C. medullaris*
*Cyathea affinis* M. Martens & Galeotti, see under *C. affinis* (J. R. Forster) Swartz
*Cyathea agatheti*, 90
*Cyathea alata*, 90, 122
*Cyathea albidosquamata*, 90
*Cyathea albidula*, see *C. rubiginosa*

## 346　Index

*Cyathea albifrons*, 49, 91
*Cyathea albomarginata*, 91
*Cyathea albosetacea*, 91
*Cyathea alderwereltii*, 91
*Cyathea alleniae*, 92
*Cyathea alphonsiana*, 92, 229
*Cyathea alpicola*, 92, 159, 160, 244
*Cyathea alpina*, see *C. alpicola*
*Cyathea alstonii*, 93
*Cyathea alternans*, 93, 227
*Cyathea amaiambitensis*, see *C. ramispina*
*Cyathea amazonica*, 93, 95, 242
*Cyathea amboinensis*, 94
*Cyathea ampla*, see *C. assimilis*
*Cyathea anacampta*, see *C. poeppigii*
*Cyathea andersonii*, 94
*Cyathea andina*, 93, 94, 276
*Cyathea aneitensis*, 95, 274
*Cyathea angiensis*, 95, 115
*Cyathea angolensis*, see *C. dregei*
*Cyathea angustipinna*, 95
*Cyathea annae*, 95
*Cyathea apiculata*, 96
*Cyathea apoensis*, 96
*Cyathea approximate*, 96
*Cyathea aramaganensis*, 96, 170
*Cyathea araneosa*, see *C. woodwardioides*
*Cyathea arborea*, 19, 47, 48, 59, 81, 84, 97, 99, 170
*Cyathea arborescens*, see *C. caudata*
*Cyathea arbuscula*, see *C. dichromatolepis*
*Cyathea archboldii*, 97, 132, 231
　　var. *horrida*, 98
*Cyathea arguta*, see *C. integra*
*Cyathea aristata*, see *Cnemidaria apiculata*
*Cyathea armata*, 84, 98, 103, 114, 130, 141, 230, 254, 263, 269, 271, 273
*Cyathea arthropoda*, 98
*Cyathea ascendens*, 98
*Cyathea aspera*, 47, 84, 97, 99, 136
*Cyathea asperula*, see *C. furfuracea*
*Cyathea aspidioides*, see *C. corallifera*
*Cyathea assimilis* Christ, see *C. oosora*
*Cyathea assimilis* W. J. Hooker, 99
*Cyathea atahuallpa*, 99
*Cyathea aterrima*, 100, 155, 237, 258
*Cyathea atropurpurea*, 100, 250

*Cyathea atrospinosa*, 100
*Cyathea atrovirens*, 100, 241, 275
*Cyathea atrox*, 101
　　var. *atrox*, 101
　　var. *inermis*, 101
*Cyathea aurea*, see *C. fulva*
*Cyathea auriculifera*, 101
*Cyathea australis*, 38, 49, 85, 101, 118, 153, 171, 172, 221
*Cyathea austroamericana*, see *C. multiflora*
*Cyathea baileyana*, 39, 102, 172
*Cyathea bakeriana*, see *C. cyatheoides*
*Cyathea balanocarpa*, 84, 103
*Cyathea barringtonii*, 103, 240, 274
*Cyathea bartlettii*, see *C. obliqua*
*Cyathea batjanensis*, 103
*Cyathea beccariana*, see *C. assimilis*
*Cyathea ×bernardii*, 84
*Cyathea bicolor*, see *C. fuliginosa*
*Cyathea bicrenata*, 98, 103, 172, 173
*Cyathea bidentata*, see *C. archboldii*
*Cyathea biformis*, 84, 103, 256
*Cyathea biliranensis*, see *C. fuliginosa*
*Cyathea binuangensis*, 87, 104, 148
*Cyathea bipinnata*, 104
*Cyathea blanchetiana*, see *C. phalerata*
*Cyathea boliviana*, 104, 264
*Cyathea bonapartii*, see *C. quindiuensis*
*Cyathea boninsimensis*, see *C. spinulosa*
*Cyathea borinquena*, 104, 241
*Cyathea borneensis*, 105
*Cyathea boryana*, see *C. andina*
*Cyathea brackenridgei*, 105, 227, 288
*Cyathea bradei*, 105, 119
*Cyathea brevifoliolata*, see *C. raciborskii*
*Cyathea brevipes*, see *C. caudata*
*Cyathea brevipinnata*, 106
*Cyathea brevistipes*, 106, 264
*Cyathea brooksii*, 106, 133, 245, 310
*Cyathea brownii*, 19, 20, 35, 38, 107, 108, 174, 175
*Cyathea brunei*, 107, 135, 147, 246, 250, 312
*Cyathea brunnescens*, 108, 120, 231, 257, 269; see also *C. nigripes*
*Cyathea brunoniana*, 108
*Cyathea brunonis*, see *C. moluccana*

*Cyathea buennermeijeri*, 108
*Cyathea burbidgei* (Baker) Copeland, see
   *C. wallacei*
*Cyathea burbidgei* Holttum, see *C.*
   *trichodesma*
*Cyathea burkei*, see *C. dregei*
*Cyathea callosa*, 109, 261
*Cyathea camerooniana*, 109
   var. *aethiopica*, 109
   var. *camerooniana*, 109
   var. *congi*, 109
   var. *currorii*, 109
   var. *occidentalis*, 109
   var. *ugandensis*, 109
   var. *zenkeri*, 109
*Cyathea capensis*, 39, 47, 109, 175
   subsp. *polypodioides*, 109
*Cyathea capitata*, 110, 175
*Cyathea caracasana*, 83, 110, 125
   var. *boliviensis*, 110
   var. *caracasana*, 110
   var. *chimborazensis*, 110
   var. *maxonii*, 110
   var. *meridensis*, 110
*Cyathea caribaea*, see *C. imrayana*
*Cyathea carrii*, 111
*Cyathea castanea*, see *C. lechleri*
*Cyathea catillifera*, 111
*Cyathea caudata*, 111, 128, 141
*Cyathea caudipinnula*, see *C. javanica*
*Cyathea celebica*, 111
*Cyathea chimborazensis*, see *C. caracasana*
*Cyathea chinensis*, 112
*Cyathea choricarpa*, see *Cnemidaria*
   *choricarpa*
*Cyathea christii*, 112
*Cyathea cicatricosa*, 112, 122
*Cyathea cincinnata*, 113
*Cyathea cinerea*, 113
*Cyathea coactilis*, 113
*Cyathea colensoi*, 35, 114, 176
*Cyathea columbiana*, see *C. multiflora*
*Cyathea commutata*, see *Cnemidaria*
   *horrida*
*Cyathea* ×*concinna*, 85
*Cyathea* ×*confirmis*, 85, 114, 143
*Cyathea conformis*, 114, 240

*Cyathea conjugata*, 98, 114
*Cyathea conspicua*, see *C. suprastrigosa*
*Cyathea contaminans*, 20, 95, 114, 154,
   177, 274
*Cyathea cooperi*, 19, 35, 35, 87, 115, 178,
   179
   'Brentwood', 34, 115, 179
   'Robusta', 34, 115
*Cyathea corallifera*, 116, 126, 264
*Cyathea corcovadensis*, 84, 116
*Cyathea cordata*, see *C. marattioides*
*Cyathea coriacea*, see *C. poeppigii*
*Cyathea costalisora*, 116
*Cyathea costaricensis*, 116, 179
*Cyathea costulisora*, 117
*Cyathea crassa*, 85, 117, 133, 138, 245,
   272, 279
*Cyathea crassifolia*, see *C. schiedeana*
*Cyathea crassipes*, see *C. quindiuensis*
*Cyathea crenulata*, see *C. polycarpa*
*Cyathea crinita*, 117, 159, 268
*Cyathea croftii*, 118
*Cyathea cucullifera*, 118
*Cyathea cunninghamii*, 20, 22, 85, 118,
   150, 180, 181, 221
*Cyathea curranii*, 89, 119
*Cyathea cuspidata*, 119
*Cyathea* subg. *Cyathea* (*Alsophila* clade),
   84
*Cyathea* subg. *Cyathea* (*Cyathea* clade), 82
*Cyathea cyatheoides*, 106, 119, 141, 266
*Cyathea cyclodium*, 120, 124
*Cyathea cyclodonta*, see *C. leucotricha*
*Cyathea cystolepis*, 120, 139
*Cyathea darienensis*, 108, 120, 231, 257,
   269
*Cyathea dealbata*, 11, 19, 30, 32, 34, 35,
   38, 120, 181, 182, 226
*Cyathea decipiens*, see *C. spinulosa*
*Cyathea deckenii*, 121
*Cyathea decomposita*, 121
*Cyathea decorata*, 122, 261
*Cyathea decrescens*, 122
*Cyathea decurrens*, 22, 83, 90, 113, 122,
   144, 183, 252, 263
   subsp. *epaleata*, 122
   var. *vaupelii*, 122

*Cyathea decurrentiloba*, see *Cnemidaria decurrens*
*Cyathea delgadii*, 24, 123, 134
*Cyathea deminuens*, 123
*Cyathea demissa*, 120, 123, 229
    var. *demissa*, 124
    var. *thysanolepis*, 124
*Cyathea dichromatolepis*, 124, 241
*Cyathea dicksonioides*, 124
*Cyathea dimorpha*, 124
*Cyathea dimorphotricha*, see *C. elmeri*
*Cyathea discophora*, 125
*Cyathea dissimilis*, 125, 148
*Cyathea dissoluta*, 110, 125
*Cyathea distans*, see *C. polycarpa*
*Cyathea divergens*, 84, 116, 125, 142, 236
    var. *divergens*, 126
    var. *tuerckheimii*, 126
*Cyathea doctersii*, 126
*Cyathea dombeyi*, 126, 249
*Cyathea dregei*, 127, 184, 185, 268
*Cyathea* ×*dryopteroides*, 59, 127, 309, 310
*Cyathea dudleyi*, 127, 152
*Cyathea dulitensis*, see *C. assimilis*
*Cyathea ebenina*, 127, 152
*Cyathea edanoi*, 111, 128, 141
*Cyathea elegans*, see *C. grevilleana*
*Cyathea elegantissima*, see *Cnemidaria decurrens*
*Cyathea elliptica*, 128, 270
*Cyathea elmeri*, 128
*Cyathea elongata*, 128
*Cyathea erinacea*, 129
*Cyathea eriophora*, 129
*Cyathea estelae*, 98, 129
*Cyathea everta*, 130, 252
*Cyathea ewanii*, see *Cnemidaria ewanii*
*Cyathea excavata*, 130
*Cyathea exilis*, 130
*Cyathea fadenii*, 130
*Cyathea falcata*, 131, 240
*Cyathea farinosa*, see *C. gibbosa*
*Cyathea fauriei*, see *C. spinulosa*
*Cyathea feani*, 131
*Cyathea feeana*, see *C. corcovadensis*
*Cyathea felina*, 131
*Cyathea fellacina*, see *C. atrovirens*

*Cyathea fenicis*, 132
*Cyathea ferruginea*, 132
*Cyathea ferrugineoides*, see *C. ferruginea*
*Cyathea firma*, see *C. divergens*
*Cyathea floribunda*, see *C. dombeyi*
*Cyathea foersteri*, 98, 132, 231
*Cyathea formosana*, see *C. metteniana*
*Cyathea francii*, see *C. intermedia*
*Cyathea frigida*, 133, 238
*Cyathea fructuosa*, see *C. loheri*
*Cyathea fugax*, 133
*Cyathea fulgens*, 85, 106, 117, 133, 138, 245, 272, 279
*Cyathea fuliginosa*, 133
*Cyathea fulva*, 83, 84, 123, 134, 140, 234, 266, 267
*Cyathea funebris*, see *C. albifrons*
*Cyathea furfuracea*, 114, 134, 185, 201
*Cyathea fusca*, 134, 277
*Cyathea fuscopaleata*, see *C. moluccana*
*Cyathea gardneri* W. J. Hooker, 108, 135, 147, 246, 250
*Cyathea gardneri* (W. J. Hooker) Lellinger, see *Alsophila gardneri*
*Cyathea geluensis*, 135
*Cyathea gibbosa*, 99, 135
*Cyathea gigantea*, 136, 186, 243, 265
*Cyathea glaberrima*, 136
*Cyathea glabra*, 135, 136, 243, 265
*Cyathea glabrescens*, see *C. squamulata*
*Cyathea gleichenioides*, 137, 145, 158
*Cyathea gracilensis*, see *C. parvula*
*Cyathea gracilis*, 52, 81, 137, 152
*Cyathea gracillima*, see *C. macgillivrayi*
*Cyathea grandifolia*, see *Cnemidaria grandifolia*
*Cyathea grandis*, see *Cnemidaria mutica*
*Cyathea gregaria*, 137
*Cyathea grevilleana*, 85, 117, 133, 138, 245, 272, 279
*Cyathea guatemalensis*, see *Cnemidaria decurrens*
*Cyathea guianensis*, see *C. cyatheoides*
*Cyathea guimariensis*, see *C. dichromatolepis*
*Cyathea hainanensis*, 138
*Cyathea halconensis*, 138

# Index 349

*Cyathea halonata*, 120, 139
*Cyathea hancockii*, 139
*Cyathea harrisii*, 134, 139
*Cyathea haughtii*, 140, 261
*Cyathea havilandii*, 140
*Cyathea hemichlamydea*, see *C. borneensis*
*Cyathea hemiepiphytica*, 140, 149
*Cyathea henryi*, 140
*Cyathea heterochlamydea*, 111, 128, 141
*Cyathea hirsuta*, 87, 98, 119, 141
*Cyathea hodgeana*, 141, 231
*Cyathea holdridgeana*, 126, 141
*Cyathea holstii*, see *C. mossambicensis*
*Cyathea holttumii*, see *C. elliptica*
*Cyathea hooglandii*, 142, 225
*Cyathea hookeri*, 142, 186
*Cyathea hornei*, 142
*Cyathea horrida*, see *Cnemidaria horrida*
*Cyathea horridipes*, see *C. alderwereltii*
*Cyathea horridula*, 143
*Cyathea hotteana*, 85, 114, 143, 310
*Cyathea howeana*, 122, 143
*Cyathea humilis*, 144
  var. *pycnophylla*, 144
*Cyathea hunsteiniana*, 144, 239
  var. *acuminata*, 144
*Cyathea hymenodes*, 145
*Cyathea iheringii*, see *C. phalerata*
*Cyathea imbricata*, 137, 145, 158
*Cyathea impar*, 145, 240
*Cyathea imrayana*, 145
*Cyathea inaequalis*, 146
*Cyathea incana*, 146
*Cyathea incisoserrata*, 146, 151
*Cyathea incurvata*, see *C. gardneri*
*Cyathea indrapurae*, see *C. apiculata*
*Cyathea inquinans*, 146
*Cyathea insignis*, 108, 135, 147, 246, 250
*Cyathea insulana*, 147
*Cyathea insularum*, 147
*Cyathea integra*, see *C. tripinnatifida*
*Cyathea integrifolia*, see *C. speciosa*
*Cyathea interjecta*, see *C. albifrons*
*Cyathea intermedia*, 148, 187
*Cyathea intramarginalis*, 125, 148
*Cyathea* ×*irregularis*, 85
*Cyathea jamaicensis*, 148

*Cyathea javanica*, 126, 149, 244
  var. *rigida*, 149
*Cyathea junghuhniana*, 149, 250
*Cyathea kalbreyeri*, 140, 149, 231
*Cyathea kanehirae*, 150
*Cyathea karsteniana*, see *Cnemidaria karsteniana*
*Cyathea kemberangana*, see *C. polypoda*
*Cyathea kermadecensis*, 150, 188
*Cyathea khasyana*, 150
*Cyathea kinabaluensis*, see *C. moluccana*
*Cyathea kingii* (C. B. Clarke in Beddome) Copeland, see *C. lurida*
*Cyathea kingii* Rosenstock, see *C. werneri*
*Cyathea klossii*, 150
*Cyathea klotzschiana*, see *C. pungens*
*Cyathea kohautiana*, see *Cnemidaria grandifolia*
*Cyathea korthalsii*, see *C. hymenodes*
*Cyathea kuhnii*, see *C. falcata*
*Cyathea laciniata*, see *C. aneitensis*
*Cyathea lasiosora*, 151, 257, 276
*Cyathea latebrosa*, 126, 146, 151, 189, 190
  var. *indusiata*, see *C. hymenodes*
*Cyathea latevagens*, 152
*Cyathea latipinnula*, 152
*Cyathea lechleri*, 127, 137, 152
*Cyathea ledermannii*, 152, 270
*Cyathea leichhardtiana*, 86, 102, 153
*Cyathea lepidocladia*, 153
*Cyathea lepifera*, 115, 153
*Cyathea leprieurii*, see *Cnemidaria cruciata*
*Cyathea leucofolis*, 154
*Cyathea leucolepis*, 154
*Cyathea leucotricha*, 154, 264
*Cyathea* ×*lewisii*, 84
*Cyathea liebmannii*, see *Cnemidaria decurrens*
*Cyathea lindsayana*, see *C. grevilleana*
*Cyathea lobata*, see *C. apoensis*
*Cyathea lockwoodiana*, 100, 155, 237, 258
*Cyathea loddigesii*, see *C. australis*
*Cyathea loerzingii*, 155
*Cyathea loheri*, 155, 234
*Cyathea longipaleata*, see *C. muelleri*
*Cyathea longipes*, 156
*Cyathea lucida*, see *Cnemidaria decurrens*

*Cyathea lunulata*, 31, 156, 191
    subsp. *vitiensis*, 156
*Cyathea lurida*, 157
*Cyathea macarthurii*, 157
*Cyathea macgillivrayi*, 157
*Cyathea macgregorii*, 137, 145, 158
*Cyathea macrocarpa*, 158
*Cyathea macrophylla*, 158
    var. *quadripinnata*, 158
*Cyathea macropoda*, 93, 158, 160, 244
*Cyathea macrosora*, 159
    var. *reginae*, 159
    var. *vaupensis*, 159
*Cyathea madagascarica*, 159
*Cyathea magna*, 117, 159, 268
*Cyathea magnifolia*, 93, 159, 160, 244
*Cyathea manniana*, 31, 84, 160, 192
*Cyathea marattioides*, 160, 239, 258, 271
*Cyathea* ×*marcescens*, 85, 118, 192, 221
*Cyathea marginalis*, 221, 260
*Cyathea marginata*, 221
*Cyathea masapilidensis*, 221
*Cyathea maxonii*, see *C. caracasana*
*Cyathea mearnsii*, see *C. halconensis*
*Cyathea media*, 222
*Cyathea medullaris*, 19, 20, 22, 24, 30, 31, 34, 35, 38, 43, 47, 131, 156, 193, 194, 195, 222
    var. *tripinnata*, see *C. mertensiana*
*Cyathea megalosora*, 222
*Cyathea melanoclada*, see *C. hornei*
*Cyathea membranulosa*, see *C. caracasana*
*Cyathea meridensis*, see *C. caracasana*
*Cyathea mertensiana*, 223
*Cyathea mesocarpa*, see *C. dichromatolepis*
*Cyathea mesosora*, 223
*Cyathea metteniana*, 223
*Cyathea mexiae*, see *Alsophila gardneri*
*Cyathea mexicana*, 32, 196, 197, 224, 311
    var. *boliviensis*, see *C. caracasana*
*Cyathea microchlamys*, 224
*Cyathea microdonta*, 224
*Cyathea microlepidota*, 225
*Cyathea microphylla*, 225, 229
*Cyathea microphylloides* Domin, see *Trichipteris microphylla*

*Cyathea microphylloides* Rosenstock, 142, 225
*Cyathea mildbraedii*, 225
*Cyathea milnei*, 121, 197, 226
*Cyathea mindanensis*, see *C. fuliginosa*
*Cyathea minita*, see *Cnemidaria grandifolia*
*Cyathea minor*, 85, 87, 133, 138, 226, 264, 272, 310
*Cyathea modesta*, 226
*Cyathea mollis*, see *C. trichophora*
*Cyathea moluccana*, 32, 93, 227
*Cyathea monstrabila*, see *C. dissoluta*
*Cyathea moorei*, see *C. macarthurii*
*Cyathea moseleyi*, 105, 227
*Cyathea mossambicensis*, 227
*Cyathea mucilagina*, 228, 242, 248, 257
*Cyathea muelleri*, 35, 228
*Cyathea multiflora*, 48, 89, 92, 228, 248, 257, 272
*Cyathea multisegmenta*, 225, 229
*Cyathea mutica*, see *Cnemidaria mutica*
*Cyathea myosuroides*, 229
*Cyathea nanna*, 124, 229
*Cyathea naumannii*, see *C. lunulata*
*Cyathea negrosiana*, 229
*Cyathea neocaledonica*, see *C. vieillardii*
*Cyathea nesiotica*, 98, 230
*Cyathea nicklesii*, 230
*Cyathea nigra*, see under *C. lasiosora*
*Cyathea nigrescens*, see *C. arborea* or *C. woodwardioides*
*Cyathea nigricans*, 32, 230
*Cyathea nigripes*, 108, 120, 141, 230, 241, 247, 257, 269, 276
    var. *brunnescens*, see *C. brunnescens*
    var. *nigripes*, 231
*Cyathea nigrolineata*, 98, 132, 231
*Cyathea nigropaleata*, 231
*Cyathea nigrospinulosa*, see *C. tripinnatifida*
*Cyathea nilgirensis*, 231
*Cyathea nockii*, 232
*Cyathea nodulifera*, 149, 232
*Cyathea notabilis*, 232
*Cyathea novae-caledoniae*, 198, 233
*Cyathea novoguineensis*, see *C. geluensis*

# Index

*Cyathea obliqua*, 233
*Cyathea obscura*, 233
*Cyathea obtusa*, see *Cnemidaria grandifolia*
*Cyathea obtusata*, see *C. borneensis*
*Cyathea obtusiloba*, 233
*Cyathea ocanensis*, see *C. caracasana*
*Cyathea ogurae*, 234
*Cyathea oinops*, 156, 234
*Cyathea oldhamii*, see *C. khasyana*
*Cyathea oligocarpa*, see *C. delgadii*
*Cyathea olivacea*, see *C. hornei*
*Cyathea onusta*, 234
*Cyathea oosora*, 235
*Cyathea opizii*, see *C. humilis*
*Cyathea orientalis*, 235
*Cyathea ornata*, see *C. khasyana*
*Cyathea pachyrrhachis*, 235
*Cyathea palaciosii*, 235
*Cyathea paladensis*, 236
*Cyathea paleacea*, see *C. havilandii*
*Cyathea paleata*, see *C. apiculata*
*Cyathea paleolata*, see *C. phalerata*
*Cyathea pallescens*, 126, 236, 259
*Cyathea pallida*, see *C. dichromatolepis*
*Cyathea pallidipaleata*, 236
*Cyathea panamensis*, see *C. petiolata*
*Cyathea papuana*, 236
*Cyathea parianensis*, 100, 155, 236, 258
*Cyathea parksii*, 199, 237
*Cyathea parva* Copeland, 237
*Cyathea parva* (Maxon) Tryon, see *Alsophila parva*
*Cyathea parvifolia*, see *C. caracasana*
*Cyathea parvipinna*, 237
*Cyathea parvula*, 84, 237
*Cyathea patellifera*, 238
*Cyathea pauciflora*, 133, 238
*Cyathea paulistana*, see *C. phalerata*
*Cyathea percrassa*, 238
*Cyathea perpelvigera*, 144, 239
*Cyathea perpunctulata*, 239
*Cyathea perrieriana*, 160, 239, 258, 271
*Cyathea persquamulata*, see *C. subdubia*
*Cyathea persquamulifera*, 240
*Cyathea petiolata*, 103, 114, 131, 145, 240, 249, 255
*Cyathea phalaenolepis*, 240, 272, 277

*Cyathea phalerata*, 101, 105, 124, 240, 310
  var. *iheringii*, 240
*Cyathea phegopteroides*, 231, 241, 247
*Cyathea philippinensis*, 241
*Cyathea physolepidota*, 241
*Cyathea piligera*, see *C. surinamensis*
*Cyathea pilosa*, see *C. delgadii*
*Cyathea pilosissima*, 94, 228, 241
*Cyathea pilulifera*, 89, 119, 242
*Cyathea pinnata*, see *C. moluccana*
*Cyathea pinnula*, 242, 276
*Cyathea plagiostegia*, 89, 242
*Cyathea platylepis*, 243
*Cyathea podophylla*, 136, 137, 199, 243, 265
*Cyathea poeppigii*, 244
*Cyathea polycarpa*, 93, 149, 159, 244
  var. *rigida*, see *C. javanica* var. *rigida*
*Cyathea polypoda*, 244
*Cyathea ponapeana*, see *C. lunulata*
*Cyathea portoricensis*, 59, 85, 106, 117, 133, 138, 245, 272, 279, 309, 310
*Cyathea praecincta*, 245
*Cyathea princeps*, 49, 108, 135, 147, 200, 201, 245, 250, 312
*Cyathea procera*, 246, 248
*Cyathea producta*, see *C. caracasana*
*Cyathea propinqua*, 246
*Cyathea pruinosa*, 246
*Cyathea pseudoalbizzia*, see *C. robinsonii*
*Cyathea pseudomuelleri*, 247
*Cyathea pseudonanna*, 247
*Cyathea pteridioides*, see *C. lepifera*
*Cyathea pubens*, 185, 201, 231, 241, 247
*Cyathea pubescens*, 85, 248, 309
*Cyathea pulcherrima*, 246, 248
*Cyathea pulchra*, see *C. obscura*
*Cyathea pumila*, see *C. albidosquamata*
*Cyathea punctata*, 228, 248, 257
*Cyathea punctulata*, 248
*Cyathea pungens*, 84, 126, 240, 245, 249, 274
*Cyathea pycnoneura*, 249
*Cyathea quadripinnatifida*, see *C. celebica*
*Cyathea quindiuensis*, 108, 135, 147, 246, 249
*Cyathea quitensis*, see *C. poeppigii*

*Cyathea raciborskii*, 149, 250
*Cyathea ramispina*, 100, 250
*Cyathea ramosii*, see *C. trichophora*
*Cyathea rapaensis*, see *C. affinis*
*Cyathea rebeccae*, 39, 251
*Cyathea recommutata*, 251
*Cyathea recurvata*, 251
*Cyathea reducta*, see *C. glabra*
*Cyathea regularis*, see *C. serratifolia*
*Cyathea ridleyi*, see *C. squamulata*
*Cyathea rigens*, 130, 251
*Cyathea rigida*, see *C. havilandii*
*Cyathea robertsiana*, 122, 202, 252
*Cyathea robinsonii*, 252
*Cyathea robusta*, 35, 202, 253
*Cyathea roraimensis*, see *Cnemidaria roraimensis*
*Cyathea rosenstockii*, 253
*Cyathea rubella*, 253
*Cyathea rubiginosa*, 254
*Cyathea rufa*, 98, 254
*Cyathea rufopannosa*, 254
*Cyathea ruiziana*, 254, 264
*Cyathea runensis*, 254, 271
*Cyathea rupestris*, 255
*Cyathea saccata*, 255
*Cyathea sagittifolia*, 103, 240, 255, 274
*Cyathea salletii*, 255
*Cyathea sangirensis*, see *C. felina*
*Cyathea sarasinorum*, 256
*Cyathea sarawakensis*, see *C. alternans*
*Cyathea sartorii*, see *C. divergens*
*Cyathea scandens*, 84, 104, 256
*Cyathea schanschin* Jenman, see *C. harrisii*
*Cyathea schanschin* Martius, see *C. fulva*
*Cyathea schiedeana*, 108, 120, 228, 231, 248, 256, 262
*Cyathea schizochlamys*, see *C. sumatrana*
*Cyathea schlechteri*, 257
*Cyathea schliebenii*, 257
*Cyathea schlimii*, 151, 257, 276
*Cyathea sechellarum*, 203, 257
*Cyathea semiamplectens*, 258
*Cyathea senex*, 258
*Cyathea senilis*, 100, 155, 237, 258
*Cyathea sepikensis*, see *C. geluensis*
*Cyathea serratifolia*, 160, 239, 258, 271

*Cyathea* ×*sessilifolia*, 84
*Cyathea sessilipinnula*, see *C. suluensis*
*Cyathea setchellii*, see *C. vaupelii*
*Cyathea setifera*, 259
*Cyathea setulosa*, 259
*Cyathea sherringii*, see *C. caracasana*
*Cyathea sibuyanensis*, 259
*Cyathea simplex*, 236, 259
*Cyathea sinuata*, 84, 203, 259
*Cyathea sipapoensis*, 221, 260
*Cyathea smithii*, 22, 24, 35, 38, 85, 203, 204, 205, 260
*Cyathea solomonensis*, 89, 260
*Cyathea speciosa*, 72, 122, 261, 310
*Cyathea spectabilis*, see *Cnemidaria spectabilis*
  var. *longipinna*, see *Cnemidaria spectabilis*
  var. *trinitensis*, see *Cnemidaria spectabilis*
*Cyathea* subg. *Sphaeropteris* (*Sphaeropteris* clade), 86
*Cyathea spinifera*, see *C. alderwereltii*
*Cyathea spinulosa*, 84, 109, 205, 261
*Cyathea squamulata*, 261
*Cyathea squamulosa*, 257, 262
*Cyathea stelligera*, see *C. cunninghamii*
*Cyathea sternbergii* Domin, see *C. corcovadensis*
*Cyathea sternbergii* Pohl, see *C. arborea*
*Cyathea steyermarkii*, 55, 262
*Cyathea stipipinnula*, 262
*Cyathea stipularis*, 84, 98, 262
*Cyathea stokesii*, 122, 263
*Cyathea stolzei*, 263, 272
*Cyathea straminea*, 104, 106, 116, 254, 263
*Cyathea strigosa*, 155, 264
*Cyathea stuebelii*, 264, 310
*Cyathea stuhlmannii*, see *C. humilis*
*Cyathea subarborescens*, see *Cnemidaria uleana*
*Cyathea subbipinnata*, see *C. elliptica*
*Cyathea subcomosa*, see *C. elmeri*
*Cyathea subdubia*, 136, 137, 243, 264
*Cyathea subincisa*, see *Cnemidaria speciosa*
*Cyathea submarginalis*, see *C. praecincta*

*Cyathea subsessilis*, 265, 273
*Cyathea subtripinnata*, 265
*Cyathea subtropica*, 265
*Cyathea suluensis*, 266
*Cyathea sumatrana*, 266
*Cyathea superba*, see *C. surinamensis*
*Cyathea suprastrigosa*, 134, 266
*Cyathea surinamensis*, 119, 266
*Cyathea tahitensis*, see *C. affinis*
*Cyathea taiwaniana*, see *C. spinulosa*
*Cyathea tenera*, 84, 134, 266
*Cyathea tenggerensis*, 205, 267
*Cyathea tenuicaulis*, 267
*Cyathea ternatea*, 267
*Cyathea teysmannii*, 268, 270
*Cyathea thomsonii*, 268
*Cyathea tijucensis*, see *C. poeppigii*
*Cyathea tomentosa*, 117, 159, 268
*Cyathea tomentosissima*, 206, 268
*Cyathea tortuosa*, 108, 120, 231, 269
*Cyathea trichiata*, 98, 269
*Cyathea trichodesma*, 270
*Cyathea trichophora*, 128, 270
*Cyathea tricolor*, see *C. dealbata*
*Cyathea trinidadensis*, see *C. delgadii*
*Cyathea tripinnata*, 158, 268, 270
*Cyathea tripinnatifida*, 255, 270
*Cyathea truncata*, 88, 271
*Cyathea tryonorum*, 98, 271
*Cyathea tsilotsilensis*, 160, 239, 258, 271
*Cyathea tuerckheimii*, see *C. divergens*
*Cyathea tussacii*, 85, 117, 133, 138, 245, 271, 279
*Cyathea uluguruensis*, see *C. humilis*
*Cyathea umbrosa*, see *C. lepifera*
*Cyathea underwoodii*, see *C. fulva*
*Cyathea urbanii*, 226, 272
*Cyathea ursina*, 229, 240, 263, 272
*Cyathea usambarensis*, see *C. manniana*
*Cyathea valdecrenata*, 272
*Cyathea vandeusenii*, 273
*Cyathea vaupelii*, 265, 273
*Cyathea veitchii*, see *C. lunulata*
*Cyathea venezuelensis*, 273
*Cyathea vernicosa*, see *C. villosa*
*Cyathea verrucosa*, 115, 274
*Cyathea vestita*, see *C. delgadii*

*Cyathea vieillardii*, 95, 206, 274
*Cyathea vilhelmii*, see *C. platylepis*
*Cyathea villosa*, 101, 241, 274
*Cyathea vitiensis*, see *C. lunulata*
*Cyathea vittata*, 275
*Cyathea walkerae*, 275
  var. *tripinnata*, 275
*Cyathea wallacei*, 275
*Cyathea weatherbyana*, 95, 276
*Cyathea welwitschii*, 276
*Cyathea wendlandii*, 151, 231, 242, 257, 276
*Cyathea wengiensis*, 277
*Cyathea werffii*, 240, 277
*Cyathea werneri*, 135, 277
*Cyathea whitmeei*, 277
*Cyathea wilkesiana*, see *C. whitmeei*
*Cyathea willdenowiana*, see *C. pungens*
*Cyathea williamsii*, 278
*Cyathea* ×*wilsonii*, 84
*Cyathea womersleyi*, 278
*Cyathea woodwardioides*, 85, 114, 117, 133, 138, 143, 245, 272, 278
*Cyathea woollsiana*, 35, 206, 278
*Cyathea xanthina*, see *C. squamulata*
*Cyathea yungensis*, see *C. quindiuensis*
*Cyathea uannanensis*, see *C. chinensis*
*Cyathea zakamenensis*, 279
*Cyathea zambesiaca*, see *C. thomsonii*
*Cyathea zamboangana*, 280
Cyatheaceae, 22, 23, 25, 28, 49, 50, 51, 52, 59, 69, 81
Cyatheales, 52
Cyatheocaulis, 25
Cystodiaceae, see Dicksoniaceae
Cystodium, 50, 51, 52, 59, 280, 306
*Cystodium sorbifolium*, 280, 281
  subsp. *solomonensis*, 282
*Davallia berteriana*, see *Dicksonia berteriana*
*Davallia dubia*, see *Calochlaena dubia*
de Candolle, Augustin Pyramus, 48
*Dennstaedtia*, 282
*Deparia*, 56
Dickson, James, 48
*Dicksonia*, 25, 28, 50, 51, 52, 59, 63, 282, 306

*Dicksonia antarctica*, 19, 20, 29, 30, 34, 35, 38, 39, 42, 207, 284, 289
*Dicksonia arborescens*, 11, 97, 208, 282, 285
   var. *minor*, 286
*Dicksonia archboldii*, 286, 292
*Dicksonia baudouini*, 208, 286
*Dicksonia berteriana*, 287
*Dicksonia berteroana*, see *D. berteriana*
*Dicksonia blumei*, 287, 291
*Dicksonia brackenridgei*, 288
*Dicksonia chrysotricha*, see *D. blumei*
*Dicksonia coniifolia*, see *Culcita coniifolia*
*Dicksonia deplanchei*, see *D. baudouini*
*Dicksonia externa*, 209, 288
*Dicksonia fibrosa*, 19, 20, 22, 35, 38, 42, 58, 210, 211, 284, 286, 288
*Dicksonia ghiesbreghtii*, see *D. sellowiana*
*Dicksonia gigantea*, see *D. sellowiana*
*Dicksonia glauca*, see *Cibotium glaucum*
*Dicksonia grandis*, 289
*Dicksonia herbertii*, 289, 294
*Dicksonia hieronymi*, 290
*Dicksonia javanica*, see *Cibotium schiedei*
*Dicksonia karsteniana*, see *D. sellowiana*
*Dicksonia lanata*, 38, 212, 282, 290
*Dicksonia lanigera*, 291
*Dicksonia ledermannii*, see *D. grandis*
*Dicksonia lobulata*, see *D. sellowiana*
*Dicksonia mollis*, 287, 291
*Dicksonia schlechteri*, see *D. grandis*
*Dicksonia sciurus*, 286, 292
*Dicksonia sellowiana*, 212, 213, 284, 292, 294
*Dicksonia sorbifolia*, see *Cystodium sorbifolium*
*Dicksonia squarrosa*, 30, 34, 35, 38, 39, 58, 204, 213, 214, 286, 293
*Dicksonia steubelii*, 292, 293
*Dicksonia straminea*, see *Calochlaena straminea*
*Dicksonia thyrsopteroides*, 215, 294
*Dicksonia youngiae*, 39, 290, 294
Dicksoniaceae, 15, 20, 22, 23, 25, 28, 49, 50, 51, 52, 55, 59, 60, 63, 79, 280, 282, 297, 305
Dicksonieae, see Dicksoniaceae

*Diplazium*, 56
*Diplazium dietrichianum*, 56, 215
*Diplazium esculentum*, 56
*Diploblechnum*, 57
*Diploblechnum fraseri*, 57
*Disphenia*, see *Cyathea*
*Disphenia orientalis*, see *Cyathea orientalis*
'ehu'ehu, see *Sadleria cyatheoides*
*Erboracia*, 25
ethnobotany, 29
fern spike, 26
Flinders, Matthew, 48
fossils, 25
fronds, 20, 21
gametophyte, 16, 17, 41, 161
Gaudichaud-Beaupré, Charles, 66
golden chicken fern, see *Cibotium barometz*
*Gondwanopteris*, 57
gully tree fern, see *Cyathea cunninghamii*
*Gymnosphaera nicklesii*, see *Cyathea nicklesii*
*Gymnosphaera squamulata*, see *Cyathea squamulata*
hairs, 21, 22
hapu, see *Cibotium menziesii*, *C. nealiae*
hapu'u, see *Cibotium chamissoi*, *C. glaucum*
Hawaiian tree fern, see *Cibotium chamissoi*
*Hemistegia*, see *Cnemidaria*
*Hemitelia*, see *Cyathea*
*Hemitelia amabilis*, see *Cnemidaria amabilis*
*Hemitelia andina*, see *Cyathea andina*
*Hemitelia apiculata*, see *Cnemidaria apiculata*
*Hemitelia australis*, see *Cyathea leichhardtiana*
*Hemitelia bella*, see *Cnemidaria bella*
*Hemitelia choricarpa*, see *Cnemidaria choricarpa*
*Hemitelia* subg. *Cnemidaria*, see *Cnemidaria*
*Hemitelia conformis*, see *Cyathea conformis*

*Hemitelia costaricensis*, see *Cyathea costaricensis*
*Hemitelia crenulata*, see *Cyathea raciborskii*
*Hemitelia cruciata*, see *Cnemidaria cruciata*
*Hemitelia cyatheoides*, see *Cyathea cyatheoides*
*Hemitelia decorata*, see *Cyathea decorata*
*Hemitelia decurrens*, see *Cnemidaria decurrens*
*Hemitelia dissimilis*, see *Cyathea dissimilis*
*Hemitelia firma*, see *Cyathea mexicana*
*Hemitelia karsteniana*, see *Cnemidaria karsteniana*
*Hemitelia ledermannii*, see *Cyathea macrophylla*
*Hemitelia macarthurii*, see *Cyathea macarthurii*
*Hemitelia macrocarpa*, see *Cyathea macrocarpa*
*Hemitelia multiflora* var. *sprucei*, see *Cyathea cyatheoides*
*Hemitelia mutica*, see *Cnemidaria mutica*
*Hemitelia nervosa*, see *Cnemidaria nervosa*
*Hemitelia perpunctulata*, see *Cyathea perpunctulata*
*Hemitelia petiolata*, see *Cyathea petiolata*
*Hemitelia platylepis*, see *Cyathea platylepis*
*Hemitelia quitensis*, see *Cnemidaria quitensis*
*Hemitelia roraimensis*, see *Cnemidaria roraimensis*
*Hemitelia spectabilis*, see *Cnemidaria spectabilis*
*Hemitelia squamulosa*, see *Cyathea squamulosa*
*Hemitelia suprastrigosa*, see *Cyathea suprastrigosa*
*Hemitelia surinamensis*, see *Cyathea surinamensis*
*Hemitelia uleana*, see *Cnemidaria uleana*
*Hemitelia weatherbyana*, see *Cyathea weatherbyana*
heruheru, see *Leptopteris superba*
Holttum, Richard, 53, 54
Hooker, William, 66

Hymenophyllospidaceae, 50
*International Code of Botanical Nomenclature*, 47
*Ipomoea batatas*, 30
katote, see *Cyathea smithii*
Kaulfuss, Georg Friedrich, 49, 66
korau, see *Cyathea medullaris*
Krajina, Vladimir, 66, 68
kumara, see *Ipomoea batatas*
kuripaka, see *Dicksonia fibrosa*
lacy tree fern, see *Cyathea robertsiana*
lamb, vegetable, 32, 33, 65
Lellinger, David B., 54
*Leptopteris*, 28, 52, 58, 60, 295, 300, 308
*Leptopteris alpina*, 296
*Leptopteris fraseri*, 296
*Leptopteris hymenophylloides*, 216, 295, 296
*Leptopteris superba*, 216, 296, 297
*Leptopteris wilkesiana*, 296
L'Héritier de Brutelle, Charles-Louis, 47, 48
Liebmann, Frederik, 49
life cycle, 15, 16
Linden, Jean Jules, 34, 49
Linden, Lucien, 49
Linnaeus, Carl (father and son), 47
Linnean Society, 48
*Lomaria*, 57
*Lomaria nuda*, see *Blechnum nudum*
*Lomariocycas*, 57
*Lophosoria*, 25, 50, 51, 52, 297
*Lophosoria pruinata*, see *L. quadripinnata*
*Lophosoria quadripinnata*, 35, 217, 297, 298, 299
  var. *contracta*, 299
*Lophosoria quesadae*, 299
Lophosoriaceae, see Dicksoniaceae
*Lophosoriorhachis*, 25
Loxsomataceae, 50
mamaku, see *Cyathea medullaris*
man tree fern, see *Cibotium chamissoi*
maquique, 31, 173
*Marattia*, 26, 57
Marattiaceae, 57
Marattiales, 26
Menzies, Archibold, 68

Metaxyaceae, 50, 51
Mexican tree fern, see *Cibotium schiedei*
*Microstegnus*, see *Cnemidaria*
*Nephelea*, see *Cyathea*
*Nephelea polystichoides*, see *Alsophila polystichoides*
*Nephelea tryoniana*, see *Alsophila tryoniana*
ngutungutu kiwi, see *Leptopteris superba*
*Nishidicaulis*, 25
Norfolk tree fern, see *Cyathea brownii*
*Oguracaulis*, 25
*Oncyhiopsis*, 25
*Osmunda*, 28, 29, 52, 58, 60, 295, 299, 307
*Osmunda banksiifolia*, 300
*Osmunda cinnamomea*, 300
*Osmunda claytoniana*, 300
*Osmunda* fiber, 29
*Osmunda javanica*, 300
*Osmunda lancea*, 300
*Osmunda regalis*, 217, 299, 300, 301
*Osmundacaulis*, 28, 218
Osmundaceae, 50, 52, 58, 60, 295, 299, 307
Osmundales, 52
*Palaeosmunda*, 28
paleae, see scales
palma de montaña, see *Cyathea princeps*
*Panicularia*, see *Thyrsopteris*
passionvine hopper, see *Scolypopa australis*
penewar jambi, see *Cibotium barometz*
*Phytophthora*, 42
phytoplasma, 43
*Pinonia splendens*, see *Cibotium chamissoi*
*Pinonia*, see *Cibotium*
*Pinus radiata*, 29
Plagiogyriaceae, 50, 51
*Pneumatopteris pennigera*, 58, 218
*Polypodium*, 47, 48
*Polypodium affine*, see *Cyathea affinis*
*Polypodium alternans*, see *Cyathea alternans*
*Polypodium arboreum*, see *Cyathea arborea*
*Polypodium armatum*, see *Cyathea armata*
*Polypodium asperum*, see *Cyathea aspera*
*Polypodium atrovirens*, see *Cyathea atrovirens*

*Polypodium barometz*, see *Cibotium barometz*
*Polypodium capense*, see *Cyathea capensis*
*Polypodium corcovadense*, see *Cyathea corcovadensis*
*Polypodium dealbatum*, see *Cyathea dealbata*
*Polypodium felinum*, see *Cyathea felina*
*Polypodium horridum*, see *Cnemidaria horrida*
*Polypodium lunulatum*, see *Cyathea lunulata*
*Polypodium medullare*, see *Cyathea medullaris*
*Polypodium microdonton*, see *Cyathea microdonta*
*Polypodium procerum*, see *Cyathea pungens*
*Polypodium pungens*, see *Cyathea pungens*
*Polypodium quadripinnatum*, see *Lophosoria quadripinnata*
*Polypodium taenitis*, see *Cyathea corcovadensis*
*Polypodium unisorum*, see *Sadleria unisora*
ponga, see *Cyathea dealbata*
potato, sweet, 30
prickly tree fern, see *Cyathea leichhardtiana*
Prince of Wales feathers, see *Leptopteris superba*
pua'a, see *Sadleria cyatheoides*
*Pythium*, 42
rabo de mico, see *Cyathea princeps*
rainbow fern, see *Calochlaena dubia*
*Rhizoctonia*, 42
rhizome, 17, 18
rot (bacterial, crown, fungal, and root), 42
rough tree fern, see *Cyathea australis*, *Dicksonia squarrosa*
royal fern, see *Osmunda regalis*
Sadler, Joseph, 49
*Sadleria*, 52, 57, 60, 301
*Sadleria cyatheoides*, 49, 218, 219, 301, 302

*Sadleria hillebrandii*, 303
*Sadleria pallida*, 220, 303
*Sadleria rigida*, see *S. pallida*
*Sadleria souleyetiana*, 303, 304
*Sadleria squarrosa*, 301, 304
*Sadleria unisora*, 304
*Sadleria wagneriana*, 304
sapsucking insects, 43
scales, 21, 22
scaly tree fern, see *Cyathea cooperi*
*Schizocaena*, see *Cyathea*
*Scolypopa australis*, 43
Scythian lamb, see *Cibotium barometz*
silver fern, see *Cyathea dealbata*
skirted tree fern, see *Cyathea* ×*marcescens*
slender tree fern, see *Cyathea cunninghamii, C. robertsiana*
Smith, James Edward, 48
soft tree fern, see *Cyathea smithii, Dicksonia antarctica*
Solander, Daniel, 48
Sowerby, James, 48
sori, 23
*Sphaeropteris*, 48, 50, 51; see also *Cyathea*
*Sphaeropteris aciculosa*, see *Cyathea aciculosa*
*Sphaeropteris aeneifolia*, see *Cyathea aeneifolia*
*Sphaeropteris agatheti*, see *Cyathea agatheti*
*Sphaeropteris albidosquamata*, see *Cyathea albidosquamata*
*Sphaeropteris albifrons*, see *Cyathea albifrons*
*Sphaeropteris albosetacea*, see *Cyathea albosetacea*
*Sphaeropteris alternans*, see *Cyathea alternans*
*Sphaeropteris angiensis*, see *Cyathea angiensis*
*Sphaeropteris angustipinna*, see *Cyathea angustipinna*
*Sphaeropteris aramaganensis*, see *Cyathea aramaganensis*
*Sphaeropteris arthropoda*, see *Cyathea arthropoda*
*Sphaeropteris assimilis*, see *Cyathea assimilis*

*Sphaeropteris atahuallpa*, see *Cyathea atahuallpa*
*Sphaeropteris atrospinosa*, see *Cyathea atrospinosa*
*Sphaeropteris atrox*, see *Cyathea atrox*
*Sphaeropteris auriculifera*, see *Cyathea auriculifera*
*Sphaeropteris australis*, see *Cyathea leichhardtiana*
*Sphaeropteris binuangensis*, see *Cyathea binuangensis*
*Sphaeropteris brackenridgei*, see *Cyathea brackenridgei*
*Sphaeropteris bradei*, see *Cyathea bradei*
*Sphaeropteris brunei*, see *Cyathea brunei*
*Sphaeropteris brunoniana*, see *Cyathea brunnescens*
*Sphaeropteris capitata*, see *Cyathea capitata*
*Sphaeropteris carrii*, see *Cyathea carrii*
*Sphaeropteris celebica*, see *Cyathea celebica*
*Sphaeropteris concinna*, see *Cyathea felina*
*Sphaeropteris cooperi*, see *Cyathea cooperi*
*Sphaeropteris crinita*, see *Cyathea crinita*
*Sphaeropteris cuatrecasassi*, 311
*Sphaeropteris curranii*, see *Cyathea curranii*
*Sphaeropteris discophora*, see *Cyathea discophora*
*Sphaeropteris elliptica*, see *Cyathea elliptica*
*Sphaeropteris elmeri*, see *Cyathea elmeri*
*Sphaeropteris elongata*, see *Cyathea poeppigii*
*Sphaeropteris excelsa*, see *Cyathea brownii*
*Sphaeropteris feani*, see *Cyathea feani*
*Sphaeropteris fugax*, see *Cyathea fugax*
*Sphaeropteris fusca*, see *Cyathea fusca*
*Sphaeropteris gardneri*, see *Cyathea gardneri*
*Sphaeropteris glauca*, see *Cyathea contaminans*
*Sphaeropteris hainanensis*, see *Cyathea hainanensis*
*Sphaeropteris hirsuta*, see *Cyathea surinamensis*

*Sphaeropteris horrida*, see *Cyathea princeps*
*Sphaeropteris inaequalis*, see *Cyathea inaequalis*
*Sphaeropteris insignis*, see *Cyathea insignis*
*Sphaeropteris insularum*, see *Cyathea insularum*
*Sphaeropteris integra*, see *Cyathea integra*
*Sphaeropteris intermedia*, see *Cyathea intermedia*
*Sphaeropteris intramarginalis*, see *Cyathea intramarginalis*
*Sphaeropteris ledermannii*, see *Cyathea macrophylla*
*Sphaeropteris lepifera*, see *Cyathea lepifera*
*Sphaeropteris leucolepis*, see *Cyathea leucolepis*
*Sphaeropteris leucotricha*, see *Cyathea leucotricha*
*Sphaeropteris lockwoodiana*, see *Cyathea lockwoodiana*
*Sphaeropteris lunulata*, see *Cyathea lunulata*
*Sphaeropteris magna*, see *Cyathea magna*
*Sphaeropteris marginata*, see *Cyathea marginata*
*Sphaeropteris medullaris*, see *Cyathea medullaris*
*Sphaeropteris megalosora*, see *Cyathea megalosora*
*Sphaeropteris mertensiana*, see *Cyathea mertensiana*
*Sphaeropteris microlepidota*, see *Cyathea microlepidota*
*Sphaeropteris moluccana*, see *Cyathea moluccana*
*Sphaeropteris moseleyi*, see *Cyathea moseleyi*
*Sphaeropteris nigricans*, see *Cyathea nigricans*
*Sphaeropteris novae-caledoniae*, see *Cyathea novae-caledoniae*
*Sphaeropteris obliqua*, see *Cyathea obliqua*
*Sphaeropteris obscura*, see *Cyathea obscura*
*Sphaeropteris papuana*, see *Cyathea papuana*
*Sphaeropteris parianensis*, see *Cyathea parianensis*
*Sphaeropteris parksii*, see *Cyathea parksii*
*Sphaeropteris parvifolia*, see *Cyathea deminuens*
*Sphaeropteris parvipinna*, see *Cyathea parvipinna*
*Sphaeropteris persquamulifera*, see *Cyathea persquamulifera*
*Sphaeropteris philippinensis*, see *Cyathea philippinensis*
*Sphaeropteris pilulifera*, see *Cyathea pilulifera*
*Sphaeropteris polypoda*, see *Cyathea polypoda*
*Sphaeropteris procera*, see *Cyathea procera*
*Sphaeropteris propinqua*, see *Cyathea propinqua*
*Sphaeropteris pulcherrima*, see *Cyathea pulcherrima*
*Sphaeropteris quindiuensis*, see *Cyathea quindiuensis*
*Sphaeropteris robinsonii*, see *Cyathea robinsonii*
*Sphaeropteris robusta*, see *Cyathea robusta*
*Sphaeropteris rosenstockii*, see *Cyathea rosenstockii*
*Sphaeropteris runensis*, see *Cyathea runensis*
*Sphaeropteris samoensis*, see *Cyathea whitmeei*
*Sphaeropteris sarasinorum*, see *Cyathea sarasinorum*
*Sphaeropteris* subg. *Sclephropteris*, 53, 54
*Sphaeropteris senex*, see *Cyathea senex*
*Sphaeropteris setifera*, see *Cyathea setifera*
*Sphaeropteris sibuyanensis*, see *Cyathea sibuyanensis*
*Sphaeropteris sipapoensis*, see *Cyathea sipapoensis*
*Sphaeropteris* subg. *Sphaeropteris*, 53, 54
*Sphaeropteris squamulata*, see *Cyathea squamulata*
*Sphaeropteris stipipinnula*, see *Cyathea stipipinnula*

*Sphaeropteris strigosa*, see *Cyathea strigosa*
*Sphaeropteris subsessilis*, see *Cyathea subsessilis*
*Sphaeropteris suluensis*, see *Cyathea suluensis*
*Sphaeropteris tenggerensis*, see *Cyathea tenggerensis*
*Sphaeropteris teysmannii*, see *Cyathea teysmannii*
*Sphaeropteris tomentosa*, see *Cyathea tomentosa*
*Sphaeropteris tomentosissima*, see *Cyathea tomentosissima*
*Sphaeropteris trichodesma*, see *Cyathea trichodesma*
*Sphaeropteris trichophora*, see *Cyathea trichophora*
*Sphaeropteris tripinnata*, see *Cyathea tripinnata*
*Sphaeropteris tripinnatifida*, see *Cyathea tripinnatifida*
*Sphaeropteris truncata*, see *Cyathea truncata*
*Sphaeropteris vaupelii*, see *Cyathea vaupelii*
*Sphaeropteris verrucosa*, see *Cyathea verrucosa*
*Sphaeropteris vittata*, see *Cyathea vittata*
*Sphaeropteris wallacei*, see *Cyathea wallacei*
*Sphaeropteris werneri*, see *Cyathea werneri*
*Sphaeropteris womersleyi*, see *Cyathea womersleyi*
*Sphaeropteris zamboangana*, see *Cyathea zamboangana*
sporangia, 23, 40
spore, 23, 39, 40
sporophyte, 16, 17, 41
Stolze, Robert, 69
*Tempskya*, 26, 27
*Thamnopteris*, 28
Thelypteridaceae, 15, 50, 58
Thyrsopteridaceae, see Dicksoniaceae
Thyrsopteridales, 305
*Thyrsopteris*, 50, 51, 52, 59, 305
*Thyrsopteris elegans*, 305, 306

*Todea*, 28, 52, 58, 60, 295, 300, 307
*Todea africana*, see *Todea barbara*
*Todea barbara*, 58, 220, 307, 308
*Todea fraseri*, see *Leptopteris fraseri*
*Todea hymenophylloides*, see *Leptopteris hymenophylloides*
*Todea papuana*, 58, 307
*Todea superba*, see *Leptopteris superba*
*Trichipteris*, see *Cyathea*
*Trichipteris bipinnata*, see *Cyathea bipinnata*
*Trichipteris conjugata*, see *Cyathea conjugata*
*Trichipteris cyclodium*, see *Cyathea cyclodium*
*Trichipteris lechleri*, see *Cyathea subtropica*
*Trichipteris leucolepis*, see *Cyathea leucofolis*
*Trichipteris mexicana*, see *Cyathea valdecrenata*
*Trichipteris microphylla*, 312
*Trichipteris nanna*, see *Cyathea nanna*
*Trichipteris nigra*, see *Cyathea lasiosora*
*Trichipteris nigripes* var. *brunnescens*, see *Cyathea brunnescens*
*Trichipteris pinnata*, see *Cyathea stolzei*
*Trichipteris procera*, see *Cyathea pungens*
*Trichipteris pseudonanna*, see *Cyathea pseudonanna*
*Trichipteris pubescens*, see *Cyathea pubens*
*Trichipteris steyermarkii*, 55, and see *Cyathea venezuelensis*
*Trichomanes squarrosum*, see *Dicksonia squarrosa*
*Trichosorus*, see *Lophosoria*
trunk, 17, 18, 38
Tryon, Rolla, 49, 54, 78
tuokura, see *Dicksonia lanata*
vegetable lamb, 32, 33, 65
weki, see *Dicksonia squarrosa*
weki-ponga, see *Dicksonia fibrosa*
wig tree fern, see *Cyathea baileyana*
woolly fern, see *Cibotium barometz*
woolly tree fern, see *Dicksonia antarctica*
*Zalesskya*, 28